Guide to Manuscript Revision

ab .... Spell out abbreviation (M6b)

adv .... Use adverb form (S1c)

agr .... Make verb agree with subject

(or pronoun with antecedent) (S4a, S4c)

ap .... Use apostrophe (M4b)

cap .... Capitalize (M4a)

coll .... Use less colloquial word (U3c)

d .... Improve diction (W2)

dev .... Develop your point (C3b)

div .... Revise word division (M6a)

DM .... Revise dangling modifier (S4b)

frag .... Revise sentence fragment (M1a)

gr .... Revise grammatical form or construction (U1)

awk .... Rewrite awkward sentence (S4)

lc .... Use lowercase (M4a)

MM .... Shift misplaced modifier (S4b)

P .... Improve punctuation (M1-3)

¶ .... New paragraph (C2)

no¶ .... Take out paragraph break (C2)

ref .... Improve pronoun reference (S4c)

rep .... Avoid repetition (U2a)

sl .... Replace slangy word (U3c)

sp .... Revise misspelled words (M5)

st .... Improve sentence structure (S4)

t .... Change tense of verb (U1d)

American English Today

American English Today

General Editor and Senior Author: **Hans P. Guth**

Contributing Author, 7–9: Edgar H. Schuster

Third Edition

WEBSTER DIVISION/McGRAW-HILL BOOK COMPANY
New York   St. Louis   San Francisco   Dallas   Atlanta

Editorial Development: *John A. Rothermich*

Managing Editor: *Hester Eggert Weeden*

Design: *Bennie Arrington*

Production: *Judith Tisdale*

Acknowledgments—see page 397

Library of Congress Cataloging in Publication Data

Guth, Hans Paul, date
    Exploring English.

    (Their, American English today; [1])
    Includes index.
    SUMMARY: A seventh grade text offering instruction in the areas of composition, word study, grammar, usage, and speech.
    1. English language—Grammar—1950–   2. English language—Composition and exercises. [1. English language—Grammar. 2. English language —Composition and exercises] I. Schuster, Edgar Howard, date joint author. II. Title.
[PE1408.G933 1980 vol. 1] [PE1112] 808'.042s [428'.2] 79-26231
ISBN 0-07-025017-0

The Authors

HANS P. GUTH

General Editor and Senior Author

Dr. Guth is a widely published teacher-scholar who writes about effective communication with the authority that comes from successful practice. He is widely known for his work in workshops and in-service meetings for teachers of language and composition. His first book on the teaching of English, *English Today and Tomorrow*, was widely praised and hailed as a "milestone" and as a book "with no equal in its field." His recent book for teachers, *English for a New Generation*, has been called "a book that every teacher of the language arts should read." Through his college textbooks—especially the widely used rhetoric handbook, *Words and Ideas* (Wadsworth)—Dr. Guth has become known as a leading authority on teaching composition to today's students. He has spoken at numerous regional and national conferences and has taught in institutes sponsored by Stanford University, University of Illinois, and University of Hawaii.

EDGAR H. SCHUSTER

Contributing Author, Grades 7–9

Dr. Schuster is Language Arts Coordinator for the Allentown (Pa.) School District. He had taught English in both urban and suburban high schools in the Philadelphia area. He has also taught at the college level. He has written articles for professional journals, including the *Clearing House*, the *English Journal*, and *Educational Leadership*. Dr. Schuster has been a Master Teacher at Harvard University and is a recipient of a Lindback Foundation Award for Distinguished Teaching. He is the principal editor of *American Literature*, the Grade 11 text of McGraw-Hill's *Themes and Writers* anthology series.

Consultants and Contributors

Student Writing	**Gabriele Rico,** *San Jose State University*
Cultural Minorities	**Carol Kizine,** *Kansas City Public Schools*
Teaching Suggestions	**Barbara Johnston,** *San Jose, California*
Testing and Measurement	**William Kline,** *California Test Bureau*
Graphics	**Herbert Zettl,** *San Francisco State University*

The Authors and the Publishers also thank the following teachers who evaluated manuscript, provided hundreds of examples of student writing, and tried out *American English Today* in their classrooms:

Marge Archer, Lawrenceville, New Jersey
James Conway, St. Louis, Missouri
Jeanne Irwin, Los Angeles, California
Cherry Mallory, Kansas City, Missouri
Donald Mayfield, San Diego, California
Virginia McCormick, Allentown, Pennsylvania
Jane McGill, Chula Vista, California
Janet Minesinger, Columbia, Maryland
Nancy Mitchell, Lakewood, California
Richard E. Roberts, Clinton Corners, New York
Margaret Timm, Bay City, Michigan
Marilyn Walker, Salem, Oregon

To the Teacher

American English Today, Third Edition, offers solid productive work in the basic areas of language and composition. Its aim is to provide materials that are intelligible, workable, and motivating for today's students. The following are key features of the new Third Edition:

1. More varied, effective, and interesting exercises than any competing series.

2. A functional, plain-English approach designed to help students defeated by awkward, elaborate terminology or theory.

3. Streamlined, compact presentation for efficient study and reference.

4. A positive, constructive teaching program systematically developing the students' skills and proficiencies.

5. Frequent provision for measurement of student achievement, with new unit review exercises, diagnostic tests, and achievement tests. A new section on how to take tests, complete with sample tests, appears in the resource chapter of each volume.

6. High-interest materials designed to help teachers overcome students' resistance to English as a subject.

7. Effective use of charts and other visuals designed to help students take things in at a glance.

8. A positive, habit-building program for teaching standard English.

9. Proven step-by-step instruction in the process of composition.

10. Special attention to familiar trouble spots and problem areas for students.

Chapter Table of Contents

TABLE OF CONTENTS

Chapter 3

COMPOSITION: How We Write

Chapter 4

USAGE: Using Standard English

Chapter 5

MECHANICS: The Written Page   273

Chapter 6

ORAL LANGUAGE: Speaking to a Group

Chapter 7

RESOURCES: The Library, Study Skills, Taking Tests

To the Student

Everybody uses language all the time. This book is designed to help you understand it better, and to help you make better use of it. How can you get the most from this book? How can you get the most from your study of English in class?

Remember the following advice:

(1) *Find things out for yourself.* When you study the way language works, say, "Let me see for myself." When you study the way writers write, say, "Let me take a look at a piece of writing." You will forget much that you are told. You will remember what you have discovered for yourself.

(2) *Learn by asking questions.* If something you are told does not make sense, try to find out more about it. Don't be satisfied unless you can say: "Yes, I see. Now I understand how this fits in. Now I know what purpose this serves."

(3) *Learn from what you do.* A person can be a great lover of music and yet never learn how to sing or play an instrument. Try not to be just a spectator. Try not to be just a consumer, who listens when other people talk, who reads what other people write. Use every opportunity to talk to a group. Volunteer to write up a program or resolution. Learn from practice. Try things out.

Chapter 1

Words
Building Your Vocabulary

Chapter Preview 1

IN THIS CHAPTER:

- What we learn from names.

- What we learn from words with similar and opposite meanings.

- How familiar roots help us understand words.

- How we learn new words to serve our practical needs.

- What kinds of information dictionaries give us about words.

Learn new words and put them to good use.

Our lives are filled with words. What would family life be like if we could not express feelings, make requests, and argue with one another? What would school be like if we did not have words for instruction and conversation? What would business and government be like without words for memos, inquiries, and directions?

As you study and learn new words, remember that words serve several major purposes:

(1) Words serve our practical needs. They direct us to the right turnoff, the right building, the right office. They tell us how to operate a machine or how to open a jar of fruit. They tell us what we want to know about the weather, prices, school rules, and traffic laws. They enable us to conduct our business at a club meeting, a rummage sale, or a school assembly.

(2) Words express our feelings. What do you say when you are angry, or happy, or sad? Much of the talking we do does not get practical results, but it makes us feel better (and sometimes worse). In turn, we spend much of our time listening to others expressing *their* feelings, ideas, and attitudes. Words help us understand how other people think and feel.

(3) We enjoy words and often entertain ourselves with them. People of all ages enjoy rhymes, jingles, riddles, or proverbs. People are pleased when they come up with a witty remark or the right reply.

Study the names we give to people, things, and places.

One of the most basic functions of language is to give names to the people and things we encounter every day. Often these names come to us from a faraway past. They often tell us something about our history.

For instance, where did Americans get their names for places and people? Our place names and personal names in many ways mirror the varied history of this country. Here are some familiar sources of American names:

(1) Many names remind us of the original native Americans. For instance, *Massachusetts* is an Indian word that meant "by the big hill." The state of Delaware is named after a tribe. The city of Pontiac was named after a chief of the Ottawa tribe.

(2) Many names remind us of the British who were among the first to settle in the new continent. States like Georgia, Maryland, and the Carolinas were named after British kings and queens. Cities like Boston and Cambridge have old English names.

(3) Many names remind us of early explorers and settlers other than English. Albuquerque was named after a Portuguese explorer of the fifteenth century. Santa Fe, the city of the "Holy Faith," was named by Spanish missionaries. Detroit has a French name, reminding us that the French influence was once strong around the Great Lakes.

(4) Many names were brought to this country by people from many parts of the world. The name *Caudill* was originally *Caudillo,* which in Spain was the word for "leader." The name *Zimmerman* came from Germany, where it meant "carpenter." Names like *Hayakawa* and *Yamagami,* common in Hawaii and on the West Coast, came from Japan.

Other national or ethnic groups are represented in the names of such everyday things as food. Okra is a vegetable whose name is still very close to its original West African name, nkruma. Scones were first baked in Scotland. Coleslaw was first made in Holland.

The exercises on the following pages will give you a chance to ask: "What's in a Name?"

WHAT'S IN A NAME?
How did Americans name places in the New World?

When New Orleans was the Capital of the Spanish Province of Luisiana. 1762 — 1803 This street bore the name CALLE REAL

↑ ALBUQUERQUE
ESPAÑOLA →
TAOS →

TOWN LINE PENOBSCOT

SAGUARO NATIONAL MONUMENT

4

Giving Things Names

We can often guess at the nationality of someone's grandparents by looking at the *family name*. Where did the ancestors of the following people live? Write the place of origin or the original nationality after the number of the name. (What helps you guess? If you don't know, how can you find out?) For three of these, bring to class several similar names from the same group.

EXERCISE 1

1. Ericson
2. Gerber
3. Garcia
4. Van Houten
5. Di Giuglio
6. Epstein
7. Muradian
8. Wong
9. Laporte
10. Yanitelli
11. Paganopolis
12. McGraw
13. Roskowsky
14. O'Hara
15. Harrington
16. Hittenberger
17. Czermak
18. Romanoff
19. Semanski
20. Perez

Many people have a family name that once described an occupation. What kind of work is named by each name in this list? If you know the answer (or can guess), write it after the number of the word. (Do you know any names that could be added to this list? What are they?)

EXERCISE 2

1. Butler
2. Carter
3. Fowler
4. Cooper
5. Wright
6. Wainwright
7. Page
8. Miller
9. Mason
10. Dyer
11. Porter
12. Smith
13. Weaver
14. Chandler
15. Carpenter
16. Tinker
17. Clark
18. Shepherd
19. Reeve
20. Constable

The pioneers who explored and settled our country had to gives names to thousands of *places*. How did they go about this task? Find out about our American names by studying questions that appear on the next page. Write down brief notes for class discussion.

EXERCISE 3

Words

1. What do the following American place names have in common? Can you explain how each of these places was named?

Washington	Cicero
Williamsburg	Lincoln
Maryland	Charleston
Jackson Corners	Madison
Jamestown	Houston

2. What do the following American place names have in common? Where did they come from?

Cairo	Cambridge
New Jersey	New York
New Orleans	Memphis
Athens	Syracuse

3. What do the following American place names have in common? What accounts for the differences between them?

San Antonio	San Pedro
St. Louis	Santa Clara
San Francisco	San Mateo
Santa Maria	

4. What do the following names have in common?

Mohawk River	Penobscot Bay
North Dakota	Cherokee Trail
Mohave Desert	Oneida Lake
Sioux Falls	

EXERCISE 4

People often give their names to a product or activity. Whose name is preserved in each of the following? Find the answer for *ten* of these in a dictionary. Write one sentence about each.

1. hooligan	11. guppy
2. boycott	12. gardenia
3. Levis	13. diesel
4. tawdry	14. chesterfield
5. bowie knife	15. graham cracker
6. leotard	16. dahlia
7. mackintosh	17. sequoia
8. volt	18. poinsettia
9. sandwich	19. zinnia
10. wisteria	20. watt

Study the meanings of words and of the building blocks that help us make up words.

When we learn new words, we try to fix their meanings firmly in our minds. We look at how they are used in a sentence. We look at them together with words that mean the same. Sometimes we look at *parts* of a word that help us understand or remember its meaning.

W2
WORDS AND
THEIR MEANINGS

Study words with the same meaning and words with opposite meanings.

Several words often have the same or a very similar meaning. In building up our vocabulary, this fact helps us move from one word to the other. Words that have the same or a very similar meaning are called **synonyms.** Synonyms "name something together." *Start* is a synonym of *begin. End* is a synonym of *finish.*

To help fix the meaning of a word in our minds, we sometimes look at a word with the *opposite* meaning. Words that have opposite meanings are called **antonyms.** *End* is an antonym of *begin. Hot* is an antonym of *cold. Lenient* means the opposite of *harsh* or *strict.* Remember:

W2a
Synonyms and
Antonyms

(1) Our language often gives us a choice of several synonyms for an idea or thing. Here are some groups of synonyms that we can use in talking about the world of work:

work	job, employment, position
fire	dismiss, lay off, terminate
tool	instrument, implement, utensil
pay	compensation, wage, salary
vacation	break, leave, furlough, holiday

(2) Synonyms do not always mean exactly the same. They may have different shades of meaning. *Harsh* and *strict* mean roughly the same. But *harsh* is the stronger word; it means "very strict" or "too strict." Synonyms may have slightly different uses. We can give either "directions" or "instructions" on how to assemble a piece of furniture. But when we give a traveler "directions," we make it clear that these are instructions on how to find a place.

(3) Dictionaries often provide both synonyms and antonyms. To explain the word *fragile,* the dictionary may use

the word *breakable*. Often dictionaries provide a brief comparison of synonyms after a regular dictionary entry. Here is a comparison of synonyms for *excuse*. Study it and explain the differences in your own words:

> **Syn.** *v.t.* 3 **Excuse, pardon, forgive** mean to free from blame or punishment. **Excuse** means to overlook less important errors and faults: *He excused our failure to reply.* **Pardon** is used in a similar manner, but it can also mean to free from punishment due for serious faults, wrongdoing, or crimes: *The governor pardoned him and restored his civil rights.* **Forgive** suggests more personal feelings, and emphasizes giving up all wish to punish for wrong done: *I am sure his rudeness was unintentional, and I forgive him for it.*
>
> —*Thorndike Barnhart Advanced Dictionary*

EXERCISE 1

A. After the number of each of the following words, write down another word that means the same or nearly the same. (Compare your choices with those of your classmates.)

EXAMPLE: rapid   (Answer) *quick*

1. error	11. assist
2. jail	12. journey
3. examine	13. allow
4. shrewd	14. prohibit
5. goal	15. security
6. mercy	16. illegal
7. protect	17. demand
8. construct	18. wealthy
9. wood	19. attorney
10. rock	20. collect

B. After the number of each of the following words, write down another word that means the *opposite*. (Compare your choices with those of your classmates.)

EXAMPLE: determined   (Answer) *undecided*

21. excited	26. profit
22. ancient	27. suspicion
23. complicated	28. temporary
24. hostility	29. bashful
25. contaminated	30. eager

EXERCISE 2

Look at the italicized word in each sentence. In the list of *synonyms* at the end, find a word that means the same, or nearly the same. Write it after the number of the sentence.

EXAMPLE: The builders complained about *interference* by the city.
(Answer)   *meddling*

1. We returned the table because of a *flaw* in the wood.
2. Doctors had discovered a new *remedy* for this illness.
3. Pat tried to *assemble* the model car without help.
4. Things do not just *vanish* without a trace.
5. Customers often *waver* before signing the contract.
6. The rudder makes the boat *alter* its direction.
7. The company will move to its new *location* in May.
8. The museum will *exhibit* treasures from ancient Egypt.
9. They decided to *bolster* the strength of their border patrols.
10. The new *regulations* were posted on the bulletin board.
11. These safety measures have had very little *effect*.
12. The tribes along the coast used to *barter* salt against furs.
13. Rivalry between members of a family can cause a *conflict*.
14. The highway was always *congested* on a weekend.
15. The doctor's office changed the date for my *examination*.
16. The reporters refused to *identify* their sources.
17. The students had presented several *legitimate* complaints.
18. The box had a *transparent* plastic cover.
19. Everyone was asked not to *discard* old cans and bottles.
20. The accident was the result of an *unfortunate* decision.

SYNONYMS:

change	disappear	see-through	quarrel
result	display	trade	put together
rules	address	strengthen	crowded
cure	hesitate	name	throw away
defect	checkup	unlucky	justifiable

Look at the italicized word in each sentence. In the list of *antonyms* at the end, find a word that means the opposite. Write it after the number of the sentence.

EXERCISE 3

EXAMPLE: My uncle was always *affectionate* with us children.
(Answer)   *harsh*

1. The accident happened in very *dense* fog.
2. The team was trying to strengthen its *offense*.
3. They explained that the insult had not been *deliberate*.
4. A potter needs *nimble* fingers.
5. Teachers should do more to counteract *prejudice*.
6. Marion made a *determined* effort to lift the heavy cover.
7. We were afraid such a well-known athlete would be *arrogant*.
8. She has been very *secretive* about her future plans.
9. Julio had been taught to treat old people with *respect*.

10. Very young children are helpless and *vulnerable*.
11. The parents wanted to *believe* the excuses given them by the son.
12. Elected officials have a right to their own *private* lives.
13. The child dragged along by its sister started to *resist*.
14. My friend has a record of *failure* as an inventor.
15. Chinese painters often used very *delicate* lines.
16. Until her illness, my aunt had always been an *optimist*.
17. The judge decided that the driver had been *negligent*.
18. The owner had to *dismiss* most of her employees.
19. Heat causes metals to *expand*.
20. When the band marched in, the audience broke into *spontaneous* applause.

ANTONYMS:

coarse	awkward	public	unintentional
open	protected	careful	rehearsed
thin	pessimist	humble	halfhearted
yield	tolerance	contract	defense
hire	contempt	success	doubt

EXERCISE 4

Study the words in the following pairs. What do the words in each pair have in common? How are they different? Prepare to help explain the differences in class discussion.

1. paddling and rowing
2. scribble and scrawl
3. a wage and a salary
4. a street and a road
5. trotting and running
6. a kingdom and an empire
7. a discussion and a debate
8. a newcomer and an outsider
9. listen and overhear
10. imitate and mimic

W2b

Word Roots

Study the building blocks that help us make up words.

Often a part of a word is repeated in several other words. Look at the syllable *leg* in the following words: Something is *legal* when it is according to the law. Something is *illegal* when it is against the law. A *legislator* is a person who helps make laws. The shared syllable often appears in words that have something to do with the law. It helps us understand a group of related words.

Remember:

(1) Often a familiar word root helps us understand the meaning of a word. The same **root** can serve as the main or basic part of several different words. For instance, several English words use the root *flex*, which means "bend." A *flexible*

rod can be bent. An *inflexible* person will not yield or bend. Here are ten familiar roots, with their meanings and examples:

ROOT	MEANING	EXAMPLES
ceed, cede	go, come	When hikers *proceed*, they *go* forward. Someone who *concedes* the truth *comes* around to admitting something is true.
frac, frag	break	A *fractured* arm has been *broken*. A *fragment* is a piece that has *broken* off.
lib	free	*Liberty* is another word for *freedom*. To *liberate* people means to set them *free*.
mit, miss	send	When we *remit* money by mail, we *send* a check or money order. People on a *mission* have been *sent* to do a task.
mob	move	A *mobile* home can be *moved*. An *automobile* is a "self-*moving*" vehicle.
pel	push	A person who is *expelled* is *pushed* out. An insect *repellent pushes* away insects.
port	carry	*Transportation carries* people to their destination. When we *portage* a canoe, we *carry* it.
rect	right	When we *correct* something, we set it *right*. A *rectangle* has four *right* angles.
temp	time	A *temporary* employee has been hired only for a *time*. A *contemporary* lives at the same *time* as someone else.
tract	pull	A *tractor pulls* farm machinery. A sale that *attracts* customers *pulls* them in.

Words

(2) Often a common prefix helps us understand the meaning of a word. A **prefix** is a part we attach at the beginning of a word to change its meaning. The prefix *re–* often means "back." When we *return* something, we give it back. A *rerun* brings back an old program. Here are ten familiar prefixes:

PREFIX	MEANING	EXAMPLES
co–, con–	together	When we *cooperate,* we work *together*. At a *conference,* many people come *together*.
dis–	opposite, apart	*Disagree* means the *opposite* of agree. *Discomfort* is the *opposite* of comfort. When we *disassemble* something, we take it *apart*.
ex–	out, out of	When we *exhale,* we breathe *out*. We *export* products when we sell them and ship them *out of* the country.
in–, im–	in, into	When we *inhale,* we breathe *in*. When we *import* goods, we bring them *into* the country from abroad.
inter–	between, among	*International* trade is trade *between* nations. An *interstate* highway runs *between* states.
post–	after, later	When we *postpone* a meeting, we put it off until *later*. A *postscript* is written *after* the rest of a letter.
pre–	before	A *preview* lets us see something *before* others do. A *pretest* tests what you know *before* you study something.
re–	back	When we *return* a gift, we give it *back*. When we put a car in *reverse,* we make it go *back*.

PREFIX	MEANING	EXAMPLES
sub–	below	*Subzero* temperatures go down *below* zero. A *submarine* can travel *below* the surface of the ocean.
trans–	across	A *transatlantic* flight *crosses* the Atlantic. A *transmitter* sends signals *across* large distances.

NOTE: Some prefixes have several *different* meanings. The prefix *in–* or *im–* often means "opposite" or "not": *informal* (the opposite of formal), *impossible* (not possible).

(3) Often a common suffix helps us understand a word. A suffix is a part we attach at the end of a word to change its meaning. The suffix *–less* means "without": *hopeless* (without hope), *penniless* (without money). Here are a few suffixes:

SUFFIX	MEANING	EXAMPLES
-cide	kill	A *pesticide kills* pests. *Homicide* is the *killing* of another person.
-ette	small	A *kitchenette* is a *small* kitchen. A *dinette* is a small dining area.
-fy	make	We *purify* water to *make* it pure. We *justify* a decision to *make* it seem right.

The italicized word in each of the following sentences uses a familiar word root. Find the right meaning for the word in the list at the end. Write the meaning after the number of the sentence.

EXERCISE 1

EXAMPLE: She adjusted the projector so the movie could *proceed.*
(Answer) *go on*

1. The black ants *repelled* the attack of the red ants.
2. Check to see if your name and address are *correct.*
3. Jokes may *distract* attention from more serious matters.
4. The plane is *propelled* by a stream of air.

5. Queen Elizabeth *succeeded* Queen Mary.
6. Long negotiations may *precede* the settlement.
7. She took her *portable* typewriter along on the trip.
8. The information we had was *fragmentary*.
9. The flood waters had already started to *recede*.
10. Changes in temperature had made the metal *contract*.
11. The candidate started to *mobilize* his supporters.
12. They always contributed *liberally* to fund-raising efforts.
13. Illegal immigrants were *deported* to their own countries.
14. We read about Amelia Earhart in *contemporary* newpapers.
15. The horse gave the tribes of the plains greater *mobility*.
16. Her grandmother had been a *liberated* slave.
17. The impact had *fragmented* the windshield.
18. Please enclose your *remittance* in the envelope.
19. We will try to *rectify* the error.
20. Please *transmit* the completed application.

MEANINGS:

set free	of that time	exactly right
freely	pushed forward	come before
go down	money sent	ability to move
send	shipped back	came after
set right	pull together	in bits and pieces
shattered	easy to carry	pushed back
pull away	make move	

EXERCISE 2

The italicized word in each of the following sentences uses a familiar *prefix* or *suffix*. Find the right meaning of the word in the list at the end. Write the meaning after the number of the sentence.

EXAMPLE: The dentist *extracted* the tooth.
(Answer) *pulled out*

1. A driver's license will *expire* if it is not renewed.
2. The phone company had *disconnected* the telephone.
3. The drivers took a *preliminary* look at the sunken treasure.
4. We use loudspeakers to *amplify* sound.
5. Even the strongest supporters of the team were *discouraged*.
6. On public television, no commercials *interrupt* the programs.
7. Because of the fine weather, we decided to *extend* our vacation.
8. The company has an *exclusive* contract for the new toys.
9. The police and the fire department tried to *coordinate* their efforts.
10. Most of the wreck was *submerged* in the sand.
11. Mustangs are horses that have *reverted* to their wild ways.
12. There was a long *intermission* after the first part of the concert.
13. The two partners had to *cosign* the documents.

14. The workers began to *dismantle* the scaffolding.
15. Scientists were *predicting* a major earthquake.
16. The group helped *rehabilitate* former prisoners.
17. Tourists broke all records for *transatlantic* travel.
18. Several kinds of *insecticide* had been banned.
19. Her parents had lived in *postwar* Europe.
20. His family had *immigrated* from Samoa.

MEANINGS:

gone back	keeping others out
sign together	take apart
unhooked	telling beforehand
bring back to normal	without confidence
make bigger	break in between
across the Atlantic	after war
come into the country	covered
make work together	before the main effort
stretch out	pause
insect killer	run out

Each of the numbered words in this exercise is followed by three choices. Which choice gives the right meaning of the word? Write the letter for the right choice after the number of the word.

EXAMPLE: *7 c*

1. illegal	a. unlawful	b. delayed	c. new
2. furlough	a. allow	b. furrow	c. vacation
3. fragile	a. breakable	b. broken	c. elastic
4. remit	a. push back	b. send	c. repeat
5. temporary	a. to be sold	b. reluctant	c. for a time
6. dismantle	a. expose	b. take apart	c. ship back
7. inhale	a. buy abroad	b. breathe in	c. pull out
8. postpone	a. put off	b. push up	c. draw in
9. precede	a. go around	b. come before	c. shrink
10. location	a. time zone	b. attempt	c. address
11. remedy	a. repetition	b. excuse	c. cure
12. congested	a. crowded	b. digested	c. automatic
13. alter	a. repeat	b. change	c. trade
14. liberate	a. register	b. teach	c. set free
15. expel	a. push out	b. exterminate	c. force
16. cooperate	a. unhook	b. work together	c. stitch up
17. amplify	a. increase	b. join	c. lose faith
18. predict	a. recognize	b. break up	c. tell ahead
19. dismiss	a. sign up	b. fire	c. ban
20. spontaneous	a. required	b. far away	c. unrehearsed

WORDS SERVE OUR NEEDS

W3

**WORDS ON
THE JOB**

Study words that help people do their work.

Language helps the world do its work. To do something right, we often need to know the words connected with the task. We learn new words the first time we try to repair our own bicycle, or the first time we use a sewing machine. We learn new words when we learn how to drive, or when we become interested in woodwork or pottery.

Most tasks and most jobs bring with them their own **technical terms**—exact words for the tools and activities they require.

Here are two examples:

awl   "a tool consisting of a rounded wooden handle and a long metal point, used by a shoemaker to make holes in leather for sewing, or by a carpenter to make holes in wood (for screws, for instance)"

scalpel   "a small, straight, very thin-bladed knife used by doctors in surgery to make very precise cuts"

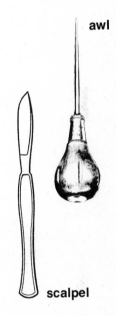

awl

scalpel

Remember:

(1) Some words are truly "specialist's words," new to many outsiders. When talking to an optometrist, we learn words like *retina* and *cornea*. When talking to a carpenter, we learn words like *auger* and *bit*. When you encounter such words, learn to ask questions like "How do you spell that word? What does it mean?"

Here is how your dictionary might explain a "specialist's word":

> **cau ter ize** (kô′tər īz), *v.,* **-ized, -iz ing.** burn with a hot iron or a caustic substance. Doctors sometimes cauterize wounds to prevent bleeding or infection.
>
> —*Thorndike-Barnhart Advanced Junior Dictionary*

(2) A common word is often used with a special meaning on a particular job. A dressmaker uses the word *eye* to mean the hole in a needle for thread, or the loop in which to fasten a hook. A watchmaker uses the word *balance* for a special wheel that helps regulate the movement of a clock.

(3) A word often changes its meaning as it moves from one job to another. The same italicized word has two very

different meanings in each of the following pairs. In each case, are the two meanings in any way related?

Reception was poor until we bought our new *antenna*.
The beetle stopped and wiggled one *antenna*.

The carpenter took the *plane* out of the toolbox.
The *plane* stopped for refueling.

The shoes were designed to help with fallen *arches*.
The architect has designed a row of graceful *arches*.

Here is how a high school dictionary lists two different meanings of the same word:

an ten na (an ten′ə), *n., pl.* **-ten nae** *for 1;* **-ten nas** *for 2.* **1.** one of two feelers on the head of an insect, lobster, etc., **2.** long wire or wires used in television and radio for sending out or receiving electromagnetic waves; aerial. [< L *antenna*, originally, sailyard]

—Thorndike-Barnhart High School Dictionary

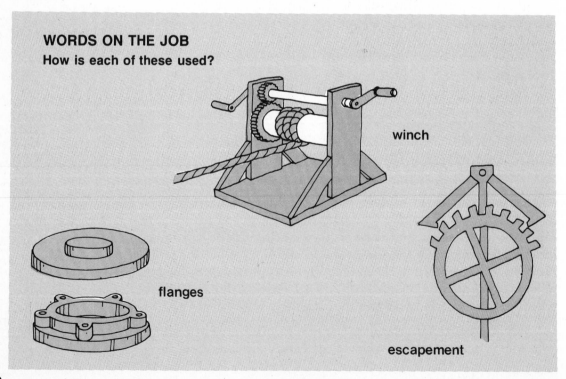

WORDS ON THE JOB
How is each of these used?

winch

flanges

escapement

Choose *ten* of the following tools or devices. Write one sentence about each to describe it or explain its use.

1. a chisel
2. a crowbar
3. a plumb line
4. an easel
5. a thimble
6. a vise
7. a plane
8. a scalpel
9. a tripod
10. a pendulum
11. a telescope
12. a monkey wrench
13. a power saw
14. a trowel
15. a squeegee

Look at the italicized words in the following sentences. Find the right meaning for each word in the list at the end. Write the meaning after the number of the word.

EXAMPLE: The owner was looking for *clerical* help.
(Answer) *for office work*

1. Unfortunately the ticket was no longer *valid*.
2. Blazing heat *alternated* with extreme cold.
3. I can take the day off if I find a *substitute*.
4. In a cold climate, homes need *insulation*.
5. The store sent an *invoice* with the lamp.
6. The chemicals started to *contaminate* the water supply.
7. The turnout was only fifty percent of the *eligible* voters.
8. The agent said our reservations had been *confirmed*.
9. The factory refused to take back the *merchandise*.
10. We carefully assembled the *rations* for the long trip.
11. The second *installment* on the record player will soon be due.
12. If the item is damaged, ask for a *reduction* in price.
13. The crops were larger because of improved *irrigation*.
14. She asked for an *extension* of her vacation.
15. Higher pay and shorter hours were the main *incentives*.
16. Cotton had been replaced by *synthetic* fibers.
17. The product was sold on an *experimental* basis.
18. The law banned garments made from *inflammable* materials.
19. Customers were asked to state their *preference*.
20. The older buildings had begun to *deteriorate*.

MEANINGS:
took turns
get worse
poison
more time
things for sale
bill
watering
reasons for effort
can participate
lowering

artificial
protecting layer
burning easily
tryout
food portions
part payment
good for use
replacement
first choice
made final

Words

Some words change in meaning as they move from one job to another. Fill in the missing explanation in each of the following pairs. (Write on a separate sheet of paper.)

1. To a salesclerk, a *deposit* is money put down by a customer who plans to buy something.
   For a person working with chemicals, a *deposit* is _____ .

2. A doctor will put a broken leg in a *cast*.
   For people working in the theater, the *cast* is _____ .

3. In a newspaper, a *column* is a short piece giving opinions or advice, written regularly by the same writer.
   To a builder, a *column* is _____ .

4. To a builder, a *pool* is a big tank of water for swimming.
   For commuters, a car *pool* is an arrangement that _____ .

5. A school *board* is a group in charge of the local schools.
   Someone offering room and *board* offers a place to live and _____ .

6. To a cook, an *apron* is something to wear over clothes.
   For an airplane mechanic, an *apron* is _____ .

7. For a motorist, a *radiator* is a cooling device that keeps the engine from overheating.
   For a janitor in an old building, a *radiator* is _____ .

8. For a hunter, a *trap* is a device that catches animals.
   For a plumber, a *trap* is _____ .

9. To a sailor, a *cape* is a piece of land jutting out into the ocean.
   To a tailor, a *cape* is _____ .

10. To a doctor, a *vein* is a blood vessel.
    To a miner, a *vein* is _____ .

11. To an electrician, a *wire* is a thin strand of metal.
    To a messenger, a *wire* is _____ .

12. For a clerk in a hardware store, a *basin* is a kind of container.
    For a geography teacher, a *basin* is _____ .

13. For people who like to fish, a *pole* is a fishing rod.
    For an electrician, a *pole* is _____ .

14. To a violinist, the *strings* are wires across an instrument.
    To a music critic, the *strings* are _____ .

15. To an office worker, a *staple* is a metal clamp used to clip paper together.
    To a dietician, a *staple* is _____ .

Pretend you have been invited to replace the manager of an employment agency for one day. How well do you understand the terms and expressions that you might need on the job? Prepare some brief notes for class discussion.

EXERCISE 4

1. What is the difference between *personal* and *personnel?*
2. Is every "clerk" a "clerical" worker?
3. What kind of jobs do people usually call "professions"?
4. Is there a difference between "apprentice" and "trainee"?
5. What is the difference between "skilled" and "semiskilled" labor?
6. What is the difference between a "mechanic" and a "technician"?
7. What do people mean by "service occupations"?
8. Explain in one sentence each what kind of work is done by a receptionist, a stenographer, and a cashier.
9. What is the difference between a physician and a surgeon?
10. What is the difference between a pilot and a navigator?

Do you have a friend or relative whose *job talk* would not make sense to many outsiders? Or have you studied the words of some occupation or technical field as part of a hobby? Choose five important terms connected with the job or technical field. Give a brief explanation for each.

EXERCISE 5

Learn how to use the dictionary.

A dictionary is a book of words. It collects a wealth of information about words. You will use it mainly to find the meaning of words. But it also tells you how words are spelled and pronounced. Often it tells you something about the history of a word. It tells you where a word came from, or how it was first used. You may even use a dictionary to find out how something looks, for most dictionaries have pictures for some of the words they explain.

W4

USING THE DICTIONARY

Learn how to find words in the dictionary.

Each word explained in a dictionary is called an **entry.** Dictionaries list entries in alphabetical order. All the words

W4a

Finding Words

EXPLANATION OF DICTIONARY ENTRIES

Key to the parts of a dictionary entry

① the entry word, printed in boldface type; often called *main entry* or simply *entry* (shows how the word is spelled and divided in writing)

② the pronunciation, in parentheses; often called the *respelling*

③ grammatical label, abbreviated, in italic type

④ any irregular forms, in small boldface type

⑤ the word's meanings (special phrases in boldface type)

⑥ usage label such as *informal, slang, dialectal*

⑦ the origin of the word, in square brackets

⑧ synonyms keyed by number to the definition to which they apply

⑨ usage notes dealing with words frequently confused and similar problems

⑩ words derived from the entry word; often called *run-on entries* or simply *run-ons*

---

an them (an′thəm), *n.* **1.** song of praise, devotion, or patriotism: *"The Star-Spangled Banner" is the national anthem of the United States.* **2.** piece of sacred music, usually with words from some passage in the Bible. [< VL *antefna* < LL < Gk. *antiphona* antiphon.]

(labels ① ② ③ ⑤ ⑦)

buy (bī), *v.,* **bought, buy ing,** *n.* —*v.* **1.** get by paying a price: *You can buy a pencil for five cents.* **2.** buy things. **3.** bribe: *It was charged that two of the jury had been bought.* **4. buy off,** get rid of by paying money to. **5. buy out,** buy all the shares, rights, etc., of. **6. buy up,** buy all that one can of; buy. —*n.* **1.** *Informal.* thing bought; purchase. **2.** *U.S. Informal.* a bargain. [OE *bycgan*]
Syn. *v.* **1. Buy, purchase** mean to get something by paying a price. **Buy** is the general and informal word: *A person can buy anything in that store if he has the money.* **Purchase** is used in more formal style and suggests buying after careful planning or by business dealings or on a large scale: *The bank has purchased some property on which to construct a new building.*
Buy is used with *from,* not *off of*: *He bought it from a stranger he met on the street.*

(labels ① ② ③ ④ ③ ⑤ ⑥ ⑦ ⑧ ⑨)

pro tec tive (prə tek′tiv), *adj.* **1.** being a defense; protecting: *the hard protective covering of a turtle.* **2.** preventing injury to those around: *a protective device on a machine.* **3.** guarding against foreign-made goods by putting a high tax or duty on them: *a protective tariff.* —**pro tec′tive ly,** *adv.* —**pro tec′tive ness,** *n.*

(labels ① ② ③ ⑤ ⑩)

protective coloring, a coloring some animals have that makes them hard to distinguish from the things they live among, and so hides them from their enemies.

(labels ① ⑤)

—*Thorndike Barnhart Dictionary*

beginning with *a* are listed first. Then come all words beginning with *b*, and so on. The words under *a* or *b* or any other letter are alphabetized by their second letter, third letter, or whichever letter is the first to be different. Here, for example, is a sample of alphabetized *a* words:

a	a*bd*omen	a*bi*de
*aa*rdvark	a*be*d	a*bi*lity
a*ba*ck	a*be*t	a*bj*ure
a*bb*ot	a*bh*or	a*bl*aze

Remember:

(1) Use guide words to help you find entries quickly. **Guide words** appear in the upper left- and right-hand corners of each page. Or there may be a guide word in the upper left corner of one page and another in the upper right corner of the facing page. (Sometimes both guide words for a page may appear in the upper left corner.) One guide word will be the first word on its page. The other guide word will be the last word on its page.

Here is part of a dictionary page with only the guide words and a sampling of the entry words for that page:

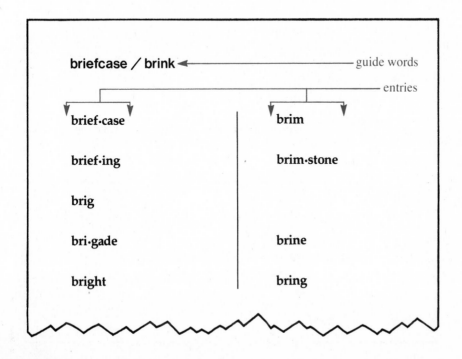

By looking at the guide words, you can quickly tell if a word you are looking for is on that page. Suppose you are looking up *fiction*. If the guide words are *fever* and *field,* you know you will find *fiction* on that page. You would not, however, find *feud* or *ferry* on the same page. Nor would you find *fierce* or *fight*.

(2) Know the most common ways the same sound may be spelled. Many English words are not spelled the way they sound. The more unusual or difficult a word is, the better the chance that the spelling will also be unusual. Words like *chaos* or *chemistry* do not appear under *k* but under *ch*. Words like *ghost* and *ghastly* do not follow *go* and *gas* but appear under *gh*. Study the following chart of possible spellings for common English sounds. Often, you will have to look for a new word under two or three different spellings.

A SPELLING CHART

CONSONANTS

SOUND	SOME POSSIBLE SPELLINGS
(f)	*f*it, *ph*ase, lau*gh*
(g)	*g*et, *g*uest, *gh*ost
(h)	*h*er, *wh*ose
(j)	*j*ack, *g*em, ju*dg*e
(k)	*c*at, *k*ing, *ch*emist, cli*qu*e
(n)	*n*ot, *kn*ight, *gn*aw
(r)	*r*an, *wr*ing, *rh*ythm
(s)	*s*it, *c*ent, *sc*ience, *ps*alm
(sh)	*sh*e, *ch*ef, spe*c*ial, ten*s*ion, na*t*ion, con*sc*ious, *s*ure
(t)	*t*ool, *tw*o, *Th*omas
(z)	*z*ero, *X*erox

VOWELS

SOUND	SOME POSSIBLE SPELLINGS
(ey)	*a*ble, m*ai*l, b*ay*, gr*ey*, *eigh*t
(ee)	b*e*, s*ee*, s*ea*, rec*ei*ve, rel*ie*f, cl*i*que
(ī)	*i*ce, fr*y*, *eye*, l*ie*, *ai*sle
(i)	l*i*d, h*y*mn
(u)	*u*nit, *Eu*rope, f*ew*, barbec*ue*, v*iew*
(aw)	*a*ll, p*aw*

Write the words below in alphabetical order as you would find them in a dictionary. Use your own paper.

front	gain	fate	imply	increase
grip	grace	from	grass	hem
herb	horse	help	fear	heat
idle	house	group	feast	glass
fare	income	humor	game	fast

The following words all start with the letter *s*. Alphabetize them as you would find them in a dictionary. Use your own paper.

seam	sew	snail	speed	spin
seat	severe	sever	steer	smile
shadow	safe	sour	smear	steel
shade	shy	sacred	sail	snow
smart	seven	sneak	steal	small

Assume that the guide words on a page of a dictionary are *clog* and *clutch*. Which of the following words would you find on that page? Write the words that you would find on your own paper.

close	coast	clod	clown	clone
cleat	cling	clutter	clothes	coat
cigar	clamp	cite	cluster	cloud

Look at the words in the right-hand column below, and match each of them with the proper guide words in the left-hand column. Write the letter of each word next to the number of the guide words that would include or bracket the word.

1. notify/nuclear	A. network
2. numeral/nylon	B. nice
3. nose/notice	C. noise
4. news/nick	D. navy
5. nip/noise	E. nap
6. nerve/neutral	F. nothing
7. niece/nine	G. next
8. nag/narrow	H. native
9. nasal/nature	I. noun
10. nautical/near	J. nurture

Words

EXERCISE 5

Use the spelling chart to help you find each of the following in a dictionary. Write the correct spelling of the word after its number. Each word is written roughly the way it sounds.

1. (gastlee)
2. (rath)
3. (conseeted)
4. (jiraff)
5. (sintillating)
6. (krome)
7. (vishis)
8. (tekneek)
9. (jigantik)
10. (simpathi)
11. (fotograf)
12. (klover)
13. (retreeve)
14. (gardyen)
15. (sharade)

W4b

Basic Information

Learn how to read the main parts of dictionary entries.

Each entry in a dictionary arranges information in a very similar pattern. Study the following example of a dictionary entry. Then study the explanations that follow it.

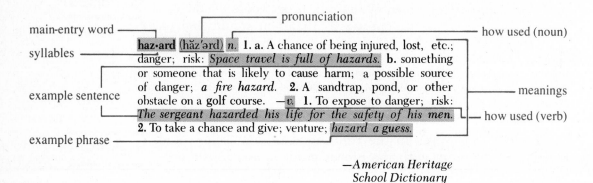

—*American Heritage School Dictionary*

Remember:

(1) Entries are divided into syllables. A small dot or extra space separates one syllable from another. Knowing the separate syllables helps you to divide a word at the end of a line in your own writing. Below is the word "commercial" as it appears in one dictionary. Notice that it may be divided between the *m*'s or between the *r* and the *c:*

com·mer·cial

(2) The way to say, or pronounce, a word is shown after the word itself. When there is more than one right pronunciation, a dictionary will show them. For instance, which of the two following pronunciations of *lever* do you use?

(lev′ər)   or   (lē′vər)

For more on pronunciation, see **W4d.**

(3) A grammatical label for a word appears next. What kind of word is it—how is it used in a sentence? Is it used as a noun, like *car* or *engine?* Is it used as a verb, like *blacken* or *organize?* Many words can be used two or more different ways in a sentence. The entry might first list meanings for *light* used as a noun (The *light* went on). Then the entry might list meanings for *light* used as a verb (It will *light* up the room).

Here are some abbreviations for kinds of words:

n. for *noun*	*pron.* for *pronoun*
v. for *verb*	*prep.* for *preposition*
adj. for *adjective*	*con.* for *connective* (or *conjunction*)
adv. for adverb	

See **S1** for more on kinds of words in a sentence.

(4) One or more meanings are given for the word. Often dictionaries give the most common meaning first. They then go on to some of the more unusual or specialized meanings. Here for instance is the likely order of meanings for a word like *foot:*

1. part of the body
2. lowest part; for instance, of a hill
3. twelve inches
4. foot soldiers, or infantry
5. part of a line of poetry

To find a difficult or unusual meaning, you will often have to keep on reading through several more familiar meanings of a word.

(5) Example sentences or phrases often follow meanings. These show us words in action. They will often help you to decide which meaning of a word you want. Suppose, for example, you want to know the meaning of *resist* in the sentence

"This material will resist stains." Here are the example sentences from one dictionary for this word:

re·sist (ri zist´) *v.t.* **1.** to refrain from yielding to; abstain from: *She found it difficult to resist his charms.* **2.** to repel or oppose: *The nation was unable to resist the invasion.* **3.** to withstand the action or effect of: *This metal resists corrosion.*

—*Macmillan Dictionary*

The example sentence for the third meaning has something to do with a substance *holding up* against the action of something like a chemical. The third meaning is the right one: to withstand, to hold up under something that might be damaging.

EXERCISE 1

Look up each of the following words in a dictionary. Show where they could be divided at the end of a line. Write the words on your own paper, using hyphens to show all of the possible breaks for each word.

1. division
2. dictionary
3. ridiculous
4. maturity
5. regulation
6. permission
7. responsibility
8. similarity
9. individuality
10. librarian

EXERCISE 2

After each sentence below, there are three possible meanings of the italicized word. Pick the letter of the meaning that fits the sentence. Write that letter on your paper after the number of the sentence.

1. We could hear the *report* of the gun from the next room.
   a. description of an event
   b. a loud noise
   c. fame or reputation

2. The actor *portrayed* General Washington in the play.
   a. make a likeness of, as by drawing
   b. picture in words
   c. act the part of a character

3. He grabbed the bottle by its *neck*.
   a. a part of the body
   b. a thin upper part of a thing
   c. a narrow strip of land

4. John has a *natural* smile.
   a. not forced; sincere
   b. inborn; native
   c. of or referring to natural science

5. The golfer used an *iron* instead of a wood.
   a. a silver-gray metal
   b. a metal-headed club
   c. an appliance used to press clothes

6. The workers *heaved* the heavy load.
   a. raise or lift with effort
   b. lift and throw with effort
   c. rise and fall

7. The twins are birds of the same *feather*.
   a. an outgrowth that covers the bodies of birds
   b. kind or sort
   c. mood or state of health

8. Ben Franklin once worked as a *devil*.
   a. a printer's helper
   b. a wicked or cruel person
   c. an unlucky, pitiful person

9. We tied the boat to the *cleat*.
   a. a piece of metal or rubber on a shoe
   b. a strip of wood or metal to prevent slipping
   c. an object of metal shaped like the top of a T

10. Don't *cloud* the argument by using big words.
    a. make confused or vague
    b. make sad or troubled
    c. cover as if with a cloud

EXERCISE 3

After each sentence below there are three example phrases or sentences for the italicized word. Pick the letter of the sentence or phrase that fits the italicized word. Write that letter on your paper after the number of the sentence.

1. Claire found a good *match* for her new skirt.
   a. *She made a bad match when she married him.*
   b. *a wrestling match*
   c. *The gloves are a good match for the bag.*

2. The teacher's explanation was *obscure* to most students.
   a. *The meaning of this poem is obscure.*
   b. *He's visiting an obscure little fishing village.*
   c. *an obscure back room*

3. Because of the emergency, the mayor was *recalled* from his vacation.
   a. *to recall the past*
   b. *The ambassador was recalled to his own country.*
   c. *His license was recalled for reckless driving.*

4. I hope this cup of tea will *settle* my nerves.
   a. *Quebec was settled by the French.*
   b. *to settle an argument*
   c. *He took a pill to settle his stomach.*

5. The roof is *supported* by large beams.
   a. *That chair won't support your weight.*
   b. *He's not able to support a family yet.*
   c. *His religion supported him after her death.*

6. His confession *washed* away his guilt.
   a. *to wash one's face*
   b. *to be washed of one's sins*
   c. *The boat washed ashore during the storm.*

7. She entered two *events* at the track meet.
   a. *the events leading to the American Revolution*
   b. *In the event of rain, the game will be postponed.*
   c. *We hope to win the figure-skating event.*

8. Only the best five players were given a *letter.*
   a. *the letters of the alphabet*
   b. *the letter of the law*
   c. *a football letter*

9. Have you seen the November 15th *issue* of *Time?*
   a. *to die without issue*
   b. *They discussed the issue for hours.*
   c. *the latest issue of a magazine*

10. The legislature is *invested* with the power to make laws.
    a. *to invest $300 in stocks*
    b. *to invest time in one's work*
    c. *The police are invested with the authority to make arrests.*

EXERCISE 4

Each italicized word below is used in a narrow or special sense. Look each word up in a dictionary. Find the meaning that fits the sentence. Write the meaning on your paper next to the number of the sentence.

1. We loved to swing on the *glider* on our porch.
2. The sailboat was on a good *tack.*

3. The lawyer was permitted to read from her *brief.*
4. Did the golfer actually have an *eagle* on the first hole?
5. How many *kisses* did you eat after lunch?
6. The counselor helped Jane to *map* her future.
7. It is dishonest to *pirate* another author's work.
8. What gift are you going to bring to the *shower?*
9. The score of the first tennis set was six to *love.*
10. For Thanksgiving dinner we always pull out the *leaves* of the table.

Learn the finer points about dictionary entries.

No two dictionaries are exactly alike. But all of them deal in some way with the special items discussed below. If you have a dictionary handy as you read this, check to see how it handles the following points:

(1) Run-on entries usually appear in boldface type. A **run-on entry** is a word that has the same basic meaning as its main-entry word. But it has a different ending or a different use in a sentence. Run-on entries are normally the very last item you will find in a dictionary entry, as you can see from the example below:

> **short‧sight‧ed** (shôrt′sī′tid), *adj.* 1. unable to see far; near-sighted. 2. lacking in foresight; having or showing little care for the future: *a reckless short-sighted young man; a short-sighted decision.* —**short′-sight′ed‧ly,** *adv.* —**short′-sight′ed‧ness,** *n.*
>
> —*Random House School Dictionary*

The run-on entries here are "short-sightedly" and "short-sightedness." If you know the meaning of the main-entry word, you should also understand the meaning of any run-on entry of that word. *(Short-sightedly* means "done in a short-sighted way.")

(2) Look-alike or sound-alike words are listed as separate main-entry words. Ash, for example, is a powdery gray material that is left over after something has been burned. But *ash* can also mean a certain kind of shade tree. A dictionary will show homonyms such as these separately. Each is given a number, usually printed after the entry.

Here is another example. Notice that in this case the words are also pronounced differently but still, however, spelled the same.

> **gill**[1] [gil] *n.* The organ for breathing of fishes and other animals that live under water. Oxygen is removed from water as it passes through the gills, and carbon dioxide is discharged.
> **gill**[2] [jil] *n.* A liquid measure equal to ¼ pint, or half a cup.
>
> — *The Harcourt Brace Intermediate Dictionary*

Whenever you see a word marked[1], be sure to remember that it will be followed by another marked[2], and sometimes one marked[3], and so on. Unless you check all the numbered words, you may not find the proper definition.

NOTE: Homonyms that sound alike but are not spelled alike, such as *hear* and *here, buy* and *by,* will appear in alphabetical order in the dictionary.

See **M5c** for confusing pairs.

(3) Idioms often follow the last meaning of a word. An **idiom** is a group of words, or an expression, that has a special meaning of its own. Often, that meaning cannot be guessed from just the separate words that make up the idiom. Here are the idioms listed after the entry word "place" in one dictionary:

> **give place, a.** make room. **b.** yield; give in.
> **in place, a.** in the proper or usual place; in the original place. **b.** fitting, appropriate, or timely.
> **in place of,** instead of.
> **know one's place, a.** act according to one's position in life.
> **out of place, a.** not in the proper or usual place. **b.** inappropriate or ill-timed.
> **take place,** happen; occur.
>
> — *Thorndike-Barnhard High School Dictionary*

(4) Almost all dictionaries use some usage labels. Usually, these labels are printed in italics and appear directly after the number of the meaning to which they apply.

A **usage label** tells us that a word is in some way limited in its use. Here, for example, are the last two definitions in one dictionary of "hack²" as a noun:

> 5. *Informal.* a. taxicab. b. taxicab driver.
> 6. *British.* a. horse kept for hire or for general work. b. horse for riding.
> *—Macmillan Dictionary*

The usage labels here are "Informal" and "British." The particular labels used in a dictionary and their meanings are usually given in the front part of the book. Here is a list of familiar usage labels:

Nonstandard—not used in educated English
Informal—chatty, fit for casual talk
Slang—*very* informal or disrespectful
Archaic—very old-fashioned
Obsolete—no longer used today
Regional—used only in part of the country

Regional labels may be broken down into the specific places where the expression is commonly used—*Southwestern U.S.* or *New England,* for example. In addition, labels like *British* and *Scotch* and foreign language labels are commonly used in dictionaries.

(5) Often a dictionary will tell us something about the history of a word. Where was it first used? What did it mean at first? How did its meaning change over the centuries? Often word history appears in square brackets. Some dictionaries give it *before* the current meanings of a word. Others leave it to the end.

Here are two sample entries that tell us where a word came from and how it came to have its current meanings:

ko sher (kō′shər), *adj.* **1** right or clean according to Jewish ritual law: *kosher meat.* **2** dealing in products that meet the requirements of Jewish ritual law: *a kosher butcher.* **3** SLANG. all right; fine; legitimate: *It's not kosher to change the rules once the game has started.* —*v.t.* make kosher; prepare (food), clean (utensils), etc., according to the Jewish ritual law. [< Hebrew *kāshēr* proper]

kow tow (kou′tou′), *v.i.* **1** kneel and touch the ground with the forehead to show deep respect, submission, or worship. **2** show slavish respect or obedience. —*n.* act of kowtowing. [< Chinese *k'o-t'ou,* literally, knock (the) head]
—Thorndike Barnhart Advanced Dictionary

WORDS FROM AROUND THE WORLD

Where does each of these words come from? What does it mean?

wigwam

gondola

mantilla

igloo

catamaran

machete

The sign < means "comes from." Common abbreviations for languages that have supplied words to us are as follows:

L.   Latin
Gk.   Greek
F.   French
G.   German
Sp.   Spanish
It.   Italian
Scand.   Scandinavian

NOTE: The introductory materials in a dictionary will explain these and similar abbreviations used in its pages.

Which of the following words are listed as main entries in your dictionary? Which are run-on entries? Write ME after the number of each main entry. Write RO after the number of each run-on entry.

EXERCISE 1

1. imaginative   6. antiquity
2. racial   7. specialist
3. retailer   8. tidiness
4. shaky   9. twirler
5. slowly   10. vocally

Write on a sheet of paper the run-on entries for each of the following words. After studying the meanings of the main-entry words for each, use any five of the run-on entries in a sentence of your own.

EXERCISE 2

1. creative   6. forceful
2. frail¹   7. solid
3. superstitious   8. mobilize
4. tyrannical   9. inherit
5. annual   10. perfect

(NOTE: In some dictionaries the words above may themselves be listed as run-on entries. In that case, find the main-entry word, and list the run-ons for it.)

Each of the following words is a homonym. Write each word on your paper. Then look it up in a dictionary. After

EXERCISE 3

each word, write the basic meanings of the different main entries.

1. bay   6. band
2. mean   7. gorge
3. down   8. loom
4. row   9. minute
5. port   10. do

EXERCISE 4

For each italicized word below, find in your dictionary the homonym that best fits the meaning. On a piece of paper, write the meaning of the homonym that fits.

EXAMPLE: Which kind of *mail* would a knight wear?
(Answer) *a suit of armor*

1. What kind of *line* would concern a tailor?
2. Which *key* might interest a scuba diver?
3. Which *pupil* would interest an eye doctor?
4. What kind of *ply* concerns a carpenter?
5. Which *let* might concern a tennis player?
6. What kind of *bat* bites?
7. What kind of *bass* might bite?
8. Which *buffet* would you find in a restaurant?
9. What *low* might concern a rancher?
10. What sort of *mold* might bother a diner?

EXERCISE 5

Each sentence below contains an idiom—an expression with a special meaning. Look up the italicized word in each sentence. Find the idiom and write it on your paper.

EXAMPLE: If you don't *shake* a leg, we'll be late.
(Answer) *shake a leg*

1. He said we had to hold the *line* on expenses.
2. The coach said we had to *go* for broke.
3. Actors and actresses are in the public *eye*.
4. It's wise to *set* aside money for retirement.
5. How long do you think I will *put* up with you?
6. The general manager was *kicked* upstairs.
7. I hope someone will *come* up with a good idea.
8. We'll have to *make* do with our old car for another year.
9. The British kept a stiff upper *lip* during the war.
10. I hope you didn't get up on the wrong side of the *bed*.

EXERCISE 6

Look up the following words in the front part or in the main part of your dictionary. On your own paper, write the meaning of each, using your own words. If you find more than one meaning, use the one that deals with the use of words or language.

1. archaic   3. informal   5. obsolete   7. slang
2. dialect   4. nonstandard   6. poetic   8. vulgar

EXERCISE 7

In each sentence below the italicized word or words are used in a special way. Look up the word or expression in your dictionary. Next to the number of the sentence, write the usage label given in your dictionary for the intended meaning. (If there is no label, write *No.*)

EXAMPLE: I don't want to hear any more of your *lip*.
(Answer)   *Slang*

1. I'm *game* for a roller-coaster ride if you are.
2. Here come the police; now we're in a *jam*.
3. He bought a new loom for his *bonny*.
4. Do you think he *kenned* my meaning?
5. I'm going to *kibitz* at the card game.
6. It's *Dutch treat* tonight at dinner.
7. We hope *you all* will be coming to the dance.
8. Our team is a *cinch* to win tomorrow.
9. A *bobby* could arrest someone but carried no gun.
10. It's time we *hit the road*.

EXERCISE 8

Find a dictionary that will tell you what language each of the following comes from. Write the language after the number of the word.

1. chauffeur   6. symphony   11. algebra
2. gymnasium   7. motor   12. corral
3. smorgasbord   8. soprano   13. raccoon
4. ballet   9. ski   14. bazaar
5. coleslaw   10. pretzel   15. clique

Let a dictionary show you how to pronounce a word.

W4d

Guide to Pronunciation

Dictionaries show us how to say new or difficult words. After the ordinary spelling of a word, they "respell" it in parentheses to show how the word sounds. The "sound spelling" of the word leaves out all letters that we do not hear when the word is spoken. For instance, the *gh* is left out in words like *night* and *through.* But in addition, dictionaries need special ways of showing the sound of words. Here are some sample respellings:

bare·foot (bâr′foot′)   **cat·tle** (kat′əl)   **row·boat** (rō′bōt′)

Remember:

(1) The sound spelling always uses the same letter or symbol for the same sound.   In ordinary spelling, we use the letter *i* in the word *lid* and in the word *hide.* But the sound is quite different each time. Most dictionaries use the letter *i* to show only the sound in words like *lid, it, lip,* and the like. They use a different way of showing the sound in words like *hide* or *time.* Usually, they use the letter *i* with a long line over it: ī.

Here are other similar pairs:

a	hat, bat, cap	ā	age, page, late
o	hot, not, rot	ō	open, code, road
e	let, bed, pen	ē	equal, be, seat

Sometimes, a single dot or a double dot over a letter helps us tell two sounds apart:

e	let, best	ė	term, learn
ů	full, put	ü	rule, move

For some sounds, dictionaries use a pair of letters: *ch* stands for the first sound in *church* and *child.* Another pair, *zh,* may stand for the sound in the middle of the words *measure* and *leisure.*

Many dictionaries use an upside-down *e* for sounds like the *a* in *about,* the *e* in taken, and the *u* in circus. The sound is called *schwa* and looks like this: ə.

(2) The sound spelling shows what part of the word is loudest or stands out most.   We say that a syllable that stands out is **stressed,** or **accented.** In words like *about* and *around,* the second part stands out. In words like *outlaw* and *soundtrack,* the first part stands out.

Most dictionaries use a heavy mark for the strongest stress: ′. They use a weaker mark for weaker or second-strongest stress: ′. They use no mark for a syllable that is unstressed. Here are some words with both strongest and weaker stress:

cof′fee cake′	pre dom′i nate′
fas′ci nate′	sat′is fac′tion
gear′shift′	San′ Fran cis′co
im′po lite′	trans′at lan′tic
match′book′	un′re served′

NOTE: Some dictionaries make the stress mark come *before* the stressed part of the word. Some make the stress mark come *after* the stressed part.

(3) *Often there is more than one right way to say a word.* When a dictionary lists more than one pronunciation, they are equally good. Dictionary makers generally list the more widely used pronunciation first.

Study the sample pronunciation key reprinted with this section. What sound does each symbol stand for?

A PRONUNCIATION KEY

a	hat, cap	j	jam, enjoy	u	cup, butter
ā	age, face	k	kind, seek	ů	full, put
ä	father, far	l	land, coal	ü	rule, move
		m	me, am		
b	bad, rob	n	no, in	v	very, save
ch	child, much	ng	long, bring	w	will, woman
d	did, red			y	young, yet
		o	hot, rock	z	zero, breeze
e	let, best	ō	open, go	zh	measure, seizure
ē	equal, be	ô	order, all		
ėr	term, learn	oi	oil, voice	ə	represents:
		ou	house, out		a in about
f	fat, if				e in taken
g	go, bag	p	paper, cup		i in pencil
h	he, how	r	run, try		o in lemon
		s	say, yes		u in circus
i	it, pin	sh	she, rush		
ī	ice, five	t	tell, it		
		th	thin, both		
		ᴛʜ	then, smooth		

—Thorndike-Barnhart Advanced Dictionary

Words

Using the pronunciation key printed with this section, say the following pronunciations out loud. After the number of each, write the word the pronunciation item stands for.

1. kärv
2. kėrv
3. drôn
4. droun
5. ə fekt′
6. fens
7. glas′ē
8. hid′n
9. ish′ü
10. nē
11. līn
12. māt
13. uᴛʜ′ər
14. frāz
15. kwik
16. ri vyü′
17. sī′əns
18. sun
19. ᴛʜō
20. yü nīt′

Using the pronunciation key printed with this section, write the pronunciation of each of the following words. Include accent marks where appropriate.

1. high
2. know
3. cream
4. arise
5. extent
6. whole
7. army
8. flower
9. thumb
10. thus

Copy the words below on your paper, keeping the syllable divisions shown. Then put in the strong and, if necessary, weaker stress marks. When you are finished, check your answers in a dictionary.

1. a board
2. but ter fly
3. co ed u ca tion
4. con trast (noun)
5. con trast (verb)
6. dis a gree
7. e lec tric
8. en trance (noun)
9. ex clude
10. hold o ver
11. in con sist ent
12. laugh ter
13. mem or y
14. net work
15. par tic u lar
16. re sist
17. text book
18. un der stand
19. va ri e ty
20. with out

The following words may be pronounced in more than one way. On a sheet of paper, write the pronunciation that you normally use. Use the pronunciation key. Then compare your results with your classmates'.

1. amateur
2. corridor
3. creek
4. either
5. envelope
6. horror
7. often
8. mathematics
9. tomato
10. welfare

Match each word in the left-hand column with its meaning in the right-hand column. Put the right letter after the number of the word.

UNIT REVIEW
EXERCISE

1. example phrase

A. a word that helps us find a word on a page of a dictionary

2. regional

B. a label telling that a word is most commonly used in a particular place

3. run-on entry

C. a label telling that a word is in some way limited in its use

4. pronunciation

D. a word defined in a dictionary

5. usage label

E. another way of spelling a word

6. variant spelling

F. a word that appears after the meanings of a root word

7. main entry

G. a word that sounds like or looks like another word but has a different meaning

8. guide word

H. the way to say a word

9. idiom

I. an illustration of the meaning of an entry

10. homonym

J. a combined expression with a meaning of its own

FOR FURTHER
STUDY

MORE ABOUT NAMES

When we want to name people or things, we often have a choice. Sometimes we encounter new names for things already familiar. Sometimes we have to learn new names for new things. The following activities will give you a chance to explore the ways we choose and change names.

ACTIVITY 1

We often find that a person or thing goes by several different names. Why do we often have several names for the same person or thing? Investigate the cases of double identity on the next page. (Your teacher may ask you to choose one or more of these for a brief report.)

1. What is an alias? Who uses it, and why?

2. What happens when a name is "Anglicized"? Do you know the real names of any current movie stars? Can you tell why the star changed his or her name? Can you find out the real names of such movie and television greats as Marilyn Monroe, Rock Hudson, John Wayne, Kirk Douglas, Lucille Ball, Woody Allen?

3. What is a pen name? Find out the real names of several of the following: Mark Twain, George Eliot, George Orwell, Lewis Carroll.

4. In Africa and other parts of the world, many English and French place names have disappeared in recent years—*Léopoldville* and *Stanleyville,* for example. Can you explain why? On the maps of Europe, what has happened to *St. Petersburg, Stalingrad, Danzig?* Do you know of any place names that were changed at one time or another in your own country or state? Can you explain why?

5. In recent years, some prominent black athletes and writers have changed their names, such as Cassius Clay to Muhammad Ali, or LeRoi Jones to Imamu Amiri Baraka. Why? Where do the new names come from? What other such names do you know?

6. Terms of endearment are special names we call people in order to show affection. Parents often have special affectionate names for children. Friends call each other by friendly nicknames. What "terms of endearment" and nicknames do you know? Do you know any nicknames for famous people in history? Have you had any nicknames—and how did you feel about them?

ACTIVITY 2

Acronyms are a special kind of substitute name. Many acronyms start out as simple abbreviations. We say "UN" and know that the letters stand for "United Nations." But sometimes the new concentrated word takes over, and the original longer name is forgotten.

Explain what the following acronyms originally stood for. Use each acronym in a sentence to show that you understand its meaning (Choose *ten.*)

EXAMPLE: NASA—*National Aeronautics and Space Adminis-
tration.*
*NASA directs the space probe programs in the
United States.*

1. AC
2. FBI
3. UNESCO
4. UNICEF
5. AFL
6. CIO
7. LP
8. emcee
9. CARE
10. ZIP
11. RCA
12. scuba
13. radar
14. veep
15. GI
16. USSR
17. C.O.D.
18. laser
19. Seabee
20. TVA

BONUS: Explain five other acronyms you know. Can you
find any that have become known very recently? (Pool
your list with those of your classmates to make a chart of
current acronyms.)

Different words for the same thing may get different
reactions. *Youngster* sounds warm and welcoming; *juve-
nile* sounds cold and impersonal. *Slender* shows approval;
skinny often shows disapproval. We say that synonyms
that produce different reactions have different **connota-
tions.** In each of the following pairs, which synonym would
you choose? Be prepared to explain the difference in atti-
tude that the two words show. (Prepare brief notes for
class discussion.)

ACTIVITY 3

1. If you had an unusual uncle, would you prefer to have him
   called a *character* or a *crank?*
2. Would you prefer to be called *ambitious* or *pushy?*
3. Do you think people with much money would prefer to be
   called *rich* or *well-off?* Does it make any difference?
4. Where would you rather live—in a *cabin* or a *shack?* Why?
5. When you introduce a student from Great Britain, would
   you call him a *visitor* or a *foreigner?* Why?
6. What do the words *immigrant* and *pilgrim* have in common?
   Is there any difference in the way people react to these two
   words?

7. If you were writing advertising copy for a new beauty cream, would you advise customers to *rub it on* or *smooth it on?*
8. If you want to disapprove of a good friend's misguided plan, would you call it *silly* or *impractical?*
9. Would you call an aunt who is careful with her money *tight* or *economical?*
10. Would you call a friend who rarely takes chances *timid* or *careful?*
11. Does it make a difference whether a newspaper calls someone a *union boss* or a *labor leader?*
12. Would you rather be called *shy* or *inhibited?*
13. Would you rather be called a *student* or a *pupil?* Does it make any difference?
14. Would you rather be described as *sprawling* in an easy chair or as *relaxing* in it?
15. What is the difference between *nosy* and *curious?*

ACTIVITY 4

Science fiction often takes us into the world of the future. What new words, and new uses of old words, will we encounter as we move ahead into a new and different world? The following selection from a science-fiction story uses many terms that were unknown to readers fifty years ago. Many of these terms have become familiar to today's newspaper readers.

Study the passage, paying special attention to the italicized words. Answer the questions that follow the passage.

> The suits we use on the station are completely different from the *flexible* affairs men wear when they want to walk around on the Moon. Ours are really baby *space* ships, just big enough to hold one man. They are stubby *cylinders,* about seven feet long, fitted with low-powered *propulsion* jets, and have a pair of *accordion*-like sleeves at the upper end for the *operator's* arms.
>
> As soon as I'd settled down inside my very exclusive space *craft,* I switched on *power* and checked the *gauges* on the tiny instrument panel. All my *needles* were well in the safety zone, so I gave Tommy a wink for luck, lowered the *transparent hemisphere* over my head and sealed myself in. For a short trip like this, I did not bother to check the suit's *internal* lockers, which were used to carry food and

special equipment for *extended* missions. As the *conveyor* belt *decanted* me into the *air lock,* I felt like an Indian *papoose* being carried along on its mother's back. Then the pumps brought the pressure down to zero, the outer door opened, and the last traces of air swept me out into the stars, turning very slowly head over heels. The *station* was only a dozen feet away, yet I was now an independent planet —a little world of my own. I was sealed up in a tiny, *mobile* cylinder, with a *superb* view of the entire universe, but I had practically no freedom of movement inside the suit.

—Arthur C. Clarke, "The Haunted Space Suit"

1. Explain why the following words mean something different from what they would have meant fifty years ago:

space   needle
craft   lock
power   station

2. Explain briefly the meaning of each of the following words:

cylinder   transparent
accordion   internal
operator

3. What picture does the author bring to mind when he says he was "decanted" into the air lock? What does it feel like to be carried like a "papoose"? How well do these two comparisons fit?

4. Study the two choices that follow each term. Write down the meaning the term has in the passage.

   a. *flexible*—lightweight; can be bent
   b. *transparent*—can be seen through; is made of glass
   c. *mobile*—attached to a cable; movable
   d. *hemisphere*—half of a circle; half of a globe
   e. *propulsion*—thrust; obstacle
   f. *internal*—inside; orally
   g. *superb*—very good; very bad
   h. *conveyor*—carrier; messenger
   i. *gauge*—scale; warning light

Chapter 2

Sentences
Building Good Sentences

Chapter Preview 2

Make words work together in a complete sentence.

Words without grammar are like the building materials for a house. They are like materials ready for use before the carpenters or the bricklayers have gone to work. In building

GRAMMAR MAKES WORDS FIT INTO A SENTENCE

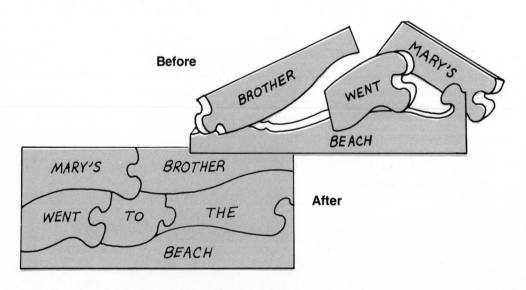

a sentence, we do what a carpenter does: We use the right materials, and we put them to the right use.

How do we discover the way English grammar works? We look at English sentences and ask:

- What kinds of words do we use?
- How do we make words fit into a sentence?
- What do we add to a sentence to make it carry more freight?

Work your way through the following preview activities. When you finish them, you will have learned some basic things about how English grammar works.

To use words in an English sentence, we have to put them in the right order. The words in each of the following groups could go together as part of a sentence. Put the words in each group in the right order. Then write them after the number of the group.

PREVIEW EXERCISE 1

EXAMPLE: mountain famous a climber
(Answer)   *a famous mountain climber*

1. frisky two puppies
2. close my friend without
3. not have might happened
4. young player the violin
5. best soccer world's the team
6. have earlier should called
7. old-fashioned an theater movie
8. cafeteria the usual lunch
9. tomorrow will call you
10. popular gymnast the Russian
11. very message this urgent
12. in paintings the museum oil
13. special a very sale
14. for starving assistance artists
15. typing your right practice away
16. straight entrance to the nearest go
17. can locked outside from the be
18. accident badly victim a injured
19. at the will them airport meet
20. stairs those wooden new

**PREVIEW
EXERCISE 2**

Often, putting words in the right order is not enough. We may have to change a word somewhat to fit it into its slot in the sentence. We may have to add links like *the* or *a* or *an* to help the sentence run smoothly. In each of the following groups of words, make the least possible changes that would turn each group into a smoothly running English sentence.

EXAMPLE: Motorist honk at pedestrian.
(Answer) *The* motorist honk*ed* at *the* pedestrian.

1. Grandfather tell us story.
2. Jean behavior was child.
3. Give me back knife.
4. Principal has notify all parent.
5. Mario had add tomato to salad.
6. Water was warm than usual.
7. Food was always salt.
8. Last year Gina join band.
9. They had travel during vacation.
10. Emily was the tall of player.

S1

**WORDS IN A
SENTENCE**

Know the major kinds of words that we use in an English sentence.

Pay phones have different slots for quarters, dimes, and nickels. Sentences have different slots for different kinds of words. One of the most basic things we learn when we learn to talk is to put the right kind of word in the right place. Several major kinds of words help us build the typical English sentence.

S1a

**Nouns:
Label Words**

Know the clues that help us recognize nouns.

A **noun** is a naming word. The typical English noun is a label for people, places, things, or ideas. *Shirt* is a noun because we can use it as a label for a piece of clothing. *Happiness* is a noun because we can use it to label a feeling. Our language uses several kinds of noun signals. These tell us: "This is a labeling word," or "Naming word coming next."

(1) Look for the words that work as noun signals. Suppose you read the following message: SHIP SINKS QUICKLY. Is it about a sinking SHIP? Or is it about SINKS that somebody

THE ENGLISH SENTENCE: A Bird's-Eye View

KINDS OF WORDS:

Noun	*The owner* of *this car* is *a friend.*
Pronoun	*She* told *everyone* about *our* party.
Verb	I *painted* the table I *had bought.*
Adjective	The *new* chair was very *expensive.*
Adverb	*Today* she drove *carefully.*
Connective	Kevin *and* Helga had left.
Preposition	We turned *to* the right *at* the corner.

THE COMPLETE SENTENCE:

S–V	Her friend left.
S–V–O	The dog bit the stranger.
S–LV–N	Joan is a student.
S–LV–Adj	The grass is green.
S–V–IO–O	Jim gave me the money.

THREE KINDS OF SENTENCES:

Statement	The parade will start at ten.
Question	Can my friends join the club?
Request	Clear the sidewalk.

WELL-BUILT SENTENCES:

Agreement	*The record* of our meetings *was* lost.
Modifiers	*Smiling happily,* I *got into the boat.*
Pronoun Reference	*Martha* smiles when *she* does *her* work.

COMBINED SENTENCES:

Coordination

First Source:	The Russians first orbited the earth.
Second Source:	Americans first orbited the moon.
Result:	The Russians first orbited the earth, *but* Americans first orbited the moon.

Subordination

First Source:	Jean left the room.
Second Source:	I walked in.
Result:	Jean left the room *before* I walked in.

Relative Clause

First Source:	Edgar loved *Anna.*
Second Source:	*Anna* became his wife.
Result:	Edgar loved Anna, *who* became his wife.

wants shipped? We cannot tell, because some of the *signals* are missing. We can see the difference when the missing signal is added:

The ship sinks quickly.
Ship *the* sinks quickly.

The word *the* here works as a signal that says: *"This one* is the labeling word—This one is the noun." We call noun signals like *the* **noun markers.** In each of the following sentences, a different noun marker tells us that the word *hit* is used as a noun:

A hit won the game.	*My* hit won the game.
His hit won the game.	*Their* hit won the game.
That hit won the game.	George got *those* hits.
Her hit won the game.	George got *our* hits.

Here is a complete list of noun markers. There are three different kinds:

ARTICLES: a, an, the
POSSESSIVE PRONOUNS: my, yours, his, her, its, our, their
POINTING PRONOUNS: this, that, these, those

NOTE: Noun markers do not always tell us that the noun is coming right away. Can you tell which words after the markers are nouns in the following sentences?

A good hit won the game.
Ship the new sinks quickly.
That cheap perfume smells terrible.
We took a short walk.

(2) Look for the endings that signal nouns. Noun markers come *before* nouns and are *detached* from them. Endings come *after* nouns and are *attached* to them. The most common ending signaling nouns is the *–s* or *–es* that means "more than one." We call the plain form for "one of the kind" the **singular** form. We call the form for "more than one" the **plural** form. Look at the examples below and on page 53.

SINGULAR: A *hit* will win the game.
PLURAL: *Hits* will win the game. (more than one hit)

SINGULAR: We saw the *church*.
PLURAL: We saw the *churches*. (more than one church)

SINGULAR: She found the missing coin.
PLURAL: She found the missing *coins.*   (more than one coin)

SINGULAR: Our *hero* won the game.
PLURAL: Our *heroes* won the game.   (more than one hero)

(3) Look for special endings that turn other words into nouns.   When we want to label the people that govern us, we call them our *government.* When we label a person who governs a state, we use the word *governor.* When we want to label a happy feeling, we can call it *happiness.* The endings *–er* or *–or, –ment,* and *–ness* help us to make up labels. They help us turn other words into nouns.

Find all examples of these noun-making endings in the following sentences:

The banker made an investment.
A sailor received the shipment.
The teacher had an argument with the manager.
The jailer was known for meanness and dullness.
The auditor checked the payments.
We thanked the photographer for her kindness.

Nouns help us talk about someone or something. They fit into the blank space in a *test pattern* like the following:

EXERCISE 1

Let's talk about ———————.
Let's talk about a (an) (the) ———————.

Test the words in the following list to see which of them could be used as nouns. If a word fits easily or naturally into one of the test frames, write *yes* after the number of the word. If it does not fit, write *no.*

EXAMPLE: holiday   (Answer)   *yes*

1. house	11. for	21. went
2. station	12. sadly	22. are
3. tree	13. boot	23. kindness
4. hummingbird	14. truth	24. office
5. easily	15. strongly	25. very
6. criticize	16. college	26. path
7. honesty	17. took	27. regulation
8. because	18. step	28. advertise
9. neighborhood	19. delay	29. without
10. dinosaur	20. party	30. refrigerator

NOUNS LABEL OCCUPATIONS

Tailor

Judge

Photographer

Find all the nouns in the following sentences. Write the nouns after the number of each sentence. Follow the instructions for each group of ten.

A. Find all nouns by looking for their *noun markers.* Write down the noun marker with the noun.

EXAMPLE: My aunt owns a store.
(Answer)   *my aunt, a store*

1. Our relatives are coming for a visit this week.
2. My uncle is a comedian.
3. His hair sticks out like the spokes on a wheel.
4. That lady next to him is his wife.
5. Those suitcases in our hallway are their luggage.
6. Are your relatives as odd as mine?
7. Their cat will bring its kittens along.
8. An idea has just occurred to her.
9. She will use our den for her nursery.
10. These visits are always welcome.

B. Find all nouns by looking for the *plural –s* (or *–es*) that tells us "more than one."

EXAMPLE: Beggars can't be choosers.
(Answers)   *Beggars, choosers*

11. My parents like cats.
12. Her cousins had friends with cars.
13. Trees lined the streets.
14. The fans in the cheap seats were booing.
15. She took pictures of the floats in parades.
16. Librarians keep books on huge shelves.
17. During the cold winter months, birds fly to warmer countries.
18. My brothers take lunch boxes full of sandwiches and cookies.
19. Collectors of rare coins check the dates of old pennies.
20. Knights used to fight monsters and dragons.

Many nouns that name *occupations* use *–er* or *–or* as a noun-making ending. Find such a noun for each of the blank spaces in the sentences on the following page. Write the noun after the number of the sentence. Make sure each noun you choose has the *–er* or *–or* ending. (Use either the singular or the plural form as required.)

EXAMPLE: A ――――― repairs shoes.
(Answer)   *shoemaker*

1. A _____ plows and plants.
2. A _____ plots the course of a plane.
3. A _____ builds buildings.
4. The _____ unplugged our toilet.
5. A _____ has to like the sea.
6. The _____ tried to ring the number again.
7. Many _____ still make pants and jackets.
8. _____ choose the news stories for the front page.
9. A _____ tames wild animals.
10. An _____ checks the quality of fresh meats.
11. The _____ in a play have to memorize the script.
12. _____ make rolls, pies, and cakes.
13. A _____ uses a camera to make pictures.
14. A _____ helps people choose furniture, wall decorations, and drapes for a home.
15. All _____ use ladders and brushes.
16. A _____ delivers sermons.
17. A _____ sells jewels.
18. A _____ supervises other workers.
19. A _____ prints books.
20. A _____ conducts the orchestra.

EXERCISE 4

Make nouns (or new nouns) from the following words by adding one of these endings: *–er*, *–or*, *–ment*, or *–ness*. Write the new noun after the number of the original word. (Adjust the spelling as necessary.)

1. make	6. buy	11. enjoy	16. resent
2. treat	7. sell	12. sweet	17. play
3. sail	8. content	13. lend	18. calm
4. ride	9. round	14. heat	19. agree
5. friendly	10. investigate	15. govern	20. tender

EXERCISE 5

Which of the numbered words in the following sentences are nouns? Write *Yes* after the number of the word if the word shows one of the three main noun signals: (1) It follows a noun marker. (2) It has the plural *–s* or *–es* to show more than one. (3) It has one of the noun-making endings. If the word is not a noun, write *No* after the number of the word.

EXAMPLE: Odysseus had fought with the (1) **Greeks** against the (2) **city** of Troy.
(Answer) *(1) Yes (2) Yes*

1. The (1) **adventures** of Odysseus after the (2) **end** of the war make great (3) **stories.**
2. His (4) **travels** (5) **lasted** ten (6) **years.**
3. Odysseus first (7) **went** to the (8) **land** of the Lotus-Eaters, who ate (9) **flowers.**
4. Some of his men shared the (10) **food,** which made them feel great (11) **happiness.**
5. They (12) **quickly** (13) **lost** all desire to return to their (14) **homes.**
6. Odysseus had to (15) **drag** those (16) **sailors** away and tie them to the (17) **ships.**
7. He (18) **ordered** the rest of his (19) **crew** not to taste the (20) **plant.**
8. He was a strict (21) **leader** (22) **to** his followers.
9. He did not tolerate (23) **disagreement.**
10. However, he also showed his (24) **comrades** much (25) **kindness.**

Know how pronouns take the place of nouns.

A **pronoun** is a word that can take the place of a noun. Look at how pronouns take the place of nouns in the following pairs:

NOUNS: *Tommy* likes *animals.*
PRONOUNS: *He* likes *them.*

NOUNS: *The books* are on *the desk.*
PRONOUNS: *They* are on *it.*

In the first pair, pronouns replace nouns alone. In the second pair, pronouns replace nouns and their markers. *They* takes the place of *the books. It* replaces *the desk.*

Pronouns help us to be brief. They help us to avoid repeating ourselves. Without pronouns, you would have to write sentences like this:

NOUNS ONLY: Mahalia asked Mahalia's father when Mahalia and Mahalia's father would be leaving.

With pronouns, you can say the same thing like this:

WITH PRONOUNS: Mahalia asked *her* father when *they* would be leaving.

Remember: Pronouns are often briefer substitutes for nouns. Know the main kinds of pronouns:

(1) The **personal pronouns** *usually take the place of nouns that point to persons.* Instead of using your own name, you may use *I* or *me*. Instead of using the name of another person, you may use such personal pronouns as *you, he, him, she,* or *her. We, us, they,* and *them* are personal pronouns that refer to more than one person. *It* and sometimes *they* and *them* are personal pronouns that may point to things as well as to people.

See **U3a** for subject forms and object forms of pronouns.

(2) **Possessive pronouns** *tell us what belongs to whom.* They take the place of nouns that show where or to whom something belongs:

NOUNS: *Jack's* books are on *Susan's* desk.
POSSESSIVE PRONOUNS: *His* books are on *her* desk.

My, your, his, her, its, our, and *their* are possessive pronouns that are followed by a noun. *Mine, yours, his, hers, its, ours,* and *theirs* are possessive pronouns that we can use *without* a noun. We use them alone:

My books are here; *Grace's and Lola's books* are there.
Mine are here; *theirs* are there.

(3) **Pointing pronouns (demonstrative pronouns)** *point out which one or ones.* The pointing pronouns are *this, these, that,* and *those.* They may be used to point to things. *This* and *these* often point to things close at hand. *That* and *those* often point to things further away. Suppose there were two pencils on a desk. You could use pointing pronouns to tell which is which:

This is mine; *that* is yours.

See **U1b** for uses of possessive and pointing pronouns.

(4) The **indefinite pronouns** *do not point to someone or something specific.* Compare the following sentences. Indefinite pronouns are used in the second one.

DEFINITE: The *quarterback* threw the *ball* to the fullback.
INDEFINITE: *Somebody* threw *something* at our car.

The indefinite pronouns are *somebody, someone, something; anybody, anyone, anything; everybody, everyone, everything; nobody, no one, nothing.*

FOUR KINDS OF PRONOUNS

PERSONAL PRONOUNS	I	me
	you	you
	he	him
	she	her
	it	it
	we	us
	they	them
POSSESSIVE PRONOUNS	my	mine
	your	yours
	his	his
	her	hers
	its	its
	our	ours
	their	theirs
DEMONSTRATIVE PRONOUNS (POINTING)	this	these
	that	those

INDEFINITE PRONOUNS	somebody (someone)	something
	anybody (anyone)	anything
	everybody (everyone)	everything
	nobody (no one)	nothing

In each sentence below, there is one pronoun. Write it on your paper next to the number of the sentence. (Your teacher may also ask you to label the pronouns: personal, possessive, pointing, and indefinite.)

EXERCISE 1

EXAMPLE: Everybody loves vacations.
(Answer) *Everybody*

1. Everyone should visit a place like Acadia National Park.
2. Rangers showed us slide programs at night.
3. These showings can be very interesting.
4. Ours was about rocks and glaciers.
5. During the day, we explored the island.
6. Sand Beach is its only ocean beach.
7. A few people went into the icy waters up to their knees.
8. That was deep enough for most people.

9. Nobody went swimming.
10. Thunder Hole is really something to see.
11. My friends watched the ocean hit the rocks.
12. On a stormy day, this scene is spectacular.
13. Mount Cadillac is the highest point on our coast.
14. Anyone can drive to the top of the mountain.
15. This trip is a great experience.
16. On a clear day, I can see for miles.
17. What is your favorite pastime?
18. Mine is watching gulls glide through the air.
19. They are very graceful birds.
20. Someone in need of a good vacation should go to Maine.

EXERCISE 2

Pronouns take the place of nouns. Because of this, you can use a pronoun substitution test as another way of finding nouns. Try putting a pronoun in place of the italicized words below. Use only *he, him, she, her, it, they,* or *them.* The test should work for only one of the two words. That word will be the noun. Write the noun and the pronoun that replaced it on your paper next to the number of the sentence. (Remember that pronouns take the place of nouns *and* their noun markers.)

EXAMPLE: *The children* were playing *happily.*
(Answer)   The children (They)

1. Who has *already* read *the poem?*
2. *Our cats* are always *playing.*
3. *Susan* learned to drive *quickly.*
4. *Little* birds eat *worms.*
5. *My friends* are giving a *big* party.
6. *Did* you see *monkeys* at the zoo?
7. You *should* read *her novel.*
8. *Elephants* never *forget.*
9. *The actress* played two roles *in* the movie.
10. *Drivers* must turn left *ahead.*

S1c

**Verbs:
Action Words**

Know the clues that help us recognize verbs.

A noun can help us point to a baby, a car, a dog, a cat, a girl, a boy. The names of all of these would be nouns. Another major kind of word helps us set these nouns in *motion.* The words in this group are **verbs.** In the following sentences, the verbs are italicized. The verbs are the words that make something happen:

The baby *cried.*
The car *sped* away.
A dog *barked.*
The cat *jumped.*
The boy *combed* his hair.

The girl *parked* her bike.
The bridge *collapsed.*
A wire *snapped.*
A guard *sounded* the alarm.
The rock *smashed* the window.

WHAT VERBS TELL US

See how many verbs you can find by filling in the blank spaces below. Each time fill in *one single word*. Write the verbs for each question after the number of the question.

EXAMPLE: Engines *start.* What else do engines do?
They _____, _____, and _____.
(Answer) *stop, stall, roar*

1. Planes *leave.* What else do planes do?
They _____, _____, and _____.

2. Ballplayers *pitch.* What else do ballplayers do?
They _____, _____, and _____.

3. Dogs *bark.* What else do dogs do?
They _____, _____, and _____.

4. Children *play.* What else do children do?
They _____, _____, and _____.

5. Teachers *teach.* What else do teachers do?
They _____, _____, and _____.

6. Singers *sing.* What else do singers do?
They _____, _____, and _____.

7. Athletes *practice.* What else do athletes do?
They _____, _____, and _____.

8. Audiences *applaud.* What else do audiences do?
They _____, _____, and _____.

9. People who make clothes *sew.* What else do they do?
They _____, _____, and _____.

10. Guests at a party *talk.* What else do they do?
They _____, _____, and _____.

Verbs do not *always* show something in action. Some verbs merely tell us that something exists. Or they tell us that something is in a certain position or condition:

The country *surrounds* the city.   Bears *hibernate*.
The lamp *dangles* from the ceiling.   The rain *continued*.

Several kinds of signals help us recognize verbs:

(1) Look for the forms that help verbs show differences in time. The most basic difference between a noun and a verb is that verbs "tell time." There is something built into the verb that answers questions like:

"Is this going on now?"
"Did this already happen?"
"Is this going to happen?"

By just looking at the verb, we can label each of the following statements "now," "past," or "future":

NOW: My brother *likes* milk.
          The moon *circles* the earth.

PAST: Lindbergh *crossed* the Atlantic.
          The North *fought* the South.

FUTURE: The weather *will improve*.
          My sister *will meet* us at the gate.

We call the forms that show differences in time forms for different **tenses.** With many verbs, we can change tense by means of different endings. We attach these endings to the plain form of the verb: *bark, jump, like, continue.*

The three most commonly used verb endings are *–es* (or *–s*), *–ed* (or *–d*), and *–ing*. We attach the *–es* or *–s* when we talk about one single "third party," with "action now." The *–s* shows **present** time when we are talking about one single person or thing:

Benny (one person) *practices* often.
The key (one thing) *fits* the lock.
Time (one thing) *flies* quickly.
That girl (one person) *looks* lovely.

The *–ed* or *–d* ending added to verbs shows **past** time:

Benny *practiced* yesterday.
Jim *suggested* a good plan.

The governor *freed* the prisoners.
I *worked* on a model airplane.

The *–ing* ending added to verbs often shows *ongoing* time and *continuing* time (**progressive** time—things are "in progress"):

Benny is *practicing*.
He was *thinking* about it all day.
I am *working* on a model airplane.
They were *planning* a picnic.

See **U1c** and **U1d** for more on verb forms.

NOTE: Sometimes we do not add an ending to show past time. With some verbs, the whole word changes to show the difference:

PRESENT: We *see* them often.
PAST: We *saw* them last year.

PRESENT: We always *bring* a lunch.
PAST: In grade school, we always *brought* a lunch.

(2) Look for the auxiliaries that work as verb markers. Often the verb is just a single word. But often we use "verb helpers," like the *will* that helps us show future time:

The time *will come*.
Spring *will return*.
The bus *will leave* at eight.

We call verb helpers like *will* **helping verbs** or **auxiliaries.** Here is a list of helping verbs:

FORMS OF *be:*   am, is, are, was, were
FORMS OF *have:*   have, has, had
OTHER AUXILIARIES: will (would), shall (should), can (could), may (might), must

Each of the following statements uses a different helping verb to help make up the complete verb:

Astronauts *have visited* the moon.
The witness *will testify* in the afternoon.
One fool *can spoil* a party.
The principal *may resign*.
They *were testing* the engine.
The tenants *had barricaded* their doors.
Her father *is circulating* a petition.

(3) Look for the special endings that help us make up new verbs. Endings like *–en, –ize,* and *–fy* help us make new verbs from other words. What do we do when we make something sharp? We *sharpen* it. What do critics do? They *criticize.* What do burglars do? They *burglarize* apartments. Use the verb-making endings *–en, –ize,* and *–fy* to make up the verbs missing in the following sentences:

(sweet) Sugar substitutes _____ many soft drinks.
(memory) _____ the poem by tomorrow.
(test) Who will _____ for the defense?

NOTE: You may need to adjust the spelling when you add the verb-forming ending. Before you make *memory* a verb, you have to drop the *y* from it. Then you get *memorize.* With *test,* you must add an *i* to get *testify.*

EXERCISE 1

We use verbs to talk about something we want to do, or something that may happen. We can therefore use a *test frame* like the following to find out if a word can be used as a verb:

Let's _____.
Let's _____ it.
Let it _____.

Try each of the following words. Write *Yes* after the number of the word if it fits easily or naturally into one of the test patterns. Write *No* if it does not fit.

EXAMPLE: rain (Let it *rain.*)
(Answer) *Yes*

1. begin	11. melt	21. ask
2. without	12. beautiful	22. hungry
3. airplane	13. happiness	23. describe
4. try	14. park	24. lower
5. finish	15. cheap	25. investigate
6. soak	16. walk	26. goal
7. solution	17. watch	27. approve
8. report	18. unwrap	28. return
9. sing	19. dry	29. continue
10. discuss	20. there	30. athlete

In each of the following sentences, change the italicized verb *from present to past*. After the number of the sentence, write the form that shows something happened in the past. (Write a single word.)

EXERCISE 2

EXAMPLE: The principal *talks* to the ringleaders.
(Answer)   *talked*

1. My brother always *congratulates* me first.
2. Sometimes we *watch* the waves all day.
3. We often *receive* a friendly letter from my aunt.
4. In the spring we *organize* a carnival.
5. My sisters *bring* their own tent.
6. Some people in Ireland *believe* in elves and goblins.
7. My grandmother *lives* across the street from us.
8. The hikers *see* deer and sometimes a bear.
9. The clerk *adds* up the bill.
10. The operator *repeats* the telephone number.
11. The mechanic *overhauls* the engine.
12. Chemicals *pollute* the river.
13. My relatives *recognize* me right away.
14. The course *teaches* students how to save energy.
15. The townspeople *choose* the names themselves.
16. All my friends *walk* to school.
17. Cooking an old-fashioned stew *takes* time.
18. Rehearsals *begin* in the spring.
19. Sudden noises *frighten* our pets.
20. In the fall, the geese *fly* south.

Find the verbs in the following sentences by looking for the *helping verbs* that serve as verb markers. Write the complete verb after the number of the sentence. Include the helping verb.

EXERCISE 3

EXAMPLE: Most people have read many articles about food.
(Answer)   *have read*

1. Your food can show things about you as a person.
2. Doctors have tested their patients.
3. They are discovering new facts.
4. Patients under stress will eat eggs.
5. These patients had disliked eggs before.
6. People may overeat in times of worry.
7. Some persons simply must raid the refrigerator.
8. Usually, they are worrying about their problems.
9. Worriers may go overboard on health foods.

10. Hearty eaters were enjoying life.
11. Picky eaters may have problems.
12. Researchers have studied kinds of food, too.
13. Favorite foods could be a clue to character.
14. Young children should eat meat.
15. Kind people are eating salads.
16. Shy people may eat starchy foods.
17. Quiet people might like vegetables.
18. Persons with a sense of humor should like desserts.
19. Happy people would like desserts also.
20. I am watching my food for clues to my personality.

EXERCISE 4

Sometimes *more than one* helping verb helps us make up the complete verb. In each of the following sentences, two and sometimes three helping verbs are part of the complete verb. Write the complete verb after the sentence number.

EXAMPLE: You should have called the office.
(Answer) *should have called*

1. I should be leaving soon.
2. The campers could have cleaned the site better.
3. Someone has been leaving strange messages.
4. We may have passed the turnoff.
5. Those men must have taken my coat.
6. Henry could have caught cold.
7. Hester should have joined us.
8. I will be seeing her in August.
9. Kate has been flying her kite all day.
10. You must have been reading all afternoon.
11. That drawing can be duplicated.
12. His car should have been sold.
13. Janis has been elected to the council.
14. John should have known the answer.
15. The referee should have been following the play.
16. The boys should have scrubbed the floor.
17. A stranger has been following me.
18. The day will be remembered.
19. Joan should have been offered the job.
20. Karen has been listening well.

EXERCISE 5

Add one of the following endings to each word in parentheses to make a new verb: *–en, –fy, –ize*. Make sure the new verb fits the blank space in its sentence. Write the new verb after the number of the sentence. (Adjust or change spelling as necessary.)

EXAMPLE: *(strength)* Athletes try to ⸏⸏⸏⸏⸏⸏ their muscles.
(Answer) *strengthen*

1. *(simple)* The teacher should ⸏⸏⸏⸏⸏⸏ the instructions.
2. *(short)* We had to ⸏⸏⸏⸏⸏⸏ our stay.
3. *(just)* Students will have to ⸏⸏⸏⸏⸏⸏ their absences.
4. *(special)* The store will ⸏⸏⸏⸏⸏⸏ in china and glassware.
5. *(capital)* The other teams ⸏⸏⸏⸏⸏⸏ on our mistakes.
6. *(height)* Scriptwriters try to ⸏⸏⸏⸏⸏⸏ suspense.
7. *(legal)* This state will never ⸏⸏⸏⸏⸏⸏ gambling.
8. *(author)* The city must ⸏⸏⸏⸏⸏⸏ construction.
9. *(note)* Libraries ⸏⸏⸏⸏⸏⸏ us of overdue books.
10. *(light)* The assistant will ⸏⸏⸏⸏⸏⸏ our work load.

Which of the numbered words in the following sentences are verbs? Write *Yes* after the number of the word if it shows one of the following verb signals: (1) It has changed its form to show past tense. (2) It follows a helping verb, or auxiliary. (In addition, some of the verbs may show a typical verb-making ending.) If the word is not used as a verb, write *No*.

EXERCISE 6

EXAMPLE: Odysseus and his crew (7) **traveled** far and (8) **wide.**
(Answer) *(7) Yes (8) No*

1. After he had (1) **visited** the Lotus-Eaters, Odysseus (2) **reached** a (3) **mysterious** land.
2. He (4) **explored** the cave of the Cyclops, a one-eyed giant.
3. While the men were (5) **looking** around the cave, the Cyclops (6) **returned.**
4. The Cyclops could (7) **frighten** anyone who (8) **saw** him.
5. When the monster (9) **asked** who they were, Odysseus knew he should (10) **answer.**
6. "You should (11) **obey** the gods," Odysseus said, "and treat your guests well."
7. But the monster was (12) **thinking** only about (13) **food.**
8. He (14) **swallowed** two men (15) **quickly.**
9. He could (16) **eat** the others at a later (17) **time.**
10. But we should (18) **realize** that Odysseus had a (19) **cunning** mind.
11. Very (20) **soon,** Odysseus had (21) **organized** his escape.
12. He would (22) **destroy** the monster's (23) **sight.**
13. He could (24) **put** the giant to sleep with wine.
14. The men (25) **escaped** by hanging beneath the giant's sheep.

S1d

**Adjectives:
Degree Words**

Know the clues that help us recognize adjectives.

The word *adjective* originally meant "next to" or "next door to." An **adjective** is a word that we often find *next to* a noun:

NOUN MARKER	ADJECTIVE	NOUN
the	*big*	house
a	*strong*	wind
our	*simple*	solution
my	*favorite*	program
a	*cheap*	meal
an	*old*	car

Each of these adjectives tells us more about the noun that follows it. The adjective tells us "which one" or "what kind": Which house? The *big* one. What kind of meal? A *cheap* meal. We say that the adjective **modifies** the noun. It adds something to the meaning of the noun.

Several kinds of signals help us tell adjectives apart from nouns or verbs:

(1) Many adjectives fit in after words that show degree. If we have a usual degree of heat, we can simply say that it is hot. But if the heat gets intense, we say that it is *very* hot. Words like *very* are **intensifiers.** They help us step up (or in some other way change) the degree of heat, cold, and the like. In each of the following, two words have been put between the noun marker and the noun. The first of the two words is an intensifier. It tells us: "Adjective coming." The second word is the adjective:

a *very funny* story
a *rather quiet* evening
a *quite simple* solution
a *more dangerous* assignment

the *most competent* candidate
a *fairly successful* attempt
an *extremely contagious* disease
a *really helpful* hint

(2) Many adjectives can show a change in degree by a change in the word itself. Many adjectives use the endings *–er* and *–est* to show degree. In each of the following sets, the first form is the plain or ordinary form of the adjective. The second is the **comparative** form: We use it in comparisons to

show that something is "more so" than something else. The third is the **superlative** form: We use it when something stands out from all the rest. It is at the highest or lowest point on the scale:

PLAIN: Susan is *calm.*
COMPARATIVE: Susan is *calmer* than her brother.
SUPERLATIVE: Miriam is the *calmest* person in the family.

PLAIN: Beans were *cheap.*
COMPARATIVE: Beans were *cheaper* than meat.
SUPERLATIVE: Beans were the *cheapest* food we could buy.

**LANGUAGE
IN ACTION**

WHAT ADJECTIVES TELL US

See how many adjectives you can find by filling in the blank spaces below. Each time fill in *one single word.* Write the adjectives for each sentence after the number of the sentence.

EXAMPLE: Mules are very _____, very _____, and very _____ .

(Answer)   *strong, patient, stubborn*

1. Jet planes are very _____, very _____, and very _____ .

2. Screen cowboys used to be very _____, very _____, and very _____ .

3. When peaches are just right, they are very _____, very _____, and very _____ .

4. Tigers are very _____, very _____, and very _____ .

5. Some people like cars that are very _____, very _____, and very _____ .

6. I dislike movies that are very _____, very _____, or very _____ .

7. People can be very _____, very _____, or very _____ .

8. Food may taste too _____, too _____, or too _____ .

9. Music may also be too _____, too _____, or too _____ .

10. A story may be quite _____, quite _____, or quite _____ .

Not all adjectives simply add these endings. With some adjectives, we change the whole word. What words would you use to fill the blanks in the following sets?

Your idea is good.
Your idea is _____ than anyone else's.
Your idea is the _____ that I have ever heard.

I have a bad cold.
My cold is _____ than yours.
This is the _____ cold I've ever had.

Here are the three forms for several unusual adjectives:

PLAIN:	good	bad	little	far
COMPARATIVE:	better	worse	less	farther
SUPERLATIVE:	best	worst	least	farthest

NOTE: Many adjectives with two syllables, and those with three syllables or more, use *more* and *most* instead of the endings *–er* and *–est:*

a *cautious* driver	a *fantastic* story
a *more cautious* driver	a *more fantastic* story
the *most cautious* driver	the *most fantastic* story

(3) Special endings help us make up new adjectives. Endings like *–able, –ible, –ous, –ful,* and *–less* help us make new adjectives from other words:

(remark)	Dorothy had a *remarkable* dream.
(horror)	She was threatened by a *horrible* witch.
(marvel)	The scarecrow was a *marvelous* friend.
(cheer)	The tinman was a *cheerful* companion.
(spine)	The lion was a *spineless* coward.

Notice the adjustment in *spelling* that is necessary in pairs like the following:

sense—sensible	beauty—beautiful
believe—believable	penny—penniless

See **S2d** for adjectives after linking verbs.

EXERCISE 1

Suppose someone asks: "Can this word be used as an adjective?" Try out the word in a *test frame* like the following. If the word fits naturally into both slots in one of these patterns, it is a true adjective.

The _____ one was very _____.
The _____ ones were very _____.

Try out the following words. If the word fits *both* slots in one of the test patterns, write *Yes* after the number of the word. If the word does not fit, write *No*.

1. dark	11. scary
2. spooky	12. corpse
3. howl	13. pale
4. ghost	14. screams
5. helpless	15. dungeon
6. coffin	16. screech
7. horrible	17. skeleton
8. chains	18. smelly
9. dead	19. monstrous
10. wild	20. bones

In the following sentences, find all adjectives that meet one of the following tests: (1) They follow an intensifier like *very*. (2) They use the special form for comparative or superlative. After the number of the sentence, write all adjectives that meet one or both of these tests. (Include the intensifier with the adjective.)

EXERCISE 2

EXAMPLE: My older sister had a very special vacation.
(Answer) *older, very special*

1. Our parks are among the most beautiful places in the world.
2. The Grand Canyon is a quite spectacular sight.
3. A walk into the canyon is rather different from easier hikes.
4. The grade is extremely steep.
5. On a very hot day, water is really necessary.
6. Even on a fairly cool day, the more cautious climbers will prepare themselves.
7. The hardest part is the climb back up.
8. The climbers are quite happy to be on more even ground again.
9. Yosemite has some of the grandest scenery of the parks.
10. Tourists may stay in the lower valley, which is very crowded in the summer.
11. More adventurous visitors go up to the higher levels.
12. The best choice is to go backpacking into the wilderness.
13. The most enjoyable vacations for me are spent outdoors.
14. The most famous parks are often far away from the quickest vacation routes.

15. Most roads to our parks are very good, but some are rather bumpy.
16. One of the worst roads leads to Baxter State Park in Maine.
17. Stones would bounce up from the extremely rocky surface.
18. The roads in Acadia National Park—one of the most unusual parks in the country—are quite good.
19. The road to Mount Cadillac is extremely scenic and more gradual than one might expect.
20. It may be quite foggy at the top, however.

EXERCISE 3

Turn each word in parentheses into an adjective. Use one of the following adjective-making endings: *–ible, –able, –ous, –ful, –less.* Make sure the new adjective fits into the blank in its sentence. Write the new adjective after the number of the sentence. (Adjust or change spelling as necessary.)

EXAMPLE: *(heart)* Scrooge was a _____ employer.
(Answer) *heartless*

1. *(break)*   Everything in the box was _____ .
2. *(hope)*   We are in a _____ situation.
3. *(cheer)*   Trudy is the most _____ girl in the class.
4. *(pain)*   A visit to the dentist can be _____ .
5. *(wash)*   Her new blouse is _____ .
6. *(depend)*   Their service is very _____ .
7. *(poison)*   We were warned about _____ snakes.
8. *(wonder)*   It was a _____ trip.
9. *(digest)*   We had an easily _____ meal.
10. *(use)*   A flashlight without batteries is _____ .
11. *(fame)*   Emily Dickinson is a _____ poet.
12. *(like)*   Rufus is a _____ cat.
13. *(work)*   The plan is _____ .
14. *(punish)*   The crime was _____ by a prison sentence.
15. *(sense)*   It was a _____ murder.
16. *(remark)*   That speech was _____ .
17. *(profit)*   They had a _____ business.
18. *(prosper)*   She came from a _____ mining town.
19. *(success)*   We were celebrating the _____ climb.
20. *(return)*   You should save all _____ bottles.

EXERCISE 4

Look at the numbered words in the following sentences. Write *Yes* after the numbers of the words that are being used as adjectives. Write *No* after the numbers of the words that are not being used as adjectives.

1. Science-fiction writers tell us (1) **wonderful** stories about future (2) **worlds.**
2. They make very (3) **strange** happenings quite (4) **believable.**
3. One of the (5) **weirdest** tales (6) **takes** place on the (7) **planet** of Mars.
4. Many Martians were quite (8) **happy** in a world of (9) **colorful** dreams.
5. Their (10) **dreams** were more (11) **real** than the dreams people had on Earth.
6. The (12) **pictures** in these (13) **powerful** dreams were (14) **visible** not only to the dreamer but also to other people.
7. Instead of watching (15) **spooky** movies, the Martians were (16) **always** watching these quite (17) **mad** dreams.
8. Finally a (18) **spaceship** from Earth made the first (19) **successful** trip to this very (20) **distant** planet.
9. The people on Mars were quite (21) **sure** that the spaceship was a (22) **fantastic** dream.
10. The (23) **unlucky** astronauts protested against this (24) **mistake.**
11. They faced a (25) **hopeless** task.

Know the clues that help us recognize adverbs.

The word *adverb* means "with the verb." **Adverbs** often appear next to a verb, just as adjectives often appear next to a noun. The italicized words in the following sentences are all adverbs. Look at how they cluster around a verb like *leave* or *stopped.* We say that the adverbs **modify** the verb. They add something to its meaning.

The workers	*always* leave *quickly.*
Jim	has *never* stopped *there before.*
The girl	ran *away suddenly.*
The clock	*slowly* struck *twice.*
The dogs	were barking *loudly* and *angrily.*

Adverbs have several things in common with adjectives. Many adverbs can follow a word like *very: very quickly,* quite *suddenly,* rather *slowly.* Many adverbs have special forms for comparative and superlative:

COMPARATIVE:	He went *earlier.*	Cook it *more slowly.*
SUPERLATIVE:	She went *earliest.*	Cook this one *most slowly.*

The points on the following page will help you tell adverbs apart from adjectives:

WHAT ADVERBS TELL US

How many different adverbs do you know that would fill the blank in each of the following? After the number of each statement, write *three* adverbs that could fill the blank space. Try to find different words for each set. Use only single words with the *–ly* ending.

EXAMPLE: People drive _____ . *(How?)*
(Answer)   *carefully, recklessly, cautiously*

1. People talk _____ . *(How?)*
2. Customers buy _____ . *(How?)*
3. Listeners answer _____ . *(How?)*
4. People walk _____ . *(How?)*
5. People complain _____ . *(How?)*
6. Workers work _____ . *(How?)*
7. People behave _____ . *(How?)*
8. Crooks operate _____ . *(How?)*
9. Athletes perform _____ . *(How?)*
10. Weather changes _____ . *(How?)*
11. Voters vote _____ . *(How?)*
12. Movies end _____ . *(How?)*
13. Announcers speak _____ . *(How?)*
14. People smile _____ . *(How?)*
15. Equipment works _____ . *(How?)*

(1) Adverbs tell us how, when, or where.   The verb tells us what is happening. The adverb tells us how, when, or where:

HOW?   Antelopes run *swiftly*.
          The dog growled *threateningly*.
          The winner smiled *happily*.
          The coach shouted *furiously*.

WHEN?   The rain has stopped *now*.
          Winter will come *soon*.
          My relatives *sometimes* visit us.
          The bus *always* stops at the corner.

WHERE?   The line starts *here*.
          You should wait *outside*.
          We lived *there* for many years.
          My brothers sleep *upstairs*.

(2) Many adverbs have the –ly *ending.* This ending is especially common with adverbs that tell us how: *slowly, carefully, eagerly, sadly, luckily.* Often we can add the ending –*ly* to turn an adjective into an adverb:

ADJECTIVE	ADVERB
Her *quick* reaction surprised me.	We opened the door *quickly*.
His *kind* words were welcome.	He talked to us *kindly*.
The *sudden* stops shook us up.	The bus stopped *suddenly*.

Adjustments in *spelling* are sometimes necessary when we add the –*ly* ending. Remember the following pairs especially:

happy—happily	probable—probably
lazy—lazily	true—truly
sensible—sensibly	helpful—helpfully

NOTE: Sometimes, we change the whole word instead of merely adding the adverb ending to it. Sometimes, we need *no* added ending, and adjective and adverb forms are exactly the same:

ADJECTIVE	ADVERB
She was a *good* player.	She played *well*.
We took the *fast* train.	The train went *fast*.
Make a *right* turn.	Remember to turn *right*.
We rode the *early* bus.	The bus left *early*.

See **U3c** on using the right adverb forms.

(3) Adverbs can often move around in a sentence. Many sentence parts are locked into one spot in the sentence. Adverbs, however, are able to shift their place more freely than other kinds of words:

She stops here *often*.
She *often* stops here.
Often she stops here.

Sentences

In how many different places can you put the adverb in each of the following sentences?

(suddenly)   Tom ran out of the house.
(painfully)   He pulled himself up the cliff.
(quickly)   She hid the note in her book.
(frantically)   They were digging in the soft ground.
(finally)   The shovel struck a hard object.

EXERCISE 1

Suppose someone asks you: Can this word be used as an adverb? Try the word out in the following *test pattern:*

Somebody did something _____ . *(How? When? Where?)*

Try out each of the following words. Write *Yes* after the number of the word if it fits easily into the blank space in the test pattern. Write *No* if it does not fit.

1. here	16. ice
2. yesterday	17. backwards
3. dogs	18. often
4. late	19. but
5. slowly	20. garage
6. organize	21. foolishly
7. reluctantly	22. badly
8. gratefully	23. fast
9. gratitude	24. repeat
10. outside	25. well
11. twice	26. meanwhile
12. fish	27. right
13. again	28. soon
14. hurriedly	29. invite
15. before	30. secretly

EXERCISE 2

Turn each word in parentheses into an adverb. Or leave the word unchanged if the word can be used as an adverb as it is. Write the adverb after the number of the sentence. Make sure the word you write would fit into the blank space in its sentence.

EXAMPLE: *(eager)*   The newcomers waved _____ .
(Answer) *eagerly*

1. *(rare)*   We _____ have snow here.
2. *(hasty)*   The note had been written _____ .
3. *(right)*   The meat had been cooked just _____ .

4. *(fortunate)* _____ no one was hurt.
5. *(sincere)* They _____ regretted the incident.
6. *(fast)* Basketball players move _____ .
7. *(loose)* The rope had been knotted _____ .
8. *(daily)* Our newspaper is published _____ .
9. *(simple)* She explained the problem _____ .
10. *(strict)* Everything was _____ regulated.
11. *(nervous)* The contestants were waiting _____ .
12. *(hard)* Everyone had worked extremely _____ .
13. *(recent)* Her uncle had died _____ .
14. *(doubtful)* He looked at me _____ .
15. *(quiet)* We filed out the door _____ .
16. *(thankful)* I smiled at him _____ .
17. *(childish)* They were always giggling _____ .
18. *(threatening)* The thug gestured _____ .
19. *(desperate)* The braves fought _____ .
20. *(grave)* The elders listened _____ .

Find the adverbs in the following sentences. After the number of the sentence, write all adverbs used in it. Make sure the words you write down tell us how, when, or where.

EXERCISE 3

EXAMPLE: Sometimes the train stops suddenly.
(Answer) *sometimes, suddenly*

1. Lucy often got the right answers.
2. Don throws a curve ball well.
3. Sarah missed class frequently.
4. The defendant answered the questions willingly.
5. Jim always drives his car fast.
6. He seldom made a mistake.
7. Our best player has never hit a home run.
8. Suddenly he went outside.
9. Jane sometimes treats her friends badly.
10. The police were looking everywhere.
11. We were slowly pushing the car forward.
12. The city reluctantly canceled the meeting.
13. They are going away soon.
14. The children went inside early.
15. The crowd was still talking excitedly.
16. Rita skillfully spliced the strands together.
17. My friends often shop downtown.
18. We watched the election returns hopefully.
19. The rider mounted the horse awkwardly.
20. We can now meet there again.

S1f
Connectives and Prepositions

Learn how connectives and prepositions work.

The major building blocks of the English sentence are nouns, pronouns, verbs, adjectives, and adverbs. These words are the bricks we use to build sentences. But we sometimes need other words to hold the bricks together. Two important kinds of "mortar words" are connectives and prepositions.

Learn the most common connectives and prepositions and how they work:

(1) Connectives join words or larger parts to each other. A **connective** is a joining word. If you connect another car to a train, you have a longer train. In language, too, we build longer units by using connectives. For example, we can use the connective *and* to make one long sentence out of two shorter ones:

SEPARATE: Snakes live in the desert. Lizards live in the desert.
JOINED: Snakes *and* lizards live in the desert.

Connectives join words or sentence parts of the same kind. A connective may also be used to join two sentences:

SINGLE SENTENCE: The queen gave the order.
SINGLE SENTENCE: The knight obeyed.
JOINED SENTENCE: The queen gave the order, *and* the knight obeyed.

The most common connectives are *and, but,* and *or.* In addition to joining words and larger units, these words also signal meanings. *And* often shows we are adding more of the same. *But* shows contrast: We are going on to something different. *Or* gives us a choice.

ADDITION: The coach will start Vera *and* Pat.
CONTRAST: The coach will start not Tex *but* Andy.
CHOICE: The coach will start Ron *or* Greg.

See **S5** for other connectives and their meanings.

(2) Prepositions tie a noun or pronoun to the rest of a sentence. **Prepositions** are words like *at, by, for, from, in, of, on, to,* and *with*. Often such a word stands in front of the noun or pronoun it brings into a sentence. The combination of the preposition and its noun or pronoun is called a **prepositional phrase.** The following are examples of prepositional phrases. Can you see that prepositions, like connectives, also signal meanings?

at the desk	*for* their daughter
by the river	*from* Detroit
in the ocean	*of* the week
on our table	*with* a knife
to me	*like* everybody

Prepositions help us tell where things are in time or space. Something can happen *before* something else, or *after* something else. Something can be *above* something else, or *below* something else. Something can be *before* you or *behind* you. All these italicized words are prepositions.

A PREPOSITION CHART

THE MOST COMMON PREPOSITIONS:

at	from	on
by	in	to
for	of	with

OTHER USEFUL PREPOSITIONS:

about	behind	over
above	below	since
across	beside	through
after	between	toward
against	during	under
among	except	until
around	into	upon
as	like	within
before	off	without

Each sentence below contains one connective. Find it, and write it on your paper next to the number of the sentence.

EXERCISE 1

1. I wanted to pet the cat, but it ran away.
2. You need a dime and a quarter to operate that machine.
3. Mabel or Georgia should be our next class president.
4. The hero was brave but weak.
5. Should we go out or stay at home?
6. Pat rented a canoe, and Miriam rented a sailboat.
7. This morning, we can clean the rugs or windows.
8. Bette washed her mother's and father's cars.
9. My sister likes rock, but my brother likes classical music.
10. He tried to find gold at the end of the rainbow and did.

Sentences

EXERCISE 2

Decide what connective—*and, but,* or *or*—is needed in each blank space in the following story. Write the missing connective after the number of the sentence.

1. The thirsty crow wanted some water _____ other liquid.
2. He found water, _____ it was in a deep pitcher.
3. He pushed his bill in, _____ it would not fit.
4. Should he break the pitcher, _____ was there another way?
5. He tried to break it, _____ he could not.
6. Then he tried to turn it over _____ pour the water out.
7. Finally, he picked up a pebble _____ dropped it in.
8. Each time he added a pebble _____ stone, the water rose.
9. Soon the water was high enough, _____ he drank some.
10. This is a fable by Aesop, called "The Crow _____ the Pitcher."

EXERCISE 3

Each sentence below contains one prepositional phrase. Find each phrase. Then write the preposition that introduces the phrase after the sentence number. (Your teacher may ask you to write the noun that goes with the preposition.)

1. The Greek army could not enter the city of Troy.
2. It was surrounded by a wall.
3. At night the Greeks built a horse.
4. The horse of wood had a hollow belly.
5. They filled the horse with soldiers.
6. The other Greek soldiers sailed away from Troy.
7. The horse was left for the Trojans.
8. They thought it was a gift from the gods.
9. The people brought the horse into the city.
10. The guards on duty let the horse pass.
11. In the evening, the Greek soldiers left the horse.
12. They climbed up the walls and overpowered the guards.
13. The bravery of these men was obvious.
14. They then sent a message to their ships.
15. The ships were not really at sea.
16. They had been waiting behind rocks.
17. The Greeks within the city opened the gates.
18. Through the gates poured their comrades.
19. Naturally the Trojans were taken by surprise.
20. They were no match for the Greeks.

EXERCISE 4

What preposition could you use to fill the blank space in each of the following sentences? After the number of the sentence, write a preposition that could fill the blank. Use a *different* preposition as often as you can. (Your teacher may ask you to compare answers with your classmates.)

EXAMPLE: There was agreement _____ the five survivors.
(Answer) *among*

1. I'll talk to you _____ lunch.
2. Someone wrote a message _____ the wall.
3. Everyone was _____ the party.
4. Don't walk in the rain _____ an umbrella.
5. She hit the ball _____ the fence.
6. Potatoes grow _____ the ground.
7. Tomatoes grow _____ the ground.
8. The rank _____ captain is lieutenant.
9. Who was sitting _____ you?
10. We are not leaving _____ tomorrow.
11. Islands are surrounded _____ water.
12. She looked _____ an athlete.
13. I'm selling my bike _____ twenty dollars.
14. My uncle _____ Georgia is visiting us.
15. We threw pennies _____ the well.
16. They were driving _____ Chicago.
17. The cover _____ my book is torn.
18. The car turned _____ the road.
19. Our team is playing _____ Central High.
20. I had not seen them _____ yesterday.

Look at each numbered word in the following sentences. After the number of the word, write the abbreviation that shows how the word is used. Use these abbreviations:

UNIT REVIEW EXERCISE

N	Noun
Pro	Pronoun
V	Verb (or part of a complete verb)
Adj	Adjective
Adv	Adverb
Con	Connective
Prep	Preposition

EXAMPLE: During his travels, Odysseus (7) **visited** many (8) **islands.**
(Answer) *7V, 8N*

1. One (1) **famous** adventure brought the (2) **traveler** to the island of Circe.
2. She was a (3) **powerful** goddess who (4) **imprisoned** her (5) **visitors.**

3. The (6) **sailors** explored (7) **her** island (8) **cautiously.**
4. The goddess at first (9) **treated** them (10) **well** (11) **but** then turned them (12) **into** animals.
5. Their leader escaped from the island (13) **and** told the (14) **story** to Odysseus.
6. "She sings the (15) **sweetest** music that (16) **I** have (17) **heard,"** he said.
7. "She is very (18) **dangerous,** and (19) **she** has (20) **tricked** my (21) **foolish** companions."
8. Nothing could (22) **persuade** Odysseus to leave his (23) **followers.**
9. A (24) **god** came (25) **from** Mount Olympus and (26) **brought** help.
10. He brought protection (27) **against** the (28) **magic** of the goddess.
11. Her (29) **strongest** drugs lost their (30) **power.**
12. Odysseus met (31) **his** enemy (32) **confidently.**
13. She (33) **looked** at him (34) **with** surprise when he (35) **attacked** her.
14. She (36) **swore** an (37) **oath** that she would (38) **plot** no more.
15. Odysseus left her island (39) **and** again traveled (40) **restlessly** across the sea.

S2
THE COMPLETE SENTENCE

Know the basic parts needed to make a complete English sentence.

What makes a complete sentence? The normal English sentence has at least two basic parts. At least two basic parts are needed to give us the complete message:

INCOMPLETE: Wood _____ . (What about wood?)
COMPLETE: Wood floats.

INCOMPLETE: Coyotes _____ . (What about coyotes?)
COMPLETE: Coyotes howl.

Sometimes three or even four basic parts are needed for a complete message. In the following examples, three or four basic parts are needed for a complete sentence:

INCOMPLETE: Clouds bring _____ . (What?)
COMPLETE: Clouds bring rain.

INCOMPLETE: Mary gave Brian _____ . (What?)
COMPLETE: Mary gave Brian directions.

Study the five most common ways we put basic parts together in a complete English sentence.

FIVE COMMON SENTENCE PATTERNS
A Summary

The following sentence patterns give us the basic frames for nearly all the sentences we read, write, or speak:

PATTERN ONE: *S–V:* Our friends have left.

This is the "Doer"—Action pattern. What the subject *(S)* does is shown by the verb *(V)*.

PATTERN TWO: *S–V–O:* The batter hit the ball.

This is the "Doer"—Action—Goal pattern. The direct object is the target or the result of the action shown by the verb.

PATTERN THREE: *S–LV–N:* My friend is a mechanic.

The noun (or pronoun) following the verb puts a label on the subject. It is connected to the subject by the linking verb.

PATTERN FOUR: *S–LV–Adj:* The apple looks ripe.

The adjective following the verb tells us more about the subject. It is connected to the subject by the linking verb.

PATTERN FIVE: *S–V–IO–O:* Ann sent her friend a letter.

This is the "Doer"—Action—Destination—Object pattern. The indirect object tells us *where* something is headed.

Study sentences made up of a subject and a verb.

To make a "bare-minimum" statement in English, we need only two basic parts. First, we mention something that can be a topic for discussion: birds, or cars, or children, or pollution. We focus on this topic as if to say: "Here—this is what I want to talk about." Then we go on to make a statement about the topic. We act as if someone asked: "Well—what *about* birds?" Or, "What *about* cars?"

SUBJECT AND VERB:
Some verbs tell the whole story.

We call the sentence topic the **subject** of the sentence. We call the part that makes a statement the **predicate** of the sentence.

SUBJECT	PREDICATE
Birds	sing.
Cars	stall.
Children	play.
Pollution	smells.

In the normal English sentence, the predicate makes a statement about the subject. In the first of several common sentence patterns, a single basic part can give us the whole predicate. Remember the following points about Pattern One sentences:

(1) The subject is typically a noun—alone, or with a noun marker. The subject may be *singular* (we talk about *one* of a kind) or *plural* (we talk about *more* than one). Here are Pattern One sentences showing the different kinds of subjects:

Glass breaks.
Children play.
The hyena laughed.
My friends approved.
This material shrinks.

Pronouns are words that can take the place of a noun. We use them as shortcut words when we know who (or what) is being talked about. *I, you, he, she, it, we,* and *they* are pronouns that can replace a noun as the subject of a sentence:

I know. | *They* play. | *It* shrinks.

(2) In a Pattern One sentence, a complete verb by itself can make up the whole predicate. The verbs in Pattern One are verbs that can "tell the whole story." The verb may be a single word. Or it may have one or more auxiliaries that help make up the complete verb:

SUBJECT	VERB
Monkeys	*chatter.*
The lion	*had roared.*
The bears	*were sleeping.*
The seals	*could have barked.*

We call verbs that "tell the whole story" **intransitive** verbs. After an intransitive verb, nothing further is needed to complete the sentence.

(3) The subject-verb pattern gives us the basic frame for an actual sentence. We can build up a Pattern One sentence by adding parts that do not change the basic frame. The frame can stand by itself, but we can also attach *optional* parts. For instance, we can build up the subject by putting an adjective before the noun. We can build up the predicate by having adverbs go with the verb.

The following Pattern One sentences have been *expanded* by the addition of such optional parts. Can you still see the basic *S–V* frame? Point out each of the added parts:

S	V
The ship	finally sank.
Angry people	shout.
My clever brother	quickly hid inside.
The bell	always rings twice.
His rich old aunt	suddenly died.
The English butler	smiled icily.
Our detective	had blundered again.

Sentences

(4) *Usually, the subject comes before the verb.* The position before the verb is "subject territory." If subjects were not put in their proper slot, the sentence machinery would start to malfunction. What is wrong with the following sentences?

Her tooth pulled the dentist.
The daisy picked the girl.
The pancake ate the boy.

EXERCISE 1

How many animal noises can you identify? Complete each of the following *S–V* sentences by adding the right verb. Each time use a verb that gives the right sound or noise for that animal. Use a single word as your complete verb. Write the verb after the number of the sentence.

EXAMPLE: Cats _____ .
(Answer)   *meow*

1. Dogs _____ .
2. Horses _____ .
3. Hyenas _____ .
4. Snakes _____ .
5. Lions _____ .
6. Ducks _____ .
7. Canaries _____ .
8. Crickets _____ .
9. Roosters _____ .
10. Hens _____ .
11. Bees _____ .
12. Donkeys _____ .
13. Owls _____ .
14. Frogs _____ .
15. Elephants _____ .
16. Mice _____ .
17. Lambs _____ .
18. Turkeys _____ .
19. Geese _____ .
20. Pigeons _____ .

EXERCISE 2

Find the basic parts in each of the following *S–V* sentences. After the number of the sentence, write down the noun or pronoun that is the subject of the sentence. (Include any noun marker.) Then write down the complete verb. (Include any helping verbs.) Leave out all added optional parts.

EXAMPLE: The colorful fair finally ended.
(Answer)   *The fair ended.*

1. Heavy rains will arrive tonight.
2. A light plane was landing.
3. The fans always cheer loudly.
4. The new calculator works well.
5. I always walk there.
6. The same cable has snapped again.

7. Things may change later.
8. Our new trees have really grown.
9. His older sister may be jogging.
10. The fire always burns brightly.
11. That Egyptian mummy will sleep forever.
12. His food spoiled long ago.
13. The dogs ran away frequently.
14. They often leave early.
15. Those foolish boys are smoking again.
16. His high voice rose even higher.
17. My older brother seldom sleeps late.
18. The nosy detective has been snooping around.
19. The quiet old town was sleeping peacefully.
20. The savage headhunters had been hunting nearby.

In the following *S–V* sentences, each predicate makes a statement about the wrong subject. For each subject, find the predicate that should go with it. After the number of each sentence, write a sentence that makes good sense.

EXERCISE 3

1. The cook purrs almost constantly.
2. The store was barking ferociously.
3. The weed is baking now.
4. Their house may have been stealing.
5. The car will close early today.
6. Our telephone was running around wildly.
7. The child is growing everywhere.
8. The criminal burned down quickly.
9. My dog rings frequently.
10. His cat is stalling again.

Study sentences where an object follows the verb.

S2b

Verb and Object

Read the following statements. Which sound complete as they stand? Which need more information before the message is complete?

The girls left _____
The train arrived _____
The boy carried _____
The students demanded _____

The first two statements give us a complete message: Somebody left. Something arrived. But the other two statements make us ask: The boy carried _____ (what?) The students demanded _____ (what?) With verbs like *carry* or *demand,* the sentence usually has to *go on* to a third basic part:

COMPLETE: The boy carried *a cat.*
COMPLETE: The students demanded *a vacation.*

When we need a basic part after the verb, we call it a **completer** (or **complement**). In a second common sentence pattern, the completer is a noun. (Sometimes it is a pronoun that takes the place of a noun.)

The following points will help you recognize Pattern Two sentences:

(1) Pattern Two sentences often take us from a "doer" through what is done to a goal or a target. The verb carries the action across to a target or receiver. We can ask questions like: What is this action aimed at? Who is at the receiving end? What is the product or result?

"DOER"	ACTION	TARGET OR RESULT
The coyote	hunted	mice.
A stranger	shoved	my friend.
The sheriff	questioned	the suspect.
My sister	was painting	the mailbox.
The campers	had cooked	their hamburgers.

The verbs in this second pattern *go on* to something else. We call them **transitive** verbs.

(2) The completer in a Pattern Two sentence is typically a noun or a pronoun. We call the completer in Pattern Two the **object.** It names the object or target of an action. Or it names the result of a process. The object names a person, place, or thing *different from* the subject:

SUBJECT	VERB	OBJECT
The dog	bit	*the man.*
Our family	visited	*the Capitol.*
The horse	ate	*an apple.*

Pronouns can replace nouns as objects of sentences. But we use a different set of pronouns in object positions from those that we use in subject positions. What pronouns would you use to replace the objects in the three sentences above? The object pronouns are the following: *me, you, her, him, it, us,* and *them.* (*You* and *it* do double duty as subject pronouns.) In the following sentences, pronouns serve as objects:

My audience liked *it.*
My sisters hated *me.*
Our teachers encouraged *us.*
Her grandmother invited *her.*

See **U3a** for more on subject forms and object forms.

(3) *The S–V–O skeleton may be fleshed out in various ways.* The three basic parts provide only the most basic frame. In this pattern, adjectives may tell us more about the subject *and* about the object. Adverbs, as always, can answer questions like *How? When?* and *Where?* about the action shown by the verb.

The following Pattern Two sentences have been *expanded* by the addition of optional parts:

The *hungry* coyote hunted mice.
The students demanded a *longer* vacation.
The campers had *already* cooked their hamburgers.

EXERCISE 1

For each of the following sentences, find a verb that would complete the sentence. Write the verb after the number of the sentence. Each time, use one single word. Make sure each completed sentence fits the *S–V–O* pattern.

EXAMPLE: Mail clerks _____ mail.
(Answer) *sort*

1. Mechanics _____ cars.
2. Doctors _____ patients.
3. A thermometer _____ your temperature.
4. Volunteers _____ blood.
5. Truckers _____ trucks.
6. Tailors _____ clothes.
7. Lawyers _____ clients.
8. Newspapers _____ news.
9. Messengers _____ telegrams.

10. Secretaries _____ letters.
11. The weather bureau _____ the weather.
12. Detectives _____ crimes.
13. Pilots _____ airplanes.
14. Architects _____ buildings.
15. A refrigerator _____ food.
16. Engines _____ fuel.
17. Our government _____ laws.
18. Jewelers _____ bracelets.
19. Turbines _____ electricity.
20. Dairies _____ milk.

EXERCISE 2

For each of the following, write down the basic *S–V–O* pattern. Leave out all optional parts. Include any noun marker with the subject and the object. Include any helping verb with the verb.

EXAMPLE: Tall waves always pounded the rocky shore.
(Answer) *Waves pounded the shore.*

1. Proud braves once hunted the buffalo.
2. They owned beautiful horses.
3. Storytellers often told the old stories.
4. The young people learned the ancient customs.
5. Great chiefs had united hostile tribes.
6. White settlers were already crossing the plains.
7. Their powerful guns were destroying the huge herds.
8. Brave warriors fought the soldiers fiercely.
9. Everywhere the tribes lost their lands.
10. Native Americans today remember their past.

EXERCISE 3

The following African story explains how the god of the Yao tribe left the earth. The name of their god was Mulungu. All of the sentences that tell the story are either Pattern One or Pattern Two. After the number of each sentence, write either *S–V* or *S–V–O*. Remember that the object answers the questions *Whom?* or *What?* after the verb. It does not answer the questions *When? Where?* or *How?*

EXAMPLE: The people set traps.
(Answer) *S–V–O*

1. Originally the earth lacked people.
2. Only Mulungu lived.

3. Many beasts surrounded their god.
4. They were living happily.
5. A chameleon found a human pair.
6. The animal had never seen these creatures.
7. The chameleon reported its discovery.
8. Mulungu waited patiently.
9. The animals watched the newcomers.
10. The people made fires.
11. Soon the bush was blazing.
12. The animals ran away.
13. The people set clever traps.
14. The hunters killed animals.
15. Mulungu left this earth.
16. A little spider helped him.
17. The spider spun a fine web.
18. It led upwards.
19. Mulungu climbed it sadly.
20. He left the people behind.

Study sentences where a linking verb pins a label on the subject.

S2c

Linking Verb and Noun

Study the following pairs of sentences. In the first sentence in each pair, somebody does something that is aimed *at someone else.* In the second sentence, only one person appears. The same person appears before and after the verb:

DIFFERENT: My father met *my friend.*
SAME: My father is *my friend.*

DIFFERENT: His sister asked *a guide.*
SAME: His sister was *a guide.*

DIFFERENT: My cousin will need *a dentist.*
SAME: My cousin will be *a dentist.*

When the two people are the same, the second noun tells us more about the first. It serves as a label that we can pin on the subject of the sentence. In a Pattern Three sentence, the verb is used to pin a label on the subject. Remember:

(1) Pattern Three sentences are built on an Item-Linker-Label model. They do the kind of work that zoo keepers do when they paste labels on the different cages. The completer in a Pattern Three sentence is a noun we can use to identify each different specimen:

ITEM	LINK	LABEL
This animal	is	a zebra.
This monkey	is	a baboon.
These birds	are	parakeets.
This specimen	may be	a coyote.
Those apes	were	gorillas.

(2) Only very few verbs are used in Pattern Three. We call these verbs **linking verbs.** In most Pattern Three sentences, the linking verb is one of the many forms of *be: am, is, are, was, were, will be, has been, had been,* and the like.

In the typical Pattern Three sentence, a form of *be* is followed by a second noun that completes the basic pattern, as shown in the chart:

SUBJECT	LINKING VERB	NOUN
Her car	is	a Ford.
The nurses	are	volunteers.
These thieves	were	professionals.
Our coach	had been	a champion.

Some other common linking verbs are *become* and *remain:*

Elizabeth	became	a queen.
My cousin	will remain	our leader.

(3) The S–LV–N skeleton may be fleshed out in various ways. As with the other patterns, optional parts may be added to the basic frame. Can you find all the added parts in the following Pattern Three sentences? Can you still see the basic frame? (Identify each added part.)

Her older sister once was a guide.
Those big apes are probably young gorillas.
Their relatives had always remained poor peasants.

Remember: Both of the nouns in a Pattern Three sentence point to the same person or thing.

For each blank space, find a noun that would complete a Pattern Three sentence. Include a noun marker where necessary. Write the noun after the number of the sentence. Write on a separate sheet of paper.

EXERCISE 1

EXAMPLE: Tennis is _____.
(Answer) *a sport*

1. Checkers is _____.
2. Spiders are _____.
3. Christianity is _____.
4. Japan is _____.
5. Dolphins are _____.
6. A trombone is _____.
7. A trombonist is _____.
8. The Romans were _____.
9. Tadpoles become _____.
10. Hawaii became _____.
11. A veteran has been _____.
12. George Washington had been _____.
13. The states had been _____.
14. Adolescents will be _____.
15. A cathedral is _____.
16. Glaciers are _____.
17. Cancer remains _____.
18. Washington, D.C., has remained _____.
19. Atlantis may have been _____.
20. The President must be _____.

For each of the following, write down the basic *S–LV–N* sentence. Leave out all optional parts. Include any noun markers or helping verbs with the basic parts.

EXERCISE 2

EXAMPLE: Holidays are very special times.
(Answer) *Holidays are times.*

1. Chanukah is a favorite Jewish holiday.
2. The earliest Chanukah was a religious celebration.
3. The Maccabees were famous Jewish rebels.
4. Their enemies had become powerful overlords.
5. Their goal was complete freedom.
6. The victory must have been an unforgettable event.
7. Familiar holidays are often anniversaries.
8. Sometimes a holiday becomes a true popular festival.
9. Important birthdays may become official holidays.
10. Very old holidays remain a worldwide tradition.

EXERCISE 3

What is the basic pattern in each of the following sentences? After the number of the sentence, put the right abbreviation:

S–V
S–V–O
S–LV–N

EXAMPLE: The driver sighted an unidentified object.
(Answer) *S–V–O*

1. Frieda will be our new secretary.
2. The singer was entertaining our guests.
3. Our former home was a cooperative apartment.
4. They are going away now.
5. The girl was an excellent artist.
6. His grandparents had been farmers.
7. The squad demolished the bridge.
8. True happiness should be our goal.
9. The lecturer rarely spoke plainly.
10. The animals have been waiting patiently.
11. My cousin is directing traffic downtown.
12. Wonder drugs may produce remarkable cures.
13. The first page has mysteriously disappeared.
14. The building had been a warehouse.
15. My friends are good athletes.
16. We have been looking everywhere.
17. The sprinter was constantly breaking records.
18. The old man had been their chief suspect.
19. Prices were gradually rising.
20. Their aim was complete freedom.

S2d

Linking Verb and Adjective

Study sentences where an adjective follows the linking verb.

Look at the sentences in each of the following pairs. The first sentence in each pair is a Pattern Three sentence. The completer after the verb is a noun. The linking verb pins a label on the subject. In the second sentence, an adjective follows the verb instead:

This ape is a gorilla.
Gorillas are *huge*.

She is our leader.
Our leader is *courageous*.

Pat Greene is the manager.
The manager is *new*.

This flower is an orchid.
Orchids are *beautiful*.

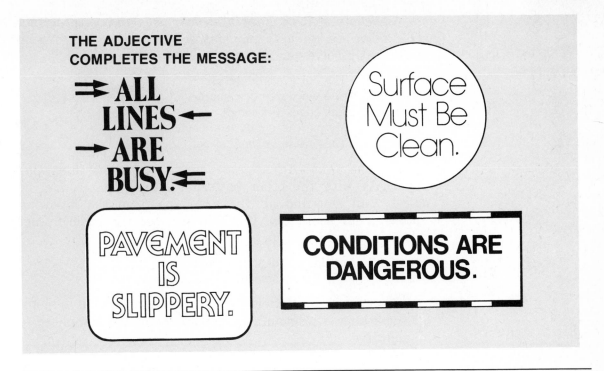

In the fourth common sentence pattern, an adjective follows the linking verb. It serves as the third basic part of the sentence and completes the sentence. Remember:

(1) As with Pattern Three, the most common linking verb in Pattern Four is a form of be. In other words, the verb in a Pattern Four sentence is usually a form like *am, is, are, was, were,* or *has been.* Then, instead of a noun, an adjective follows. Remember that most adjectives are degree words that fit in after *very:* very *huge,* very *new,* very *beautiful.*

SUBJECT (S)	LINKING VERB (LV)	ADJECTIVE (Adj)
The windows	are	*open.*
Electricity	is	*dangerous.*
Her relatives	were	*wealthy.*
Donations	have been	*generous.*
The search	will be	*thorough.*

(2) Many Pattern Four sentences use linking verbs that show what we do with our five senses. They use linking verbs that involve our senses of sight, touch, and so on:

SIGHT: The shirt *looked* faded.
HEARING: The voice *sounded* hoarse.
TOUCH: The edges *feel* rough.
TASTE: My pancakes *will taste* better.
SMELL: These flowers *smell* sweet.

(3) The S–LV–Adj skeleton may be fleshed out in various ways. As with the other patterns, optional parts may be added. Can you find all the added parts in the following Pattern Four sentences? Can you still see the basic frame? (Identify the added parts.)

Captive gorillas are usually sullen.
Hungry wolves are sometimes dangerous.

Remember: In Pattern Three, the completer is a noun (or sometimes a pronoun). In Pattern Four, the completer is an adjective.

EXERCISE 1

For each blank space, find an adjective that could complete a Pattern Four sentence. Write the adjective after the number of the sentence. Write only one single word for each blank.

EXAMPLE: Clowns are _____ .
(Answer)   *funny*

1. Ants are _____ .
2. Glass is _____ .
3. Salesclerks should be _____ .
4. Cafeteria lunches should be _____ .
5. Flavoring may be _____ .
6. The dinosaurs were _____ .
7. Pups are _____ .
8. The pioneers were _____ .
9. Bridges may be _____ .
10. A speaker should sound _____ .
11. Her story might have been _____ .
12. The new building looked _____ .
13. Lemons always taste _____ .
14. A prisoner must feel _____ .
15. Velvet feels _____ .

16. A voice may sound _____.
17. My relatives are usually _____.
18. Soil can be _____.
19. Winners are often _____.
20. Friends should be _____.

For each of the following items, write down the basic Pattern Four *(S–LV–Adj)* sentence. Leave out all optional parts. Include any noun markers or helping verbs with the basic parts.

EXERCISE 2

EXAMPLE: Our favorite stories may be very old.
(Answer) *Our stories may be old.*

1. Folktales are sometimes very simple.
2. Fate seems unkind.
3. The monsters always sound gruesome.
4. The wicked witches are usually very ugly.
5. The innocent princess naturally looks very beautiful.
6. The prince is handsome.
7. The villains can be extremely cruel.
8. Sometimes a younger sister is very kind.
9. The older sisters may be mean.
10. Stepmothers, of course, are always evil.
11. A poor peasant may suddenly become rich.
12. The good people will usually be lucky.
13. The defeated villains are unhappy.
14. Fortunately the ending will usually be happy.
15. The moral of the story is direct.

What is the basic pattern in each of the following sentences? After the number of the sentence, put the right abbreviation:

EXERCISE 3

   S–V
   S–V–O
   S–LV–N
   S–LV–Adj

EXAMPLE: Guinea pigs are good pets.
(Answer) *S–LV–N*

1. The man talked angrily.
2. Our dog looks happy now.

3. The soldier sounded the alarm too late.
4. Justice should be impartial.
5. The wealthy old man disinherited his family.
6. Experience is the best teacher.
7. Their conversation sounded silly.
8. The boy tasted the cookies.
9. Our cookies always taste good.
10. The machine must be working well now.
11. My father has always been a Democrat.
12. You should have been holding my hand.
13. Their party was a failure.
14. The problem sounded familiar.
15. Her speech was a great success.
16. The crowd suddenly pushed forward.
17. That kind old lady could be your grandmother.
18. Honesty is its own reward.
19. The show closed quite suddenly.
20. The children looked sleepy.

S2e

The Indirect Object

Study sentences that include an indirect object.

Look at the sentences in each of the following pairs. The first sentence in each pair is complete. We have filled in an object, and it completes the sentence. In the second statement in each pair, we have filled in an object, but the sentence is still not complete:

Uncle Jim bought candy.
Uncle Jim bought the children _____ (what?)

Simon offered a dime.
Simon offered the beggar _____ (what?)

Grandmother mailed a parcel.
Grandmother mailed her daughter _____ (what?)

The king granted permission.
The king granted his knights _____ (what?)

The second sentence in each pair needs a *second* completer before the message makes sense. In the fifth common sentence pattern, two completers follow the verb:

Uncle Jim bought *the children candy.*
Simon offered *the beggar a dime.*
Grandmother mailed *her daughter a parcel.*

Remember:

(1) Pattern Five sentences use an additional completer.
After the verb, we put in an additional completer that shows *where* something is headed:

"DOER"	ACTION	DESTINATION	OBJECT
My aunt	gave	*Sue*	a bicycle.
Businesses	send	*their customers*	bills.
My friend	offered	*the hikers*	a ride.
They	told	*me*	a secret.
Sam	passed	*his mother*	the salt.

Pattern Two sentences head directly for the object. Pattern Five sentences fill in the destination first. The noun (or pronoun) that shows the destination is called the **indirect object** (IO).

PATTERN TWO:	He bought flowers.
PATTERN FIVE:	He bought *his mother* flowers.

PATTERN TWO:	The boy mailed the letter.
PATTERN FIVE:	The boy mailed *us* the letter.

PATTERN TWO:	We sold the house.
PATTERN FIVE:	We sold *our friends* the house.

PATTERN TWO:	Sally told a lie.
PATTERN FIVE:	Sally told *the teacher* a lie.

(2) Only a limited number of verbs can be used in Pattern Five. They are the kind of verbs that show we are passing something on, or handing it over. Here are some typical examples:

S	V	IO	O
The bank	*loaned*	my sister	the money.
Carol	*has written*	her friend	a letter.
Their parents	*left*	them	a fortune.
Frances	*will teach*	the group	songs.
The messenger	*handed*	our leader	a note.

Pattern Five verbs include *give, send, offer, teach, grant, write, leave, pass, sell, buy, hand, tell,* and *pay.*

(3) The S–V–IO–O skeleton may be fleshed out in various ways. Can you see the basic frame in each of the following sentences? Identify the added parts:

> My father always gave the children long lectures.
> Mother finally told us the sad truth.
> The ad promised interested tourists a wonderful vacation.

NOTE: When an object follows a verb, it becomes a basic part of the sentence. The object comes into the sentence without any connecting link (though it may bring a noun marker with it). The object of a verb does *not* follow a preposition— a word like *of, to, at, with,* or *for.* In these examples, an additional noun is linked to the sentence by a preposition:

S–V:	Her cousin worked *for the railroad.*
S–V–O:	My friend sold programs *at the games.*
S–LV–N:	The band is the pride *of our school.*
S–LV–Adj:	The stranger was mean *to cats.*
S–V–IO–O:	She gave us a map *with directions.*

EXERCISE 1

Which of the following sentences can you complete by filling in two completers? After the number of the sentence, write the two missing parts. Use only nouns, alone or with a noun marker. If the verb does not fit Pattern Five, write *No* after the number of the sentence.

EXAMPLE: Insurance gives _____ _____.
(Answer) *people protection*

1. Employers ask _____ _____.
2. Teachers teach _____ _____.
3. Merchants offer _____ _____.
4. My parents knew _____ _____.
5. Parents should give _____ _____.
6. The band was marching _____ _____.
7. Tourists may send _____ _____.
8. The engine overheated _____ _____.
9. Pharmacists sell _____ _____.
10. Commercials promise _____ _____.
11. People may lend _____ _____.
12. The city pays _____ _____.
13. Rainfall cleans _____ _____.
14. Peddlers sold _____ _____.
15. The governor can grant _____ _____.

16. The fans were cheering _____ _____.
17. The host passed _____ _____.
18. The police officer was handing _____ _____.
19. Grandchildren should write _____ _____.
20. This country sells _____ _____.

Write *Yes* after the number of the sentence if it follows Pattern Five *(S–V–IO–O)*. Write *No* if it does not.

EXAMPLE: The clerk showed us the camera.
(Answer)   *Yes*

1. A neighbor lent my family a tent.
2. The ranger explained the slides to the campers.
3. The guide showed our group the giant trees.
4. The campgrounds are crowded in August.
5. A small store sells the campers supplies.
6. My older sister had given us advice.
7. We sent our friends postcards.
8. Visitors often see deer in the park.
9. Raccoons steal food at night.
10. My parents had promised us a trip.
11. Sylvia handed the cook the charcoal.
12. I passed my brother the catsup.
13. The wind was rustling in the trees.
14. A ranger was selling the campers tickets.
15. Parents should teach their children a love of nature.
16. The stars in the sky can be very beautiful.
17. The woods are a different world.
18. People should offer their friends a ride.
19. Scouts teach newcomers the lore of the outdoors.
20. You should buy a friend a book about wild animals.

Look for the basic pattern in each of the sentences on the following page. Put the right abbreviation after the number of each sentence:

S–V
S–V–O
S–LV–N
S–LV–Adj
S–V–IO–O

EXAMPLE: The Micmac Indians tell an ancient story.
(Answer)   *S–V–O*

Sentences

1. Hunger stalked the tribe.
2. The wind was always blowing fiercely.
3. The choppy waters bothered the tribespeople.
4. Their favorite food was eels.
5. The chief gave his youngest child a hard task.
6. The young warrior must calm the winds.
7. The traveler started a long trip.
8. He finally saw a large bird.
9. The bird was the storm-king.
10. It was flapping its wings violently.
11. Its wings created the storms.
12. The young champion broke the huge wings.
13. The news gave the tribe new hope.
14. Now the sea became very calm.
15. Scum covered the water everywhere.
16. The eels again escaped their hunters.
17. The young hero brought the storm-king medicine.
18. Its wings soon flapped again.
19. The winds were now slower.
20. The fishing was more successful.

S3
ADAPTING THE SIMPLE SENTENCE

Study the ways we can change a sentence to make it serve a different purpose.

The basic sentence patterns serve us well when we give other people information. We use them to make a *statement*. We use them to tell others something:

Time is money.
The time has come.
You are wasting my time.

But language also serves other purposes. Often, we are trying to find something out. We ask a *question*. We turn to others for information:

What time is it?
Do you have the time?
Is it time yet?

Often we use language to ask others to do something. We make a *request:*

Tell me in time. | Save your time.

Study some of the ways we change or adapt simple statements to make them serve other purposes.

Know the ways we can change statements to questions or requests.

We can often change the meaning of a sentence by simply *rearranging* some of its parts:

STATEMENT: The driver *has told* the boys.
QUESTION: *Has* the driver *told* the boys?

STATEMENT: The food *is ready.*
QUESTION: *Is* the food *ready?*

Or we can change the meaning of a sentence by adding something or *taking something out:*

STATEMENT: *Custodians* lock the doors.
REQUEST: Lock the doors!

STATEMENT: *Bicycle riders* look out for cars.
REQUEST: Look out for cars!

THREE KINDS OF SENTENCES

STATEMENTS: The British army has surrendered at Yorktown.

Russia sold Alaska to the United States.

Hawaii became a state.

QUESTIONS: Was George Washington already commander-in-chief?

Do you remember Valley Forge?

Have you heard of Harriet Tubman?

REQUESTS: Look up the date of the battle.

Study the maps of the new territories.

Learn more about American history.

The first three of the following rules help us turn statements into simple questions. The fourth rule helps us turn statements into simple requests:

(1) If one or more auxiliaries are part of the verb, we can shift the first auxiliary to the beginning of the sentence. Using this rule, make questions of the following. (The first auxiliary has been italicized in each sentence.)

The doctor *will* see me.
Joe *is* sending us a package.
You *have* seen your friend.
The expedition *has* reached the North Pole.
Maria *could* have been a lawyer.

(2) If there is no auxiliary, we can add do, does, *or* did *to the sentence.* Then we shift this added auxiliary to the beginning of the sentence. Here are examples of this two-step rule in action:

SOURCE: The horse seems healthy.
STEP ONE: The horse *does* seem healthy.
STEP TWO: *Does* the horse seem healthy?

SOURCE: The trains run on Sundays.
STEP ONE: The trains *do* run on Sundays.
STEP TWO: *Do* the trains run on Sundays?

SOURCE: The earth shook.
STEP ONE: The earth *did* shake.
STEP TWO: *Did* the earth shake?

(3) If there are no auxiliaries and the verb is a form of be, *we simply shift the verb to the beginning of the sentence.* Find the form of *be* in each of the following sentences. Then change each sentence to a question by moving that form:

Nancy was your leader.
The scouts were always alert.
Those girls are good listeners.
The children are hungry.

(4) We can often turn a statement into a request by leaving out the subject. We then use the plain or ordinary form of the verb as the **request form:**

STATEMENT: Guests should park outside.
REQUEST: *Park* outside.

Adapting the Simple Sentence

STATEMENT: You will report for practice at three o'clock.

REQUEST: *Report* for practice at three o'clock.

NOTE: Although the subject has been left out, such requests are still complete sentences. We say that *you* is understood as the subject of a request sentence. (We are talking *to* someone, and that person is expected to do what we ask.)

Turn each of the following statements into a question. Add no new words, except a form of *do* where necessary.

EXERCISE 1

EXAMPLE: The rain has stopped.
(Answer) *Has the rain stopped?*

1. The batter had watched the pitcher.
2. The passengers boarded the airplane.
3. He thinks about her constantly.
4. The workers are repairing the roof.
5. The police officer should have arrested the suspect.
6. George's family bought a new car.
7. The judge gave the boys a second chance.
8. She will close the store early tonight.
9. The student finished his homework.
10. The sun was sinking slowly.
11. The dog looks very sick.
12. Her story was interesting.
13. He should have parked his car outside.
14. The flowers were beautiful.
15. His answers seem silly.
16. Her brother told her the news.
17. They expect a great crowd tonight.
18. The reviewer liked the novel.
19. We lost the bet.
20. They were always good friends.

Turn the following questions back into statements. Add no new words. Take out the form of *do* where necessary.

EXERCISE 2

EXAMPLE: Does the library close early?
(Answer) *The library closes early.*

1. Has she told the driver?
2. Is the car ready?
3. Will you bring me the book?
4. Is that boy the leader?

5. Did he look unhappy?
6. Has the boy found his coat?
7. Does the bus stop here?
8. Are our friends going?
9. Do the stores close at eight?
10. Can we afford the prices?

EXERCISE 3

Write ten sentences that do one of the following:

- Give advice for a camping trip, or the like.
- Give pointers for a sightseeing trip through a town or city.
- Tell someone how to take care of a bicycle, a garden, or the like.

Each time use a request sentence.

EXAMPLES: Plant bulbs in the fall.
Prune trees in the winter.
Clean your garden of debris in the spring.

S3b

The Passive

Know how to change a sentence from active to passive, or from passive to active.

Many English sentences move from the "doer" through the action to the target. They start with somebody who is active or with something that moves:

ACTIVE: *The dog* chased the rabbit.
ACTIVE: *The prince* kissed Cinderella.
ACTIVE: *The spaceship* reached Mars.

The passive sentence turns this usual pattern around. It pulls the target or the receiver out in front:

PASSIVE: *The rabbit* was chased by the dog.
PASSIVE: *Cinderella* was kissed by the prince.
PASSIVE: *Mars* was reached by the spaceship.

A passive person is somebody who "lets things happen." In the passive sentence, the spotlight is on somebody who lets things happen. Or the spotlight is on something that has things happen to it.

To make a passive sentence, we start with sentences that are either Pattern Two *(S–V–O)* or Pattern Five *(S–V–IO–O)*. We then go through several steps:

(1) We make the subject and object trade places;

A dragon guards the entrance.
The entrance ——————— *a dragon.*

The sisters hated Cinderella.
Cinderella ——————— *the sisters.*

(2) We change the verb to a form that uses a form of be. In other words, we switch to a form that uses *am, is, was, were,* or the like. Then we put the word *by* after the verb:

A dragon guards the entrance.
——————— *is guarded by* ———————.

The sisters hated Cinderella.
——————— *was hated by* ———————.

When the active verb already has an auxiliary, we put a form of *be* between the auxiliary and the main verb:

The school *has announced* a contest.
——————— *has been announced by* ———————.

(3) We use the complete passive sentence, or we omit the original subject:

ACTIVE: A dragon guards the entrance.
COMPLETE PASSIVE: The entrance is guarded *by a dragon.*
SHORT PASSIVE: The entrance is guarded.

ACTIVE: The school has announced a contest.
COMPLETE PASSIVE: A contest has been announced *by the school.*
SHORT PASSIVE: A contest has been announced.

ACTIVE: The voters have reelected the President.
COMPLETE PASSIVE: The President has been reelected *by the voters.*
SHORT PASSIVE: The President has been reelected.

The best way to recognize the "short passive" is to see if you can fill in a phrase that tells us "by *whom?*" or "by *what?*"

NOTE: When a sentence has *two* objects, the *first* one usually goes out in front as the new subject. Watch the word *Jim* move in the following sentence:

ACTIVE: My uncle offered *Jim* a job.
COMPLETE PASSIVE: *Jim* was offered a job by my uncle.
SHORT PASSIVE: *Jim* was offered a job.

Sentences

Can you show how the first object goes out in front when you turn the following into passive sentences? For each, find the complete passive first, and then the short passive:

The wizard gave the tinman a watch.
The wizard gave the lion a medal.
The wizard gave the scarecrow a diploma.

EXERCISE 1

Most of the following statements can be turned into passive sentences. Write each passive sentence after the number of the original statement. If the statement cannot be turned into a passive sentence, write *No*.

EXAMPLE: Dutch pioneers had settled the area.
(Answer) *The area had been settled by Dutch pioneers.*

1. The police arrested the suspect.
2. A thief took my keys.
3. The owner banned bare feet.
4. The painting was an excellent landscape.
5. My older sister sent Jean a gift.
6. The father warned the child.
7. Students published the newspaper.
8. The dogs will rescue the lost climber.
9. You should go out more often.
10. An expert had copied the painting.
11. My aunt left a fortune.
12. Your mother should have signed the form.
13. Jean was looking very sad.
14. The dog carried the newspaper.
15. My sister offered my brother her bicycle.
16. A stranger gave Giorgio the money.
17. He has been searching everywhere.
18. A kindly couple adopted the orphan.
19. She can sometimes look very angry.
20. The store had promised customers a refund.

EXERCISE 2

Turn each of the following passive sentences back into an active statement. Write the active statement after the number of the original sentence.

EXAMPLE: Congratulations were sent by the mayor.
(Answer) *The mayor sent congratulations.*

1. The bad news was brought by Tim.
2. My family is often visited by relatives.
3. The squad has always been led by a sergeant.
4. The house was invaded by termites.
5. The game should have been called by the umpire.
6. The grand old mansion was bought by the Brown family.
7. The visitors must have been seen by the guard.
8. Carol is always teased by those girls.
9. His ear was grazed by the bullet.
10. The guests were offered a homemade cake by the hosts.

Some of the following statements have been turned into passive sentences. In some of them, the original subject has been dropped from the sentence. Put the right abbreviation after the number of the sentence:

EXERCISE 3

A   for active sentence;
CP for complete passive;
SP for short passive.

EXAMPLE: The plans for the new gymnasium must be approved by the school board.

(Answer) *CP*

1. Friendship is often praised.
2. Friends do things together.
3. Our group explored the playground.
4. Sometimes friends are separated.
5. The letter had been written by a friend.
6. Sometimes people become friends very slowly.
7. Your parents will like your new friend.
8. Contestants are encouraged by their friends.
9. Her friend lent her the money.
10. Rachel had invited her friends.
11. Her friends have been invited to a party.
12. Friends may be envied by outsiders.
13. My friend was offered a free book.
14. She always shares things with me.
15. My apologies were accepted.
16. My feelings had been hurt by these remarks.
17. Trouble puts friendship to the test.
18. The members will be notified by a printed announcement.
19. My brother finally found new friends.
20. His remarks have hurt my feelings.

UNIT REVIEW EXERCISE

In which of the following has a simple sentence been changed or adapted to make it serve a special purpose? After the number of each sentence, put one of the following abbreviations:

A for active statement;
P for passive statement (either short or complete passive);
Q for question;
R for request.

EXAMPLE: The rules have been changed.
(Answer) *P*

1. The alarm was sounded by the sentry.
2. A small leak will sink a great ship.
3. Cyclists should wear helmets.
4. Fasten your seat belt before takeoff.
5. Books have been stolen from the library.
6. Could the instructions have been wrong?
7. The town was leveled by an earthquake.
8. Follow the directions carefully.
9. A package was left for you earlier today.
10. My teeth were checked by a very good dentist.
11. The early morning has gold in its mouth.
12. These coupons can be redeemed at their stores.
13. New laws have reduced smog.
14. The road will be widened soon.
15. Can you remember your earliest friends?
16. Return these tools to the shed.
17. Birds can cause serious accidents.
18. The new show was canceled by the network.
19. Does your grandmother live with you?
20. Memorize these numbers.

S4

WELL-BUILT SENTENCES

In a well-built sentence, put the right parts in the right place.

A sentence is not merely a group of words placed next to one another. The words in a sentence are *related*. Verbs, for example, are related to their subjects. Adjectives and adverbs are related to the words they modify. Pronouns are related to the words they stand for.

If these relationships are well worked out, the sentences will hold together well. They will be easy to read. If the relationships in a sentence are shaky, the sentence will seem off balance. It may confuse the reader.

Learn to construct your sentences carefully.

Make the verb agree with the subject of the sentence.

The subject and the verb are the main supports of a sentence. When the sentence is constructed right, subject and verb fit together and are locked in place. In many sentences, subject and verb are "locked together" by **agreement.** Agreement means that subject and verb *change their forms together*.

Agreement makes us choose between *is* and *are, was* and *were, has* and *have.* One person *is* talking, or *was* talking. Several people *are* talking, or *were* talking. One person *tells* the story or *does* the work. Several people *tell* the story, or *do* the work. *Is, was, does,* and *tells* are **singular** forms. We use them when we are talking about *one* of a kind. *Are, were, tell*, and *do* are **plural** forms. We use them in talking about *several,* or *more* than one.

Remember:

(1) Whenever you have a choice, select matching forms to make the subject and verb agree. When there are no auxiliaries, the subject agrees with the main verb. When there are auxiliaries, the subject agrees with the first auxiliary. In each of the following pairs, subject and verb change their forms together:

SINGULAR: That girl *sings* well.
PLURAL: Those girls *sing* well.

SINGULAR: That man *repairs* television sets.
PLURAL: Those men *repair* television sets.

SINGULAR: My brother *asks* foolish questions.
PLURAL: My brothers *ask* foolish questions.

SINGULAR: The camper *was* doing the laundry.
PLURAL: The campers *were* doing the laundry.

SINGULAR: The prisoner *has* escaped.
PLURAL: The prisoners *have* escaped.

See **U1c** on choosing the right verb forms.

(2) Match your subject and verb even when other words come between them. Remember that the verb agrees with its subject, not simply with the word in front of it. When the verb is separated from its subject, do not make the verb agree with the word nearest to it:

The health of your pets *is* your responsibility.
(What is your responsibility? Their health *is*.)

Riding the fast-moving rafts *was* exciting.
(What was exciting? Riding them *was*.)

Look at the wedge that separates the verb from its subject in each of the following. In each case, the verb agrees with the subject as if the wedge were not there:

SUBJECT		VERB	
The speed	of our canoes	*was*	amazing.
Runoff	from the mountains	*swells*	the rivers.
Tickets	for the game	*are sold*	here.
Passing	these tests	*is*	easy.
Donations	to this charity	*have fallen*	off.

(3) Check for agreement when there is more than one subject. The word *and* adds one thing to another. When two subjects are joined by *and,* the result is a plural:

PLURAL: The jeep *and* the camper *were* parked near the entrance.
PLURAL: My brother *and* sister *have* both gone to school here.

The word *or* gives us a choice. It may be a choice between two singulars:

SINGULAR: The flour *or* the milk *was* spoiled.
SINGULAR: Our cat *or* our dog *finishes* the leftovers.
PLURAL: Shorts *or* bare feet *are* not allowed.

(4) Know how to handle special agreement problems. Use the words *each, either,* and *neither* as singulars. Use the expression *a number of* as a plural when it means "several":

SINGULAR: *Each* of the witnesses *has* told the same story.
SINGULAR: *Either* answer *is* right.
PLURAL: *A number of* people *were* still waiting.

Many nouns ending with *–ics* look like plural nouns. But they often stand for a single area or thing. Use them as singulars if you can replace them with *it,* not with *they:*

SINGULAR: Mathematics *is* a hard subject. (*It* is.)
SINGULAR: Politics *has* always interested her. (*It* has.)
SINGULAR: Athletics *offers* many opportunities. (*It* does.)

In each of the following sentences, is the subject singular or plural? Choose the verb form that agrees with the subject. Write it after the number of the sentence.

EXERCISE 1

EXAMPLE: The oars for the boat (was/were) missing.
(Answer) *were*

1. Two pieces of the puzzle (was/were) lost.
2. The swimmer in the middle of the lake (was/were) shouting.
3. Physics (teaches/teach) us about electricity.
4. The report from the weather bureau (is/are) bad.
5. The girl and her dog often (passes/pass) by here.
6. Pieces of glass (was/were) scattered on the walk.
7. The design of these engines (is/are) completely new.
8. My uncle or my aunt (has/have) always helped me.
9. Reading these instructions (confuses/confuse) me.
10. Filling in this form (takes/take) time.
11. Younger brothers or sisters often (needs/need) help.
12. The noise of the spectators (bothers/bother) the players.
13. Each of the winners (receives/receive) a trophy.
14. A number of people (has/have) complained.
15. Athletics (takes/take) time and money.
16. The voices of small birds (wakes/wake) us up in the morning.
17. Several days of rain (has/have) caused a mudslide.
18. Food for the prisoners (was/were) bad.
19. Either answer (makes/make) no sense.
20. The color and the shape of the figure (was/were) strange.

In each of the following sentences, is the subject singular or plural? Select the verb form that agrees with the subject. Write it after the number of the sentence.

EXERCISE 2

EXAMPLE: The customs of many tribes (has/have) disappeared.
(Answer) *have*

1. Each of the tribes (has/have) its own traditions.
2. A dance or a feast (brings/bring) everyone together.

3. Joining in the ceremonies (is/are) a great privilege.
4. A number of tribes (stages/stage) rain dances.
5. A mask and a drum (is/are) prized possessions.
6. The members of a tribe (was/were) planning a sun dance.
7. A former holy man (tells/tell) the story.
8. The purpose of the dances (is/are) a new beginning.
9. First, scouts (is/are) sent out.
10. The holy man of the tribe (is/are) searching for a sacred tree.
11. Young girls (carries/carry) the tree.
12. Mounted warriors (gathers/gather) around the sacred place.
13. The ponies of the warriors (rears/rear) in the dust.
14. The members of the tribe (eats/eat) plenty at the big feast.
15. The spirit in the skies (hears/hear) the prayers.
16. Reading about the old ways (is/are) a pleasure.
17. A book with beautiful pictures (helps/help) the reader.
18. Sometimes a painter or a photographer (has/have) preserved a rare scene.
19. The pictures in an exhibit (reminds/remind) us of old times.
20. Libraries in most schools (has/have) many books about the old ways.

S4b
Using Modifiers

Build up simple sentences by fitting modifiers into the right places.

The basic sentence patterns are made up of parts that the sentence cannot do without. A complete sentence needs at least a subject and a verb. Many sentences need an object to complete the statement begun by the verb. Beyond these essential parts, we can add other words if we wish. We call such optional parts **modifiers.** They "modify" the basic meaning of the sentence: They add to it, or limit it, or change it in some other way.

In each of the following pairs, the added parts are modifiers:

BARE: That baby wants a bottle.
MODIFIED: That *crying* baby *probably* wants a bottle *of milk*.

BARE: The team scored.
MODIFIED: The *visiting* team scored *in every inning*.

In addition to adjectives and adverbs, we use two major kinds of modifiers to build up a sentence:

(1) Prepositional phrases are made up of prepositions and their objects. Prepositions are "link" words like *at, by,*

for, from, in, to, on, and *with.* We use prepositions to link an additional noun (or pronoun) to the rest of the sentence. (The added noun is the **object** of the preposition.) Look at how the prepositions do their job in the following sentences:

	PREPOSITIONAL PHRASE
Robin Hood lived	*in the forest.*
Robin took money	*from the rich.*
He gave money	*to the poor.*
The sheriff had a warrant	*for his arrest.*

Sometimes, the prepositional phrase carries additional modifiers along with it:

Uncle Bert arrived *in a blue sedan.*
The box *with pretty pink ribbons* is yours.

In all of these sentences, the prepositional phrase fits in clearly and naturally. But look at the following sentence. Who has the rock, Bert or the boy?

CONFUSING: Bert threatened the boy *with the rock.*
(Who had the rock?)

SOME MODIFIERS ARE IN THE WRONG PLACE

WANTED
YOUNGSTER
NEEDED TO CLEAN
FISH ABOUT
15 YEARS OLD

To the
Memory of

Abraham Beaulieu

Accidentally shot
4th April 1844

As a mark of affection
from his brother.

Erected
to
the Memory of

Jean Macfarlane

Drowned in
the Water of Lieth

By a few
affectionate friends.

Rewrite such sentences to clarify their meaning:

CLEAR: *With the rock,* Bert threatened the boy.
CLEAR: The boy *with the rock* was threatened by Bert.

(2) A verb form ending in –ing *may serve as a modifier.* The usual place for the –*ing* forms is after an auxiliary as part of a complete verb:

VERB: The crowd *was cheering* the team on.
VERB: The team *has been winning.*

But the verb forms ending in –*ing* can be lifted out of this usual position and used to modify nouns. They then take the place of adjectives:

MODIFIER: The *cheering* crowd got to its feet.
MODIFIER: Fans support a *winning* team.

When a word like *cheering* is used to modify a noun, it is no longer a part of the verb. We call such former verbs **verbals.** We call *cheering* an –*ing* verbal.

Verbals may carry along *additional* modifiers of their own. Look at the following sentences:

Cheering wildly, the crowd urged the team on.
We then had a team *winning most of its games.*

Like other modifiers, verbals have to point clearly to what they modify. Sometimes they appear in the wrong place and seem to point the wrong way. We then call them **misplaced** modifiers. Sometimes what they point to has been left out. We then call them **dangling** modifiers:

MISPLACED: *Blaring loudly,* she turned off the radio.
(What was blaring?)
CLEAR: She turned off the *loudly blaring* radio.

DANGLING: *Cheering wildly,* the team was urged on.
(The *team* was cheering?)
CLEAR: Cheering wildly, *we* urged the team on.

DANGLING: *Waiting patiently,* his sister was taking a bath.
(She waited in the tub?)
CLEAR: *While* he *was waiting patiently,* his sister was taking a bath.

(3) A second kind of verbal can also be used as a modifier. The verb forms that usually follow *have (has, had)* can also be used to modify a noun:

VERB: The leaves *had fallen.*
VERBAL: She was raking the *fallen* leaves.

VERB: Marion *has finished* the model.
VERBAL: I admired the *finished* model.

Again, the verbal may bring other material with it. The result is a verbal phrase:

> I looked at the model, *finished just in time.*
> *Written hastily,* the message was hard to read.

NOTE: The technical term for *falling* and *fallen, finishing* and *finished* is **participle.** With the other material they bring into the sentence, they make up a "participial phrase."

In the list at the end, find the *prepositional phrase* that would best fill the blank in each sentence. Write the completed sentence after its number.

EXERCISE 1

EXAMPLE: _____, the pyramids attracted robbers.
(Added phrase) with their many treasures
(Answer) *With their many treasures, the pyramids attracted robbers.*

1. The birds _____ are pelicans.
2. Mountain climbers use crampons _____.
3. _____, a canoe trip can be miserable.
4. An umpire may have to check a disputed call _____.
5. Stoplights _____ prevent accidents.
6. Whalers _____ speared the whales.
7. The rescuers threw a rope _____.
8. _____, the numbers on the dial light up.
9. Visitors reach the park _____.
10. Some scientists are looking for messages _____.

ADDED PHRASES: in the dark
              to the marooned survivors
              in the rulebook
              with hand-held harpoons
              for steep slopes
              with the huge beaks
              by an all-weather road
              from outer space
              without waterproof baggage
              at school crossings

Sentences

In the list at the end, find the *verbal* or *verbal phrase* that would best fill the blank in each sentence. Write the completed sentence after its number.

EXAMPLE: Americans are protecting their _____ wildlife.
(Added verbal) endangered
(Answer) *Americans are protecting their endangered wildlife.*

1. Pelicans are big, clumsy birds _____.
2. Florida has six thousand pairs _____.
3. The eggs are laid in nests _____.
4. _____, the parent birds keep the nest warm.
5. Pelicans _____ fly over shallow waters.
6. _____, the birds catch fish.
7. Insecticides _____ hurt the birds.
8. Wildlife workers are saving the ____ birds.
9. Fish take in poisons in ____ waters.
10. Other states are bringing the pelicans back, _____.

ADDED VERBALS OR VERBAL PHRASES:

threatened
searching for food
diving clumsily into the water
living in the Southeast
washing off farmlands
taking turns
made out of sticks
raising young birds each year
transplanting young birds from Florida
polluted

In each of the following pairs, which sentence is the *clearer* one? Write the letter of the clearer sentence after the number of the sentence. (Prepare to explain the difference.)

1. (a) The doctor kept on visting patients with the flu.
   (b) The doctor with the flu kept on visiting patients.

2. (a) Climbing slowly, the summit was reached.
   (b) Climbing slowly, we reached the summit.

3. (a) He chased the dog without a shirt.
   (b) Without a shirt, he chased the dog.

4. (a) Sleeping soundly, the burglar stole our television set.
   (b) The burglar stole our television set while we were sleeping soundly.

5. (a) Grinding loudly, we came to a complete halt.
   (b) Grinding loudly, the car came to a complete halt.

6. (a) In pajamas, I greeted the guest.
   (b) I greeted the guest in pajamas.

7. (a) Wrapped in cellophane, we put the food in the freezer.
   (b) We wrapped the food in cellophane and put it in the freezer.

8. (a) Rushing for the bus, he lost his hat.
   (b) Rushing for the bus, his hat fell off.

9. (a) The FBI trapped the thief with false banknotes.
   (b) The thief with the false banknotes was trapped by the FBI.

10. (a) Seeing the baby, she reminded me of my daughter.
    (b) Seeing the baby, I was reminded of my daughter.

11. (a) The food in the refrigerator was waiting for our friends.
    (b) The food was waiting for our friends in the refrigerator.

12. (a) Shouting loudly, the whole town was soon awake.
    (b) Shouting loudly, Paul Revere soon woke the whole town.

13. (a) With his girl friend, Alan admired the portrait of Lincoln.
    (b) Alan admired the portrait of Lincoln with his girl friend.

14. (a) Reaching for the mustard, my plate fell off the table.
    (b) Reaching for the mustard, I knocked my plate off the table.

15. (a) A cane has been lost by an old man with a carved ivory head.
    (b) An old man has lost a cane with a carved ivory head.

Build up each of the following sentences. Use *at least one* prepositional phrase or verbal (or verbal phrase).

EXERCISE 4

EXAMPLE: An arrow hit the soldier.
(Answer)   An arrow hit the *running* soldier *in the chest*.

1. The Apaches rode their horses.
2. The settlers fired guns.
3. The warriors shouted.
4. The tribes moved.
5. Their chiefs concluded treaties.
6. Trappers had found gold.
7. The railroad brought trade.
8. Outlaws were roaming the West.
9. Towns grew.
10. Americans will study the story.

S4c

**Pronoun
Reference**

Make pronouns point clearly to what they stand for.

A pronoun typically takes the place of another word (or words). A pronoun is clear when we know what it has replaced. Often the word it has replaced appears earlier in the same sentence. Look at the italicized pronouns in the following sentences. Each points back, or *refers,* to the noun italicized earlier in the sentence:

> *Sheila* said that *she* would go to the party.
> Mike showed us *the painting,* and we praised *it.*
> José has *books* but no place to store *them.*

In these sentences, the pronouns point clearly to what they stand for. But sometimes the meaning of a pronoun is not so clear. We say that the **reference** of the pronoun is unclear or confusing. The pronoun does not point or refer clearly to one thing or another. Look out for the following:

(1) Make sure the meaning of the pronoun is clearly spelled out. Make sure an *it* or a *they* points to something mentioned earlier. (Sometimes the pronoun points to something mentioned in an earlier sentence.)

CONFUSING: They were arguing, but I didn't hear *it.* (What is *it?*)
CLEAR: They were having *an argument,* but I didn't hear *it.*

CONFUSING: Sam would like a career in the army, but *they* do not earn much money. (Who are *they?*)
CLEAR: Sam would like a career in the army, but *soldiers* do not earn much money.

(2) If there are two possible meanings for the pronoun, show clearly which is the right one. When something has two possible meanings, we say it is **ambiguous.** Change sentences when they have a possible double meaning:

AMBIGUOUS: *Iris* asked *her mother* if *she* could go.
(*Who* could go—Iris or her mother?)
CLEAR: *Iris* asked *her mother's* permission to go.
To find out if *her mother* could go, *Iris* asked *her.*

AMBIGUOUS: *Fred* discussed the problem with *the counselor* after *he* returned.
CLEAR: After *the counselor* returned, *Fred* discussed the problem with *him.*

(3) Make sure a this *or a* which *points clearly to one thing rather than another.* Sometimes several things or ideas have been mentioned, and the *this* or the *which* does not point clearly enough. Add the necessary information:

CONFUSING: The law would ban ownership of guns. *This* makes my uncle very angry. (Is he angry about people owning guns, or about the law that will ban them?)

CLEAR: The law would ban ownership of guns. *This proposed ban* makes my uncle very angry.

CONFUSING: I failed the very difficult exam, *which* I had predicted. (Did you predict how difficult it was, or that you would fail it?)

CLEAR: As I had predicted, the exam was very difficult. I failed it.

In each of the following pairs of sentences, one sentence is clearer than the other. Write on your paper the letter of the *clearer* sentence.

EXERCISE 1

1. (a) After we finished the game, we put the pieces away.
   (b) After we finished the game, we put them away.

2. (a) When he threw the alarm clock at the television set, it was broken.
   (b) He broke the alarm clock when he threw it at the television set.

3. (a) My friends were smoking cigarettes, but I don't like them.
   (b) My friends were smoking, but I don't like cigarettes.

4. (a) The boys told the girls that they couldn't dance.
   (b) The boys admitted that they couldn't dance.

5. (a) Wipe your mouth and throw it away.
   (b) Wipe your mouth and throw the napkin away.

6. (a) He brought baskets for berries, but we hadn't found any.
   (b) We hadn't found any berries, though he brought baskets for them.

7. (a) After I paid the bill, the store delivered the package.
   (b) After I paid the bill, the store delivered it.

8. (a) The children were watching the monkeys while they were running all over the place.
   (b) While the monkeys were running all over the place, the children were watching them.

9. (a) When he pulled the dog's leash, it snapped.
   (b) When he pulled the leash, the dog snapped.

10. (a) Having been vice-president last year, Bella expected it again this year.
    (b) Having been vice-president last year, Bella expected to be reelected this year.

11. (a) After reading for an hour, she finally put it down.
    (b) After reading the book for an hour, she finally put it down.

12. (a) The coach promised Charles that he would call all the plays during the game.
    (b) The coach promised that Charles would call all the plays during the game.

13. (a) Chris was interested in politics, but she seldom believed what they said.
    (b) Chris was interested in politics, but she seldom believed what politicians said.

14. (a) Martin liked the sport coat better than the suit, although the suit was expensive.
    (b) Martin liked the sport coat better than the suit, although it was expensive.

15. (a) After my cousins brought home the fish, we cleaned them.
    (b) We cleaned the fish that my cousins brought home.

EXERCISE 2

What is wrong in each of the following statements? Rewrite each sentence so that its meaning is clear. Say what you think the writer *meant* to say.

1. When the magician pointed at Fred, he frowned.
2. Susan goes to baseball games, but she doesn't understand it.
3. Don talked politics with his father, yet he didn't say whom he was supporting.
4. Many girls reported for spring practice. This is something new.
5. When Father spoke to Jake, he was very upset.
6. The teacher offered statistics to support the points, but they were not clear to me.
7. Mary asked her friend to visit her before her vacation.
8. Sue admired doctors and wanted to make it her profession.
9. Frannie's mother is a good painter, and she will be recognized some day.
10. If they don't ship enough cages for the animals, send them back.

122

Which of the following are well-built sentences? In which is there a problem that should be set right? After the number of each sentence, put the right abbreviation:

S   for satisfactory;
AGR   for unsatisfactory agreement;
MOD   for misplaced or dangling modifier;
REF   for unsatisfactory pronoun reference.

EXAMPLE: The main event at these fairs is the judging.
(Answer) *S*

1. The principal and my teacher are going to have a meeting.
2. A meeting after school hours are always poorly attended.
3. Stopping suddenly, the other car hit us in the rear.
4. Bundled up, a few spectators were shivering in the cold rain.
5. The new members of the band were trying on their uniforms.
6. Looking down, the floor of the canyon appeared far below.
7. The passenger told the driver he did not know the way.
8. Each of the swimmers swims two hours every day.
9. Athletics sounds glamorous, but their dreams seldom come true.
10. Soccer was once little known, but it has become very popular.
11. Training for the Olympics takes time.
12. My friend argued with the waiter in his wet bathing suit.
13. The strength of her hands were surprising.
14. After Karen returned, she told her mother everything.
15. The birds circling over the pier were scavenging for food.
16. Either road is dangerous at this time of the year.
17. Fred said that he had had an argument with a friend.
18. Crowded into the back seat, the trip took a long time.
19. Opening the door, we noticed a musty smell.
20. Hurrying away from the station, a passenger was left behind.

Join related ideas in a larger combined sentence.

A short single sentence often gives us only part of the story: "The crew abandoned the ship."

Often our reaction to such a statement is: "Tell me more!" One way to "tell more" is to bring in additional statements and join them onto the original sentence. This way we can answer questions like the following:

WHEN?   The crew abandoned the ship *when the boiler blew up.*

WHERE?   The crew abandoned the ship *after it reached the coast.*

WHY? The crew abandoned the ship, *for gold had been found in Nevada.*

WHAT KIND? The crew abandoned the ship, *which had been built in 1927.*

In much sentence building, we take several ideas that go together. We then work them into a single larger sentence. Study ways of writing combined sentences that will "tell us more."

S5a

Coordination

Use coordinating connectives to combine related ideas.

Coordination is the simplest method of combining several ideas. When we coordinate the work of two people, we make them "work together." We can make two statements work together by using connectives like *and* and *but:*

FIRST SOURCE: The French settled in Louisiana.
SECOND SOURCE: The Spanish settled in New Mexico.
RESULT: The French settled in Louisiana, *and* the Spanish settled in New Mexico.

FIRST SOURCE: The Russians first orbited the earth.
SECOND SOURCE: Americans first orbited the moon.
RESULT: The Russians first orbited the earth, *but* Americans first orbited the moon.

The two statements in each pair could appear as separate sentences. When they combine, they still have their own subjects and verbs. But they are part of a larger combined sentence. We call sentences that become part of a new combination **clauses.** Each of the "result sentences" above is made up of two clauses joined by a connecting word like *and* or *but.* We call these connectives **coordinators.** They simply take two statements as they are and tie them together. Six common coordinators, or **coordinating connectives,** are *and, but, so, for, or,* and *yet:*

The party was dull, *so* we left.
Jim rarely plays ball, *for* he hates sports.
Helen must work harder, *or* she will lose the job.
He waved, *yet* the waiter paid no attention.

The connective shows *how* the two clauses are related:

(1) And *shows addition.* We add something similar:

ADDITION: Mother made iced tea, *and* Father made lemonade.
ADDITION: My sister fed her goldfish, *and* my brother fed his cat.

(2) And *and* so *may be used to show result.* We can usually substitute *therefore* or *as a result* for the connective:

RESULT: The detective found the missing link, *and* he was able to solve the crime. (as a result)
RESULT: I lived near Boston, *so* I know about the concerts on the Esplanade. (as a result)

(3) But *and* yet *show contrast.* The second idea points the opposite way from the first:

CONTRAST: We caught ten fish, *but* we threw them all back.
CONTRAST: They had little money, *yet* they enjoyed themselves.

(4) For *shows that the second clause gives a reason for the first.* It tells us why:

REASON: We got wet, *for* we had neither raincoats nor umbrellas.

(5) Or *shows choice.* Either statement may be right, but not both:

CHOICE: I may work on the farm, *or* I may move to town.
CHOICE: You should graduate from high school, *or* you will not get a good job.

NOTE: A coordinator joins two clauses only loosely. They could easily be separated again. We call the two clauses **independent** clauses. Things are independent when they are free to go their own way.

See **M2a** on using the comma with coordinators.

How are the two statements in each of the following pairs related? What connective would you choose to join them in a larger combined sentence? After the number of the pair, write the coordinator that would fit best.

EXERCISE 1

EXAMPLE: Her father was Hawaiian.
              Her mother was Portuguese.
(Answer) *but*

1. Our team put up a good fight.
   The other team won.

2. Nancy changed out of her working clothes.
   She was going out for dinner.

3. Father likes the mountains.
   Mother likes the seashore.

4. We had better win the game.
   The coach will be angry.

5. The leopard was a fierce fighter.
   The hunters had guns.

6. The manager threw in the towel.
   The boxer was being badly beaten.

7. Pollution must be controlled.
   Human beings cannot survive.

8. I threw a rock at the creature.
   It swam away.

9. The accident could have been avoided.
   It was too late.

10. The candidate shook everyone's hands.
    She wanted to be elected.

11. The fog was heavy.
    The airport was shut down.

12. Scuba divers carry weights.
    Their buoyancy pushes them back to the surface.

13. The roads were narrow.
    Drivers were driving at breakneck speed.

14. Water was precious.
    Desert surrounded us on every side.

15. She explained the problem patiently.
    The customer got angry anyway.

16. The hikers had no forks.
    They used their hands.

17. Fires start easily in August.
    The underbrush is dry.

18. Millions of dinosaurs lived on the earth.
    They died out.

19. A guard protects the property during the day.
    Dogs guard it at night.

20. Bears look clumsy.
    They move fast.

For each of the following, write a second clause that would answer the question in parentheses. Start your clause with a coordinator. Make sure the clause has its own subject and verb.

EXERCISE 2

EXAMPLE: Streetcars need tracks, _____ . (But?)

(Answer) *but buses use the regular roadway.*

1. My friends love rock 'n' roll, _____ . (But?)
2. President Truman came from Missouri, _____ . (And our current President?)
3. You should train for a job, _____ . (Or?)
4. Our neighbors sold their house, _____ . (Why?)
5. Police patrolled the streets, _____ . (So?)
6. My uncle hates weddings, _____ . (But?)
7. Girls now dress like boys, _____ . (And boys?)
8. People laughed at the Wright brothers, _____ . (But?)
9. Nuclear power stations produce radioactive wastes, _____ . (So?)
10. Elections cost millions, _____ . (Why?)

Often, a coordinator joins two sentences that have been *expanded* by modifiers. Can you still see the coordinator at work? After the number of each sentence, write the subject and complete verb of both clauses. Include the connective. Leave out all completers and modifiers.

EXERCISE 3

EXAMPLE: We pulled up by the side of the road, for the horses needed rest.

(Answer) *We pulled up, for the horses needed.*

1. The hikers had built an open fire, so the hut was full of smoke and fumes.
2. The dog was bigger than I, and it enjoyed more privileges.
3. She sat down, and the sound of applause filled the air.
4. The road was becoming slippery, yet the cars hardly slowed down.
5. Sometimes Lonnie arrived home from school with me, and she would sit on the couch watching. (Alice Munro)
6. I love freedom, but freedom needs limits.
7. We traveled on foot, or sometimes we would rent a donkey.
8. He was a big man with pink cheeks and sleepy eyes, and he dressed in full army regalia. (Gordon Parks)
9. In the 4A his long legs fitted under the desk, so he began his education there. (Mario Suarez)
10. Now you will feel no rain, for each of you will be shelter to the other. (Apache Wedding Blessing)

S5b

Subordination

Use subordinating connectives to combine related ideas.

When we coordinate two things, each is about equally important. When we *subordinate* one to the other, one becomes less important or second in rank. In some combined sentences, one part is the main part of the structure or gives us the main point. The other part is second in importance. In the following, the subordinated part is italicized:

You will receive the books *after you sign the order.*
I love ice cream, *although it is fattening.*

When a clause has been subordinated, it *can no longer stand by itself.* Suppose someone says: "After you sign the order." Your question would be: "After I sign—then what?" We expect a main statement, or **main clause,** to go with the subordinated part. We call the less important part the **dependent** clause. It depends, or "leans," on the main part of the sentence.

Connectives like *if, after,* and *although* are **subordinating connectives,** or **subordinators.** Among the most common subordinators are *if, when, where, unless, because, after, before, until,* and *though* (or *although*). Look at how these connectives join two clauses. Each clause has its own subject and verb:

FIRST SOURCE: The party had just started.
SECOND SOURCE: The Smiths arrived.
RESULT: The party had just started *when* the Smiths arrived.

FIRST SOURCE: They came to the United States.
SECOND SOURCE: They treasured freedom.
RESULT: They came to the United States *because* they treasured freedom.

FIRST SOURCE: The teacher recommended the book.
SECOND SOURCE: The students read it.
RESULT: The teacher recommended the book *before* the students read it.

FIRST SOURCE: Jean left the room.
SECOND SOURCE: Her friend walked in.
RESULT: Jean left the room *after* her friend walked in.

The connective shows *how* the two clauses are related:

(1) After, before, when, *and* until *show time.* Like many adverbs, they answer the question *When?*

TIME: I watch television *after* I have done my homework.
TIME: The doctor will see you *when* she returns from the hospital.
TIME: You should not count your chickens *until* they are hatched.

(2) Where *shows place or location:*

PLACE: The cat was hiding *where* no one could find it.

(3) Because *shows a reason or cause:*

REASON: The letter came back *because* I forgot the stamp.

(4) If *and* unless *show conditions.* They help us show under what condition something will or will not be done:

CONDITION: I will go to the movie with you *if* you pay.
CONDITION: I will meet you at noon *unless* it rains.

(5) Though (*or* although) *shows contrast.* Often the part that starts with *although* points in the opposite direction from the main statement.

CONTRAST: You have to take the test again, *although* you took it last year.
CONTRAST: Dad bought a new car, *though* we really could not afford it.

NOTE: Coordinators start a clause that must follow the clause to which it is joined. Subordinators start a clause that *may* follow the main clause. But the dependent clause may also *come before the main clause* in the sentence.

AFTER: We usually have a Coke *after the coach leaves.*
BEFORE: *After the coach leaves,* we usually have a Coke.

Here are other examples with the dependent clause first:

Although Jennie likes ice cream, she rarely eats it.
When I was not quite six years old, an old man came down San Benito Avenue. (William Saroyan)

When two sentences have been *co*ordinated, this change is not possible:

(IMPOSSIBLE: *And* my brother was six, I was eight.)
(IMPOSSIBLE: *But* the well was dry, I went out for water.)

See **M2b** on using commas with dependent clauses.

Sentences

How are the two statements in each of the following pairs related? What connective would you choose to join them in a larger combined sentence? After the number of the pair, write the subordinator that would fit best. (Be ready to read some of the completed sentences out loud in class.)

EXAMPLE: Molten lava flows down the hillsides.
The volcano erupts.

(Answer) *after*

1. Newspapers carry big headlines.
It rains in our state.

2. We did not recognize Tom.
He was wearing sunglasses.

3. Everybody was asleep.
I came home at midnight.

4. I don't want any lemonade.
You put ice in it.

5. The picnic was canceled.
The weather was fine.

6. I will go.
You are ready.

7. We pitched the tent.
The ground was level.

8. He took his dog for a walk.
They both went to bed.

9. I want to read another chapter.
The library closes.

10. We will stay in the cottage.
The summer ends.

11. Huge herds of buffalo traveled over the prairie.
The settlers arrived.

12. Pet rabbits easily become sick.
They are well cared for.

13. The roof leaked again.
It had been repaired.

14. The engineers blasted tunnels.
The grade was too steep.

15. Contestants can win many prizes.
They know the right answers.

16. The post office will return your letters.
    You put stamps on them.

17. The state has put up a sign.
    The Spanish explorers first reached land.

18. The conversation stops.
    The bells are ringing.

19. The champion lost the bout.
    He was the favorite.

20. Students graduate.
    They fulfill all requirements.

For each of the following statements, write a second statement that would answer the question in parentheses. Use a subordinator each time to tie the two statements together. (Compare answers with your classmates.)

EXERCISE 2

EXAMPLE: The plane sat on the runway for two hours _____.
          (Why?)
(Answer) *because the fog was rolling in.*

1. I will answer the question _____. (When?)
2. Jim drops dishes all the time _____. (Why?)
3. The principal will approve the trip _____. (On what condition?)
4. Congress will defeat the measure _____. (Except on what condition?)
5. The meeting will begin promptly _____. (When?)
6. Tim will not take a summer job _____. (For how long?)
7. America owes its tribes a great deal _____. (Why?)
8. Phil was accused of the crime _____. (In spite of what?)
9. You should be vaccinated against smallpox _____. (Prior to what?)
10. People used kerosene in lamps _____. (Until when?)

Often a subordinator links two sentences that have been *expanded* by modifiers. Can you still see the subordinator at work? After the number of each sentence on the following page, write the subject and the verb of both clauses. Include the connective. Leave out all completers and modifiers.

EXERCISE 3

EXAMPLE: The swallows arrive in Capistrano when spring returns.
(Answer) *The swallows arrive when spring returns.*

1. A long, skinny man sat on the stoop when we approached the building.
2. The airline will save you a seat if you confirm your reservation in time.
3. Eagles may become extinct unless our current efforts succeed.
4. We will hold the parade if the weather improves somewhat.
5. The dough will rise after it is put in a warm place.
6. You should not insult the alligator until you have crossed the river. (African proverb)
7. Their eyes are blind to this magnificent sight because it is so familiar to them. (Helen Keller)
8. No player should ever give up until the last player is out.
9. My relatives are happy when they talk about the Old Country.
10. Pioneers are exciting people because they are excited about their land. (Harry Golden)

EXERCISE 4

In which of the following combined sentences can the *second clause come first?* Rewrite each such sentence, putting the dependent clause first. (Put a comma where the main clause starts.) If the second clause cannot come first, write *No* after the number of the sentence.

EXAMPLE: You should come to Utah if you like magnificent scenery.
(Answer)   *If you like magnificent scenery, you should come to Utah.*

1. The captain survived, although the ship went down.
2. The twins shouted after Jim locked them in the closet.
3. His father had lost his job, so the family went hungry.
4. My relatives serve a huge meal when the family gets together.
5. Dr. Frankenstein was a genius, but he misused his talents.
6. The clock stopped because the electricity was cut off.
7. She will not marry him unless he changes his ways.
8. His grandmother was Irish, and his grandfather was Dutch.
9. We cannot use the car until the radiator is fixed.
10. A church now stands where the saint died.

S5c
Relative Clauses

Combine related ideas by using relative pronouns.

A special way of subordinating one clause to another is to turn it into a relative clause. Look at what the italicized part adds to each of the following sentences:

We need machines *that work.*
She likes girls *who are interested in sports.*
He bought a tractor, *which replaced his mules.*

Look at the words that link each relative clause to the main clause—*who, which,* and *that.* We call these words **relative pronouns.** They perform a double function. First, like a connective, they link, or "relate," two clauses to each other. But they also do a job *within* the second clause. Like a pronoun, they take the place of a noun (or a pronoun) in the second clause.

Remember:

(1) A relative pronoun replaces part of the second clause. To link two sentences by a relative pronoun, we start with two sentences that have one noun (or pronoun) *in common.* The relative pronoun then replaces this shared part in the second clause:

FIRST SOURCE:	Edgar loved *Anna.*
SECOND SOURCE:	*Anna* became his wife.
RESULT:	Edgar loved Anna, *who* became his wife.

FIRST SOURCE:	I lost *the notebook.*
SECOND SOURCE:	I had just bought *the notebook.*
RESULT:	I lost the notebook *that* I had just bought.

FIRST SOURCE:	Columbus discovered *America.*
SECOND SOURCE:	He mistook *America* for India.
RESULT:	Columbus discovered America, *which* he mistook for India.

(2) A relative clause often interrupts the main clause:

FIRST SOURCE:	*The snake* was nonpoisonous.
SECOND SOURCE:	*The snake* had bitten him.
RESULT:	The snake *that had bitten him* was nonpoisonous.

FIRST SOURCE:	*Columbus* called the natives "Indians."
SECOND SOURCE:	*Columbus* was looking for India.
RESULT:	Columbus, *who was looking for India,* called the natives "Indians."

(3) Who *points to people;* which *points to things and ideas.* That *can take the place of either of these two:*

The girl __*who*__ invited us
Their house, __*which*__ was really only a shack
The man __*who*__ called
The car __*that*__ had stalled
The phone, __*which*__ had been ringing
Jim, __*who*__ was my best friend
The teachers __*who*__ were on duty
The cars __*which*__ had been parked

NOTE: In strictly formal English, *whom* takes the place of *who* when the pronoun is the object or target of the action:

> She wrote to her grandmother, *whom* she dearly loved.
> The picture showed the official *whom* the President had appointed.

See **M2b** on using commas with relative clauses.

EXERCISE 1

Write the following pairs of sentences as single sentences. Turn the second sentence in each pair into a relative clause.

EXAMPLE: The student will win an award.
The student writes the best essay.
(Answer) The student who writes the best essay will win an award.

1. We were waiting for the first holiday.
The first holiday was Thanksgiving.

2. The girl is my sister.
The girl is digging for clams.

3. They finally received the message.
We sent them the message two days ago.

4. The showers never came.
The weather bureau had predicted the showers.

5. The girl must be a genius.
The girl painted the picture.

6. The men tried to rescue the children.
The children were trapped in the cave.

7. The people caught very little.
The people were fishing for swordfish.

8. The books are mystery stories.
Charles likes the books.

9. A cat can be a pest.
A cat is hungry.

10. The boy finally went home.
The boy had been waiting.

EXERCISE 2

Write a relative clause to fill the blank in each of the following sentences. Make sure the clause starts with *who, which,* or *that.*

EXAMPLE: The Incas, _____ , built rich cities.
(Answer) *who lived in Peru*

1. American tourists travel to Peru, _____ .
2. The explorers _____ destroyed the Inca empire.
3. The Spaniards were looking for gold, _____ .
4. The big Spanish ships carried the treasure _____ .
5. Tourists still see the ruins of the cities _____ .
6. Spain sent missionaries _____ .
7. Some cities were hidden by mountains _____ .
8. The peasants _____ are very poor.
9. The churches _____ resemble those of Spain.
10. Half of the people _____ still speak their old Indian language.

Some sentences have optional parts. We can take out one or two of the parts, and the sentence still means exactly the same. In many sentences, a relative pronoun is such an expendable part. Try to leave out the relative pronoun in each of the following sentences. Which sentences can do without it? Write *Yes* after the number of the sentence. Write *No* if the pronoun cannot be taken out.

EXERCISE 3

1. Mr. Sanders gave the poor all the money *that he could spare.*
2. The flood *which destroyed our home* was the worst in history.
3. The food *that the knights did not eat* was thrown to the dogs.
4. The person *who rented our spare room* was a young college girl.
5. The horses *that we rented* had funny names.
6. I could not understand the answer *that she gave me.*
7. The clothes *that she bought for school* did not fit her very well.
8. The map *that we discovered* led us to the treasure.
9. The cat *that had been missing for a week* finally came home.
10. The cat *which I like best* had been missing for a week.
11. Passengers *who are not careful* may become seasick.
12. He tore up the ticket *that the officer had given him.*
13. We really liked the actor *who played Superman.*
14. The audience booed the villain *that the hero fought.*
15. Pizarro, *who had only 168 soldiers,* conquered the empire.

How have related ideas been combined in each of the following sentences? What kind of connective is used to join two clauses? After the number of each sentence on the following page, put the right abbreviation:

UNIT REVIEW EXERCISE

CO for coordinator;
SUB for subordinator;
REL for relative pronoun;
NO if there is only one clause.

EXAMPLE: We stayed inside when it rained.
(Answer) *SUB*

1. We heard a strong wind that was shaking the trees.
2. Frank solved the problem, but his method was unusual.
3. When the clock struck three, we rushed from the room.
4. Snow had piled up on the roof, and the creek had frozen solid overnight.
5. The man in the shabby overcoat was gasping for air.
6. The valley is half desert, so water is very valuable.
7. The birds that crossed overhead were wild geese.
8. We practiced during every afternoon because time was running out.
9. If the story is true, the ranch will be sold.
10. Our neighbor, who hardly ever smiled, was grinning broadly.
11. The tracks in the sand were getting fainter all the time.
12. The people in line were grumbling, for nothing moved.
13. They always locked all doors before they went to bed.
14. The shovel leaning against the shed looked very rusty.
15. I called my cousin, who works at the theater.
16. They will lose the game unless a miracle happens.
17. The water was cold, yet we all plunged in.
18. Rita checked the pegs that held the tent.
19. We should hang our provisions from a branch, or a bear will get them.
20. A stream which is divided into many channels has little depth. (Fulton J. Sheen)

FOR FURTHER STUDY

DOUBLE-DUTY WORDS

In an English sentence, as in a football game, there are many specialized jobs to do. Some words, like a player who kicks only field goals, are *specialized*. They perform only one limited function. But others are more *versatile*. They can do different jobs in different sentences.

The following assignments will give you a chance to discover several kinds of double-duty words.

We can often make a word serve *both* as a noun and as a verb. In each of the following sentences, the italicized word is used as a noun. For each, write a second short sentence in which the same word, *without a change in form,* is used as a verb. (Use a verb marker, or auxiliary, with it, if you wish.)

EXAMPLE: We bought a *farm.*
(Answer)   They *farm* their land.

1. *Smoke* was pouring from the chimney.
2. The *light* was very dim.
3. He called the *police.*
4. *Dust* had settled on the shelves.
5. He met the man at the *station.*
6. *Fire* had destroyed the buildings.
7. He had had little *demand* for the book.
8. This *plan* will be revised.
9. They beat a hasty *retreat.*
10. The troops had halted their *advance.*

Some words can serve as *three* kinds of words: noun, verb, and adjective. Take the word *double,* for instance:

NOUN: The star needed a *double.*
VERB: They *doubled* his salary.
ADJECTIVE: The print showed a *double* exposure.

In the following list, find five words that can serve all three of these functions. Use each word in three short sentences, each time using the word as a different kind of word. (Attach the *–s, –ed,* or *–ing* as needed—but no others.)

light, rival, dark, duplicate, gold, gray, cool,
warm, yellow, white, sudden, brief, right

Some English verbs work only in Pattern One. We always just *arrive;* we never arrive *somebody.* Some English verbs work only in Pattern Two. We usually annoy *somebody;* we don't just annoy. But some English verbs work both ways, as shown on the following page:

s–v: The clock *stopped.*
s–v–o: Grandfather *stopped the clock.*

How many of the following verbs work both ways? Write a pair of short sentences for each verb in the list below, using the word in both patterns. Write *No* if a word will not work in one of the patterns. (Compare your sentences with those of your classmates.)

1. finish   5. shout   9. play
2. agree   6. notice   10. circle
3. dive   7. begin
4. read   8. mail

ACTIVITY 4

Be with its many forms (*am, is, are, was, were*) is one of the most versatile verbs in the language. Can you take inventory of the uses of *be?* How does a form of *be* function in each of the following sentences? What job does it do in each sentence? How does it fit into the pattern of the sentence? (Be prepared to describe each use in class.)

1. Often a name *was* originally a mistake.
2. A new name may *be* wrong.
3. America *was* named by a mapmaker.
4. In his opinion, Amerigo Vespucci *was* the discoverer of our continent.
5. "Dutch" *is* a word that at first meant "German."
6. People from Holland *were* called "Dutch" by mistake.
7. We *are* calling people "Indians" who never came from India.
8. Perhaps our whole continent should *be* called "Columbia."
9. We should *be* calling a Dutchman a "Hollander."
10. For a time, the English *were* using terms like "Red Indian" or "American Indian" for Native Americans.
11. The wrong names *are* still here.
12. A name *is* right if we know its intended meaning.
13. A wrong name becomes right if it *is* still there after many centuries.
14. Former mistakes resulting from incorrect translations *are* everywhere in our language.
15. Key West *was* once a Spanish word that meant "bone island."

Like many other words, the words used as subordinators do double duty. For instance, *after, before,* and *until* are subordinating connectives only when they join two sentences, each with its own subject and verb. These same words are also used as prepositions. After the number of the sentence, write SUB if the word is used as a subordinator. Write PREP if the word is used as a preposition.

1. *After* a long delay, the bus was moving again.
2. We waited for you *until* noon.
3. We waited for them *until* they arrived.
4. *After* the price of eggs soared, we ate cereal.
5. We didn't buy any eggs *before* the trip.
6. I saw her just *after* she spoke to him.
7. We had reached our destination *before* the rain started.
8. The accused men appeared *before* the judge.
9. The lawyer left *before* the judge arrived.
10. The park was cleaned up *after* the picnic.

Chapter 3

Composition
How We Write

Chapter Preview 3

Learn how to put together a paper that has something to offer to the reader.

Composition is the art of "putting things together." A pep talk, or a sermon, is an *oral* composition. A letter to the editor, or an article in *Reader's Digest,* is a *written* composition. A composition does not just happen, the way a conversation does. When you write a letter or a paper, you have to plan. You need to collect material and pull it together.

Your finished composition must offer something that will make your reader pay attention. Here are some of the things that make readers pay attention:

(1) Your paper may tell people something that they want to know.   People are curious. They want to know about new superjets, or about how ants communicate, or about lost tribes living on the Amazon River. One way to hold the attention of a reader is to *find out* about something that is interesting, or to *explain* something that is difficult.

(2) Your paper may tell your readers something about yourself.   Most people are interested in other people. Many books are written about famous people in history. Many readers buy magazines with articles about celebrities or other people in the news. Many readers are interested in the thoughts and feelings of other people like themselves.

(3) Your paper may make a point. People listen when someone speaks out on an issue close to their hearts. They take notice when someone contradicts their own views. They get excited when someone challenges their prejudices.

Discuss the following questions with your classmates. Share your reactions to things you have read. Think about what the writer had to offer you as a reader.

1. Have you recently read about someone especially likable or admirable? Describe the person. Or, have you recently read about a person you *dis*liked or disapproved of? Why did you judge the person the way you did?

2. Do you ever read about something in which you have a *special interest?* For instance, do you read about a sport, a hobby, an occupation, or a special kind of achievement? What kind of people share your interest? When a writer writes something for these people, what do they expect? What do they like?

3. When you read a newspaper, what catches your attention? Describe something in a newspaper or magazine that you felt especially good about. Describe something that made you angry.

MAKE SURE YOUR MESSAGE GETS THE ATTENTION OF THE READER

PHOTOGRAPHY STUDIO

If you are not Good-Looking We Will Make You So

ENTER

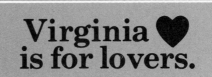

HEAR THE BISHOP
Services in George and Human's Hall tomorrow, Sunday, at 11 A.M. and 8 P.M.

PLEASE LEAVE YOUR NAMES
WITH THE USHER

C1
GETTING READY

Get as much writing practice as you can.

Writing takes more planning—and more work—than talking does. But it has to become almost as much a habit. A carpenter who is still worried about how to hold the hammer cannot do much work.

What you need most as a beginning writer is *enough practice*. Write as often as you can. Athletes do not use their skills only when actually in a contest or a game. They exercise constantly. They limber up before the big event. Here are some limbering-up exercises you can do as a writer.

(1) Tell your reader something about yourself. Study the following short passage as a model for a similar passage of your own. In your own words, explain what the passage is about. Why do you think the writer remembered the incident? Do you think it would have meant as much to you?

> I remember that in my first year at camp I wore an ill-fitting Boy Scout hat. One of the counselors, a boy five years my senior who seemed to me to belong already to the grown-up world of authority, began, in a pleasant way, to tease me about the hat. Every morning for a week he led us to the abandoned logging road and clocked us as we walked and trotted a measured mile. My hat was anchored down by a heavy chin strap. It flopped and sailed about my head as I ran to the finish line. The boy began to laugh at me. He waved his arms and called out, "Come on, you rookie!" The other kids took it up, and Rookie became my first nickname. I loved it. I tingled when someone called it out. I painted it on my belt, carved it in my packing case, inked it into my hatband, and began to sign it to my letters home.
> —Thomas Sancton, "The Silver Horn," *Harper's*

(2) Explain a difference. Study the following model passage. What difference does the passage explain? How did the girl who wrote the passage show or explain the difference? Why is the difference important?

```
               Living Color


     The sensations you feel when bicycling
through the country on a crisp, clear morning
are quite different from the feeling you have
when riding in a closed car.  When you are
```

riding a bike, you feel every bump you pass
over. You can see every rock, rut, and ridge
in the road. You can see the many different
colors and kinds of grass along the side of
the road. From a car, the grass becomes one
long continuous green blur, and often even
this won't be noticed. When driving in a car,
you are more likely to pay attention to the
radio than to notice the sights and smells
around you. When you are in a cər, you don't
see the powdery fluffs of clouds in the clear
blue sky. You don't notice the small animals
and even insects that make their homes along
the roadway. You don't have the invigorating
feeling you get when you are pedaling the bike
and gulping in the clean air.

(3) Write a letter that asks for advice. Many people write
to columnists who offer advice. One of the earliest such col-
umns appeared in the Yiddish-language newspaper the *Jewish Daily Forward,* published in New York. Newly arrived
immigrants wrote to this column for advice. Here is a letter
written to that newspaper in 1909. Does it remind you of similar letters, or of people with similar problems? (Your teacher
may ask you to write an imaginary letter in answer to this
letter. What would you say to help or comfort the writer?)

Dear Editor,
    I am a young man of twenty-two and have every reason to be
happy, but I am unhappy because nature saw fit to give me red
hair. Because of the color of my hair, I endure many insults in
the shop and on the street. When I hear someone say to me,
"Hello, Red!" I am hurt and offended.
    I am unhappy and lonely, and I've even consulted doctors
about it. One of them advised me to dye my hair. Another told
me not to do it because, first of all, it has a bad effect on the
scalp, and, secondly, the color would not be natural.
    I would be very thankful to you if you could advise me in this
situation.

                                        Respectfully,
                                        Unhappy

(4) Keep a diary or a journal. Two or three times a week, write down some of the things you do and think about. Write down some of the things that make you happy, and some of the things that make you angry. Often, when something special happens to you, you will want to tell somebody. Tell your diary. When you are unjustly blamed for something, you will want to tell your side of the story. Tell your journal.

As you write in your journal, try to answer the two following questions:

- *"What did I actually see?"* Suppose you were to open a photo album that covers a trip to Hawaii. You would be disappointed if instead of pictures of beautiful sites and spectacular views, you found only empty squares with the words *beautiful* and *spectacular* written in. Your journal will have many such empty squares if you always rely on words like *wonderful, great,* and *beautiful* to describe the things you have seen. Fill in the empty squares with details—describe the colors and shapes that *made* something beautiful or wonderful or spectacular.

- *"What did I actually hear?"* We come to know people by listening not only to *what* they say but also to *how* they say it. Make people come to life in the pages of your journal by *quoting* them. Try to remember their actual words and favorite expressions.

EXERCISE 1

Try *automatic writing* as a limbering-up exercise. Simply keep pen or pencil moving—for ten or fifteen minutes, or twenty. Just fill line after line. Repeat the same word at first, if necessary, or the same slogan, like "No Smoking" or "Don't shove." Then, as your mind starts wandering, write down some of the thoughts that come into your head. Put down on paper what you happen to think at the moment. Move on from one idea to another as they come to mind.

EXERCISE 2

Start your *journal*. Start by writing a few short journal entries two or three times a week. At first, write about your daily routine: What are some of the things you do every day, and why? Describe some of the places you pass on the way to school. Describe some of the people you see—a bus driver, a principal, a janitor. Start writing about some of the things that you look forward to, and those that you try to avoid. Write about some of the things that bother you, and those that make you glad.

People write about what they see. They write to tell us what they think. But they also write to tell us about their *feelings*. Look at the following short poem by a student. Do you recognize the writer's feelings? Write several sentences of your own that start: "It's a good feeling to . . ."

EXERCISE 3

```
              Good Feelings


It's a good feeling
To sleep late on a Saturday morning
To eat the last spoonful of a hot fudge
        sundae
To go on a vacation
To do gymnastics and perfect a stunt
To have someone say something nice about you
. . . and to be loved.
```

Use a paragraph to take care of one major point.

C2

WRITING A PARAGRAPH

In a paragraph, *several related sentences work together*. They work together to put across an idea, or to create an impression. Paragraphs are to writing what steps are to a staircase. They are what rooms are to a building, or what cinder blocks are to a wall. A paragraph gives us a chance to do justice to one thing at a time. It enables us to cover one definite part of the ground we have mapped out.

Whenever you write a paper that is longer than half a page, break it up into paragraph units. The paragraph breaks will give your reader the feeling that you know what you are doing. You are taking care of one thing at a time. You are moving forward one step at a time.

C2a

Learn to focus your paragraph on a single topic.

The first requirement for writing a good paragraph is to limit your territory. You cannot map out everything you know about pets, or cars, or American history in a few sentences. You have to split up a large subject. You have to do justice to one limited part at a time. When you buy a booklet about the care of rabbits, the general subject will be divided into more limited topics: kinds of rabbits; feeding of rabbits; breeding; diseases. In a similar way, the separate paragraphs in a longer paper enable you to treat *one part* of a larger subject.

Study the following model paragraphs. Like a well-focused camera, each takes aim at a limited target. Answer the following questions about each of the paragraphs:

1. How has the writer limited the topic? Sketch out in your own words the area the paragraph covers.
2. What material has the writer used? In your own words, summarize the information in each paragraph.
3. What additional questions would you have liked to ask the writer? If the writer could have included one or two more sentences, what would you have liked to see included?

PARAGRAPH ABOUT A SPORT:

Surfing was invented in countries with huge flat beaches and large waves. The surfer's basic equipment is a rounded-off board about as long and as wide as the surfer's body. The board has a fin that helps guide it. The surfer, standing up, uses the board to ride the waves as they come in toward the shore. Then the surfer has to swim back out, sometimes as much as half a mile, and wait for the next big wave. Surfers need a good sense of timing and a natural sense of balance. They also need much time and a love of the outdoors.

PARAGRAPH ABOUT A PERSON:

Billie Jean King won her first big victory in international tennis in 1966. She went on to win 19 titles in singles and doubles play. She equaled the record set by the legendary Elizabeth Ryan. When Billie Jean King was 31 years old, she won the Women's Singles Championship for the sixth time. About 15,000 spectators saw her defeat a young Australian challenger in a match that took barely 40 minutes. In 1977, Billie Jean staged a remarkable comeback in the first Masters Tournament for women.

PARAGRAPH ABOUT A PLACE:

Much of the California desert seems dead to a person who rides through it on a dirt bike or a jeep. But the dry land comes to life for someone who walks quietly through a desert canyon. Many different animals manage to survive in the desert. They include the bighorn sheep, the badger, and the desert tortoise. Hikers can see the tracks of the kit fox and the ground nest of the horned lark. They can see a blotchy lizard dart under a log, while a red-tailed hawk glides silently above. The spadefoot toad buries itself in the loose soil for a long period of time. But when the desert rain finally falls, it becomes active, heading for the nearest pond. It croaks noisily until the sun soaks up the shallow water.

The following questions will help you find limited topics for your own paragraphs. Answer each question in a single sentence. (Your teacher may ask you to write a paragraph on the most promising of your limited topics.)

EXERCISE 1

1. What is the most difficult (easiest) (nicest) thing about living with a brother or sister?
2. What do you like best about your favorite kind of movies?
3. What is the most common problem that young people have with pets?
4. Which athlete or sports figure have you known about longest, or which do you know best?
5. With what musical instrument or kind of sport are you most familiar, and why?
6. What kind of housework do you like least, or what kind do you do best?
7. What place do you know or remember that is most nearly like original wilderness untouched by human hands?
8. What character in a book, movie, or television program do you like exceptionally well?
9. What have you recently watched or read that had an unexpected sad (happy) ending?
10. What for you is the best thing about a vacation?

Every writer has to learn to *gather material.* As a preliminary exercise, bring together everything you know or remember about one of the following topics. Write quickly. Put

EXERCISE 2

things down as they come to mind, without sorting them out. Title your collection "Everything I Know About _____." Fill in one of the following:

ants	nuts
the desert	wells
buffaloes	vacant lots
tennis	bait
soccer	banjos
square dancing	pyramids
pottery	flags
frogs	bottles

C2b
The Topic Sentence

Sum up the main idea of your paragraph in a topic sentence.

A citizen speaking before the school board may have five minutes to present arguments, give statistics, even tell a joke. But what the people in the room really want to know is: "What is the point? What have you come to tell us?" They want the key idea to stand out.

An effective speaker knows how to sum up the main point:

KEY IDEA: "The school board is spending too much on excursions and camping trips."

KEY IDEA: "Outsiders are responsible for most of the violent incidents in our schools."

KEY IDEA: "Driver education starts a year too early for most students."

What goes for a short speech also goes for a paragraph. Sometimes we simply present our facts. We let our readers draw their own conclusions. But most of the time we come right out and say *what the point of the paragraph is*. We give the gist of the paragraph in one key sentence.

The sentence that sums up the main point is called the **topic sentence.** In many paragraphs, the very first sentence is the topic sentence. It gives the key to the rest of the paragraph. In other paragraphs, an introductory sentence or two leads up to the topic sentence.

Remember:

(1) Learn to recognize topic sentences in your reading. In the following paragraph, the first sentence is the topic sen-

tence. Can you show that it sums up everything the writer tells us in the paragraph?

Robert E. Lee had outstanding qualities as a leader. He was, first of all, a strong leader who treated his soldiers as human beings, not as machines of war. A more popular leader couldn't be found. Secondly, Lee was a brilliant strategist. Usually his strategy was a series of quick moves which bewildered and scattered the Union forces. Sometimes, he split his army into two forces in order to trap and outflank the Northern forces. Thirdly, Lee was a gentleman. This was shown when he admitted defeat with dignity and asked his soldiers to work peacefully for a united nation.

(2) Learn to write a good topic sentence. How do we produce a topic sentence? We produce a topic sentence when we say to ourselves: "Stop! Let me sum up what I have just observed." Let's say you spent a day at the beach. Off and on during the day, you saw members of a local motorcycle club. One wore the kind of boots paratroopers wear in old war movies. Another had an old World War II medal—the Iron Cross. Another wore a kind of army jacket. During the day, you saw other bits of old military uniforms, medals, even an old army helmet. When you tell a reader what you have seen, you would report all these details. But you would also add it all up. Your topic sentence would *sum up:* It would give the reader the main point.

TOPIC SENTENCE: Members of some motorcycle clubs wear old odds and ends from military life—boots, jackets, medals, belts.

In one sentence each, answer each of the following questions. Each time write one complete sentence that could become the topic sentence of a paragraph.

EXERCISE 1

1. What is one sure way to start a quarrel or a fight?
2. What kind of style in clothes is most popular with students your age this year?
3. What quality is needed most to help make students popular with their friends?
4. What makes a movie or television performer seem insincere or unconvincing?
5. What do people seem to miss most when they move from one place to another?

Composition

Each of the following groups of sentences gives details that might appear together in a paragraph. How do the details add up? How would you *sum up* what the details show? Write a topic sentence for each paragraph. (Write on a separate sheet.)

1. TOPIC SENTENCE: _____.
   Streetcars were clanging and screeching along the tracks.
   Jackhammers were ripping up the pavement.
   Impatient drivers were tooting their horns.
   The engines of heavy trucks were roaring.
   A motorcycle rider was gunning his engine.

2. TOPIC SENTENCE: _____.
   The paint was gone from the wooden buildings.
   Most of the wooden sidewalks had rotted away.
   A few broken-down chairs were left in some of the rooms.
   Weeds grew between the houses.

3. TOPIC SENTENCE: _____.
   The quarterback faked well.
   The running backs averaged four yards per play.
   The line opened many holes on offense.
   The defensive line held when it had to.
   Even the placekicker went six for six for the day.

4. TOPIC SENTENCE: _____.
   The boy was sprawled on the grass under a tree.
   In his hand he held a frosted glass of lemonade.
   A transistor radio played by his side.
   Occasionally, he yawned.
   From time to time he brushed away a passing fly.

5. TOPIC SENTENCE: _____.
   The fenders were crumpled in many places.
   Each window was either cracked or shattered.
   All four tires were flat.
   In some places, the paint was blistered.
   The chrome grillwork had turned to rust.
   Upholstery stuffing seeped through rips in the seats.

6. TOPIC SENTENCE: _____.
   In one place, about three hundred people were straining against the police barriers.
   Some men were in the process of overturning an automobile.
   The crash of breaking glass windows echoed through the night.
   A rifle shot broke the silence from time to time.
   A frightening roar drifted up from the crowd.

7. TOPIC SENTENCE: _____ .
   The Indian peacock wears a crown of royal blue.
   The metallic bluish-green of the neck feathers contrasts with
      the orange side feathers.
   The peacock's back is black and white.
   Long tail feathers spread out like a fan.
   "Eyes" of gold and blue spot the green tail feathers.

8. TOPIC SENTENCE: _____ .
   The grounds had been raked and leveled.
   The prancing horses stepped lightly around the ring.
   The riders didn't seem to move a muscle.
   The horses were lined up in military style.

9. TOPIC SENTENCE: _____ .
   The car has an automatic temperature control system.
   The stereophonic tape system furnishes a choice of AM or FM
      radio.
   The ventilation system changes the air even when the windows
      are up.
   The instrument panel contains a warning-light cluster and a
      lane-changing signal.
   The seat has an adjustable headrest and a reclining feature.

10. TOPIC SENTENCE: _____ .
    Bird-watchers spend hours waiting for a sighting of a rare bird.
    Tourists are fascinated by the seals on rocks and islands off
       the California coast.
    Tourists on wild-animal safaris in Africa now more often carry
       a camera than a gun.

Use relevant details to support your topic sentence.

C2c

Using Examples

The topic sentence is your promise to the reader. The supporting details make the promise good. A topic sentence without detail to back it up is like the program without the play. This paragraph makes a promise that it does not keep:

Many drivers are careless. They let their minds wander as they cruise along the streets and countryside. Some of them even fail to be courteous to other drivers. I think it is a pity that such drivers are allowed on the road.

The paragraph starts with what sounds like the main point: "Many drivers are careless." But in the next few sentences, the writer makes *other* general statements. We do not find details that show the carelessness of drivers. To be convinced, the reader needs **examples** of careless behavior:

TOPIC SENTENCE: Many drivers are careless.
First Example: Drivers eat and drink.
Second Example: They read road maps while driving.
Third Example: They keep weaving from lane to lane.
Fourth Example: They turn without signaling.

Remember:

(1) A well-developed paragraph needs specific details. Use examples that make the reader say: "Yes—I see what you mean!" The examples in the following paragraph back up the topic sentence. They show what happens in practice:

> Many car drivers are careless. I have seen many who prove by their actions that their minds are not on their driving. *Some eat and drink as they drive with one hand. Others take their eyes from the road to watch the scenery, to scold the children in the back seat, or to check a road map. Still others can't keep their minds on the road because they are upset or tired.* Equally careless are the drivers who ignore the rules of safe driving. The *most important rule that they break is to drive beyond the speed limit. These same drivers dart about in traffic without signaling to show that they are planning to turn or to move into another lane. Another dangerous habit of the speeders is tailgating.* These careless drivers don't seem to realize that they are handling machines which can produce instant death.

(2) The examples in a well-written paragraph are relevant to the main point. In the paragraph about careless drivers, examples are relevant if they show carelessness. They then tie in with the main point; they show that it is true. Behavior that does not show carelessness would be *irrelevant* —it would be beside the point.

We are sometimes annoyed by drivers who honk their horns. Such behavior may not be polite or considerate. But the driver could still be a very careful driver. Examples of inconsiderate behavior would not be relevant in a paragraph about careless driving.

(3) A good topic sentence points the paragraph in a definite direction. It guides our selection of examples. It helps us pick out the details that will fit in. Look at the following two topic sentences and the details that might back them up. Can

you see that each topic sentence causes the paragraph to move in a completely *different* direction?

TOPIC SENTENCE 1: Beth's bedroom is furnished in Early American.
Details: pine bed and dresser
braided rugs
ruffled muslin curtains
Hitchcock chair and desk
walls and woodwork painted Williamsburg blue

TOPIC SENTENCE 2: Beth's bedroom looks like a disaster area.
Details: bed unmade
closet door ajar
clothes on the floor
dresser top littered
drawers gaping open
books piled on chair

EXERCISE 1

Each of the sentences below is a general statement. Complete each one by filling in the word (or words) of your choice. Below each version you have chosen, write four or five specific details that could be used to support the statement.

1. School is like a _____ (jail) (circus) (kindergarten) (factory).
2. American cars are _____ (huge) (clumsy) (luxurious) (changing).
3. Parents are too _____ (strict) (easygoing) (stingy) (busy).
4. Our neighborhood is _____ (quiet) (unsafe) (old) (very new) (average).
5. Dogs are _____ (messy) (friendly) (pests) (very different from one another).

EXERCISE 2

Use each of the following skeleton outlines for a "made-to-order" paragraph. Find relevant details or examples that would fit into the blank spaces. Write your completed paragraphs on a separate sheet of paper.

1. Anyone who has seen a few Western movies has no trouble recognizing the villain. First of all, the bad guy looks like a bad guy. He _____. He _____. Secondly, the villain talks like a villain. He _____. He _____. Finally, he acts as one would expect an evildoer to act. He _____, or he _____.

2. Our faces often show what is on our minds. When we smile at someone, that person knows that _____ . If we frown, _____ . When we give someone a blank look, _____ . People get many different messages from the expressions on our faces. When we stare, we show that _____ . When we avoid someone's eyes, we show that _____ .

3. Photographers for popular magazines like to take pictures of animals that are different or unusual. They take pictures of the giraffe because it _____ . We see many pictures of elephants because they _____ . We see pictures of the kangaroo because it _____ . Many photographs show animals like _____ because _____ .

C2d
The "How" Paragraph

Learn to write paragraphs that explain how.

The most practical kind of paragraph *explains* something. It tells readers something they want to know. Some paragraphs of explanation begin with sentences like these:

The team used a three-point strategy for winning the game.
Each student at some time tests a teacher.
My cousin taught me how to read a road map.
I have found a way to earn money for Christmas presents.

These topic sentences all make the same kind of promise to the reader: Each topic sentence shows that the writer's purpose is to explain *how to do something*. In order to develop each topic sentence, the writer must select details that will show the process involved in doing that particular thing. Remember:

(1) A "how" paragraph includes necessary details. Many "how" paragraphs include needed information about materials, tools, and procedures. Can you show that there is very little in the following paragraph that could have been left out?

    Potting a spider plant can be simple and re-
laxing if you follow the directions below. First,
you should acquire the tools and materials. You
need newspaper, a pot, soil, charcoal, a piece of
broken clay pot, and scissors. Lay the newspaper
on the table to catch the dirt. A piece of clay

pot is used over the hole of the pot; add the
charcoal, then half-fill the pot with soil. Make
a hole in the center of the dirt in which to place
the plant. Put the plant in the pot and firmly
pack the dirt around the roots and base. Add a
little water; then place it in the morning sun.
The spider plant is ready to grow and reproduce.

(2) A "how" paragraph often follows the order of events in time. We call the way things follow one another in time **chronological** order. A mechanic or a cook often has to follow the right steps in the right order in time in order to succeed.

Take a good look at the way the following paragraphs explain something and "show how." Can you *restate* these instructions in your own words? Notice the words or expressions that remind us that we are moving ahead in time:

PARAGRAPH A:

The easiest way to start a fire is to use a few fuzz sticks. Get yourself three pieces of soft, dry wood, about two inches thick. Shave one side of each piece, leaving long, ribbon-like shavings on the stick. *Now* make a little tripod, so that the shavings hang down. Build a little tepee of finger-thick dry wood all around the fuzz sticks; don't make it more than a foot across. Light the fuzz sticks with a match, and *in a moment* you'll have a vigorous and warming blaze.—Harry Zarchy, *Let's Go Camping*

LANGUAGE IN ACTION

LOST ARTS AND FORGOTTEN SKILLS

Modern machines and appliances do hundreds of things for us that people used to do for themselves. By talking to older people, or by reading books about America's past, can you find the information for a "How-to" paragraph on one of the following?

How people used to make soap
How log cabins were built
How to make your own wine
From sheep's wool to homemade clothing
Homemade butter and cheese
How to butcher a hog

PARAGRAPH B:

To make biscuits, take as much flour as you need and add some shortening. Add salt to taste. Rub all together thoroughly. *Next* add cold water slowly, as little as possible. Set the dough aside *for twenty to thirty minutes* so that it will soften a little. Press it flat, cut out the biscuits, and bake in a quick oven, one which is too hot rather than too cold. Cover up the dough *when you set it aside* to soften. The biscuits will bake *in fifteen to twenty minutes* if the oven is not too hot.—Ella E. Myers, *Home Cook and Recipe Book*

(3) Some "how" paragraphs follow the order from simple to difficult. Let's use the topic sentence "Each student at some time tests a teacher." Begin by listing details that tell how pupils test teachers. Your list might include:

dropping books	refusing to study
being late	being rude
slumping in seat	asking unrelated questions
leaving books in lockers	pretending inability to hear

You next decide how to organize the details. Common sense tells you that the student bent on testing the teacher will begin with the little tests, the less obvious ones, and go on to bold, daring tests that can't be ignored. Following this logic, you might organize your list in this order:

1. slumping in seat
2. dropping books
3. pretending inability to hear
4. being late
5. leaving books in lockers
6. asking unrelated questions
7. being rude
8. refusing to study

The list now goes from "little things" to "big things." This revised list can serve as a plan or guide for the paragraph. This paragraph could be the result:

Every student at some time tests a teacher. This testing may begin on the first day of school. The student may slump in the seat, drop a book noisily, or pretend not to hear. If the teacher fails these tests, the student soon goes on to bolder action. This may include coming to class late, leaving a notebook in the locker, and asking questions not related to the subject. These tests of the teacher are more obvious. After failing all these tests, the unwary teacher now gets the full treatment. This may range from rudeness to refusal to study. Some teachers don't know that their students want them to do well and to pass all the tests.

EXERCISE 1

Write a paragraph explaining how to do something that *not everybody* knows how to do. You might explain how to:

- Make your favorite cookies
- Construct a model airplane, car, or boat
- Stay up on a surfboard
- Perform a simple scientific experiment
- Change a tire on a car
- Patch a bicycle tire
- Make your own pizza
- Grow your own corn
- Build your own camera

EXERCISE 2

Usually, "how-to" instructions tell us how to deal with things and how to make things work. Can you see why it is much harder to give "how-to" advice on *how to deal with people?* Write a "how-to" paragraph on one of the following:

- How to make a newcomer welcome
- How to make a parent listen
- How to prevent a fight
- How to stop vandals
- How to make people behave on a school bus
- How to get an idea accepted

Learn to write paragraphs that explain why.

C2e

The "Why" Paragraph

Some paragraphs of explanation start with sentences like the following:

I love to play soccer.
Although the movie is old, I consider it worth seeing.
Grace wanted to quit school.
The half-hitch is a useful knot for a camper.
It takes brave people to climb mountains.

Again, each of these sentences has a promise in it. In all the sentences, the promise is to explain *why.* The paragraph promised in the topic sentence would explain the reason behind an event or the reason for a situation. It would give the reason for a choice.

(1) A "why" paragraph gives facts or explanations that will seem like good reasons to the reader. Restate in your own words what the following paragraph does to make readers say, "I can see why":

> *It takes brave people to climb mountains.* They must have the courage to face sudden changes in the weather. Warm winds may thaw the ice and snow, thereby causing avalanches. At other times sudden storms cover climbers and camps with tons of snow. The world's most challenging mountain is Mt. Everest. It is in the Himalayas in northern India. One of the dangers of climbing Mt. Everest is that the oxygen is thin and breathing becomes very difficult. The few who have successfully climbed Mt. Everest have gained worldwide fame.

(2) Sometimes we use one long example to "show why":

> *Baby-sitting is not the easiest way to earn money.* Small children are full of energy. For example, one of my former employers has a three-year-old daughter. This little girl can read all of her books, recite many nursery rhymes, do somersaults on the carpet and handstands on the sofa. Her other talents include yanking over expensive lamps and marching around the room wielding a baton. When bedtime finally comes, I have a battle on my hands. By sheer strength, I win, put her in bed, and firmly close the door. Exhausted, I take a glass of Coke in my trembling hands and head for the living room and rest. Then her whines begin.

(3) Often we have to sort out our reasons and give them in a clear order. Suppose you were asked about your favorite sport. Your answer might be, "Lacrosse is my favorite sport." Asked to explain why, you would start listing your reasons:

- I feel good after the game.
- The game is fast and rough.
- The players fight for the ball.
- The lacrosse stick is awkward.
- Much practice is needed.
- The players work as a team.
- The players push and shove.
- It's a game of bruising body contact.
- It relieves tensions.
- It doesn't matter whether you win or lose.

Next, study your list to see how you could organize it into a workable plan for writing. After making several false starts, you realize that your list contains three key reasons. The rest of the details support these key reasons:

TOPIC SENTENCE: Lacrosse Is My Favorite Sport.

   I. It requires practice and skill.
     A. The lacrosse stick is an awkward tool.
     B. Teamwork is needed to keep the ball in play.

  II. The game is fast and rough.
     A. Players push and shove.
     B. Players fight to get the ball.
     C. Bruises and bandages are common.
     D. Everybody engages in bruising bodily contact.

 III. I feel good after the game.
     A. I'm exhausted.
     B. I feel close to my teammates.

Your finished paragraph might look like this:

   <u>I love to play lacrosse.</u> I enjoy the practice needed to gain skill in using the lacrosse stick, an awkward tool. Our practice welds us into a team which is able to keep the ball constantly in play. I like the speed and roughness of the game. We push and shove as we fight to get the ball. Every player is proud of the bruises and bandages that he wears as a result of bruising bodily contact. After the game is over, I have tremendous feelings of satisfaction. I know that, win or lose, I've done my best. Furthermore, I'm exhausted and my tensions are gone. But best of all, I feel that my teammates and I have developed a special bond.

Using Your Imagination

TELL ME WHY

Before science explained to people how things work, the storyteller of a tribe had many traditional stories to explain facts of the world around them: Why the sun comes up in the east or why the weather turns cold in winter. Pretend you are one of the wise elders of a tribe. Can you make up a story to explain to the children of the tribe some of the facts about the world? Write an imaginary story to explain:

- why the moon shines at night;
- why winter brings ice and snow;
- why rivers flood;
- why there are insects;
- why humans and animals spend half the day sleeping;
- why some other fact of the natural world works the way it does.

EXERCISE 1

Each of the following sentences could be the topic sentence for a paragraph that shows why. For each paragraph, write the next sentence. Use your sentence to state one good reason why. (Your teacher may ask you to choose one of these and write a complete "why" paragraph.)

EXAMPLE: Soccer has become a very popular sport among young people.

_____.

(Answer) In soccer, many people—not just a few stars—can participate equally.

1. The number two is one of the most important numbers in human life. _____.
2. The government has set aside wilderness areas where all wildlife is protected. _____.
3. Many people now have smaller families than were common twenty years ago. _____.
4. The guitar has become a favorite musical instrument of younger people. _____.
5. Many carmakers now build smaller cars than they used to.

_____.
6. Over the years, the government has banned many substances that were added to food. _____.

7. On a modern farm, one person can take care of jobs that used to be done by several people. _____

_____ .

8. Few Americans travel long distances by train anymore. _____

_____ .

9. People living in an area often make fun of the tourists who visit there. _____ .

10. America has often been called a melting pot of many nationalities. _____ .

Write a paragraph explaining why. Choose one of the following. Explain:

- why a certain kind of animal makes a good pet;
- why you do well in your favorite subject;
- why you do poorly in your *least* favorite subject;
- why you are afraid of something you are afraid of;
- why you like to (or don't like to) travel with your family;
- why you like (or dislike) a movie, TV program, or commercial.

Learn to write paragraphs that explain what something is.

Some paragraphs of explanation begin with sentences like these:

A teaspoon is a utensil used when eating.
A police review board is a civilian agency that investigates cases of alleged improper police action.
A hurricane is a storm that is greatly feared along the eastern coast.

Each of these sentences shows that the writer's purpose is to answer the question "*What* is _____?" In each case the writer sets out to *define* something: in the first sentence, what a teaspoon is; in the second, what a police review board is; and so on. A **definition** helps us mark off something so that we can tell it apart from other things. It tells us what something is like and how it is used.

Let's assume you want to leave a record of what a button is for a future society that no longer uses buttons. (Maybe all clothes will have magnetic fasteners.) You start with a very general description: Buttons were used to hold together parts of our clothing. Then you go into details:

WHAT IT LOOKS LIKE:

- round and flat with holes in center
- size ranges from small to large
- many materials—leather, wood, plastic, etc.
- many colors

HOW USED:

- buttonholes needed in corresponding positions
- button inserted in hole

Here is a paragraph developed from this rough outline:

A button is one part of a device for holding together two parts of a garment. It is usually round and flat with two or more holes in the center. In size, buttons range from perhaps one-half inch to two or three inches across. The materials used to make buttons include mother-of-pearl, cloth, leather, metal, and glass. Sometimes these materials are used in combination. The colors of buttons range through the whole spectrum. Buttons are sewn onto one edge of a garment and then buttonholes are made in corresponding positions on the opposite edge of the garment. When the button is inserted into the buttonhole, the dress or coat or shirt is "buttoned up."

EXERCISE 1

What does each of the following "what" paragraphs tell you about the things being described? How good a close-up do you get? In your own words, summarize the information in each paragraph.

1.   Snorkels are breathing tubes that can only be used on the surface of the water. They are air tubes that fit in the mouth and connect with the air above the surface. These are extensively used in hobby-diving. If the snorkel is attached to the face mask, it must be cleared of water after a dive. One does not have to lift the head in breathing while using a snorkel. With the snorkel a diver can see underwater while swimming on the surface. In ancient times divers would use reeds in order to camouflage themselves from the enemy by remaining just under the surface of the water and breathing through them in a manner similar to that used by the hobbyist with the modern snorkel.—Erik Bergaust and William Foss, *Skin Divers in Action*

2.   A fishhook is a hook for catching fish. It is shaped like a lowercase j with the body of the letter and the dot connected. The dot is where the eye of the fishhook is located. The eye

is used to attach the hook to the fishline. The curved part of the fishhook ends in a sharply pointed barb. This barb serves two functions. It holds the bait and it hooks the fish after it has taken the bait. Fishhooks are made from light but strong steel. The diameter of most fishhooks is smaller than the wire in a typical paper clip. However, the larger the fish, the larger the fishhook needed.

3. Pioneers used candles to light their homes. Candles are slender cylinders of wax or tallow. A wick running through the length of the candle is burned to provide light. Last summer we saw candles being made. Some candles are made in molds; others are made by dipping wicks repeatedly in melted wax. Candles are available in many colors and designs.

Write a paragraph explaining what something is. Practice on something *ordinary or familiar*. Fill in as much detail as you can. Choose one:

EXERCISE 2

1. a surfboard
2. a revolving door
3. a rocking chair
4. a tornado
5. a pressure cooker
6. an elephant
7. a pulley
8. a thermostat
9. a carburetor
10. a bicycle pump

Read your paragraph to the class. Let them fill in any important details that you may have missed.

Each of the following questions could be answered in a "what" paragraph. Which question makes you say: "I know *more* about this than many other people"? Answer the question in a complete paragraph that tells the reader what you know.

EXERCISE 3

1. What is a compass?
2. What is amber?
3. What is a leprechaun?
4. What is a canoe?
5. What is a totem pole?
6. What is an amulet?
7. What is a refrain?
8. What is a glider?
9. What is a harp?
10. What is a submarine?

C3
TELLING YOUR STORY

Tell the story of an incident that meant something to you.

We often tell family or friends about something that has happened. We tell the story because in some way it *stood out* from ordinary routine. When we tell a story, we turn to people as if to say: "Listen—something happened that doesn't happen every day."

C3a
The Well-Told Story

Know how to make a story real and interesting for your reader.

What makes a good story? No two stories are put together exactly the same way. But a good storyteller has learned some of the things that attract and hold the attention of the reader. Remember the following guidelines for the art of effective storytelling:

(1) Include enough realistic detail to make the story real for your readers.   Help the readers imagine the place where the story happens. Help them see what exactly is going on in the story.

The following brief story looks at a car dump from the point of view of a car that was taken there. We need to use our imagination to help us picture ourselves in the place of the car. But the student writer also included details that help make the place and the car real for us. Point out all details that help make this story real:

```
                    The Junkyard


        I knew I would eventually end up here, in
this junkyard.  But I didn't know that it would
be this soon.

        It all began when my transmission broke.
My owner looked all across town for a transmis-
sion that would fit me, but he couldn't find
one and finally gave up all hope.
```

One week passed, and the next thing I knew,
I was being towed away to the nearest junkyard.
I was picked up with a large machine and stacked
on top of other cars. Then other cars were
stacked on top of me.

I've only been here in this dirty, depres-
sing junkyard for four weeks, and already my roof
is aching, my body is falling apart, and worst of
all, rust has conquered most of me. I wish I had
some moving room. I'm so cramped here.

However, there is one consolation. My better parts can be reused on other cars so they
won't end up in the same place as I am . . . this
junkyard I call home.

(2) Learn to follow the order of events in time. A good
storyteller takes us along as things happen. A story that follows events as they happen in time follows **chronological**
order. Though there are other ways of telling a story, a good
storyteller knows how to take us through an experience step
by step. We then feel we are sharing the experience with the
writer.

The following story by a student takes us along exceptionally well as it moves from one place to another. In your
own words, identify five or six major steps or stages through
which the story moves:

Journey to My Hideout

As the youngest sister in a big family,
I was constantly picked on and nagged at to
do better. When the nagging began to weigh
me down, I would take off to my own secret
place. I had to take a roundabout way to
insure that no one was following me. I knew
that if anyone ever discovered where it was,
it wouldn't be just mine anymore. Before I
left the house I would pull on rolled-up
blue jeans and a faded grey sweat shirt.
I'd tie my hair up into pigtails, completely

brushing out the curls Mother had spent an
hour getting in. Then I would sneak out the
back so as not to be seen, and call my big,
black sheep dog to go along. I would start
across the back yard, romping with Shep in
the thick green grass so dark and cool.
We'd eventually get to the fence surrounding
the feed lots and yards. I'd get down in
the sandy dirt and squeeze myself through
the holes. Shep would leap over and be waiting for me on the other side. We'd take off
running for the nearest barn, an old red
wooden granary. Inside, we would try to
crawl to the top of the wheat pile, never getting more than halfway up.

Upon leaving here, we had to climb another fence around the lambing yards. The
lambs always came running when they saw us,
and with ten or twenty lambs nudging against
me it was slow going. We never stopped long
and never went into the lambing barns, as
Shep scared the young lambs, and the ewes
didn't like us much either.

When we came to the far edge of the
yards, we again climbed a fence. We then
walked through the tall prairie grass until
we came to a windbreak of trees a mile long
and a mile wide. We started through these,
with Shep chasing rabbits while I picked
flowers. About halfway through, we came to
a clearing. Near the edge stood my hideout,
an old water tank. On the top was a hole
just large enough for me to crawl into. Once
inside, I pulled the lid on and sat quietly
in the cool damp darkness. Here I would sit
and think, and Shep would wait patiently outside. At suppertime, I would crawl back out.
Shep and I would walk home, and things always
seemed okay again.

(3) *Arouse the reader's curiosity.* Make your readers
wonder what will happen next—create **suspense.** A good
story often sets up some challenge or problem that makes us
say: "How will this turn out?" Often a story reaches its high
point as the challenge is met or the problem is solved.

Point out several things that readers *want* to know as they read the following excerpt from a story of adventure:

> I knew that I had to shoot. I puffed out my chest. I held my breath. I lowered the rifle in spite of myself—and noted that the rhinos were facing us, and sniffing and snorting. I lifted the rifle again, aimed it in the general direction of the rhinos, shut my eyes, yanked the trigger—and the sky fell right on top of me. The ground rose and slugged me. The crack of doom sounded over all Africa. I had never been hit so hard by anything, nor listened to such an explosion so close at hand. I knew I was lying down. I was sure that one of the rhinos had hit me broadside on. Nothing else could have hit so hard. Strange that I hadn't seen the rhino charging. They must travel faster than the eye could follow them. The rifle was gone from my hands. My jaw had been hit so hard I couldn't even feel it. My shoulder felt as though I had fallen down a mountain and landed on it.
>
> Then I was conscious that my two helpers were lifting me up. They tried to hand me the rifle again, but I wouldn't have it, now that I realized that it had knocked me over, not the charging rhinos.—Theodore J. Waldeck, *On Safari*

Read the following well-told story from a book about a pet raccoon. Then answer the following questions:

1. What details help the author make the story real for the reader? Point out half a dozen realistic details.
2. How well can the reader follow the events of the story? Summarize the events of the story as they happen in time.
3. Point out several places where the reader is made to wonder what will happen next. Describe the challenge or problem whose solution provides the high point of the story.

> I decided one day that Rascal was clean enough and bright enough to eat with us at the table. I went to the attic and brought down the family highchair, last used during my own infancy.
>
> Next morning while my father was fixing eggs, toast, and coffee, I went out to get Rascal, and placed him in the highchair beside me at the table. On his tray I put a heavy earthenware bowl of warm milk.
>
> Rascal could reach the milk easily by standing in the chair and placing his hands on the edge of the tray. He seemed to like the new arrangement and chirred and trilled his satisfaction. Except for dribbling a little milk, easily wiped from the

tray of the highchair, his table manners proved excellent, much better than those of most children. My father was amused and permissive as usual, and even petted the raccoon as we finished our meal.

Breakfast-for-three became part of the daily ritual, and we had no trouble whatsoever until . . . I gave Rascal his first sugar. Rascal felt it, sniffed it, and then began his usual washing ceremony, swishing it back and forth through his bowl of milk. In a few moments, of course, it melted entirely away, and a more surprised little raccoon you have never seen in your life. He felt all over the bottom of the bowl to see if he had dropped it, then turned over his right hand to assure himself it was empty, then examined his left hand in the same manner. Finally he looked at me and trilled a shrill question: who had stolen his sugar lump?

Recovering from my laughter, I gave him a second sugar lump, which Rascal examined minutely. He started to wash it, but hesitated. A very shrewd look came into his bright black eyes, and instead of washing away a second treat, he took it directly to his mouth where he began to munch it with complete satisfaction. When Rascal had learned a lesson, he had learned it for life. Never again did he wash a lump of sugar.
—Sterling North, *Rascal*

EXERCISE 2

Newspapers and magazines often print anecdotes—brief stories about unusual personal experiences. These anecdotes are included with news of greater importance because people enjoy reading about amusing and interesting things that happen to others. The following are shortened examples. Choose one and rewrite it in a more complete form. Add realistic details that would help make the story real for the reader. (Or you may want to look for a different anecdote in a newspaper or in a magazine like *Reader's Digest.*)

1. A newspaper carried a story about the Bishop of Guildford who asked a class of six-year-olds at a primary school, "Who am I?" One small boy answered, "You are the fish shop of Guildford."

2. A man was examining a horse's hoof when the animal kicked him in the leg. Hurt and angered, the man retaliated with a well-placed kick of his own, which broke his toe.

3. A woman working for an oil company had to phone gas stations to inform dealers of a rise in gasoline prices. She once got a wrong number without realizing it and made her announcement

to the person at the other end. Her listener laughed and asked her to delay the call to the right number till he could fill up his tank.

4. A woman wearing a leg brace removed it before going into a pool for a swim and put it back on afterwards. A little boy who had watched her asked: "Are you bionic?"

1. Write a story in which you put yourself in the place of an object, an animal, or a person other than yourself. Include enough realistic detail to make the story real for the reader. Some sample topics:

   - What It's Like to Be a Kite
   - A Day in the Life of a Bus
   - It's a Dog's Life
   - Music Teacher for a Day

2. Write a story in which you take your reader along as you move in space or time. It might be the story of a trip to a place that was unusual or hard to find. It might be the story of a tryout, contest, or other competition. Start a new paragraph when you go on from one major step or stage in your story to the next.

3. Write a story that leads up to a high point. Make sure the story includes a challenge or a problem that leaves the outcome in doubt. Make your story a true story about something that happened to you or someone you know well. Your story might be about a quarrel, a difficult task, a scary experience, a major change in your family, or the like.

WRITING TOPICS

Learn to write a story with a point.

Many stories are entertaining because of a clever remark or an unexpected twist. We are amused by them for a while and then forget them. The stories we remember are the ones that made us think. They taught us something worth thinking about or worth knowing.

Think about some event or some person that meant something special to you. Ask yourself: What have I learned from the experience? What did it teach me about other people?

C3b

The Story with a Point

Then write about the experience in a story that has a special meaning or a special point.

Remember:

(1) We often sum up the point of a story at the very beginning. We often remember for a long time the kind of embarrassing mistake that we all manage to make. In the following brief anecdote, the very first sentence tells us that this is the kind of story the writer is going to tell:

> *I never was so embarrassed in my whole life as I was last Friday.* My sister and I had gone shopping. I have always thought that she would lose her purse someday, because she is so careless with it. We were standing at a counter among many customers when I saw what I thought was Sis' purse hanging halfway out of her pocket. It seemed like a good time to teach her a lesson. I gently slid the purse out of the pocket and was about to hide it in my own pocket when my hand was seized in an iron grip. A large woman was glaring at me. Bewildered, I looked at Sis. There was her purse in her hand! I wriggled free from the real owner of the purse and lost myself in the crowd. Sis never did know what had happened, and I shall never tell her.

Do you remember a similar incident that happened to you? If you had been in the writer's place, what do you think you would have learned from this embarrassing experience?

(2) We often sum up the point of a story at the end—or let the readers discover it for themselves. The following story was told by a seventh-grader. Why do you think the people in his family remember and retell this story?

> When my brother Billy was five years old, he prided himself on being quite a fighter. His version of his fights with his friends always showed him as the best fighter and the winner. One night, with his usual enthusiasm, he told Pop how he had fought and beaten his pal Tommy that afternoon. He did a double take when Pop said, "I saw you and Tommy wrestling today—and Tommy had you down and was sitting on your back." Billy's surprise lasted only a moment. He recovered and answered cheerfully, "But, Pop, I fight better from underneath."

What if this story had just told us that two boys were wrestling? That wouldn't be news, and it wouldn't make a story. The story is in what Billy said—*before* the wrestling, and *after*. What do the things he says show about the kind of person Billy is? What is it about Billy that reminds us of the way other people act in similar situations? If you were writing this story, you might want to let your readers answer these questions for themselves. Or you might want to sum up what you thought when you watched Billy's behavior. Your final sentence might look like this:

MAIN POINT: Everyone wants very much to look good in the eyes of others—it's just that young children are more obvious about it than adults.

(3) Sometimes the meaning of an experience becomes clear as we watch something develop over a period of time. The sample stories you have studied so far deal mostly with a single event, a single incident. The following story of a friendship covers a much longer span. The point of the story is in how the friendship *changed* over the years.

In your own words, sum up the meaning that this story had for the writer. Explain what part or what stage of the story each paragraph covers.

```
         A Friend

   Miriam was my closest and dearest
friend.  She supplied me with the
security I didn't find at home.  She was
headstrong, intelligent, and beautiful.
Her slightly curly, baby-fine hair
glistened in the sun.  Her eyes sparkled
as her personality bubbled from her
petite frame.  I was the ugly duckling,
introverted and dejected.

   We were inseparable.  We went through
everything together, knowing each
other's deepest secrets and swearing in
blood never to tell them.  She even
taught me to play the piano, because she
knew how I envied her talent.

   After junior high, her family decided
that she should attend a high school in
a better neighborhood.  We corresponded
```

heavily at first; then her letters were fewer and farther between.

Seeing each other wasn't the same after this. We were each aware of the places we held in the world. Sophistication was her world; simplicity was mine.

At our last meeting, we never said good-by. We just looked into each other's eyes, trying to read our thoughts for the last time. My heart called out, "Why does it have to be this way?" She had brought me through the worst years of my life. What would I do without her?

EXERCISE 1

Write a brief story that would start with one of the following sentences. Make sure the rest of your story follows up this key sentence:

1. I had never been so frightened in my life.
2. It was my most embarrassing moment.
3. I remember the (kindest) (meanest) thing someone ever did to me.
4. I had never been put on the spot like this before.
5. I remember the luckiest moment of my life.

EXERCISE 2

Write a brief story that would *end* with one of the following statements. Does one of the following expressions remind you of something that happened to you? Tell the story.

1. I felt like a hayseed.
2. My mother (father, uncle, . . .) had the patience of a saint.
3. Boy, did I make a mistake!
4. I'll never do that again!
5. It happened out of a clear sky.
6. Appearances can be misleading.
7. How do you know when to trust people?
8. There will never be another.
9. What a temper!
10. The first time is the worst.
11. Dreams sometimes come true.
12. Don't believe everything you hear.

Write a story of several paragraphs about a *change* in your life. You might write about a change in your neighborhood, in your family, or in a person you know well.

Tell your readers what people say as well as what they do.

Often the high point of a story is something somebody does. But just as often the high point is something somebody *says*. When we can listen to what the characters in a story say, we get to know them as people. When we hear them talk, we can see what makes them do some of the things they do.

Compare the following "silent" and "talking" versions of the same story. How much is added through **dialogue**—the talk that goes back and forth between characters?

"SILENT" VERSION:

When I was five years old, I had to take afternoon naps in spite of the fact that I felt that I was too old for them. One day I slammed my door with all my strength as a way of showing my irritation. Then I decided that I would slip out of the window onto our porch and go to play with the kids next door. Several hours later, I saw a fire truck pull up to our house. As the fire fighters went in, I ran to a side window and listened. Mother was telling the fire chief that she was worried because she could hear no sounds from behind the locked door of my room. In response to a question from them, she said she couldn't reach my father at his office and she supposed he was on his way home. Just then Dad drove up. He picked me up and we entered the house together. Was Mother ever surprised and relieved!

"TALKING" VERSION:

Mother sent me, a reluctant five-year-old, to my room for my regular afternoon nap. As I turtled along, she urged me forward by saying, "Now, get a good nap. When you wake up, Daddy'll be home for supper."

"I'm too big for naps," I muttered as I slammed the door. Outside my window the summer sun sparkled and next door I could see Ted and Sarah playing Twist. The temptation was too great. I slid through the window onto our porch and seconds later I was playing Twist, too.

AN AFTERNOON AT THE PICTURE SHOW

In the old silent movies, the action would be interrupted every so often. Then a frame would appear with the words spoken by one of the characters: "Leave this house instantly!" or "He dare not mistreat a helpless child!" Even the silent movies could not do without words.

Write several "talk" frames for a short silent movie that uses one of the following story ideas, or make up your own idea.

1. Dishonest apprentice accuses banker's son of theft and turns father against the son. But another employee has seen the real thief (the apprentice).
2. Evil landlord tries to evict poor widow and orphans. They are saved by a generous stranger.
3. Poor girl helps penniless stranger who suffers from loss of memory. He regains memory and turns out to be millionaire's son.

More than two hours later, I was surprised to see a fire truck pull up to our house. Two brawny fire fighters rushed in. Curious, I crept close to the side window and listened.

"The door's locked from the inside and I haven't heard a sound. I know something terrible has happened to him," Mother was saying.

There was a low murmur from the fire fighters, then Mother again. "Nobody answers at his office. He must be on his way home. Please! Can't you get the door open faster?"

Just then Dad drove up and I ran to greet him. Swooping me up into his arms, he entered the house.

"What's going on here?"

Instead of answering, Mother dropped limply into a chair. For long seconds she kept her hands over her face. When she lowered them, she laughed happily.

When you write dialogue, remember:

(1) Make the conversation sound natural. Use words the way people would actually talk.

(2) Identify the speakers clearly. Write so that the reader always knows who is talking.

(3) Set off the exact words of the speaker with quotation marks.

See **M4c** on how to punctuate quotations.

EXERCISE 1

Read the following imaginary conversation. Does it seem real enough so you can say: "It actually might have happened like that"? Choose a well-known person that you have read about. Write an imaginary dialogue between two *bystanders* at a crucial stage in the well-known person's life.

"Thirty-eight cents," the attendant at New York's Bellevue Hospital called out, to complete the record sheet on the man who had just died.

"Thirty-eight cents. I've got it down. Find anything else in his pockets?"

"Not a thing, except some note here."

"What's it say?"

"Ah, nothin'. Just 'Dear Friends and Gentle Hearts.' "

"Yup, a dreamer. Like so many of these poor fellows they bring in here from the Bowery."

"He's better off dead. Well—got the name right? Stephen Foster, with the 'ph,' not 'v.' And make sure you make it 1864. It's past New Year's, you know."

This was the end of a man whose incomparable success still continues. He gave, and still gives, great pleasure to many Americans. Since 1848, just about every American has heard, whistled, or sung his beloved songs.—Joseph Mersand, editor, *Great American Short Biographies*

EXERCISE 2

Tell the story of something that happened to you or to someone you know well. Choose a story in which what was *said* was important—not just what was done. Try to use dialogue for at least one-third or one-half of the story.

Here are kinds of stories that often include talking:

- an encounter with a police officer;
- an argument after an accident;
- a story about someone being teased a lot;
- an attempt to explain something to a foreign visitor;
- a camp leader trying to get things under control;
- an angry coach (or an angry teacher);
- someone making excuses;
- someone unjustly accused.

C4
USING YOUR EYES

Use description to tell your reader what you see.

When you tell a story, the main question is, "What *happened?*" When you write a description, the main question is, "What was *there?*" What sights were there to see? What sounds were there to hear? What objects were there to handle or to touch? Reading a good description is the next best thing to being there.

C4a
An Eye for Detail

Use exact detail to make description come to life.

Good observers notice things. They take in **details:** the little things that make a description seem real. Read the following passage by John Steinbeck. Watch how he gradually fills in the details that make us say: "I can see it in front of me!" Pick three or four details in this account. Explain in your own words what you see.

> Then a moving figure caught Jody's eye. A man walked slowly over the brow of the hill, on the road from Salinas, and he was headed toward the house. Jody stood up and moved down toward the house too, for if someone was coming, he wanted to be there to see. By the time the boy had got to the house the walking man was only halfway down the road, a lean man, very straight in the shoulders. Jody could tell he was old only because his heels struck the ground with hard jerks. As he approached nearer, Jody saw that he was dressed in blue jeans and in a coat of the same material. He wore clodhopper shoes and an old flat-brimmed Stetson hat. Over his shoulder he carried a gunny sack, lumpy and full. In a few moments he had trudged close enough so that his face could be seen. And his face was as dark as dried beef. A mustache, blue-white against the dark skin, hovered over his mouth, and his hair was white, too, where it showed at his neck. The skin of his face had shrunk back against the skull until it defined bone, not flesh, and made the nose and chin seem sharp and fragile. The eyes were large and deep and dark, with eyelids stretched tightly over them. Irises and pupils were one, and very black, but the eyeballs were brown. There were no wrinkles in the face at all. This old man wore a blue denim coat buttoned to the throat with brass buttons, as all men do who wear no shirts. Out of the sleeves came strong bony wrists and hands gnarled and knotted and hard as peach branches. The nails were flat and blunt and shiny.—from *The Red Pony*

Remember:

(1) Move in for the close-up view. Take a good look at the difference between the following descriptions of the same scene. One gives us the general picture. The other gives us the close-up view. Point out the details that have been added to the second version that evoke vivid pictures or images in the reader's mind.

GENERAL PICTURE:

The tired dogs came down the frozen waterway. The traces of their leather harness were attached to a sled. On the sled was tied an oblong box, some blankets, a coffee pot, and a frying pan.

CLOSE-UP VIEW:

But there *was* life, abroad in the land and defiant. Down the frozen waterway toiled a string of wolfish dogs. Their bristly fur was rimed with frost. Their breath froze in the air as it left their mouths, spouting forth in spumes of vapor that settled upon the hair of their bodies and formed into crystals of frost. Leather harness was on the dogs, and leather traces attached them to a sled which dragged along behind. The sled was without runners. It was made of stout birch-bark, and its full surface rested on the snow. The front end of the sled was turned up like a scroll in order to force down and under the bore of soft snow that surged like a wave before it. On the sled, securely lashed, was a long and narrow oblong box. There were other things on the sled—blankets, an axe, and a coffee pot and frying pan; but prominent, occupying most of the space, was the long and narrow oblong box.—Jack London, *White Fang*

(2) Use accurate words for the specific details you include. The author of the passage on page 182 used several accurate words for features of the landscape. She used accurate words to name and describe features of the vegetation. She used accurate words for parts of the deer. Point out as many of these accurate words as you can.

She also used several *comparisons* to help us see the scene she describes. Can you find one or more of these comparisons?

(In the passage on page 182, Rocky and Tayo are two Indian boys who are out hunting together.)

Composition

AMERICAN LEGENDS
The Wright Brothers' Plane

(1) Pretend that you are a reporter assigned to Kitty Hawk, North Carolina, on December 17, 1903. Write a dispatch which explains what you saw and heard.

(2) Pretend that you are Orville or Wilbur Wright. Write a letter to the United States Patent Office explaining what your invention looks like and what it does.

AMERICAN LEGENDS
The Model T Ford

(1) Describe the Model T to someone who has never seen one.
(2) Tell the story of the Model T. Explore its history, reputation, and role in American life.

Rocky was standing in a small clearing surrounded by thickets of scrub oak. It was still early in the fall and only a few of the coppery yellow leaves had fallen from the oaks. Tayo had to strain to see the deer in the tall yellow grass. He crossed a narrow dry gulley, and then he could see the antlers. He approached the deer slowly. It had fallen on its right side with its forelegs tucked under its belly; the hind legs were curled under to the left as if it were still sleeping in the grass. The eyes were still liquid and golden brown, staring at dark mountain dirt and dry oak leaves tangled in the grass. When he was a little child he always wanted to pet a deer and he daydreamed that a deer would let him come close and touch its nose. He knelt and touched the nose; it was softer than cattails, and still warm as a breath.—Leslie Marmon Silko, *Ceremony*

EXERCISE 1

Study the following passage. Can you see that the writer was the kind of person who notices things? Do the following:

1. Point out all words that serve as accurate labels for features of the landscape (vegetation, etc.) that the author describes.
2. Point out all words that serve as accurate labels for the movements and activities of the animals in this passage.

In walking through the woods one day in early winter, we read upon the newly fallen snow the record of a mink's fright the night before. The mink had been traveling through the woods, not along the watercourses where one sees them by day, but over ridges and across valleys. We followed his tracks some distance to see what adventures he had met with. We tracked him through a bushy swamp, and saw where he had left it to explore a pile of rocks, then where he had taken to the swamp again, and where he had entered the more open woods. Presently the track turned sharply about, and doubled upon itself in long hurried strides. What had caused the mink to change his mind so suddenly? We explored a few paces ahead, and came upon a fox track. The mink had probably seen the fox stalking stealthily through the woods, and the sight had doubtless brought his heart into his mouth. I think he climbed a tree, and waited till the fox had passed. His tracks disappeared amid a clump of hemlocks, and then reappeared again a little beyond them. It described a big loop around, and then crossed the fox track only a few yards from the point where its course was interrupted. Then it followed a little watercourse, went under a rude bridge in a wood-road, then mingled with squirrel tracks in a denser part of the thicket.—John Burroughs, *Squirrels and Other Fur-Bearers*

Many things are so familiar that we hardly look at them anymore. We know what they are, and what they look like. What if we had to describe them to a visitor from a faraway country where the things of everyday life are different? Can you imagine a country where there is no ice or snow or lightning? Can you imagine a place where people have never seen a banana? For a visitor from such a place, jot down the details you would use to give the person a good picture of what you are describing.

EXERCISE 2

EXAMPLE: ice

It looks clear, glistening, clean.
It melts, cools, cracks, slushes.
It feels hard, slippery, cold, wet.
When you hold it, it makes your fingers go numb.

Do a similar note-taking for three of the following:

1. snow
2. lightning
3. a banana
4. sand
5. rain

6. grass
7. surf
8. a watermelon
9. corn
10. bread

Has anyone ever asked you to help tell apart two things that are very similar? Write a paragraph in which you help a visitor from faraway tell apart *one* of the following:

EXERCISE 3

1. a rat and a guinea pig
2. an eagle and a vulture
3. a horse and a donkey
4. a fly and a mosquito
5. a chicken and a duck

Write a description of a scene after you have had a chance to get a good look. Choose one of the following:

EXERCISE 4

1. dogs roaming your neighborhood
2. animals in a science lab
3. ants foraging or moving
4. bees in blossom time
5. pigeons in a public square
6. monkeys in a zoo or pet shop
7. goldfish or other fish in a bowl or tank
8. animals displayed at a fair

C4b
Using Sensory Detail

Use details that appeal to all five senses.

Movies give us sights and sounds. But there still is a big difference between seeing a harbor in a movie, and being there. When we are actually out on a pier, we *smell* the fishy smells, we *feel* the sea breeze on our skin, and we can *taste* a seafood snack that we bought.

Effective description uses many details that deal with how something looked, sounded, smelled, tasted, and felt. Details of this kind are called **sensory details.** They appeal to the senses of sight, sound, smell, taste, and touch.

Remember:

(1) Details of sight, sound, smell, taste, and touch create lively impressions in the reader's mind. Look at the italicized words in each of the following passages. Explain what each makes you see, hear, smell, or feel:

People shouted and called, laughed, cursed, whistled. Wheels with iron rims *rattled* over cobblestones. Steam *hissed.* A barrel *clattered* over loose boards. A crate *thumped,* a hatch *slammed,* a chain *clanked* off a winch.

The coarse smell of flaked fish drying by the acre in the sun and the *tang* of tarred rope and nets and the *iodine smell* of the seaweed all mingled with the fresh salt air. The gulls *soared* and *wheeled* and *screamed.*

As the afternoon wore on and the sun turned orange through the dust, the men came back from the fields. They *doused* the *parched,* cracked bodies of their water buffaloes and *murmured* contentedly, themselves, as the water ran over their own shoulders and arms.—Peggy and Pierre Streit, "A Well In India"

The boats *wedged* in the wharves *nudged* and *creaked* against the pilings. The sails *rippled* in the breeze.

(2) A good writer often makes us share in the feelings of the observer. The following passage describes the sensations and feelings of a sick person waiting at a railroad station. In your own words, explain what it felt like for the person to be there:

The man at the ticket window told him it would be twenty-five minutes before the train left on track four; he pointed out the big doors to the tracks and told Tayo he could wait out there. Tayo felt weak, and the longer he walked the more his legs felt as though they might become invisible again; then the top part of his body would topple, and when his head was level with the ground he would be lost in smoke again, in the fog again. He breathed the air outside the doors and it smelled like trains, diesel oil, and creosote ties under the steel track. He leaned against the depot wall then; he was sweating, and sounds were becoming outlines again, vague and hollow in his ears, and he knew he was going to become invisible right there.—Leslie Marmon Silko, *Ceremony*

EXERCISE 1

Point out all the sights and sounds in the following capsule descriptions of people and places. Then write three similar *one-sentence* descriptions of people and places that you have observed.

1. A contented old man with a dirty, shabby, stained uniform was humming a familiar hymn as he cleaned the long red carpet in the hallway.
2. The doctor's office is filled with the sound of magazines being flipped through, along with sniffles and coughs.
3. The dance studio has polished hardwood floors and mirrors, both reflecting the graceful movements of the class.
4. The wharf would not be the same without the peeling paint, the squawking gulls, the strong odors, and the creaking sounds of the waterlogged hulls.
5. Machines clanging, bells ringing, lights flashing, kids running to one, then another of the games: this is an arcade.

EXERCISE 2

Choose a scene or situation that brings all or most of the five senses into play. (Your teacher may send you out on a field trip for this assignment.) Pack your description with details that appeal to your sense of sight, hearing, smell, taste, and touch. Choose one:

- a motorcycle or stock car race;
- a stable at feeding time;
- the scene of a fire;
- an old-fashioned butcher shop;
- an old-fashioned circus;
- a day at the county fair;
- an open-air market;
- the kitchen of a busy restaurant;
- some other scene rich in sights, sounds, and smells.

C4c

The Overall Impression

Make your details add up to an overall effect.

The details in effective description are not just there by accident. They *reinforce* each other. They build toward an overall impression that gives unity to a paragraph or a longer passage. In a paragraph about a rainy afternoon, the details may build up until the reader feels the gloom and grayness of a boring rainy day. If the paragraph is effective, the writer does not even have to *tell* the reader that it was a gloomy day. The details have created the right impression.

Read the following passage by Gordon Parks. He describes how, at the beginning of his career as a photographer, he looked over an apartment in Chicago. How many different words can you find in the passage that all *echo* in one way or another Parks's overall impression of the place?

Mr. Reynolds took out a bunch of keys and started opening the door. "Need strong locks 'round here. Well, here's the living room," he said making a quick gesture with his hand.

I glanced at the dirty green walls, the worn carpeting, and the blistered ceiling. "Needs painting," I said, breaking the uncomfortable silence. I turned for a look at Sally. With Toni in her arms now, she stood in the doorway, unhappily observing the drab pieces of furniture.

Mr. Reynolds ignored my remark. "Here's the two bedrooms," he squeaked, pointing in their direction.

Sally didn't move. "Come on," I said, "take a look." She hesitated for a moment, then came over and peeped into the dimly lit rooms. There was the same grease-splotched paper on all the walls, and its tawdry design, imitating the worst of the Victorian era, went well with the ornate brass beds and the credit-store dressers.

"The bathroom ain't much. Just a tub and a toilet stool. Look it over if you want to." Sally passed it up. But one quick look confirmed his description. There was an old-fashioned bathtub with claw feet and a primitive-looking stool. "And here's the kitchen. Comes with a gas stove and icebox." And a lot of grease and bugs, I thought, watching him squash a big cockroach with his foot. It was a darksome, dingy place, but my family was tired and needed some place to sleep. I didn't dare ask Sally if she liked it. I just took $37.50 out of my pocket and paid the little man a month's rent. "It'll be fine," I assured her after he had gone; "just give me a week to fix it up and you won't know it."

"We'll see," she said; "we'll see."—from *A Choice of Weapons*

In two or three sentences, give a brief description of a real scene that will make your reader share one of the following feelings:

peacefulness
nervousness
sympathy
gloom
happiness

EXERCISE 1

Use details to build up one major overall impression. Describe one of the following:

1. a scene that reflects a true old-fashioned Christmas spirit;
2. a street or neighborhood that shows what it means to be rich;
3. a street or neighborhood that shows what it means to be poor;
4. a supermarket that shows Americans' love for glossy material goods;
5. a building that is ultramodern;
6. an intersection or city block that is cluttered with buildings of many different shapes and styles.

EXERCISE 2

Learn to state and defend your opinions.

We say that "everyone is entitled to his or her opinion." But we do not take every opinion seriously. Before we seriously consider someone's ideas on a subject, we want to know: "Have you *thought* about this subject? Do you know what you are talking about? What are the reasons *behind* this opinion? Why do you believe as you do?"

Much of the speaking and writing we do is devoted to stating our opinions. We want to have our say, and we want other people to listen. To make people listen to our opinions, we have to learn to do the following:

(1) Learn to distinguish opinions from facts. The following sentences all state someone's opinions. They state a *personal* opinion—someone else probably would have a different opinion on the subject. What kind of person do you think made each statement?

Brothers are messy.
Rats make good pets.
Today's teenagers have no respect for authority.
Television stations show too many war movies.

C5
HAVING YOUR SAY

Study the differences between fact and opinion in the following pairs:

FACT: At 2 P.M. the temperature was 92 degrees.
OPINION: It was an unbearably hot day.

FACT: Columbus reached the West Indies in 1492.
OPINION: Vasco da Gama was a greater explorer than Columbus.

FACT: The dress code at our school rules out bare feet.
OPINION: People should be able to wear what they please.

FACT: World War II ended in 1945.
OPINION: Prejudice against other nationalities causes most wars.

The first pair is a good illustration of the difference between a fact and an opinion based on personal preference. The thermometer registered a temperature of 92° F. That information is concrete and definite. It can be proven. It doesn't change, regardless of who reads the thermometer. The temperature of 92° F. is public knowledge. It is information that is available to all.

The statement "It was an unbearably hot day" is an opinion, a personal reaction to the temperature. Opinions about the temperature may vary from person to person. To Jane, who works best in cool, brisk weather, the temperature of 92° F. may be very hot. On the other hand, Sue may consider 92° F. perfect for a summer day.

Facts remain the same when they are checked by different people. An opinion is influenced by what one person thinks or feels. Opinions include likes and dislikes, judgments and predictions.

(2) Learn to sum up your opinion clearly and effectively. Before people can decide whether or not they agree with us, they need to know two things: What is the issue? What is the point? Practice summing up your opinion on some current question or issue in one clear sentence. Study the following examples:

Dogs can ruin a day at the beach.
It is very ignorant and cruel to make fun of someone's physical defect.
After a long trip, a famous scenic wonder may prove disappointing.
Students sometimes learn more from a good television program than from a textbook.

In a paper that defends an opinion, we often sum up the opinion in a summary sentence early in the paper. Then, as we finish the paper, we can ask ourselves: "Have I stuck to the point?" A point about the poor garbage disposal service run by the city will get lost if we keep pointing to everything else the city government has ever done wrong.

(3) *Back up your opinion with supporting details.* When the opinion is "Apple pie is the best possible dessert," we accept the opinion as a personal preference. Some people just happen to like apple pie, and others don't. But what if the writer says, "I think American Indians are treated shamefully"? Our reaction is "What makes you think so?" We want to know what is behind the opinion. We want to know what led up to it.

If a writer can support an opinion in some way, we are more likely to give it serious consideration. We may even change our own point of view. We might begin to feel the way the writer feels.

Read the excerpts that follow. *How* does the writer support the opinion stated in the first sentence?

I think American Indians are being treated badly. For one thing, most of them have to live on reservations. Many Indians live in the desert areas of Arizona and New Mexico. Here they are restricted to barren, unproductive lands. They are isolated from thriving industrial centers where they might find jobs. In comparison with the majority of Americans, their houses are primitive, and their villages lack the usual sanitary facilities. . . . Because many Americans of Indian ancestry live on reservations, other Americans have a limited and inaccurate image of them. Movies show all Indians as bloodthirsty fighters. Our history books tell us little about their heroes, their legends, their languages, or their crafts. . . .

How many separate examples of bad treatment can you find in this passage? Can you think of other examples that could have been used to back up the writer's opinion?

As you finish a short paper presenting an opinion, ask yourself: "Have I made my point stick?" You may have stated your opinion, but have you backed it up? Have you made use of facts or statistics from reliable sources? Have you made use of scenes and incidents you have seen with your own eyes?

EXERCISE 1

Which of the following statements are facts? Which state an opinion? After the number of the statement, write *F* for fact or *O* for opinion.

1. Many people in the Canadian province of Quebec speak French.
2. Most birthday cards are just plain silly.
3. Many birds migrate to warmer climates during the winter.
4. Every student should study Spanish or some other foreign language.
5. Americans must learn to save energy.
6. The air we breathe is a mixture containing oxygen.
7. Cities in California and New Mexico, like Los Angeles and Santa Fe, have Spanish names.
8. Firm parents are better for a child than easygoing ones.
9. Many art classes are a waste of time.
10. Mark Twain wrote *Tom Sawyer*.
11. The United States Military Academy is located at West Point.
12. Most teenagers and many adults do not eat enough well-balanced meals.
13. Lewis and Clark are the greatest explorers America has produced.
14. Erosion by the Colorado River created the Grand Canyon.
15. Cats make better pets than dogs.
16. The first transcontinental trains used steam locomotives.
17. Railroad travel is fun.
18. Schools should make more use of television and movies.
19. The Canadian dollar does not always have the same value as the American dollar.
20. Most of today's cartoons are not really funny.

EXERCISE 2

Look at the topics listed below. For each of these topics write down *two* sentences. Make the first sentence a statement of fact. Try to get a rock-bottom fact that no one can disagree with. (Example: Over 600 students are enrolled in our school.) Make the second sentence a statement of a personal opinion. (Example: Our school is so big that many students are like strangers to me.)

1. Parks where I live
2. Homework
3. Football
4. Candy
5. Vacations
6. Our school building
7. A recent movie
8. Current popular music
9. Brothers or sisters
10. The local newspaper

Writing About Your Reading

Pretend that your school is doing a *survey of student opinion*. Write one paragraph for each item in the following opinion inventory.

1. Should schools have a dress code for students your age? Why, or why not? What kind of rules should there be? If there are no rules, would *anything* go?
2. Should the school do more to prevent theft or fights on the school grounds? What? Why?
3. What kind of books should teachers recommend to students your age? Can you name some books that *you* would recommend, and tell why?

Read several *letters to the editor* of a local newspaper or a school paper. What are the people in the community or school excited about? What are they expressing their feelings about? Prepare for the following writing activities:

1. Find a letter that takes a strong stand. Sum up in one sentence the writer's opinion or point of view. Then write two or three *more* sentences explaining how the writer backed up the opinion.
2. Can you find a letter whose author you disagree with? Write a few short sentences telling the author *why* you disagree. Or, can you find a letter that makes you cheer? Write a few short sentences telling the writer why you agree.

When an important issue comes up in your school or community, organize a *letter-writing contest*. Have the class vote on whose letter best *backs up* the opinion of the author. Send the best letter to the newspaper, or the mayor, or your representative in the state legislature or in Congress.

Write about what you have read.

C6
WRITING ABOUT YOUR READING

We often write about what we have seen with our own eyes. We write about things that have happened to us or to people we know well. But often a writer turns for information to a book or a magazine. Often something we read makes us think. A good writer knows how to make use of what others have written.

C6a
The Book Report

Write book reports that show how well you have read a book.

The book reports you write in school have a very practical reason: Your teachers want you to develop the reading habit. They want you to learn to read books on your own. A good reader keeps learning after leaving school—by reading newspapers, magazines, books. Book reports are a practical way of showing your teachers that you have read some of the books they want you to read.

Learn to write the kind of book report that selects one major incident or one major part of the book to show something important about the book. For instance, you may want to select

- the incident that showed the most courage, the greatest kindness, the most cowardice, the most resourcefulness, the most unexpected development.
- the incident that is most like an experience you've had.
- the incident that best sums up the message that the author has for the readers.

Remember:

(1) Convince your reader that you have read the book. Include specific details that only someone who has read the book would know. The details included in the following excerpt from a book report are the kind that come straight from the source:

BOOK REPORT A:

Johnny Tremain by Esther Forbes

The incident I'll remember longest is the one in which Johnny dined at the Afric Queen. He had been without food for nearly a day, and in his pocket was John Hancock's gift of silver coins. Johnny tormented his stomach by going from tavern kitchen to tavern kitchen to find the one which smelled best. He chose the Afric Queen, where the small squabs and pastries that he saw cooking made him feel that he had swallowed a live kitten. Here he ate, filling and overfilling his stomach. He ate five squabs, each stuffed with fragrant dressing and wrapped in bacon. He ate three apple tarts, three mince tarts, three pumpkin tarts, and three plum tarts, some jellied eels, and a tipsy parson. Whenever he saw a dish being prepared for some other diner, he ordered "some of that. . . ."

(2) Bring out what the incident shows about a major character or about the feelings of the author. Answer the question of the reader who asks, "What is the point?" In your own words, what is the point about dogs that is made in the following sample report?

BOOK REPORT B:

Travels with Charley by John Steinbeck

Travels with Charley is John Steinbeck's account of his trip by camper across the United States. Steinbeck's only companion was Charley, a poodle, who unexpectedly revealed his hidden killer instinct.

This hidden part of Charley's character came to the surface when they visited Yellowstone National Park. The park ranger on duty asked Steinbeck to safeguard Charley from bears by putting him on a leash. Steinbeck assured the ranger that Charley was a dog of "peace and tranquility," even a coward. He promised that Charley would cause no trouble in the bear world. Nevertheless, he agreed to lock Charley in the cabin of the camper.

Within a mile, they met their first bear. Suddenly, Charley bared his lips and charged the door in his efforts to get at the bear. His killer instinct, probably descended from wolf ancestors, came to the fore. He repeated the spectacle each time they met bears. When they came to a bearless stretch, Steinbeck transferred Charley to the house part of the camper. But the very next time they met a bear, Charley thrashed about, growling and shrieking. Steinbeck made a hasty decision. He sped back to the entrance of the park, leaving the natural wonders—including the bears—of Yellowstone behind. He stopped at the gate only long enough to apologize to the park ranger.

That night, Charley's dreams of killing bears disturbed his sleep, but the next day he was his usual mild-mannered self.

(3) If appropriate, quote the author or a major character in the book. Your readers will like to hear the voice of the original author, quoted word for word. Or they will like to see a sentence or two actually spoken by one of the characters. They then can form a better idea of that character as a person.

In Scott O'Dell's *Island of the Blue Dolphins,* a girl lives alone on an abandoned island. She has to protect her life against a pack of wild dogs. A high point of the story is reached when she wounds their leader but then decides not to kill him. You may want to quote what she says about how it happened and how she felt:

> . . . As the girl says, "Why I did not send the arrow I cannot say. I stood on the rock with the bow pulled back, and my hand would not let go." Later, she nurses the dog back to health. He becomes her friend, and she names him Rontu, which in her language means "Fox Eyes."

EXERCISE 1

In one or two sentences each, describe briefly three or four books you have read. Include something about the subject, or the area where it takes place, or the people in it. Sum up briefly what you most liked (or disliked) about the book.

EXERCISE 2

Choose one of the following for a book report. (Your teacher may add other possible choices.)

1. Scott O'Dell, *Island of the Blue Dolphins*
2. Thor Heyerdahl, *Kon-Tiki*
3. A book about Amelia Earhart
4. Francene Sabin, *Women Who Win*
5. Stories from Farley Mowat, *The Snow Walker*
6. A book of stories about the Greek gods, retold for young readers
7. A book about mountain climbers or about a famous climb
8. A book about a famous explorer or a famous journey of discovery
9. A book about a young athlete
10. A book about a struggle against illness or misfortune

C6b

The Digest of Information

Learn to summarize information from a printed source.

There are many occasions when you have to read for information and then make a written report on what you have learned. Such assignments require you to read accurately, so that you will not distort the information you pass on. They require you to select what is important. You can then give your reader the gist of what you have read.

When you summarize material, remember a basic rule: *Never simply lift whole sentences from a book and pass them off as your own.* When you do want to *quote* a whole sentence, put it in quotation marks and tell your reader who wrote it. In writing a digest, you select important information. Then you pass it on in your own words.

Here are the steps in preparing a digest of information from a single source:

(1) Identify your purpose. Let's assume that you've recently read stories about King Arthur, Roland, El Cid, and other knights of the Middle Ages. The emphasis on the nobility has made you curious about the peasantry. In their brief appearances, they always seemed to be suffering from abuse and hard work. You decide that your report will focus on the condition of the peasant. *How badly off were they?* This central question will guide you as you locate information and take notes. You will select facts that help you answer your central question.

(2) Find a promising source. Check in the catalogue of your library under the subject heading "Middle Ages." You will probably find promising titles like the following: *Life in the Middle Ages; Priest, Knight, and Peasant; Medieval People; The Medieval Village.* Check the Table of Contents at the front of each book to see what parts of the book might be devoted to the peasant's life. Check the Index at the back of each book under headings like "peasant" and "village." Sample some of the pages most directly concerned with your chosen topic. Select the book that seems to give the best treatment to your topic.

Suppose you find the following book, which turns out to be an excellent source of information:

Williams, Jay. *Life in the Middle Ages.* New York: Random House, 1966.

Here are some sample passages:

PASSAGE A:

The peasant may have deserved merit, but in the eyes of the rest of society he was little better than a beast, ugly, brutal, and dirty. "The peasant's head is so hard that no idea can get into it," observed one writer, while another said, "The Devil himself will not take peasants because of their fearful smell." . . . Thousands of them followed their masters to war as foot soldiers, but when a count was taken of the dead after a battle, nobody troubled to reckon up the number of slain commoners.

PASSAGE B:

Many were, in actual fact, slaves. They were bound to the land and could not leave it without the lord's permission. If the land passed to a new master, the bondsmen, or serfs, went with it. They could be sold or given away; indeed, a serf could be sold partly to one master and partly to another, as when the lord of Chauvigny, when some property was divided, got half a serf named Simon Gonneau, while the abbot of La Préhée got the other half. Serfs could not marry without the consent of their master, and the children of a serf were not called his family but his "litter." Like the litter of a sow, they could be taken from their parents and sold separately. If a serf won freedom from his master, for example by marrying a free person, then the lord had to get a payment for the loss of his property. The serf's main work was on the land, although he might do other kinds of service; he was subject to all sorts of duties and taxes, and even when he died these did not end, for his family had to pay a *heriot* or death tax. This consisted of the best bit of his property—his pig, or sheep, or a brass pot, if that was all he owned. . . .

PASSAGE C:

The cottages, to modern eyes, would look like nothing more than hovels. They were made of wattle-and-daub, a kind of lattice-work of strips of wood woven together and covered with plaster which was mostly mud. Their windows, if they had any, were small holes tightly shuttered most of the time against the weather; their floors were hard-stamped earth. The roofs were usually thatched with bundles of straw carefully pegged down on a framework of wooden rafters. . . .

(3) Take notes. First, read and study the material until you understand it. Second, take brief notes in your own words. The easiest way to handle your notes is to put your *subtopics* on separate pieces of paper or on separate index cards. Then jot under each subtopic the important items which are related to it. All unrelated material should be ignored. Third, determine the order in which to arrange your information.

For example, after studying the first thirty-seven pages of Jay Williams' *Life in the Middle Ages,* your notes might look like this:

SAMPLE NOTES

I. <u>His service to his lord</u>
  – thousands were foot soldiers
  – main work was on the land
  – paid all sorts of duties & taxes
  (death tax)

II. <u>His Home</u>
  – was in the feudal village near
  manor house, church, or roadside
  (for safety)
  – cottages were hovels
    made of wattle-and-daub, lattice-
    work of strips of wood covered
    with mud plaster – windows, if
    any, were small holes – earthen
    floor – roofs, thatched with
    straw tied down on wooden rafters

III. <u>His livelihood</u>
  – poor, suffering, beggarly
  – many were slaves, bound to the land
  – farmed strips of land – grain crops
  – shared grazing lands for cattle
  – geese foraged after haying
  – few possessions:
    vegetable gardens, fruit trees,
    few animals, some hens

(4) Write the report from your notes. As you write the report, you may want to shift some facts into a better place. Note that the three subtopics form the basis for three paragraphs. A clincher sentence is added to the third paragraph.

The peasant of the Middle Ages led a miserable life. Whether born free or a slave, every peasant rendered some kind of service to the lord. The main work of peasants was on the land, but they did all kinds of other work, too. In fact, thousands of peasants served as foot soldiers. Their loss in battle was ignored since they were considered scarcely human. Peasants had to pay all sorts of duties and taxes to the lord of the manor. When the peasant died, the family even had to pay a death tax. This final tax always took the best piece of property that the peasant owned. It might be a pig or a brass pot.

Peasants' homes were always built in clusters for safety's sake. The peasant villages might be built near the manor house, near the church, or beside a well-traveled road. The houses were small and crude. They were built of wattle-and-daub, which means that strips of wood were used to make lattice-work or wattle, which was then covered with mud plaster or daub. The roofs were thatched with straw which was tied down on wooden rafters. The few windows were simply small holes in the wall. The floors were hard, well-trampled earth. At their very best, the houses were still hovels.

All of the peasants were poor and suffering and beggarly. Some were slaves or serfs bound to the land and were bought and sold with it. They raised grain on strips of land, some of it rich, some stony. When the haying was over, some peasants were allowed to turn their geese into the mowed hay fields to forage. No peasant owned more than a small vegetable garden, a fruit tree or two, a pig, and a few hens. The peasants fed everyone else, but they lived the most miserable life of all.

In an encyclopedia or similar reference work, find several pages on one of the following topics. Prepare *one* page of notes. Include the points that seem most important to you. Choose one:

- the earliest methods of farming;
- American civilizations before Columbus;
- the original inhabitants of Australia or New Zealand;
- the early history of the movies;
- the invention of radio;
- early history of the Mormons;
- brass bands;
- systems of shorthand.

Prepare a digest of information on one of the topics listed below. Draw your material from *one* major source.

1. How a Boy Became a Knight
2. The History of the Cherokee Nation
3. The Great Irish Famine
4. How the Mormons Came to Utah
5. The Story of Amelia Earhart
6. The Campaigns of General Robert E. Lee
7. The First Railroad Across the Continent
8. The Origin of Astrology
9. The Career of Joe Louis or Marian Anderson
10. Benjamin Franklin, the Scientist

Learn to write neat and effective letters.

**C7
WRITING LETTERS**

Almost everyone writes letters. You may want to write to a relative who lives some distance from you. Or you may decide to write an invitation or a get-well card to a friend. Knowing how to write good *business* letters can also help you. You may need to write a business letter asking for information. Or you may want to order tickets, magazines, or supplies by mail. In short, the ability to write a good letter is a useful, practical skill that will benefit you throughout your life.

Write personal letters that you yourself would like to receive.

**C7a
Writing Personal
Letters**

It is fun to receive personal letters. We enjoy hearing from other people. We like to know what they are thinking, what they are doing, where they have been. We like to know that they have been thinking of us.

It can also be fun to write personal letters. There are no set rules for writing such letters. You can be yourself. You can simply "talk on paper." If you write the kind of letter you would like to receive, you will write good personal letters.

Here are a few pointers:

(1) Write legibly. Have you ever received a letter that read like a puzzle? Personal letters are fun to get, but not if they cannot be read. It is frustrating to try to figure out what someone else is saying. Do not ask your reader to be a mind reader. Take the time to write legibly—or type— especially if your handwriting is poor.

(2) Be neat. Avoid crossing out or erasing many words. Do not smudge or crinkle the paper. And use neat-looking paper. Leave margins on both sides, as well as at the top and bottom. If you forget to include something, do not try to squeeze it into the margins or between lines. Include it in a P.S. instead. (We use these letters before something added at the end.)

(3) Use plain stationery and blue or black ink, or type your letters. At one time, typed letters were thought to be less personal than handwritten ones. Today, however, most people do not object to typed friendly letters.

(4) Include your address. Write your address and the date in the upper right-hand corner. Even if you are writing to a friend, include your address inside the letter. That way, it is easier for the person to write you in return.

(5) Use the right punctuation and indentation. Use a comma after the greeting of personal letters, and indent your paragraphs. It is easier to read letters with indented paragraphs.

(6) Include a final greeting, called the "closing." It might be something as simple as *Love,* or *As always.* You might close with *Your friend, Your cousin,* or with some other phrase that tells your relationship to the person to whom you are writing. Common closings for persons you do not know well are *Sincerely* or *Sincerely yours.* Be sure to use a comma after the closing.

(7) *Always sign personal letters.* Write your name even if you have typed the letter. If you are sure the person will know who you are from your first name alone, you may use it. Otherwise, sign your full name.

Here is a personal letter extending an invitation:

PERSONAL LETTER

1212 Spring Avenue
Lansing, Michigan 48903
August 15, 1981

Dear Charlie,

    It seems forever since you moved away, even though it's really been only 8 weeks. We all miss you, and we'll miss you even more when we start playing football again. I know we won't find anybody who can catch passes the way you do.

    But I've got good news. The gang is having a picnic on Sunday during the Labor Day weekend, and I asked Mom and Dad if you could stay at our house over the holiday. They said they'd be happy to have you. You could even stay the whole weekend if you liked. You can sleep in Bob's room because he'll be away at college.

    Can you come? Please say yes. The whole crowd is waiting for your answer.

Your friend,

Jim

P.S. Mom said she could pick you up at the station any time Friday or Saturday morning.

WRITING TOPICS

Here are some ideas for personal letters you could write:

1. Write a real or imaginary thank-you letter to someone who has done something special for you or your family.

2. Write a letter to a relative who does not live near you. (If you have no such relative, make one up.) Tell the person what you have been doing at home and in school. Ask what the person has been doing. If the letter is to a real relative, send it.

3. Pretend you have received a birthday present from a friend. It is something you have always wanted. Write a letter thanking the person for the gift. Be sure to name the gift and be specific about your appreciation of it.

4. Write a letter to a teacher you had in a previous grade. Tell the teacher what you are learning in seventh grade and how you like it. Send the letter if you wish.

5. Write a letter to a favorite television or sports personality. Tell why you admire the person. Ask for an autographed picture. Send the letter, care of a television station, baseball park, or the like.

6. Write a personal letter to the mayor, the head of the school board, or some other official about a policy of which you approve or disapprove. Send it. (Your school or public librarian can help you to find the proper address.)

C7b
Writing Business Letters

Write business letters that do the job.

A business letter is a letter written to or from a place of business. It usually has one of the following jobs to do:

- Order something;
- Ask for an adjustment;
- Request information.

To get the job done, you must give *clear, exact, and complete information.* Try to put yourself in the place of the person receiving the letter. If *you* received it, would you be able to do what the letter-writer is asking?

Business letters should always be written on unlined sheets of 8½-x-11-inch white paper. They should be typed, if possible.

Study the following business letter. Can you see that
it has all the qualities of a good business letter?

BUSINESS LETTER

100 Cordell Court
Olivette, Missouri   63132
June 6, 1979

Municipal Theater Association
Forest Park
St. Louis, Missouri   63112

Gentlemen:

Enclosed is a check for forty dollars ($40) to cover sixteen
seats at two dollars and fifty cents each for the performance
of "West Side Story" on Saturday, June 16.

The seats may all be in one row, or they may be in a block,
but they must be together. We would prefer the center section,
as near the front as possible.

Please send the tickets to (Miss) Sherry Milton at the above
address.

Yours very truly,

Sherry Milton

Sherry Milton, Treasurer
Future Teachers of America
Dennis Cooper High School

In addition to giving clear, exact, and complete information, a good business letter follows a definite form. The parts of this form are discussed below:

HEADING AND GREETING

(1) RETURN ADDRESS: At least an inch from the top of the page, write your own address in the upper right-hand corner. Use a comma between your city and state. Write your zip code after the state, with space but no punctuation between the two.

(2) DATE: Write the date directly under your address. Be sure to use a comma between the day and the year.

(3) INSIDE ADDRESS: Drop down about three-quarters of an inch (4 or 5 spaces, if you are typing). On the left-hand margin, write the name (if known) of the person to whom you are writing. If the name is not known, write the name of the firm. Directly below the name, write the address, city, state, and zip code of the firm —exactly as you did your own address. Note: If the person to whom you are writing has a title —such as "President"—write it next to or on a separate line from his/her name.

(4) GREETING: Drop down about a quarter of an inch (2 spaces) and write your greeting directly below the inside address. Use a colon after the greeting. If you do not know the name of the person, write "Dear Madam or Sir:"

Here is an example of how this part of a business letter should look:

```
                                           1027 Coventry Drive
                                           Oxford, Ohio  45056
                                           July 27, 1980




        General Transportation Company
        200 Industrial Highway
        Dayton, Ohio  45411


        Dear Sir or Madam:
```

BODY

⑤ SPACING:		If you are writing the letter, use normal space between the lines. Leave extra space between paragraphs. If you are typing, single-space each paragraph. Use double-spacing between paragraphs, and after the greeting.
⑥ INDENTATION:		It is always all right to indent each paragraph. Some modern business letters now use **block format**. In this format, each paragraph starts on the left-hand margin. No indentation is used.
⑦ MARGINS:		Use about a one-inch margin on each side of the page.

CONCLUSION

⑧ **CLOSING:**   Business letters usually close with "Sincerely," "Sincerely yours," "Very truly yours," or "Yours truly." (Note that each closing is followed by a comma.) The closing is placed just to the right of the center of the page, a quarter of an inch (2 spaces) below the last line of the body.

⑨ **SIGNATURE:**   Always sign your full name in blue or black ink. Below your name, type or print it. The signature should be directly below the closing.

Here is an example of the conclusion of a business letter:

I hope I will hear from you soon.

Sincerely yours,

Thomas Triandos

Thomas Triandos

ADDRESSING THE ENVELOPE

⑩ **RETURN ADDRESS:**   Put your name and complete return address in the left-hand corner of the envelope.

(11) **RECEIVER:**   Put the receiver's address in the lower right-hand quarter of the envelope. Start it at about the middle of the envelope. Use block style. Make sure the address on the envelope is the same as the inside address.

Here is an example of a properly addressed envelope:

Helen Kennedy
12 High Street
Chicago, Illinois   60636

Mrs. Nancy Johns
Circulation Manager
Chicago Newspapers, Inc.
5500 Northern Avenue
Chicago, Illinois   60634

NOTE: Examine the sample business letter on the following page. Check your letters for conventional punctuation, especially the following:

- Put a comma between *city* and *state:* Tacoma, Washington
- Put a colon after the greeting
- Put periods after Mr., Ms., Mrs. (but not Miss), M.D.
- Put a comma between *day* and *year* if the day follows the month: April 17, 1983 (but 17 April 1983).

SAMPLE BUSINESS LETTER

return address ——→ 967 Delancy Street
Kansas City, Missouri 64105
date ——→ November 4, 1980

Mr. Charles Malden
Colorful Stamps, Inc.   ⎤
1221 Fifth Avenue   ⎬—— inside address
New York, New York 10020 ⎦

Dear Mr. Malden: ◄—— greeting

    On October 5, I wrote for your offer of 500 assorted
postage stamps. I received the stamps on October 25, and
I like them very much. However, your ad in the <u>Stamp Col-</u>
<u>lector</u> of September 28 promised five free triangle stamps
with each order. My triangles did not come with the rest
of my order, and I still have not received them.

    Could you tell me the reason for the delay? If you
have overlooked my triangle stamps, please send them to
me at the above address as soon as possible.

body
indented
format

Very truly yours, ◄—— closing

Regina M. Phelps ◄—— signature

Regina M. Phelps ◄—— typed name

208

FOLDING THE LETTER

(12) **FOLDING:**

First, bring the bottom third of the letter up and make a crease. Then, fold the top of the letter down close to the crease. Make a second crease. You should then have three roughly equal rectangles. Put the second creased edge into the envelope first.

Here is a drawing of the proper way to fold and insert letters:

Folding and Inserting Letters

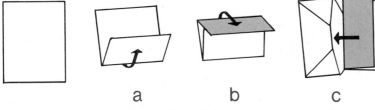

a   b   c

a. Bring the bottom third of the letter up and make a crease.
b. Fold the top of the letter down close to the crease you made in step *a*. Then make the second crease.
c. Put the creased edge you made in step *b* into the envelope first.

On a plain sheet of white paper, 8½ x 11 inches, arrange the following items in their proper positions on the page of a business letter. Correctly punctuate all items. (For the body of the letter, draw 15 straight lines. Para-

EXERCISE 1

graph these in indented style at the first, fifth, and tenth lines.)

CLOSING:	Sincerely yours
INSIDE ADDRESS:	Ms. Frances Miller/Hagen's Department Store/ Fifth Avenue at 24th Street/Albuquerque/ New Mexico/87108
GREETING:	Dear Ms. Miller
RETURN ADDRESS:	7601 Woodland Road/Atlanta/Georgia/30348
SIGNATURE:	(Use your own)

EXERCISE 2

Fold a piece of 8½ x 11 inch paper as if it were a letter. Open it up again and pretend that it is three separate envelopes. Write the following addresses, one on each third of the paper. Use a telephone book to obtain the addresses.

1. Address one envelope to the head librarian at a local public library. (Make up a name for the librarian, unless you know it.) Use your school address as the return address.
2. Address another envelope to the chief of police of your community. (Make up a name, unless you know it.) Use your own address as the return address.
3. Address a third envelope to a local medical doctor. Use a real name. Use the name of a local hospital as the return address.

EXERCISE 3

Write a letter in answer to the letter of Regina M. Phelps (page 208). Pretend you are Mr. Malden. Explain why her triangle stamps were not sent to her. Tell her what you are going to do. Make sure that your letter is clear and complete. Use the proper business-letter format.

EXERCISE 4

Find a magazine in your library to which you would like to subscribe. In the magazine, find the name and address of the person to whom you should write to obtain a subscription. Write a clear, accurate, and complete letter to that person, asking for more information about the magazine and about subscription rates. Observe proper business-letter format. Fold the letter properly. Address a real envelope or a piece of paper to the person to whom you are writing.

FOR FURTHER STUDY

USING YOUR IMAGINATION

Good writers are not always serious and business-like. They have an ear for words, and they sometimes try out the unusual or amusing things we can do with them. Good writers have to be able to use their imagination to imagine themselves in a different place, or in someone else's shoes. The following activities ask you to bring your own imagination and sense of humor into play.

ACTIVITY 1

The following poem does not have an important message. But it was probably fun to write, and it is fun to read.

> When I went out to see the sun
> There wasn't sun or anyone
> But there was only land and sea
> And lots of rain that fell on me
> And where the rain and river met
> The water got completely wet.
> —from Karla Kushkin, *In the Middle of the Trees*

Write an amusing poem that starts "When I went out . . ."

ACTIVITY 2

Readers in the Middle Ages enjoyed reading the "bestiary"—a collection of brief descriptions of real and imaginary animals. The following brief poems might form part of a modern bestiary. How can you tell they are not meant seriously? Write a poem that could become part of an amusing modern bestiary put together by the members of your class. Use one of the following as a model, or make up your own.

> Dogs in the country have fun.
> They run and run and run.
> But in the city this species
> Is dragged around on leashes.
> —from Ogden Nash, "An Introduction to Dogs"

How doth the little crocodile
  Improve his shining tail,
And pour the waters of the Nile
  On every shining scale!
                    —Lewis Carroll, "The Crocodile"

ACTIVITY 3

How often do you see a sign that was put up by someone with a sense of humor? Here are a few examples:

FIGHT SMOG—RIDE A HORSE
PAINTINGS CHEAP—ARTIST STARVING
YOUR EYES CHECKED WHILE YOU WAIT
(On a garbage truck) OUR BUSINESS IS PICKING UP
STAR VACUUM CLEANERS—WE'RE SWEEPING THE
  NATION
DON'T HONK—I AM PEDALING AS FAST AS I CAN

Collect a few such humorous inscriptions, or write your own.

ACTIVITY 4

A true story tells us something that really happened. An imaginary story is a story somebody made up. Often when we make up a story, we use details that are in some way true to life. But we give them an unusual twist. In each of the following student-written stories, what seems real? What is different or unusual? (What shows that the writers used their imagination?)

After you study these examples, write your own imaginary story. Use some real or lifelike details.

Whatever It Was

We lived in a trailer about five hundred feet from the graveyard, which really gave me the creeps.

My name was Bambie, my sister's name was Tammy, and my mother's name was Holly, or Mom as we often called her.

We had been living by the graveyard for nearly two months when Tammy got sick. This particular evening Mom had to go somewhere, so I had to stay home and watch Tammy. We went to bed early and were just going to sleep when I heard the chair in the living room fall over.

I got out Tam's knife and went out into the living room, but there was nobody there, so I went back to bed. I was just falling to sleep when I was awakened by the sound of our bedroom door opening. I then saw the strangest sight. I saw a glass of water and an aspirin come floating into the room and over to Tam. I told her to take it. After she had given the empty glass back to whatever it was, her blankets were pulled up to her chin, then the door was closed. But sometimes even now, someone or something does little things for my family.

A Short Basketball Player

The story I'm going to write about is the first thought that came into my mind. There was a short basketball player who had a lot of determination to be the best player on the floor. He was a good guard and could dribble very well. His shot was superb, but he had one handicap, which was his size. But that didn't stop him from trying. And he had the strongest determination of any person I have ever seen.

The game was about to start at center with a jump ball. He was starting at guard. The game continued slowly. By the way, I forgot to tell you his name is Jim. The game gradually got on. Jim had ten points at the end of the half. When the second half started he began to score. By the end of the third quarter, Jim had thirty points and he was getting rebounds. At the end of the game he had forty points. He was the hero. So his determination paid off.
—from B. Brenner, editor, *The Word*

ACTIVITY 5

Much writing expresses appreciation. People write about something they particularly like: gardening, stamps, a kind of person, a favorite pet, or the like. Do you sometimes feel like expressing what you think about something you do *not* like? Choose *one:*

- Not everyone likes animals, or even every animal or creature that he or she knows. Describe one animal that you are not particularly enthusiastic about. Explain why you respond the way that you do.
- Is there a kind of person or a kind of behavior that really annoys you? Explain how you feel and show why.

ACTIVITY 6

Have you ever felt that an ad or commercial was *overdone*? Can you imitate such an ad to show your reader its funny side? Study the following airline ad. Then write an ad or commercial that starts, "I always think of customers as . . ." Or, "I always think of my patients as . . ."

"I always think of the passengers as eggs. Sometimes our radar indicates a little rough air ahead. You know, the kind where you bounce a little. It has no effect on my control of the aircraft, but I'll still request clearance to get over it. Even if it means losing some time. Why?

"When I started 15 years ago, my first instructor told me something. He said, 'Always think of the passengers as thin-shelled eggs sitting back there on the floor. And your job is to get them from point A to point B without putting the tiniest crack in one of them.' I still take each bounce personally."

Captain Cliff is the kind of man who makes the best pilot because he's a concerned man. He does more than just his job. That's our way.

ACTIVITY 7

Being a reporter is hard work. But pretending that you are a reporter can be fun. Here are some activities for the amateur journalist.

1. Pretend you are a reporter covering a story about a robbery of your school during a weekend. The school's safe has been robbed, and the money in the cash register of the cafeteria has been stolen. Write down *ten questions* you would ask of the only witness to the robbery, the school janitor, who was bound and locked up by the robbers.

2. Write a short *news report* on something to which you were an eyewitness. (You may wish to assign each member of the class a different "beat" and then combine their reports in an imitation newspaper.)

Guide to Manuscript Revision

ab .... Spell out abbreviation (M6b)

adv .... Use adverb form (S1c)

agr .... Make verb agree with subject
        (or pronoun with antecedent) (S4a, S4c)

ap .... Use apostrophe (M4b)

cap .... Capitalize (M4a)

coll .... Use less colloquial word (U3c)

d .... Improve diction (W2)

dev .... Develop your point (C3b)

div .... Revise word division (M6a)

DM .... Revise dangling modifier (S4b)

frag .... Revise sentence fragment (M1a)

gr .... Revise grammatical form or construction (U1)

awk .... Rewrite awkward sentence (S4)

lc .... Use lowercase (M4a)

MM .... Shift misplaced modifier (S4b)

P .... Improve punctuation (M1-3)

¶ .... New paragraph (C2)

no ¶ .... Take out paragraph break (C2)

ref .... Improve pronoun reference (S4c)

rep .... Avoid repetition (U2a)

sl .... Replace slangy word (U3c)

sp .... Revise misspelled words (M5)

st .... Improve sentence structure (S4)

t .... Change tense of verb (U1d)

Chapter 4

Usage
Using Standard English

Chapter Preview 4

Use the right kind of English in your writing and in speaking to a group.

You can often say the same thing two different ways. Often, both ways will work equally well. Often, it will make little difference whether you say "Hi!" or "Hello!" But often your choice *will* make a difference. One choice will be right. The other choice will be wrong—or only *half*-right.

When you study **usage,** you study the choices that make a difference. In each of the following pairs, which is the right choice? Can you explain what *makes* it right?

(motorist to the judge)
(a) Well, bud, that's the silliest thing I ever heard.
(b) Well, Your Honor, I will have to disagree with that.

(tour guide to group of tourists)
(a) Them what's going get on the bus.
(b) Will those who are going with us please board the bus.

When we make the wrong choices in situations such as these, we produce the wrong reaction. People will wonder whether we have the background or the education necessary for the occasion. They will object because we do not sound serious or respectful enough.

When teachers ask for good English, they mean English that is good for serious purposes. They mean English "good for official use." To help you use good English, the following chapter deals with two basic kinds of usage choices:

(1) Learn to choose the forms and expressions of standard English. Standard English is "office English." At home, or with their friends, many Americans use *non*standard expressions. Many workers use nonstandard expressions on the job. But whenever you have any business outside your small group of friends or fellow workers, you need standard English. Standard English is the language of school, business, and government.

(2) Learn to use formal and informal English where appropriate. Within standard English, we can point out two major varieties. Formal English fits most writing and also serious discussion. In a formal committee report, you might write: "James Grimm was absent from school." Informal English is fine for friendly, relaxed talk. To a friend, you might say: "Jimmy skipped school today."

The following preview exercise deals with the most basic usage choice: between standard and nonstandard English. Which of the following sentences would be right for school English or office English? Put *S* for standard after the number of each such sentence. Which sentences would be out of place in school or office? Put *N* for nonstandard after the number of each such sentence.

EXAMPLE: She kept them rocks in a special box.
(Answer) *N*

1. I seen him yesterday.
2. He didn't do no homework last night.
3. How many men were there?
4. I hardly know them.
5. The weather is gooder today.
6. He my best friend.
7. We rarely go anywhere.
8. Tom taught himself a lesson.
9. They learning to drive.
10. Bring me those apples.
11. Charlotte never asked any questions.
12. Many women left the meeting early.
13. She look like her mother.

14. He knew everyone there.
15. I feel better now.
16. The boys was sitting on the fence.
17. Buy me some of them marbles.
18. The marbles cost twenty cents.
19. I have seen her recently.
20. My father don't remember you.
21. Suzette is our class president.
22. He gave hisself a haircut.
23. Ken usually runs more faster than that.
24. The teacher let us go home early.
25. She ain't talking to me.
26. Ben looks like his brother.
27. I borrowed the books from Laura.
28. The man he caught a big fish.
29. Some girls were sitting on the steps.
30. Frank gave them his address.
31. She returned it to the library.
32. I couldn't see it nowhere.
33. The helpers earned four dollar each.
34. Gil was sure of the answer.
35. Learn me how to do it.
36. Mother wouldn't leave me go out.
37. Mr. Hamilton could hardly get up.
38. We left on account of it was late.
39. The principal taught us how to fish.
40. We were still three mile from home.

U1

STANDARD ENGLISH: FUNDAMENTALS

Know the standard forms of English nouns, pronouns, and verbs.

The most important difference in usage is the difference between standard and nonstandard English. **Standard** English is school English, office English, and media English. You find standard English in most books, magazines, and newspapers. You hear it on news programs on radio and television. You need it when you fill in forms, write reports, or write business letters.

For many Americans, **nonstandard** English is the language of the home or of the neighborhood. It is the kind of English they hear and speak on the job. Nonstandard English is not "wrong" or inferior. For many people it is the most natural and comfortable kind of English in their everyday lives.

STANDARD ENGLISH: A Bird's-Eye View

PLURAL NOUNS:	men, women, children feet, teeth, mice knives, leaves, shelves ten years, two months

IRREGULAR VERBS:	go	went	have gone
	know	knew	have known
	bring	brought	have brought

REGULAR VERBS:	ask	asked	have asked
	solve	solved	have solved

THIRD PERSON, SINGULAR:	he knows, she drives, it works he *doesn't* know, it *doesn't* matter
COMPLETE VERBS:	she *is* waiting; we *were* sitting there; I *have* done it. where *have* you been? what *do* you know?

FORMS OF *Be*:	(Present)	I am, you are, he is, she is, it is, we are, you are, they are
	(Past)	I was, you were, he was, she was, we were, you were, they were

POINTING PRONOUNS: (demonstrative)	*this* door, *these* doors *that* trip, *those* trips
–self PRONOUNS: (reflexive)	he did it *himself;* they did it *themselves* you girls should do it *yourselves*
POSSESSIVE PRONOUNS:	*my* work and *yours* *his* glass and *hers*

COMPARISON:	he is *taller;* she is *tallest*
AVOIDING DOUBLE NEGATIVES:	he *never* said *anything;* she *could hardly* talk
An BEFORE VOWEL SOUNDS:	*an* apple, *an* hour, *an* A, *an* unusual event

Nevertheless, knowing standard English is important for people who want to hold their own in the world outside their family or group of friends. Teachers, office workers, doctors, business firms, social workers—all conduct their business in standard English. The person who cannot use standard English effectively is at a disadvantage. Do not let language put barriers in your way.

U1a
Standard Forms of Nouns

Use the standard plural forms of nouns.

Most nouns in English have at least two different forms. We use the **singular** when we talk about *one* thing. We use the **plural** when we talk about *more than one* thing:

SINGULAR:	one *girl*	one *church*	one *tree*
PLURAL:	many *girls*	many *churches*	many *trees*

SINGULAR:	one *box*	one *hero*	one *entrance*
PLURAL:	many *boxes*	many *heroes*	many *entrances*

Nouns regularly form their plurals by adding –*s* (or –*es*) to the plain form. (Note that the –*es* follows when the final letter of the plain form is *s,* or *ch,* or *x.*) But pay special attention to the following points:

(1) Some commonly used nouns have irregular plurals. Instead of the added –*s* or –*es,* there is a change in the word itself. Here are the most common irregular plurals:

SINGULAR:	one *man*	one *woman*	one *child*
PLURAL:	many *men*	many *women*	many *children*

SINGULAR:	one *foot*	one *tooth*	one *mouse*
PLURAL:	many *feet*	many *teeth*	many *mice*

(2) Some familiar, everyday nouns change f's *to* v's. Many nouns whose singulars end in *f* or *fe* form their plurals by changing the *f* to *v* and then adding –*s* or –*es.* The following are the most commonly used of these nouns:

SINGULAR:	one *half*	one *knife*	one *life*
PLURAL:	many *halves*	many *knives*	many *lives*

SINGULAR:	one *leaf*	one *loaf*	one *shelf*
PLURAL:	many *leaves*	many *loaves*	many *shelves*

(3) In standard English, the plural –s *is required for nouns that help state sums or measurements.* When talking

about money, distance, and time, nonstandard speakers often drop the plural ending. Standard English speakers do not. Compare the following pairs of sentences. Read the standard ones aloud.

NONSTANDARD: We paid eighty-five *cent*.
STANDARD: We paid eighty-five *cents*.

NONSTANDARD: She earned three *dollar* an hour.
STANDARD: She earned three *dollars* an hour.

NONSTANDARD: The town is about forty *mile* from here.
STANDARD: The town is about forty *miles* from here.

NONSTANDARD: It took three *year* to finish the building.
STANDARD: It took three *years* to finish the building.

NOTE: In standard English, the plural –s is left out when the noun is part of a combination that comes *before* another noun:

STANDARD: a *ten-dollar* shirt
STANDARD: a *three-day* trip
STANDARD: a *two-inch* layer

See **M4b** for the possessive form of nouns.

EXERCISE 1

If you have problems with plural forms, read over the following sets of sentences several times. Go back to them several times during the next few weeks. All of these sentences use the *right* form for standard English.

1. We put the *apples* in *boxes*. Many *churches* have several *entrances*. Many *neighbors* had several *cars* in their *garages*. *Bushes* lined the *roads*. There were long *lines* of *children* waiting for the *buses*.

2. *Men* and *women* worked in the plant. Several *children* had bad *teeth*. The two *women* were resting their *feet*. The children kept *mice* as *pets*. A *man* showed these *women* the way. A *woman* gave these *men* directions.

3. There were many *loaves* on the *shelves*. We used our *knives* to cut the *loaves*. They had raked the *leaves* from those *trees* all their *lives*. The two *halves* were still on the *shelf*.

4. It took us two *hours* to drive the forty *miles*. I added fifty *cents* to the two *dollars*. The strip was two *feet* long and ten *inches* wide. He has spent two *years* and three *months* in Mexico.

5. She added a ten-*cent* raise to my three-*dollar* wage. Everyone worked an eight-*hour* day. She was cutting the material into three-*inch* strips. We finished the twenty-*mile* hike in about six *hours*.

Decide whether a singular or a plural noun is needed in the answers to the following questions. Write the standard form after the number of the sentence.

1. Did the dentist pull only one tooth? No, he pulled two _____ .

2. Were there two women in the office? No, there was only one _____ .

3. Did you see a man there? Yes, I saw several _____ .
4. Was the board ten feet long? No, it was fifteen _____ long.
5. Was this child invited? No, but many other _____ were.
6. Doesn't that man look familiar? Yes, he looks like many other _____ I've seen.
7. Is he six feet tall? No, he's hardly five _____ tall.
8. How many false teeth does he have? He has about ten false _____ .

9. How many women came to the meeting? Five _____ came to the meeting.
10. Did you call both children? Yes, but only one _____ came.
11. Isn't the turnoff about a mile from here? No, it's at least two _____ .
12. Did anyone bring a knife? Yes, we have several _____ .
13. Do seat belts ever save anyone's life? Yes, they save many _____ .

14. Do you have any souvenirs for a dollar? No, everything costs at least two or three _____ .
15. Are both halves of the program equally good? No, the first _____ is more exciting.

Look at the noun in parentheses that follows each sentence. What form of that noun would you use to fill the blank in the sentence? Write the standard form for the blank space after the number of the sentence.

EXAMPLE: My younger brother has several new _____ .
(tooth)
(Answer) *teeth*

1. We were still many _____ from our goal. (mile)
2. The two _____ of the orange had disappeared. (half)
3. The voters were angry because of two new _____ . (tax)
4. Several _____ were waiting for the bus. (woman)
5. We saw a _____ in overalls next to the car. (man)
6. The flag was flying from a ten-_____ pole. (foot)
7. Most _____ love the outdoors. (child)
8. Her aunt had paid her five _____ for helping out. (dollar)
9. He had never seen a two-_____ bill. (dollar)
10. A _____ had been hired to take his place. (woman)
11. The arrow had missed the target by several _____ . (inch)
12. We just had all our kitchen _____ sharpened. (knife)
13. Three _____ were talking together on the porch. (man)
14. Five _____ separated the house from the fence. (foot)
15. The tree was dropping all its _____ . (leaf)
16. Fangs are long and sharp _____ . (tooth)
17. Her sister was fifteen _____ old. (year)
18. Both of my aunts were _____ with a sense of humor. (woman)
19. Hawks hunt _____ and other small animals. (mouse)
20. I lost my way among the _____ in the large library. (shelf)

Use the standard forms of pronouns.

Standard English uses pointing (or **demonstrative**) pronouns like *these* and *those*. It uses *–self* (or **reflexive**) pronouns like *himself* and *themselves*. It uses **possessive** pronouns like *yours* and *hers*.

Here is a chart of pronoun forms required in standard English:

POINTING (demonstrative)	*–Self* (reflexive)	POSSESSIVE (two sets)	
this that	myself yourself himself herself itself	my your his her its	mine yours his hers its
these those	ourselves yourselves themselves	our your their	ours yours theirs

SINGULAR

PLURAL

Remember:

(1) Use the standard pointing pronouns: this *and* that, these *and* those. Do not use *them* as a pointing pronoun. Expressions like *them books* or *them papers* are nonstandard. Do not put the words *here* or *there* between the pronoun and a noun. Expressions like *this here door* or *that there car* are nonstandard. Use *this* and *that* to point to one thing. Use *these* and *those* to point to several things.

Read aloud the following sentences, in which pointing pronouns are used in their standard forms:

Bring me *that book.*
Take him *this book.*
Lend her *these books.*
Leave me *those books.*

I go to *that school.*
She goes to *this school.*
My father has gone to *these schools.*
My mother has gone to *those schools.*

I saw *that man* yesterday.
I have seen *this man* before.
Who has seen *these men?*
He has seen *those men.*

(2) Use –self *and* –selves *in the right combinations.* To use the standard form of the *–self* pronouns, do two things. First, add *–self* to singular pronouns and *–selves* to plural pronouns. Secondly, choose the right combination. Only the following forms are standard:

SINGULAR: myself, yourself, himself, herself, itself
PLURAL: ourselves, yourselves, themselves

Hisself, theirself, and *theirselves* are nonstandard. Practice the standard forms by reading the following sentences aloud:

I have done *myself* a favor.
Don't get *yourself* in trouble, Bill.
Frank taught *himself* judo.
Linda had hurt *herself.*
The problem had solved *itself.*
We planned the picnic by *ourselves.*
Take care of *yourselves,* boys.
The children baked *themselves* a cake.

(3) With the exception of mine, *do not use an* –n *sound at the end of possessive pronouns.* These pronouns show where or to whom something belongs. The words *yourn, hisn, hern, ourn,* and *theirn* are nonstandard. Avoiding the *–n* forms becomes important when a possessive is used alone, *without* a following noun. Choose the *–s* forms for this use:

I did *my* homework.	I did *mine.*
Your book is there.	*Yours* is there.
He began *his* lesson.	He began *his.*
Her lesson has begun.	*Hers* has begun.
Give the cat *its* milk.	Give the cat *its.*
Our school is closed.	*Ours* is closed.
Their school is open.	*Theirs* is open.

Practice the standard form of possessive pronouns by reading aloud the following sentences:

Did he take *mine?*
No, he took *yours.*
Where is *his?*
He borrowed *hers.*
Does he want *ours?*
No, he wants *theirs.*

Mine is better than *yours.*
Ours is better than *theirs.*
Hers is better than *his.*

That book is my book, not *yours.*
These pens are our pens, not *theirs.*
This money is *his,* not *hers.*
Those records are *mine,* not *ours.*

NOTE: Do *not* add an apostrophe before the *–s* at the end of these words. Apostrophes go with the possessives of *nouns:* the *man's* hat, the *woman's* coat, the *boy's* books. But with *pronouns,* no apostrophe is used: *yours, his, hers, its, ours, theirs.*

See **U3a** for pronoun case: *I/me, he/him, we/us.*

Do you have trouble with standard pronoun forms? If so, read over the sentences in the sets on the following page several times. Read them out loud if possible. Go back to this exercise several times during the next few weeks.

EXERCISE 1

1. *This pen* doesn't write well. *That pen* writes better. *These children* went last week. *Those children* haven't gone yet. You should watch *this show*. Be careful of *that ice*. I have seen all *these pictures*. Bring me *those tools*. *This piece* doesn't fit in the puzzle. *That piece* does fit. *These students* have done good work. *Those workers* have learned their trade well.

2. He bought it *himself*. They went there *themselves*. Think of *yourself*, Tom. We saw *ourselves* in the mirror. Did you girls see *yourselves* in the mirror? He made *himself* a copy. The girls made the posters *themselves*. We congratulated *ourselves*. Practice the exercise by *yourselves*. The animal defended *itself*. George taught *himself* how to hunt.

3. They *themselves* solved all the problems. The king *himself* will speak. You *yourself* will have to make your bed. You boys *yourselves* will have to clean the room.

4. She used *her* tools, and he used *his*. They did *their* work, and we did *ours*. *Her* story was more interesting than *yours*. Sam said that *hers* was less interesting. *Our* car is newer than *theirs*. The wrench is *mine*, not *yours*. The record is *hers*, not *his*. The plan was *theirs*, not *ours*. *Mine* costs fifty cents. *Yours* is more expensive. *His* is the most expensive of all.

5. *This* bag is *mine*. *That* bag is *yours*. *These* bags are *theirs*. *Those* bags are *ours*. Don't get *those* bags mixed with *theirs*. *His* is on *that* desk. *Hers* is on *this* desk. Are *these* magazines *yours*? No, *those* magazines are *his*. Is *this* pencil *mine*? No, *that* pencil is *hers*. *Those* notes are *ours*. *These* notes are *theirs*.

EXERCISE 2

After the number of each sentence or passage, write the pronoun asked for in the instructions. Use only standard forms. (Write on a separate sheet.)

A. If the pointing pronoun in the first part of the sentence is *this*, use *that* to fill the blank, and vice versa. Do the same for *these* and *those*.

1. Don't do it *that* way; do it _____ way.
2. I wanted *those* tools, not _____ tools.
3. I like *this* album better than I liked _____ one.
4. *These* answers are wrong, but _____ answers are right.
5. I don't want *that* pie; I would like _____ one.
6. Zelda likes *these* apples, but not _____ .
7. If you take *this* road, you will get there sooner than if you take _____ one.

8. Sam collects *these* kinds of stamps, not _____ kinds.
9. *That* problem was easier to solve than _____ problem.
10. Drivers used to use *those* plugs; now they use _____ .

B. Use *myself, yourself, himself, herself, itself, ourselves, yourselves,* or *themselves* to fill the blanks:

11. Can I do that alone? Yes, you can do it _____ .
12. Will members collect the tickets? Yes, they will collect the tickets _____ .
13. Who hurt Gloria? Gloria hurt _____ .
14. Who grew the celery? The celery grew by _____ .
15. Can I build that alone? Yes, I can build it _____ .
16. Who will paint the room? You will paint it _____ .
17. Did she wire that radio? Yes, she wired it _____ .
18. Will he help deliver the papers? No, we will deliver them _____ .
19. Who bought the toys for the children? They bought them _____ .
20. Who will introduce us newcomers? You newcomers will introduce _____ .

C. Fill in *mine, yours, his, hers, its, ours,* or *theirs.*

21. This lunch is mine, isn't it? Yes, it is _____ .
22. Do these letters belong to him? No, they are not _____ .
23. Were those books hers? No, they were not _____ .
24. Was that new car theirs? No, it was not _____ .
25. Do these belong to you two? Yes, they are _____ .
26. I rode my bike to school; did you boys ride _____ ?
27. We found her coat, but I couldn't find _____ .
28. I did my work; did you do _____ ?
29. We painted our house after the neighbors painted _____ .
30. They bought a new car after we bought _____ .

After the number of each sentence, write the *–self* pronoun that would fit in the blank space. Use standard forms only.

EXERCISE 3

EXAMPLE: We had to find the right house by _____ .
(Answer) *ourselves*

1. Rita taught _____ how to play the piano.
2. You boys may get _____ into trouble.
3. Because he never got any mail, he wrote _____ a letter.
4. Will you come by _____ , Bill?
5. The children were talking among _____ .
6. The team had earned _____ its first victory.

7. The coaches _____ were amazed.
8. Why are you standing there by _____, Mary?
9. The students worked on the project by _____.
10. Tommy found _____ a new friend.
11. I am going to buy one of those bikes for _____.
12. Time solves many problems all by _____.
13. Freddy talks to _____ in his sleep.
14. They had locked _____ in.
15. Is she going to the dance by _____?
16. My grandparents _____ had built the fences.
17. You girls _____ should have filled in the forms.
18. We _____ paid for all the equipment.
19. George ate the whole pizza by _____.
20. You _____, Lillian, should have taken the package.

U1c

Irregular Verbs

Know the sets of basic forms for irregular verbs.

How often do you hear the forms below? Do you ever use them yourself? If so, learn to use the forms that take their place in standard English.

He *knowed* all the answers.
They had already *went* home.
You could have *wrote* to me.

Many of our verbs come in sets of three basic forms. Each basic form is for a different **tense.** It signals a different relationship in *time.* The first form is for action *now* (also for action taking place all the time). The "now" form is called the **present tense.** The second form is for action that is "past and done." This form is the **past tense.** The third form combines with the auxiliary *have (has, had).* It is often used for action just completed, or for *past* action that still matters *now.* Together with *have,* this form is used for the **perfect tense.** Here are typical sets of three:

PRESENT:	They *speak* Spanish.	(now or regularly)
PAST:	They *spoke* only when asked.	(in the past)
PERFECT:	I have *spoken* to Jim about it.	(recently)

PRESENT:	I *know* your brother.
PAST:	He *knew* my grandmother.
PERFECT:	I have *known* your father for many years.

PRESENT:	His parents *go* to church.
PAST:	Her aunt *went* back to Italy.
PERFECT:	The engine has *gone* dead.

At one time, most English verbs followed this pattern. But gradually a simpler pattern began to take over. For many English verbs, we now simply use the ending spelled *–ed* (or *–d*) for *both* past and perfect:

PRESENT: We *help* our neighbors.
PAST: He *helped* me last year.
PERFECT: She *has* often *helped* me.

We call the verbs that follow the simple *–ed* pattern **regular** verbs. We call the verbs that do *not* follow this pattern **irregular.** Irregular verbs go their own way. They have three basic forms that we have to learn and remember separately. Study the basic forms of common irregular verbs in the chart that goes with this section. Take up one group at a time. Make sure you know the standard forms for each of these common verbs. Remember:

*(1) Do not use the –*ed *ending with irregular verbs.* In standard English, we do not use the *–ed* (or *–d*) with *grow, know, throw, blow,* and *catch. Growed, knowed, throwed, blowed,* and *catched* are all nonstandard:

My uncle *knew* (not *knowed*) him well.
We *grew* (not *growed*) our own potatoes.
He *threw* (not *throwed*) the bat accidentally.
Doris *blew* (not *blowed*) the candle out.
She *caught* (not *catched*) the ball.

(2) Pay special attention to verbs where the standard form is different for past and perfect. The following are all past forms: *broke, went, stole, took, wore, wrote.* All the following combinations are nonstandard: had *went,* might have *took,* has *wore,* have *wrote.*

PAST	PERFECT
We *went* home.	They *have gone* back.
I *took* the test.	She *has taken* the wrong turn.
My friend *wrote* regularly.	I *have written* to the agency.

(3) Find the verbs that give you special trouble. Do you use *brang* as the past of *bring,* instead of *brought*? Do you use *run* or *begun* in the past instead of *ran* and *began*?

STANDARD FORMS: Irregular English Verbs

	PRESENT	PAST	PERFECT
GROUP 1	begin	began	have begun
	bend	bent	have bent
	blow	blew	have blown
	break	broke	have broken
	bring	brought	have brought
	buy	bought	have bought
	catch	caught	have caught
	choose	chose	have chosen
	come	came	have come
GROUP 2	dig	dug	have dug
	do	did	have done
	draw	drew	have drawn
	drink	drank	have drunk
	drive	drove	have driven
	eat	ate	have eaten
	fall	fell	have fallen
	fly	flew	have flown
	freeze	froze	have frozen
GROUP 3	get	got	have gotten, got
	go	went	have gone
	grow	grew	have grown
	know	knew	have known
	ride	rode	have ridden
	run	ran	have run
	say	said	have said
	see	saw	have seen
	sing	sang	have sung
GROUP 4	speak	spoke	have spoken
	steal	stole	have stolen
	swim	swam	have swum
	swing	swung	have swung
	take	took	have taken
	tear	tore	have torn
	throw	threw	have thrown
	wear	wore	have worn
	write	wrote	have written

Copy the set of three forms for such verbs on a card or piece of paper. Add some short sample sentences for present, past, and perfect. Study these special memory helps till the right forms have beome second nature.

Do you have trouble with basic forms of irregular verbs? Read aloud the sentences in the following sets of three several times. Come back to this exercise several times during the next few weeks.

EXERCISE 1

1. We *begin* school at 8:30.
   The movie *began* at 9 o'clock.
   I *have begun* my homework.

2. They *break* records all the time.
   Our team *broke* a record yesterday.
   Someone *has broken* a bottle.

3. Our cats *come* when we call.
   The doctor *came* this morning.
   How many people *have come* so far?

4. We always *do* our best.
   We *did* everything by ourselves.
   Donna *has done* her share.

5. We never *eat* before 6 P.M.
   They *ate* early last night.
   The children *have eaten* the cake.

6. Rains *fall* often on the plain.
   Snow *fell* yesterday.
   Both rain and snow *have fallen* today.

7. We *give* money to charity.
   The teacher *gave* the students some help.
   Pete *has given* up.

8. I *go* to the movies every Saturday.
   Last Saturday, I *went* alone.
   They *have gone* out already.

9. Cheetahs *run* fast.
   We *ran* a race yesterday.
   They *have run* out of gas.

10. She *says* that all the time.
    Last time, he *said* "no."
    The accused *has said* nothing.

11. I *see* the point now.
    She *saw* him last night.
    I *have seen* her often.

12. We always *take* the shortcut.
    Who *took* my book?
    The patient *has taken* his medicine.

EXERCISE 2

In each of the following sets, a verb appears first in the present tense (action now). Supply the past and perfect forms for the blank spaces. Write the two forms after the number of the set.

1. Winds *blow* hard along the coast. Last October, gale winds _____ down a summer cottage. Sometimes they have _____ fishing boats out to sea.

2. Hurricanes *tear* through the Everglades. Last fall they _____ up acres of almond trees. They have _____ roofs off houses.

3. Animals *run* from the storms. During last week's storm, a herd of deer _____ across the state highway. A herd has _____ as far as five miles.

4. Frightened animals *choose* a place of shelter. Three years ago, a family of porcupines _____ my aunt's basement. Wild boars have _____ tall haystacks.

5. Trees *fall* in high winds. In a thunderstorm ten days ago, a willow _____ across the pond. A tall oak has _____ in our neighbor's yard.

6. Flocks of ducks *fly* before a storm. Large flocks _____ overhead yesterday. Thousands had _____ inland before.

7. Waves *grow* in high winds. They _____ to a height of fifty feet last March. Waves in the bay have _____ to a height of sixty feet.

8. Smart people *take* cover in gales. A group _____ refuge in a local factory last year. Others have _____ shelter in schools and churches.

9. Old-timers *know* these storms. They _____ that last year's blow would come. Old Mr. James has _____ the worst storms of the past.

10. People *go* to high ground. Ten years ago, they _____ to the mainland. Some have _____ as far as fifty miles away.

After the number of each question, write the standard form that would fit the blank space in the answer. Use the same verb that is used in the question, but change its form where necessary. (Do *not* add any auxiliaries.)

EXAMPLE: Did you *wear* your coat? Yes, I _____ it.
(Answer)   *wore*

1. Did you *write* this note? Yes, I _____ it.
2. Have you *written* to her? No, I have not _____ yet.
3. Did you *tear* this out? No, Pam had already _____ it out.
4. Have you *seen* her new pet? No, I haven't _____ it yet.
5. Did anyone *see* the burglar? Yes, Jim _____ him.
6. How long ago did it *run* away? It _____ away last week.
7. How long have you *known* him? I have _____ him for years.
8. Did anyone *know* the answer? Yes, Rita _____ it.
9. Did anyone in the class *go?* Yes, Ted _____ this morning.
10. Has he *gone* away? Yes, he has _____ .
11. Did your father *drive* you home? Yes, he _____ me.
12. How many people *came* to the party? All my friends _____ .
13. Did anyone *catch* the fly? No, no one _____ it.
14. Did you *bring* your book with you? Yes, I _____ it.
15. What *blew* down the tree? The wind _____ it down.
16. Who *threw* it out? The custodian _____ it out.
17. Have you *thrown* out the rag? Yes, I have _____ it out.
18. Have you *taken* your medicine? Yes, I have _____ it.
19. Did you *speak* up? Yes, I _____ up.
20. Did you *say* no? No, I _____ yes.

Use the –s and –ed endings where appropriate when speaking or writing standard English.

Do you ever hear the following forms? Do you ever use them yourself? If so, study and practice the way *verb endings* are used in standard English.

The story *end* happily.
He *come* over here often.
She *finish* the job already.
They *was* waiting for us.

In standard English, each of the italicized verbs would need an ending—either –s (sometimes spelled –es), or –ed (sometimes spelled –d). Leaving off these endings will turn many of your verbs into nonstandard forms.

Remember:

(1) Add the –s to the present when you talk about one person or thing. The *–s* goes with the forms we use for "action now." Use it when you are talking about a single third party (or a single thing). Use a simple test: The verb has the *–s* ending when you can put one of the **third person** pronouns in place of the subject: *he, she,* or *it.*

STANDARD: My sister *works* in a drive-in. (*She* works.)
The store *closes* at five. (*It* closes.)
Her husband *sells* cards. (*He* sells them.)

There is no *–s* ending when you shift from *one* "third party" (**singular**) to *several* (**plural**). The verb has no *–s* when you can put *they* in place of the subject. Nor is there any *–s* when the subject is *I, we,* or *you:*

STANDARD: My sisters *live* at home. (*They* live there.)
The stores *close* at five. (*They* close.)

STANDARD: I often *say* "maybe."
We *live* in an old house.
You *owe* us five dollars.

Look for third person, singular, in the chart below:

		SINGULAR	PLURAL
PRESENT	**first person:**	I know	we know
	second person:	you know	you know
	third person:	he *knows*	they know
		she *knows*	
		it *knows*	

When you add the *–s, do* turns into *does. Don't* turns into *doesn't:*

SINGULAR: Smith *does* his job well. (*He* does.)
Irma *doesn't* care. (*She* doesn't.)
The price *doesn't* matter. (*It* doesn't.)

PLURAL: Her sisters *do* the work. (*They* do.)
My friends *don't* care. (*They* don't care.)

Practice using the *–s* ending by reading the following sentences aloud. Each sentence talks about one third party, with "action now."

He *asks* too many questions.
Pablo *saves* his money.
The motor *runs* better than it used to.
She *doesn't* live here anymore.
My friend *knows* the answer.
He always *says* "no."

NOW AND THEN

A. Do you have trouble with the –*s* ending? Use the –*s* ending when you tell us what *one* person does. Complete the following sets of sentences. Use the –*s* ending for each word that shows "action now."

1. A driver *walks* to her car. She *opens* the door. A driver _____ . Then she _____ . She _____ . A driver usually _____ . When she comes to a light, she _____ . A driver also _____ .
2. A teacher _____ . (Add several sentences about what a teacher does.)
3. A custodian _____ . . .
4. A pilot _____ . . .
5. A gardener _____ . . .

B. Do you have trouble with the –*ed* ending? Complete the following sets of sentences. Tell us what the following people used to do. Use only verbs that have an –*ed* ending for the past tense.

6. Cowhands *lived* on ranches. They _____ cattle. They _____ horses. They _____ hard for their wages. They _____ poachers. They _____ steers.
7. Blacksmiths *tended* forges. They _____ horseshoes. They _____ white-hot metal into shape. They _____ horses. They _____ swords. They _____ metal utensils.
8. Pioneers *started* a new life. They _____ the mountains. They _____ the streams. They _____ in new territories. They _____ their children there.
9. Sheriffs *enforced* the laws. They _____ criminals. They _____ thieves. They _____ taxes.
10. Minstrels *wandered* across the land. They _____ tales. They _____ their listeners. They _____ legends. They _____ the people.

(2) Add the –ed *(or* –d) *for the past unless the verb shows past in some other way.* Remember that many verbs show past action by a change in the verb itself: *go—went, know—knew, speak—spoke, grow—grew, catch—caught.* But most other verbs use the *–ed* ending instead. Do not leave out the *–ed* ending in sentences with regular verbs like the following:

STANDARD: Last Sunday he ask*ed* me for a ride.
Yesterday she finish*ed* early.
He call*ed* his mother at Christmas.
Fred sav*ed* my life last year.
Buffalo roam*ed* the prairies for centuries.
The club cancel*ed* our last meeting.
My sister start*ed* the engine.
The British oppos*ed* the American demand for independence.

(3) Use standard forms of be. Like other verbs, *be* has a special form for use in talking about one "third party" (third person, singular):

SINGULAR: The girl *is* his sister. (*She* is.)
PLURAL: The girls *are* his sisters. (*They* are.)

SINGULAR: Travel *is* cheaper now. (*It* is.)
PLURAL: Potatoes *are* starchy. (*They* are.)

SINGULAR: The boy *is* a camper. (*He* is.)
PLURAL: The boys *are* scouts. (*They* are.)

Be is the only English verb that has a separate form for third person singular for the present and for the *past:*

SINGULAR: The party *was* fun. (*It* was.)
PLURAL: The parties *were* fun. (*They* were.)

SINGULAR: His father *was* from Mexico. (*He* was.)
PLURAL: His parents *were* from Mexico. (*They* were.)

In addition, *be* is the only verb that has a special form for use with *I (first* person, singular): "I *am* (I'm) your friend." Remember that nonstandard English uses *is* and *was* in many situations where standard English requires other forms. *You is, we is,* and *they is* are nonstandard. *You was, we was,* and *they was* are all nonstandard.

Study the standard forms of the verb *be* in the chart on the following page:

	SINGULAR	PLURAL	
first person: second person: third person:	I am here you *are* here he is here she is here it is here	we *are* here you *are* here they *are* here	PRESENT
first person: second person: third person:	I was there you *were* there he was there she was there it was there	we *were* there you *were* there they *were* there	PAST

Practice the right forms by reading the following sample sentences out loud:

You *were* late again.
The musicians *are* getting ready.
We *were* shown to the wrong room.
They *were* in the middle of a rehearsal.
We *are* never invited.
I *am* always the first one there.
You *are* supposed to reply.

All of the examples in the following sets use the *right* verb forms for standard English. Read over the sentences in each set several times. (Read them out loud if you can.) Come back to this exercise for additional practice during the next few weeks.

EXERCISE 1

1. It *takes* about a week to drive across the country. The plane *takes* less time. My doctor *sees* many patients. Chuck *sees* the point. Jim *tells* good stories. He *tells* them to his friends. A clock *tells* time. Edith *seems* happy today. She *seems* to have recovered. Fred *looks* sad. Here *comes* the rain.

2. Emma *says* she likes the new typing teacher. I *say* the opposite. Our family *goes* everywhere together. I *go* with them.

3. The clock *doesn't* work. The engine *doesn't* start. She *doesn't* know. It *doesn't* matter. We *don't* care. You *don't* understand. He *doesn't* mind. When she *doesn't* know the answer, she says so. I *don't* know the rules, but he *doesn't* either.

4. I *expected* them yesterday. Who *called* the police? Jim *saved* his money. They *reported* to the scoutmaster. He *finished* everything on time. Jim *liked* the pie. Everybody *enjoyed* the movie. She *loved* to watch football games. Lenny *picked* up his books. It *looked* good. We *watched* them playing ball. They *raced* yesterday. The coach *timed* the runners.

5. I *am* here. You *are* there. He *is* my friend. She *is* my sister. We *are* good friends. They *are* friendly. The animal *is* hungry. The clothes *are* new. The girls *are* tired. Your shirts *are* ready.

6. I *was* absent yesterday. You *were* right. She *was* wrong. It *was* ready. We *were* sad. They *were* happy. You *were* funny. The theaters *were* closed. All of you *were* invited. The boys *were* acting silly. You *were* expected later. I *was* amazed.

EXERCISE 2

Do you know when to add the *–s* at the end of a verb? After the number of each sentence, put the right form of the word in parentheses. Use a form for the *present*—"action now." Use the form that would fit into the blank in the sentence. (Use the *–s* only if *he, she,* or *it* can take the place of the subject.)

EXAMPLE: My uncle _____ television sets. (repair)
(Answer) *repairs*

1. The show _____ at 8:30. (begin)
2. He always _____ the truth. (tell)
3. Peggy _____ adventure stories. (like)
4. They usually _____ lunch in school. (eat)
5. Those boys _____ to school on the bus. (ride)
6. Which one _____ better? (throw)
7. It _____ time to learn. (take)
8. The sign _____ "Keep Out." (say)
9. The dog always _____ for its master. (look)
10. I usually _____ better work. (do)
11. He sometimes _____ home late. (come)
12. They _____ cotton on their farm. (grow)
13. The teacher _____ how to fix it. (know)
14. They often _____ mistakes. (make)
15. My mother _____ a bus. (drive)
16. Our visitors usually _____ many fish. (catch)
17. The weather _____ good today. (seem)
18. You _____ the prize. (get)
19. Today I _____ my new job. (begin)
20. We _____ our groceries at the corner store. (buy)

Do you know when to put the *–ed* (or *–d*) at the end of a verb? After the number of each sentence, put the right form of the verb in parentheses. Use a form for the *past*. Use the form that would fit into the blank in the sentence. (Some of the verbs show their past by changes *other* than the added ending.)

EXERCISE 3

EXAMPLE: Angelina hardly ever _____ her car. (wash)
(Answer) *washed*

1. The girl _____ for an hour. (wait)
2. The students _____ the principal for a holiday. (ask)
3. They _____ that they were right. (know)
4. Jackson _____ ten dollars in dimes. (save)
5. The Johnsons _____ away for the summer. (go)
6. All the leaves _____ from the tree. (fall)
7. Jim _____ Edna to the rehearsal. (invite)
8. The farmers _____ wheat last year. (grow)
9. He never _____ with us. (argue)
10. The coach was fired because he _____ chances. (take)
11. The movie _____ almost two hours. (last)
12. He _____ much better yesterday. (look)
13. The man _____ his shoes under the sofa. (throw)
14. I _____ the gift to the store. (return)
15. He _____ us to slow down. (advise)
16. The storm _____ the shutters off the windows. (blow)
17. Love _____ into their hearts. (steal)
18. The climber _____ himself before he fell. (catch)
19. You _____ us a ride to the fair. (promise)
20. He always _____ at himself in the mirror. (stare)

Do you know the standard forms of *be?* After the number of each sentence, write a form of *be* that would fill the blank. (Use a single word each time.)

EXERCISE 4

A. Use a form that shows *present* time:

1. We _____ proud of our town.
2. Sheila _____ president of the club.
3. All my friends _____ members.
4. You _____ welcome at our meetings.
5. His parents _____ old-fashioned.
6. I _____ usually a happy person.
7. They _____ always on time.
8. The stores _____ already closed.
9. Dinosaurs _____ extinct.
10. The zoo _____ open on Sundays.

B. Use a form that shows *past* time:

11. Many people _____ already in line.
12. His comic books _____ his treasure.
13. She _____ my best friend.
14. Naturally I _____ disappointed.
15. You _____ the best of the contestants.
16. They _____ putting up a big tent.
17. Prices _____ going up and up.
18. I _____ not even on the list.
19. The Incas _____ the rulers of Peru.
20. Fortunately we _____ prepared for the snow.

U1e
Using Complete Verbs

Fill in all or part of the verb as needed in standard English.

Do you ever hear sentences like the following? Do you ever use them yourself? If so, study the way missing verbs (or parts of verbs) are filled in in standard English.

He a friend of yours?
You looking good today.
These men been here before.
Where he take you?

In sentences like these, a complete verb is needed in standard English. Remember:

(1) Fill in a form of be *when the second basic part of the sentence pins a label on the subject.* In each of the following pairs, a form of *be* makes the difference between a complete and an incomplete sentence:

NONSTANDARD: She joined the Tigers. They a social club.
STANDARD: She joined the Tigers. They *are* a social club.

NONSTANDARD: His father a realtor.
STANDARD: His father *is* a realtor.

(2) Fill in a form of be *if the* –ing *form of a verb alone makes a statement about the subject.* In standard English, the *–ing* form along cannot serve as the complete verb:

NONSTANDARD: It *getting* late.
STANDARD: It *is* (It's) *getting* late.

NONSTANDARD: Mr. Greene *looking* for you.
STANDARD: Mr. Greene *is looking* for you.

NONSTANDARD: The boys *doing* a good job.
STANDARD: The boys *are doing* a good job.

NONSTANDARD: I *going* home now.
STANDARD: I *am* (*I'm*) *going* home now.

(3) *Use a form of* have *with the perfect form of verbs.* In standard English, forms like *known, grown, thrown, gone, done,* and *been* are not used alone as the verb in a sentence. *Have, has,* or *had* is needed to complete the verb:

NONSTANDARD: He *been* here a long time.
STANDARD: He *has* (*He's*) *been* here a long time.

NONSTANDARD: They *gone* away.
STANDARD: They *have* (*They've*) *gone* away.

NONSTANDARD: They *thrown* the paper away too soon.
STANDARD: They *had* (*They'd*) *thrown* the paper away too soon.

NOTE: The shorter form (in parentheses) is the one we usually *hear* in standard English. The longer form is the one we usually *write* in standard English.

(4) *Use a form of* do *in questions when there is no other auxiliary.* Use *do, does,* or *did* to complete the verb in questions like the following:

NONSTANDARD: Where you *go* last night?
STANDARD: Where *did* you *go* last night?

NONSTANDARD: She *know* your address?
STANDARD: *Does* she *know* your address?

NONSTANDARD: Where you *come* from?
STANDARD: Where *do* you *come* from?

NONSTANDARD: What you *do* about it?
STANDARD: What *did* you *do* about it?

NONSTANDARD: When he *write* his letters?
STANDARD: When *does* he *write* his letters?

NOTE: The *do* is not needed when a word like *who* or *what* asks for the *subject* of a sentence. It is not needed when the verb is a form of *be:*

Who *wrote* the letter?
What *makes* you think so?

When *is* the library open?
Where *were* your friends?

EXERCISE 1

In each of the following sentences, a form of *be, have,* or *do* appears where it might be left out in nonstandard English. Each example shows the *right* form of the complete verb needed in standard English. Read over the sentences in each set several times. (Try reading the first three sets also with the shortened forms that we usually *hear* in standard English.) Come back to this exercise several times during the next few weeks.

1. He *is* my brother. She *is* my sister. It *is* a long walk to town. Granger *was* my best friend. It *is* very cold in here. We *are* members of the same club. I *am* the club secretary. You *are* new here.

2. I *am* writing him a note. He *is* speaking to you. They *were* talking among themselves. She *was* worrying too much. You *were* taking chances. You *are* making a mistake. I *am* going out now. It *is* working well. We *are* planning a dance. Someone *was* looking for you. The old man *is* talking to himself. A boy *was* standing beside him. You *were* driving away. You *are* learning fast.

3. I *have* seen her. You *have* not been home. We *have* gone out. Everyone *has* seen the movie. They *had* seen it. He *had* been waiting for an hour. The car *has* run out of gas. The dog *has* been taken for a walk. My sister *has* done the work.

4. Why *did* you run away? Where *does* he work? *Do* you like the new teacher? *Does* he like you? When *did* they meet? What *did* he say? Where *do* they go for lunch? What *does* she do for a living? How *do* you solve that problem? Why *did* he get so angry? What *did* they say to you?

EXERCISE 2

A. In each of the following sentences, fill in *are, have,* or *do.* After the number of the sentence, put the form needed to fill the blank. (Write on a separate sheet.)

EXAMPLE: The relatives _____ done their best to help.
(Answer) *have*

1. When _____ you want those letters?
2. Cashiers _____ people who collect money from customers.
3. His grandparents _____ gone back to Nevada.
4. _____ you listening to the same programs?
5. We _____ expecting a large crowd.
6. They _____ been here several times before.
7. The townspeople _____ seen many new fads.
8. Station wagons _____ the right cars for big families.
9. How _____ we keep the pipes from freezing?
10. Fast-food restaurants _____ serving more meals than ever.

B. In each of the following sentences, fill in *is, has,* or *does.* After the number of the sentence, put the form needed to fill the blank.

11. On what days _____ she go there?
12. The doctor _____ done everything possible.
13. A bicycle _____ a perfect gift for someone like me.
14. Everyone in my class _____ studying for the test.
15. A circus _____ coming to town.
16. Al _____ always been my best friend.
17. _____ anyone shown you the pictures?
18. Thanksgiving _____ a very traditional holiday.
19. _____ solar heating work?
20. Ann _____ gone ahead without us.

You can change each of the following sentences from non-standard to standard English by changing the italicized word. Put the right form of the italicized word after the number of the sentence.

UNIT REVIEW EXERCISE

EXAMPLE: Someone had *tore* a page from the magazine.
(Answer)   *torn*

1. You girls should introduce *yourself* to your new classmates.
2. It was still over twenty *mile* to our destination.
3. My sister and I *done* most of the work.
4. The owner had *wrote* several letters to the mayor.
5. When she was young, most people *travel* by train.
6. The driver had only *hisself* to blame.
7. You should let *them* animals out of their cages.
8. We should have *went* to the office ourselves.
9. Many kinds of flowers *growed* wild in the garden.
10. When we come in, he always *get* up to greet us.
11. I had never before earned three *dollar* an hour.
12. Someone had *stole* her watch from the locker.
13. Several cars *was* parked behind the house.
14. Our neighbor likes animals, but she *don't* like dogs.
15. They had *throwed* all the blankets in a heap.
16. When we work for her, she *pay* us well.
17. Artists *is* often trying something new.
18. The two families had reserved a big table for *theirself* in the front of the restaurant.
19. No one came to the hospital room where we *was* waiting for the specialist.
20. When I took the bus, I *need* a transfer.

U2
STANDARD ENGLISH: FINER POINTS

Learn to shift from nonstandard to standard expressions.

Do you ever use expressions like *more taller, couldn't see nothing,* and *without you agree?* If so, learn how to shift to the standard ways of saying the same thing.

U2a
Avoiding Double Forms

Avoid double negatives and other double forms.

Standard English does some jobs only once that nonstandard English does twice in the same sentence. The following sentences are nonstandard:

I did*n't* do *nothing.*
They *don't* have *no* books.
That's the *most saddest* movie I've seen.
Susan is *more nicer* than her sister.

Remember:

(1) Avoid the double negative. The **double negative** is an expression that says "no" twice. Early in the sentence, there is a word like *no,* or *not,* or *never.* But then there is another negative word like *no* or *not* or *nothing* later in the sentence. (The *not* is often shortened to *n't.*)

In standard English, take out or change the second word that says "no." Put *any* instead of *none,* or *anything (anybody)* instead of *nothing (nobody).* Put *ever* instead of *never:*

NONSTANDARD: There were*n't no* instructions with the box.
STANDARD: There were*n't any* instructions with the box.

NONSTANDARD: I do*n't* see *nobody* at the door.
STANDARD: I do*n't* see *anybody* at the door.

NONSTANDARD: They did*n't* learn *nothing* on the trip.
STANDARD: They did*n't* learn *anything* on the trip.

NONSTANDARD: *No* neighbors *never* visited us.
STANDARD: *No* neighbors *ever* visited us.

Or, try taking out the first word that says "no":

NONSTANDARD: I did*n't* see *no* way out.
STANDARD: I saw *no* way out.

NONSTANDARD: She is*n't never* going there again.
STANDARD: She is *never* going there again.

Expressions like *couldn't hardly* and *wouldn't barely* are similar to double negatives. In standard English, leave out the *not* (or *n't*):

NONSTANDARD: He *couldn't hardly* talk.
STANDARD: He *could hardly* talk.

NONSTANDARD: I *couldn't scarcely* see anything in the fog.
STANDARD: I *could scarcely* see anything in the fog.

NOTE: When the word *No* stands by itself at the beginning of a sentence, it often is not a part of the sentence pattern. Another word may then tell us "no" in the actual sentence. The following are standard:

No, I didn't find it.
No, the boys saw nothing.

(2) Use the standard forms of adjectives in comparisons. In standard English, you have two ways of changing adjectives to use them in comparisons. You may put *more* or *most* in front of the adjective. Or you may add *–er* or *–est* to the adjective. The endings are used if the adjective has only one syllable. *More* or *most* is used if the adjective has three or more syllables. Adjectives of two syllables sometimes use the endings and sometimes use *more* or *most.*

STANDARD: Ken is *taller* than his brother.
Rhoda is the *kindest* girl I know.
His plan is *simpler* than mine.
They did it the *easiest* way.

STANDARD: Jane is *more responsible* than her sister.
Fred is the *most trustworthy* boy in the class.
Please be *more careful* than that.
He is the *most awkward* boy I know.

Do not use *both* of these methods with the same adjective. Combinations such as *more taller, most kindest, more carefuller* are nonstandard. They are **double comparisons.**
Be sure you know the standard forms of these words:

good	better	best
bad	worse	worst
far	farther	farthest
little	less	least

The following are all nonstandard: *gooder, badder, worser, worsest,* and *bestest.* Also nonstandard are double forms like *more better* and *more worse.*

See **S1d** on how adjectives show degree.

(3) Avoid double plurals. We usually make the plural of a noun by adding *–s* or *–es* to the singular: one *car,* several *cars.* But the plural of *man* is *men.* The plural of *child* is *children.* The plural of *foot* is *feet. Mens* and *childrens* and *feets* are "double plurals." They have been made plural twice. Do not use such double plurals in standard English.

EXERCISE 1

All examples in the following exercise show the *right* forms for standard English. Read over the sentences in each set several times. Come back to this exercise several times during the next few weeks.

1. Fred didn't have *any* trouble. We didn't know *anybody.* He doesn't want *anything.*
2. She couldn't find *any* glue. I couldn't see *anything.* Doesn't he need *any?*
3. I don't *ever* want to see you. Aren't you *ever* coming back? She won't *ever* try again.
4. He didn't do *anything* wrong. There wasn't *anybody* home. We couldn't find it *anywhere.*
5. *I could* hardly keep my eyes open. The box *would* scarcely fit into the trunk. The money *would* barely cover expenses.
6. Tom is *more careful* than I. This was the *most wonderful* vacation we have had. This cashier is *more polite* than the other.
7. These books are *good.* That one is *better.* This one is the *best.*
8. Smoking a pipe is *bad.* Smoking a cigar is *worse.* Smoking cigarettes is the *worst* of all.
9. Cleveland is *far* from Chicago. Pittsburgh is *farther* still. New York is the *farthest* of them all.
10. Rita knows very *little* about history. Her brother knows *less.* Her father knows *least* of all.

EXERCISE 2

After the number of each question, write the form needed in the answer. (Write on a separate sheet.)

A. Write the standard form that would fit in each blank space. Use the following words only: *no, any; never, ever; nobody, anybody; nothing, anything; none.*

EXAMPLE: Are you sure you need nothing else? Yes, I don't need _____ else.

(Answer) *anything*

1. Did you bring some food? No, I didn't bring _____.
2. Did they have punch at the party? No, they didn't have _____ to drink.
3. Has anybody called me? No, _____ has called.
4. Did you ever get a letter from her? No, I _____ did.
5. Have you put a stamp on this letter? No, I couldn't find _____ stamps.
6. Do you know anything about this? No, I know _____ about it.
7. Did she ever tell anybody about it? No, she _____ told anyone.
8. Does he know the answer? No, he doesn't know _____ answers.
9. Is anything happening? No, _____ is happening.
10. Have you done any of your homework yet? No, I have done _____.

B. Write the standard form of the adjective that would best fit in the blank spaces below.

11. Does the food taste good? It tastes _____ than it did yesterday.
12. Is Chuck taller than Bill? Yes, Chuck is _____.
13. Is our track team good this year? Yes, it is the _____ team we have ever had.
14. Did you do better on the test this time? No, I did _____.
15. Which is farther from here, Montgomery or Mobile? Mobile is _____.
16. Is the weather bad today? Yes, it is the _____ that I have ever seen.
17. Do you think Glen is more independent than Ted? Yes, Glen is the _____ boy in the group.
18. Is it hot in the den? Yes, it is _____ than it is in the hall.
19. Is your new dog mean? Yes, it is the _____ we have owned.
20. Do you like the new coach? Yes, I like her _____ than the one we had last year.

You can change each of the following sentences from non-standard to standard by changing the italicized word (or words). After the number of the sentence, write the word that should replace the nonstandard form.

EXERCISE 3

EXAMPLE: My grandparents don't *never* visit us here.
(Answer) *ever*

1. We hadn't learned *nothing* during the trip.
2. Conditions were getting *worser* for much of the wildlife.
3. The newcomers *couldn't* hardly speak English.
4. Don't allow *nobody* to come into the clubhouse.
5. There was no telephone *nowhere* in the building.
6. He was the *most kindest* person we met on the trip.
7. The neighbors never gave us *no* trouble.
8. Don't *never* walk barefoot in snake country.
9. Turtles have shells with only their heads and *feets* sticking out.
10. My mother is the most *carefullest* driver in the family.
11. We ordered milk, but he didn't bring *none*.
12. My brother *can't* barely walk yet.
13. There was a special program for *childrens* and their parents.
14. The players are *more better* now than they were at first.
15. We went to visit, but we never found *no one* at home.
16. With the new machine, nothing *never* worked right.
17. Never tell *nobody* what you just heard.
18. She was the most *awkwardest* player on the team.
19. Things were getting *more worse* all the time.
20. No one wanted to give us *no* help.

U2b

Other Nonstandard Expressions

Learn ways of replacing common nonstandard expressions.

Words like *ain't* and *nowheres* are easily recognized features of nonstandard speech. If you use these words and other expressions listed below, learn how to replace them in standard English.

Remember:

(1) Avoid nonstandard use of learn *and* leave. In standard English, the teacher *teaches* and the student *learns*.

NONSTANDARD: The teacher *learned* the class math.
STANDARD: The teacher *taught* the class math.

NONSTANDARD: The experience *learned* me a lesson.
STANDARD: The experience *taught* me a lesson.

In standard English, *leave* means "to go away from." *Let* means "to permit or allow." Do not use *leave* to mean "allow." Use *let* instead.

NONSTANDARD: My parents wouldn't *leave* me go out.
STANDARD: My parents wouldn't *let* me go out.

(2) *Avoid nonstandard connectives.* The expressions *being as, being that, seeing as how,* and *on account of* are all nonstandard when they start a clause. Do not use them when what follows has its own subject and verb: being that *he lives* there; seeing as how *you have helped* us. Use the standard connective *because* instead:

NONSTANDARD:	We are calling off the meeting on account of it is snowing.
STANDARD:	We are calling off the meeting *because* it is snowing.

NONSTANDARD:	*Being as* he was our friend, we lent him the money.
STANDARD:	*Because* he was our friend, we lent him the money.

Without and *on account of* are prepositions in standard English, not connectives. They introduce nouns rather than clauses. To introduce clauses, standard English uses *unless* rather than *without:*

NONSTANDARD:	I can't go *without* my father gives me permission.
STANDARD:	I can't go *unless* my father gives me permission.
STANDARD:	I can't go *without* my father's permission. (*Without* introduces a noun.)

(3) *Know the standard uses of* a *and* an. Standard English uses *an* before words beginning with a vowel sound. It uses *a* before other words:

AN:	*an error, an apple, an inch, an hour, an A, an usher, an old trick*
A:	*a door, a game, a horse, a C, a useful idea*

(4) *Avoid starting a sentence with* the boy, he *or* the girl, she. In sentences like "The man, he didn't do anything" and "That girl, she looks tired," the subject is named twice. Leave out the *he* or *she* in standard English:

The man didn't do anything.
That girl looks tired.

NOTE: In standard English, the subject may be named twice if one is speaking directly to a person:

Susan, you should go now.

(5) *Avoid other nonstandard expressions.* Avoid the expressions in the following list:

ain't	Avoid all uses of *ain't.* Use instead some form of *be,* with *n't* or *not.* Sometimes

a form of *have* has to take the place of *ain't.*

> *I'm not* going.
> He *isn't* going, either.
> The girls *are not* (aren't) ready yet.
> We *have not* (haven't) heard from him.

don't got

Use *don't have:*

> We *don't have* the time.

irregardless

Regardless is the standard form:

> I'm going to take the job *regardless* of
>   what salary they offer.

**nowheres, some-
 wheres**

In standard English, the words *no, some, any,* and *every* combine with *where,* not with *wheres:*

> Where did you go? I went *nowhere.*
> We went *everywhere* last weekend.

off of

Use *off* or *from* instead of *off of* in standard English:

> NONSTANDARD: Did you borrow *off of* him?
> STANDARD: Did you borrow *from* him?
>
> NONSTANDARD: Take your feet *off of* the
>   sofa.
> STANDARD: Take your feet *off* the sofa.

EXERCISE 1

All of the following sentences show the *right* forms for standard English. Read over the sentences in each set several times. Come back to this exercise several times in the next few weeks.

1. We *learned* how to breathe right.
   Our teacher *taught* us how to swim.
   Where did you *learn* how to type?
   Who *taught* you to dance?

2. *Let* me take it out.
   The members wouldn't *let* Sam vote.
   If you don't *leave* now, you will be late.
   Everyone has to *leave* at eight.

3. You won't get well *unless* you rest.
   I didn't go to school yesterday *because* I was sick.
   I didn't go to school yesterday *on account of* the snow.
   She never went anywhere *without* her friend.

4. *An* old friend wrote *a* letter.
   A bad tire can cause *an* accident.
   An experienced driver would have known *an* easier way.
   He had *an* uncle and *an* aunt on *a* farm.

5. That boy *isn't* welcome here.
   The books *aren't* cheap.
   Charlie says that he *isn't* going.
   Mandy and her sister *haven't* been invited.

6. *Regardless* of what my mother says, I am going.
   She said that she would wait, *regardless*.
   I wish I had *somewhere* to go.
   She had *nowhere* to turn for help.

7. Borrow one *from* a friend.
   What answer did you get *from* him?
   We took the pie *from* the counter.
   Please take your books *off* my desk.

You can change each of the following from nonstandard to standard by changing the italicized word (or words). After the number of the sentence, write the word that should replace the nonstandard form.

EXERCISE 2

EXAMPLE: My friends don't *got* time for games.
(Answer) *have*

1. The *teacher he* told me to do it.
2. He couldn't go *without* he took his brother.
3. Since the accident, he *ain't* been the same.
4. Why wouldn't they *leave* Tom play?
5. She knew where to get *off of* the train.
6. Who *learned* her how to dance?
7. You will get *nowheres* in life unless you know how to learn.
8. The boy in the black shirt *ain't* got a chance.
9. My brother said I couldn't go, but I went *irregardless*.
10. *Learn* me how to do that.
11. *Being as* the sheriff knew us, he let us go.
12. Last Saturday, we had *a* unexpected guest.
13. We stopped skating, *on account of* the ice was too thin.
14. My *sister she* just took her driving test.

15. Sometimes *a* older brother or sister becomes a problem.
16. He let us go early, *being that* it was Saturday.
17. I tried to borrow the money *off of* my aunt.
18. The cabin has to be around here *somewheres*.
19. All that was left was *a* oatmeal cookie.
20. *Without* you help me, I will never finish the job.

UNIT REVIEW EXERCISE

Which of the following sentences are standard English? Write *S* after the number of each standard sentence. Which of the following sentences show one of the nonstandard forms or expressions you have studied? Put *N* after the number of each nonstandard sentence.

EXAMPLE: You are not allowed to drive without you pass the test.
(Answer) *N*

1. My mother taught us that nobody loses all the time.
2. Being as it was late, we ended the meeting.
3. She came to every game, irregardless of the weather.
4. You may catch cold if you leave without your coat.
5. No, the bus doesn't stop here anymore.
6. My friends and I couldn't hardly wait for the weekend.
7. Nobody in my family ever offers me a ride.
8. The new coach learned us how to use our arms.
9. The woman in charge didn't accept no excuses.
10. Ramona was kept off the team on account of her age.
11. My trip counted as an unexcused absence.
12. This building badly needs a elevator.
13. A flying fox is nothing but a large bat.
14. Nobody has taken these books off of the shelf in years.
15. You should leave her do her own work.
16. She never told us anything about her family.
17. The manager she just didn't like me.
18. The new trains are more quicker than the old buses.
19. Jim was always the most awkward of the three.
20. You shouldn't never trust a total stranger.

U3

FORMAL AND INFORMAL

Use formal standard English for formal speech and writing.

Some occasions are *formal* occasions—high school graduations, concerts of classical music, church services. On such occasions we expect people to be on their best behavior. We expect them to wear their Sunday best. On such occasions,

TALKING TURKEY

Many informal expressions are *un*original. We hear them many times. For each of the italicized expressions, write down a more formal expression—one that would mean the same thing.

1. John asked me a hard question, but I *turned the tables on him.*
2. After some pleasant conversation, the customer began *to talk turkey.*
3. I'm *in hot water* because I was late last night.
4. Usually I don't like cheese, but *once in a blue moon* I eat a lot of it.
5. Johnson was *an eager beaver* who wanted to impress his boss.
6. Ames pitched well for one season, but he turned out to be *a flash in the pan.*
7. When my uncle saw the broken pieces, I had *to face the music.*
8. No matter who argued against her, Ann *stuck to her guns.*
9. I arrived at the office on time, but I had *to cool my heels* for an hour.
10. The accusation hit me *like a bolt from the blue.*

informal dress—a T-shirt, or shorts—and casual behavior—whistling, finger-popping—are out of place. We observe the difference between formal and informal all the time:

- An office worker acts businesslike at the desk but relaxes during a coffee break.
- Students act politely in class but start horseplay between classes.

When we use standard English, we make similar changes from formal to informal. We use more **formal** English for business purposes and in public. We use it for business letters and written reports. News programs, textbooks, and magazine articles typically use a formal, businesslike kind of English. We use **informal** English for friendly conversation. Informal English is relaxed, "after-hours" English. We use informal English in writing personal letters or talking among friends.

What changes does a speaker or writer make to shift from informal talk to more formal English? In each of the following pairs, the *second* is the one you would be likely to hear from a public speaker or to read in a magazine article:

INFORMAL: Me and my brother felt awful cold.
FORMAL: My brother and I felt very cold.

INFORMAL: Us boys had a real good time.
FORMAL: We boys really enjoyed ourselves.

INFORMAL: Pablo drove slow down the path.
FORMAL: Pablo drove slowly down the path.

The following sections will help you shift from informal to more formal language when you write a paper or talk to a group.

U3a

Pronoun Case

Know the formal uses of personal pronouns.

The **personal pronouns** are words like *I, he, she,* or *we.* These words have two different forms. We use one of them when the word is the subject of the sentence. We use the other form when the word is the object or target in the sentence. Study the differences between the sentences in each of the following pairs:

SUBJECT		OBJECT
I	helped	*her.*
She	helped	*me.*
We	invited	*them.*
They	invited	*us.*
He	had believed	*me.*
I	had believed	*him.*

We say that *he* is the **subject form.** *Him* is the **object form.** Subject pronouns generally come before the verb. We could call *he* a "before" pronoun. Object pronouns generally come after the verb. We could call *him* an "after" pronoun. The object form is also the one that comes after a preposition:

She	was looking	for *him*.
I	had written	to *her*.
He	was standing	between *them*.

The difference between the subject form and the object form is traditionally called a difference in **case.** Five personal pronouns change their forms this way. (*It* and *you* stay the same regardless of where they are used.)

SUBJECT ("before") PRONOUNS	OBJECT ("after") PRONOUNS
I	me
he	him
she	her
we	us
they	them

In casual conversation, we often use these pronoun forms *informally*. Know the formal uses of these pronouns. Remember the following especially for use in all your writing and in speaking to a group:

(1) Use the right form when a pronoun is part of a combination. The pronouns in the following examples are part of a double subject, joined by *and:*

He and I cleaned the chalkboard.
Thomas and she did the dishes.
We and they always eat lunch together.

The pronouns in the following examples are part of a double object, joined by *and:*

Frank invited *Mary and him*.
The new boy met *us and them*.
The teacher called on *her and me*.

When you have subjects or objects joined by *and,* try them *separately* to decide which pronoun form to use:

FORMAL: *He and I* were working on the car.
(We would say, "He was working on the car," and "I was working on the car.")

FORMAL: The class elected *Greg and me*.
(We would say, "The class elected *me*.")

FORMAL: The umpire will solve the problem between *you and us*.
(We would say, "The umpire will solve the problem between *us*.")

Study the differences between the formal and informal sentences below. Read the formal sentences aloud:

INFORMAL: Me and John always work together.
FORMAL: *John and I* always work together.

(Note that formal English is more polite; it puts the pronoun naming the speaker *after* other nouns or pronouns.)

INFORMAL: The teacher sent Helen and I on an errand.
FORMAL: The teacher sent *Helen and me* on an errand.

INFORMAL: Lucy and him are always late.
FORMAL: *Lucy and he* are always late.

INFORMAL: I have always liked Martha and he.
FORMAL: I have always liked *Martha and him.*

INFORMAL: There is no argument between he and I.
FORMAL: There is no argument between *him and me.*

(2) When we *or* us *comes directly before a noun, use the form you would use if the pronoun stood alone.* We often use such expressions as "we Americans," "us boys," "we girls," "us members." How do you decide whether to use *we* or *us* with the nouns in formal English? One good way is to try the pronoun *without* the noun:

FORMAL: He did not really like *us* Americans.
          (He did not really like *us.*)
FORMAL: *We* members of the club did not vote.
          (*We* did not vote.)
FORMAL: Our friends gave souvenirs to *us* visitors.
          (Our friends gave souvenirs to *us.*)
FORMAL: He thought that *we* boys should help.
          (He thought that *we* should help.)

(3) After than *and* as, *use the form that would fit if you filled in the complete sentence.* In comparing two things, we often use *than* or *as* to introduce the second item in the comparison:

Ramos is as tall *as* his brother.
He is more friendly *than* his sister.
The cold hurt her less *than* her friend.

Suppose you wanted to use a pronoun in place of *his brother, his sister,* and *her friend.* To choose the right form, *complete* the second half of the sentence. Would the pronoun be a subject or an object in the completed part of the sentence?

SUBJECT: Ramos is as tall as *he* (is).
SUBJECT: He is more friendly than *she* (is).
OBJECT: The cold hurt her less than (it hurt) *him*.

EXERCISE 1

Read the following sentences several times. If you have trouble with formal pronoun forms, come back to this exercise several times in the next few weeks. All of the sentences are *formal standard English*.

1. *Nina and I* did the job. *Herb and I* found the place. *My cousin and I* went fishing. *The teacher and I* agreed. *She and I* have a plan. *He and I* fixed the car. *They and I* disagreed.

2. The picture shows *my aunt and me*. No one saw *Bill and me*. Everybody knows *Bill and her*. Somebody called *Sally and him*. No one saw *him and me*. Everybody knows *him and her*. Somebody called *her and him*.

3. They gave a surprise party for *my sister and me*. The letter is addressed to *you and her*. It's a secret between my father and *me*. It's a secret between *him and me*.

4. *We boys* went camping together. *We Americans* love our country. *We workers* should join a union. He said that *we students* should stick together. She knew that *we girls* could be trusted.

5. The principal gave *us boys* a lecture. Our hosts treated *us foreigners* well. Nobody tells *us farmers* what to do. The leader called *us boys* together. He told *us girls* that we were good students.

6. She had good news for *us hikers*. They had no chance against *us older girls*. They kept staring at *us Americans*.

7. I can run as fast as *he*. He is not as fast as *I*. They are not as good as *we*. She reads faster than *I*. I read faster than *he*. They talk more slowly than *we*. Selma studied as hard as *I*. The new girl worked as hard as *he*.

8. She paid us more than *them*. The earthquake frightened me more than *her*. The drought hurts them as much as *us*.

EXERCISE 2

Which of the sentences in each pair on the following page would be *right* in formal English? Put the letter for the right choice after the number of the pair.

EXAMPLE: (a) They always sent a Christmas gift for him and I.

(b) They always sent a Christmas gift for him and me.

(Answer) *b*

1. (a) The teacher gave us boys a second chance.
   (b) The teacher gave we boys a second chance.

2. (a) The coach appointed Chuck and I co-captains.
   (b) The coach appointed Chuck and me co-captains.

3. (a) Someone was standing between he and I.
   (b) Someone was standing between him and me.

4. (a) We girls are much better typists than them.
   (b) We girls are much better typists than they.

5. (a) Marcia and me went to the movies on Saturday.
   (b) Marcia and I went to the movies on Saturday.

6. (a) He said he would talk to we girls later.
   (b) He said he would talk to us girls later.

7. (a) My brother does as well in school as I.
   (b) My brother does as well in school as me.

8. (a) I expected you rather than them.
   (b) I expected you rather than they.

9. (a) The music teacher wanted he and I in the band.
   (b) The music teacher wanted him and me in the band.

10. (a) Us counselors knew what to do.
    (b) We counselors knew what to do.

11. (a) He and his father sometimes had a loud argument.
    (b) Him and his father sometimes had a loud argument.

12. (a) At first the other students teased we Yankees.
    (b) At first the other students teased us Yankees.

13. (a) The puppet show amused the adults more than we children.
    (b) The puppet show amused the adults more than us children.

14. (a) The rain got their blankets as wet as them.
    (b) The rain got their blankets as wet as they.

15. (a) This secret must remain between you and me.
    (b) This secret must remain between you and I.

EXERCISE 3

In each of the following sentences, choose the form that would be right in formal English. Put the right form after the number of the sentence.

EXAMPLE: My Dad and *(I/me)* are pals.   (Answer) *I*

1. Sharon left with my cousin and *(I/me)*.
2. Jimmy and *(I/me)* are going home.
3. Charlotte and *(she/her)* are having a good vacation.
4. You should call *(he/him)* and me tomorrow.
5. I have a surprise for you and *(she/her)*.
6. You and *(we/us)* should get together.
7. The principal called Danny and *(I/me)* to the office.
8. You boys and *(they/them)* will get along.
9. Between you and *(I/me)*, there isn't any disagreement.
10. What happened between him and *(she/her)?*
11. The school will send *(we/us)* officers to the conference.
12. *(We/Us)* boys could help you.
13. The present is for *(we/us)* girls.
14. He should give *(we/us)* voters some answers.
15. She said that *(we/us)* students would not be invited.
16. Pete can drive better than *(she/her)*.
17. I am as smart as *(he/him)*.
18. The illness struck her sooner than *(I/me)*.
19. Mary can play tennis almost as well as *(they/them)*.
20. Their team was faster than *(we/us)*.

Learn the formal uses of *lie/lay, sit/set, and rise/raise.*

Remember these verbs in this order: *lie/lay, sit/set, rise/ raise*. The first verb in each set *(lie, sit, rise)* is used in Pattern-One sentences only. It does not have an object. The second verb in each set *(lay, set, raise)* is generally used in Pattern-Two sentences. It comes before an object:

PATTERN ONE: *(S–V)*	The dog always *lies* at the owner's feet.
PATTERN TWO: *(S–V–O)*	The dog always *lays the paper* at the owner's feet. (*The paper* is the direct object.)
PATTERN ONE: *(S–V)*	My cousin usually *sits* next to me.
PATTERN TWO: *(S–V–O)*	My cousin usually *sets the table*. (*The table* is the direct object.)
PATTERN ONE: *(S–V)*	Dad generally *rises* at seven o'clock.
PATTERN TWO: *(S–V–O)*	Dad generally *raises the flag* at seven o'clock. (*The flag* is the direct object.)

Learn the meaning and the basic forms of each of these verbs:

(1) *Lie* means *to rest* or remain stretched out. Its basic forms are *lie* (present), *lay* (past), *have lain* (perfect). The *–ing* form is *lying*. There are no direct objects in the following sentences:

Every day, I *lie* down for an hour at noon.
Yesterday, we *lay* on the beach all day.
I have just *lain* down for a few minutes.
The guests were *lying* on the lawn.

Lay means *to put* something *down*. Its basic forms are *lay* (present), *laid* (past), *have laid* (perfect). The *–ing* form is *laying*. (The present tense of *lay* is the same as the *past tense of lie*.) Notice that there are direct objects in all of the following sentences:

Every night, I *lay* my glasses on the table.
Yesterday, we *laid* blankets on the beach.
They had just *laid* some tiles when I walked in.
They were *laying* tiles in the kitchen.

(2) *Sit* means *to be seated,* or *to take a seat*. Its forms are *sit* (present), *sat* (past), *have sat* (perfect). The *–ing* form is *sitting*. Here are some examples of this verb in sentences; notice that no direct objects are used:

Every day, Grandma *sits* in her rocking chair.
Yesterday, she *sat* there for three hours.
I have not *sat* down all day.
We were *sitting* in the office for an hour.

Set means *to put or place* something somewhere. Its forms are *set* (present), *set* (past), *have set* (perfect). The *–ing* form is *setting*. Can you find the direct object in each of the sentences below?

Every morning, I *set* the table for breakfast.
Yesterday, someone *set* the table for me.
Henry has not *set* his books here.
I was *setting* the table the wrong way.

(3) *Rise* means *to go up*. Its forms are *rise* (present), *rose* (past), *have risen* (perfect). The *–ing* form is *rising*. *Rise* does not take an object:

Every morning, I *rise* by eight o'clock.
Yesterday, the river *rose* higher.
My opinion of him has *risen.*
The sun is *rising* in the east, as usual.

Raise means *to make* something go up, or move up. Its forms are *raise* (present), *raised* (past), *have raised* (perfect). The *–ing* form is *raising.* Look for the direct objects in the following sentences.

Every morning, I *raise* the shades in the classroom.
Yesterday, the store *raised* its prices.
Who has *raised* his hand?
Mr. Jones is *raising* his children well.

NOTE: Sometimes *lay* and *set* have special meanings. They then do not follow the rule: Hens *lay.* The sun *sets.*

The following sentences show the *right* use of *lie/lay, sit/set, rise/raise* in formal standard English. Read over the sentences in each set several times.

EXERCISE 1

1. *Lie* down and rest. I *lay* down for an hour. The dog has *lain* in the corner. He was *lying* on the couch. He usually *lies* in the sun. Why did he *lie* in the shade? Why are they *lying* there? She has *lain* in the sun for an hour.

2. *Lay* your gun down. The workers *laid* the bricks. He has *laid* the note on the table. They are *laying* them now. He usually *lays* his books here. Yesterday he *laid* them over there. He has *laid* his pen on the table. She was *laying* the eggs down carefully.

3. Let's *sit* here. They *sat* on the bench. I was *sitting* on the fence. Someone has been *sitting* in my chair. Dad usually *sits* there. Who *sat* there last? Are you *sitting* alone? He has *sat* on the bench all season.

4. *Set* the table now. He *set* the package on the floor. He has *set* the clock on the bureau. Are you *setting* a date? A helper *sets* the tables. I *set* the mail on the shelf. Are you *setting* that typewriter here? I already have *set* it there.

5. *Rise* when the judge comes in. The sun *rose* early. The monster has *risen* from its grave. The river is *rising.* She usually *rises* early. The people *rose* up against him. Has the sun *risen?* We are *rising* early this morning.

6. *Raise* the blinds. The soldiers *raised* the flag. Why has she *raised* her hand? George is always *raising* his voice. He *raises* the Venetian blinds every morning. The musician *raised* his saxophone. They were *raising* vegetables. The government has *raised* taxes.

EXERCISE 2

Which of the sentences in each pair would be *right* in formal English? Put the letter for the right choice after the number of the pair.

EXAMPLE: (a) We were all sitting around the campfire.
(b) We were all setting around the campfire.
(Answer) *a*

1. (a) The builders are lying the foundation for us.
   (b) The builders are laying the foundation for us.

2. (a) We sat in the doctor's office all morning.
   (b) We set in the doctor's office all morning.

3. (a) The audience rose up and cheered.
   (b) The audience raised up and cheered.

4. (a) The camera was laying in the bright sun.
   (b) The camera was lying in the bright sun.

5. (a) Spectators were setting on the fence.
   (b) Spectators were sitting on the fence.

6. (a) The dog usually lays its head on its paws.
   (b) The dog usually lies its head on its paws.

7. (a) You should sit down your packages for a while.
   (b) You should set down your packages for a while.

8. (a) The child's balloon rose out of sight.
   (b) The child's balloon raised out of sight.

9. (a) The boy lay his head on the pillow.
   (b) The boy laid his head on the pillow.

10. (a) That ship has been laying at anchor all week.
    (b) That ship has been lying at anchor all week.

EXERCISE 3

In each of the following sentences, put the form that would be *right* in formal English. Put the right choice after the number of the sentence.

EXAMPLE: The workers were *(lying/laying)* the foundation.
(Answer) *laying*

1. When prices *(rise/raise)*, people are unhappy.
2. I always *(sit/set)* here by myself.
3. All his books were *(lying/laying)* on the floor.
4. The dog has just *(lain/laid)* down.
5. You should *(sit/set)* that plate on the hot pad.
6. The people *(rose/raised)* against the king.
7. The temperature has *(risen/raised)* to one hundred degrees.
8. Grandfather always *(sits/sets)* in the most comfortable chair.
9. They have been *(sitting/setting)* up all night.
10. He should *(lie/lay)* quietly until the doctor comes.
11. The delivery boy *(lay/laid)* the groceries on the table.
12. The neighbor is *(lying/laying)* concrete in the driveway.
13. They never *(sit/set)* the bowling pins up right.
14. The magician had *(risen/raised)* people up in the air.
15. The airplanes were *(rising/raising)* from the field.
16. The fog has *(risen/raised)* from the swamp.
17. Books were *(lying/laying)* on the floor.
18. They just *(sit/set)* around all day.
19. He *(sat/set)* his load down angrily.
20. The boy *(lay/laid)* his new stamps out in a row.
21. The workers *(rose/raised)* the house from its foundation.
22. Mother *(sits/sets)* in her favorite corner.
23. My friends *(lie/lay)* on the beach all summer long.
24. We *(lay/laid)* the fish in the sizzling frying pan.
25. The old dog just *(sits/sets)* in the warm sun all day long.

Avoid familiar informal expressions in serious speech and writing.

U3c

Avoiding Informal Expressions

All of the following are familiar informal ways of saying things. Learn the more formal way of saying the same thing. Use the more formal choice in writing and in speaking to a group.

(1) Use the adverb with the –ly ending whenever you have a choice. Informal English uses many adverbs that look like adjectives: "He had grown *considerable*." "Drive *slow*." Formal English uses separate adverb forms. Use the form with –*ly* to answer the question: "How does it work?" or "How is it done?"

Look at the adverb in sentences like the following charted on the next page.

S	V	ADVERB
My friend	drove	slow*ly*.
Some birds	sing	beautiful*ly*.

S	V	O	ADVERB
They	planned	their outing	careful*ly*.
It	helped	him	considerab*ly*.
We	did	the job	quick*ly*.

Remember that after a linking verb we usually find an adjective that is part of the S–LV–Adj pattern:

S	LV	ADJECTIVE
The windows	were	*open*.
The horse	looked	*slow*.
The music	sounded	*loud*.

Make sure to use *badly* and *well* where the adverb form is needed. After linking verbs, we use *bad* and *good* to show what something was like. But after action verbs, we use *badly* and *well* to show how something was done:

LINKING VERB + ADJECTIVE	ACTION VERB + ADVERB
The weather was *bad*.	The team played *badly*.
The news sounded *bad*.	She told the story *badly*.
Exercise is *good* for you.	They sang *well*.
The new paint looks *good*.	They covered it *well*.

Remember: Some adverbs never have the –*ly* ending: "He talked *fast*." "They do not run *much* anymore."

(2) Avoid using real, awful, mighty, *and* pretty *in combinations like* real fast *or* pretty good. *Use* really, very, *or* fairly *instead:*

INFORMAL:	The winners were *real* happy.
FORMAL:	The winners were *really* (or *very*) happy.

INFORMAL:	It had gotten *awful* cold.
FORMAL:	It had gotten *very* cold.

INFORMAL:	There had been a *pretty* good turnout.
FORMAL:	There had been a *fairly* good turnout. (or *rather* good)

These combinations show a special use of adverbs. Usually adverbs go with the verb to tell us how (or when, or where). But here the adverbs go with an adjective to tell us "how much?" (Sometimes they go with another adverb: very *badly,* fairly *well.*)

(3) *Avoid informal reference to indefinite pronouns.* In formal English, use singular pronouns to point back to the **indefinite** pronouns: *everbody (everyone), somebody (someone), nobody (no one),* and *anybody (anyone).* Indefinite pronouns do not point to any one person. In formal English, they are treated as singulars. Notice the use of *singular* pronouns in the formal examples below:

INFORMAL: Does everyone have *their* luggage?
FORMAL: Does everyone have *his* luggage?

INFORMAL: Someone forgot *their* library card.
FORMAL: Someone forgot *her* library card.

INFORMAL: Never tell anyone what *they* should do.
FORMAL: Never tell anyone what *he or she* should do.

NOTE: Many people complain that *he* is inaccurate when *everybody* or *somebody* or *nobody,* etc., may point to persons of either sex. Other people complain that *he* or *she* or *she* or *he* is awkward. To be safe, you can use a simple plural instead. Here are two examples:

SAFE: *All the people* in our group had *their* luggage.
SAFE: *Some guests* had parked *their* cars in the driveway.

(4) *Look out for some other familiar features of informal English.* Most of the following you can hear every day. Know how to change these expressions when writing a paper or speaking to a group:

• *Avoid* these kind *and* those kind. In formal English, *this kind* and *these kinds* are all right—but not *these kind.* *This* and *that* are singular. They pair off with *kind* and *sort.* *These* and *those* are plural. They pair off with *kinds* and *sorts:*

INFORMAL: I never go to *those kind* of meetings.
FORMAL: I never go to *that kind* of meeting.

INFORMAL: *These kind* of shoes are out of style.
FORMAL: *This kind* of shoe is out of style.

• *Avoid the informal use of* like. *Like* is all right as a preposition—when it does *not* precede a subject and verb:

Amanda looks *like* her mother.
George, *like* his brother, is going to college.

Do not use *like* as a connective. Formal English uses *as* or *as if* instead of *like* to start a whole clause: "Do *as* I say" (not "*like* I say").

INFORMAL: It looks *like* we are going to lose.
FORMAL: It look *as if* we are going to lose.

INFORMAL: Throw the ball *like* I taught you.
FORMAL: Throw the ball *as* I taught you.

• *Avoid the informal use of* most. In formal English, do not substitute *most* for *almost* or *nearly:*

INFORMAL: *Most* everybody knew the answer.
FORMAL: *Almost* everybody knew the answer.

INFORMAL: She scores *most* all our goals.
FORMAL: She scores *nearly* all our goals.

EXERCISE 1

Study the difference between the sentences in each of the following pairs. Choose the sentences that would be *right* in formal English. Put the letter for the right choice after the number of the pair.

EXAMPLE: (a) The door looked *as if* it had been forced open.
(b) The door looked *like* it had been forced open.
(Answer) *a*

1. (a) I bought that kind of shoe last spring.
   (b) I bought those kind of shoes last spring.

2. (a) She gave a real good speech.
   (b) She gave a very good speech.

3. (a) The plumber repaired the pipe good.
   (b) The plumber repaired the pipe well.

4. (a) He played the guitar beautifully.
   (b) He played the guitar beautiful.

5. (a) Pat pitched bad yesterday.
   (b) Pat pitched badly yesterday.

6. (a) At first the weather looked bad.
   (b) At first the weather looked badly.

7. (a) She looked rather grown-up in her new clothes.
   (b) She looked pretty grown-up in her new clothes.

8. (a) That was a mighty fine dinner.
   (b) That was a really fine dinner.

9. (a) Please drive slowly.
   (b) Please drive slow.

10. (a) Everyone did their work quietly.
    (b) Everyone did his or her work quietly.

11. (a) They shut the door quick.
    (b) They shut the door quickly.

12. (a) My Spanish is not very good.
    (b) My Spanish is not very well.

13. (a) She turned the corner very cautiously.
    (b) She turned the corner real cautious.

14. (a) His sister skated real good.
    (b) His sister skated really well.

15. (a) They did everything like their parents had taught them.
    (b) They did everything as their parents had taught them.

In each of the following sentences, which would be the *right* choice in formal English? Put the right choice after the number of the sentence.

EXERCISE 2

EXAMPLE: The food there was always *(very/awful)* spicy.
(Answer) *very*

1. People seldom wear *(these/this)* kind of hat anymore.
2. It seemed *(like/as if)* they would never stop talking.
3. I was crying *(like/as)* a baby.
4. I never saw you change your mind so *(quick/quickly)*.
5. He walked very *(good/well)* after his operation.
6. The machine worked *(good/well)*.
7. We had a *(real/very)* good Thanksgiving dinner.
8. They were having a *(fairly/pretty)* interesting conversation.
9. Somebody must have left *(his or her/their)* key in the lock.
10. Has anyone among you girls lost *(her/their)* keys?
11. No one raised *(his or her/their)* voice at the meeting.
12. She did *(most/almost)* everything by herself.
13. *(Most/Nearly)* every student passed the test.
14. We scouted the area *(good/well)*.
15. He could do nothing *(good/well)*.
16. The new band sounded very *(good/well)*.

17. We went to the baseball games *(regular/regularly)*.
18. The player was swinging the bat *(nervous/nervously)*.
19. Everyone left the restaurant *(quick/quickly)*.
20. They played the game *(like/as if)* their lives depended on it.
21. Her grandmother was *(famous/famously)* as a photographer.
22. Use it exactly *(like/as)* the directions say.
23. We had never sighted *(those/that)* kind of bird here.
24. Many of my friends had never seen a *(real/really)* zoo.
25. Cats sometimes wail exactly *(like/as)* a small child.

UNIT REVIEW EXERCISE

In each of the following sentences, which is the *right* choice for written English?

EXAMPLE: Kangaroos move naturally on two legs, *(like/as)* people.
(Answer) *like*

1. My sister and *(I/me)* are reading about Australia.
2. Much about Australia is strange for *(we/us)* Americans.
3. Most people live in big cities, *(like/as)* Americans do.
4. Others live in *(real/really)* small communities.
5. Sheep ranchers *(rise/raise)* sheep in the wide open spaces.
6. Many areas suffer *(bad/badly)* from droughts.
7. Sometimes it seems *(like/as if)* it will never rain again.
8. At other times, floods cause *(real/really)* problems.
9. Australians talk *(proud/proudly)* about their kangaroos.
10. Many kangaroos measure over five feet when they are *(sitting/setting)* on their hind legs.
11. Few animals are faster than *(they/them)*.
12. The numbers of some kinds have shrunk *(considerable/considerably)*.
13. Some species are endangered, *(like/as)* the whales.
14. But the big reds or greys are *(most/almost)* everywhere.
15. *(This/These)* kind can be seen grazing with sheep and other livestock.
16. The government controls hunters *(careful/carefully)*.
17. The aborigines hunted the *(swift/swiftly)* kangaroo for food.
18. They slept outdoors, *(lying/laying)* on the ground.
19. Life has been hard for *(they/them)* and their descendants.
20. *(We/Us)* Americans rarely hear news about Australia.
21. Some Australians are *(famous/famously)* around the world.
22. Joan Sutherland became a *(real/really)* famous singer.
23. Athletes often advertise their country *(good/well)*.
24. Australian tennis players often *(sit/set)* records.
25. A trip "down under" would be a marvelous adventure for you and *(I/me)*.

SPEAKING INFORMALLY

Informal English gives people a chance to use their sense of humor. It gives them a chance to seem clever, or to play with words. It also often gives them a chance to be less polite or less respectful than they would be in a formal situation. Study the following examples.

In the Ozark Mountains of Arkansas, Oklahoma, and Missouri, people speak a colorful variety of American English. The following sayings are drawn from the Ozark area. Can you read them with the right kind of expression? Pretend you are a colorful local character sitting near the stove in an old-time country store. Make up some sayings or phrases to go with the country sayings below.

1. I'd just as soon shin up a thorn tree with an armload of eels.
2. It's a good deal like climbin' a greased pole with two baskets of eggs.
3. He walks like he was belly-deep in cold water.
4. Her tongue was always a-waggin' like the south end of a goose.
5. He looked like the hindquarters of bad luck.
6. That man is so contrary that if you threw him in the river, he'd float upstream.
7. My brother is so unlucky, it would be money in his pocket if he'd never been born.
8. The days when I don't git to see you are plumb squandered and lost, like beads off'n a string.

When language becomes *very* informal, it becomes slang. Like all informal English, slang is "off-duty" English. We hear it on the playground, during a coffee break, or at a party. How do we *know* a word is slang? Would you agree that all of the following are slang? Do these examples have anything in common? Do they have any features that you have noticed in slang before?

wheels (car), booboo, bread (money), yuk-yuk, pad (home), sawbones (doctor), off his rocker, slurp, cracked, clink (jail)

FOR FURTHER STUDY

ACTIVITY 1

ACTIVITY 2

ACTIVITY 3

Do you ever use any of the following slang expressions? Why are they popular with people who use them? Can you tell from these examples why and when people *object* to slang? How would you react if any of these terms were applied to *you,* or to people close to you?

(physical appearance) fatso, baldy, creep, skinny
(person from rural background) hick, hillbilly, rube
(intelligence) birdbrain, stupe, dope, jerk, dumbbell, drip
(police) cop, fuzz, headbreaker
(model student) bookworm, brain, grind

ACTIVITY 4

Have you noticed how eagerly some people pick up *new* slang terms? Do you know any that seem to have become popular during the last year or so? Select three or four and explain what they mean and how they are used.

ACTIVITY 5

Members of a *group* often have their own special slang. Below is a list of contemporary words and phrases. Do you associate any of these words with a particular group? How many can you explain which are still in current use? Which ones have dropped out of the language?

bag, bit, cool, cop out, hangup, hassle, hip, out of sight, scene, split, straight, teenybopper, turn off, uptight, zap

(Can you think of any reasons why some of these terms should have survived while others have died?)

Chapter 5

Mechanics
The Written Page

Chapter
Preview 5

Know the basic rules for English punctuation and spelling.

When our system of writing was first invented, people tried to put down a letter for every sound they heard. Later, they learned to sort the letters out into words and sentences. They added marks to show how parts of a sentence went together. Look at the following sentence. What marks would you add to show the writer's meaning more clearly?

At the drive in movies are shown.

First, a hyphen would show that the word *in* belongs with *drive:* "At the drive-in movies are shown." The hyphen says, "These two words belong together." Second, we might need a mark to show that in this sentence *drive-in* and *movies* do *not* belong together:

At the drive-in, movies are shown.

The comma says, "Stop here—briefly." The brief pause shows that the words *At the drive-in* are a unit. Together, they give us the "where." Then the rest of the sentence gives us the "what." The comma shows where the main part of the sentence starts.

Readers are used to the basic rules for putting letters and other marks on the written page. To meet their expectations, you have to know how to handle commas, periods, hyphens, and other marks of punctuation. You have to know how to spell difficult words. You have to know when to capitalize. All these are part of the mechanics of writing.

How well do you know basic standards for satisfactory spelling and punctuation? Study the three possible choices for the blank space in each of the following passages. Put the letter of the best choice after the number of the passage.

DIAGNOSTIC TEST

EXAMPLE: We were watching a differ_____ program.
   a. ant   b. ent   c. int
(Answer) *b*

1. I bel_____ve everything you say.
   a. ei   b. ee   c. ie
2. My cousin lives in _____ .
   a. Shelby Iowa   b. Shelby, Iowa   c. shelby, iowa
3. Take the books back to the lib_____ .
   a. rary   b. erry   c. ary
4. The climbers put _____ goggles on.
   a. their   b. there   c. they're
5. The frost hurt the _____ damaged the blossoms.
   a. trees it   b. trees. It   c. trees, it
6. We had _____ the picnic for Saturday.
   a. plan   b. planed   c. planned
7. The oranges were _____ , and sweet.
   a. big, juicy   b. big juicy   c. big. Juicy
8. The bus _____ stop here.
   a. use to   b. useto   c. used to
9. Did you see the _____ took his wallet?
   a. person, who   b. person who   c. person. Who
10. The letter _____ make sense.
    a. dosent   b. doesnt   c. doesn't
11. I always enjoy my _____ vacations.
    a. familys   b. family's   c. families
12. We had only one _____ cat.
    a. pet. A   b. pet a   c. pet: a
13. Our club meets on _____ .
    a. Mondays   b. mondays   c. Monday's
14. My uncle was _____ had had an accident.
    a. late. He   b. late he   c. late, he

15. He asked, "What do you _____
    a. want?"   b. want.   c. want"?
16. California is famous for _____ beaches.
    a. it's   b. its   c. Its
17. I knew several _____ parents.
    a. girl's   b. girls   c. girls'
18. We watched the _____ sunset.
    a. beatyful   b. beautiful   c. beautyful
19. The party was _____ , we left.
    a. over therefore b. over, therefore c. over; therefore
20. You should help _____ they ask you.
    a. them if   b. them. If   c. them, if

M1

END PUNCTUATION

Mark the end of a sentence by a period, a question mark, or an exclamation mark.

Look at the punctuation marks with the following sentences:

Billy is talking.
Billy is talking?
Billy is talking!

All three punctuation marks stand for "Stop here." They signal the *end* of a unit of thought. The period, the question mark, and the exclamation point are called **end punctuation** for this reason.

Each mark also signals something else. The period tells us that the sentence is a *statement*. The writer is simply stating a fact. The question mark signals a *question*. It leads us to expect an answer or to give an answer. The exclamation mark signals *excitement*. The writer is telling us about something unusual, or upsetting, or important.

Without these marks, the three sample sentences would all say the same thing. With them, each sentence has a different meaning.

M1a

Sentences and Fragments

Put the period at the end of a complete sentence.

The period is the basic stop-and-go signal in writing. We use it to mark off one complete sentence from another. A complete sentence has its own subject and verb. (Remember that in a request sentence the subject has been left out. The word *you* is understood as the subject.)

SUBJECT	VERB
Dogs	*bark.*
Howard	*watched* the game.
The swallows	*will return* soon.
The balloons	*were released* together.
	Watch the game.
	Help me with the load.
	Send in your coupon.

Do not use a period to mark off a group of words that is not a complete sentence. We call an incomplete or half-finished sentence a **sentence fragment.** Avoid three major kinds of sentence fragments:

(1) Do not mark off a prepositional phrase as if it were a separate sentence. Prepositional phrases start with a preposition like *at, on, by, to, for, in, with,* and *without.* Do not cut off these phrases from the earlier sentence by inserting a period. Usually they can become part of the earlier sentence without a break:

FRAGMENT: The whole family often went fishing. *On weekends.*
COMPLETE: The whole family often went fishing *on weekends.*

FRAGMENT: We took the path up the hill. *By mistake.*
COMPLETE: We took the path up the hill *by mistake.*

FRAGMENT: You cannot cross here. *Without the owner's permission.*
COMPLETE: You cannot cross here *without the owner's permission.*

(2) Do not mark off a verb or part of a verb without a subject. Added groups of words like the following would need a subject to become a complete separate sentence:

FRAGMENT: The machine rumbled across the field. *Harvesting* the crop.
COMPLETE: The machine rumbled across the field. *It was harvesting* the crop.

FRAGMENT: I read the note. *Written* in a hurry.
COMPLETE: I read the note. *It had been written* in a hurry.

FRAGMENT: We looked up at the palm trees. *Swayed* by the breeze.
COMPLETE: We looked up at the palm trees. *They were swayed* by the breeze.

(3) Do not mark off an added noun without a verb. Added labels like the following would need a verb to turn each of them into a complete separate sentence:

FRAGMENT: The package was for Sue. *My sister.*
COMPLETE: The package was for Sue. *She is my sister.*

FRAGMENT: We met Al and Beth. *My cousins.*
COMPLETE: We met Al and Beth. *They are my cousins.*

NOTE: You can often join a fragment to the earlier sentence. You will study some of the possibilities as you study the uses of commas, colons, and dashes.

See **M2b** on dependent clauses set off as fragments.

EXERCISE 1

In some of the following, one complete sentence is followed by a period. Write *S* for satisfactory after the number of each such sentence. In others, two sentences are run together. After the number, write the last word of the first sentence, followed by a period and the first word of the other sentence, starting with a capital letter.

EXAMPLE: George ran into the room he had forgotten his books.
(Answer) *room. He*

1. Her parents worked in the fields.
2. The roof caved in the spectators screamed.
3. She and her brother are new here.
4. Paolo resisted the bandits took him along.
5. The rains came the winds blew.
6. She hit the ball it went over the fence.
7. They held a meeting after the lunch.
8. They held a meeting first they ate lunch.
9. Winter always brought heavy snow.
10. I could not solve the problem Jim helped me.
11. We waited for an hour he finally returned.
12. The astronaut shared the rocket with an electronic brain.
13. He read a book she wrote a letter.
14. I went to the telephone around the corner.
15. You can leave now I will call you later.
16. It is late we are tired of waiting.
17. Huck Finn went down the Mississippi on a raft.
18. People will leave our planet they will live on space stations.
19. The criminal was found guilty he was sent to prison.
20. You should read the book it is a good adventure story.

Which of the following pairs are two complete sentences? Write *C* for complete after the number of each such pair. In which of the pairs is the second part a sentence fragment? Write *F* for fragment after the number of the pair.

EXERCISE 2

EXAMPLE: Egypt has famous pyramids. They were built as tombs. (Answer) *C*

1. The Nile is a big river. Flowing through Egypt.
2. The Bible often mentions Egypt. It is close to Palestine.
3. The Pharaohs ruled the country. They were mighty kings.
4. They built great temples. On the banks of the Nile.
5. The country was rich. It produced much grain.
6. Bookkeepers kept records. In picture writing.
7. These people invented paper. The word itself came from Egypt.
8. They built warships. Rowed by large crews.
9. Their builders built the mighty pyramids. Without modern equipment.
10. They moved huge blocks of stone. We know little about their methods.
11. The pyramids were sealed. Many treasures were hidden inside.
12. The treasure might include a boat. For the trip to the other world.
13. Jars held fruit or oil. Food for the trip.
14. Grave robbers opened the tombs. They stole the treasures.
15. Some tombs were well hidden. Modern explorers found them.
16. Museums exhibit the treasures. Large crowds have seen them.
17. Many articles are made from precious materials. Gold and ivory.
18. Famous sculptures show us the faces. Of the dead rulers.
19. A big new dam has backed up the Nile. Some temples were covered by water.
20. Find Egypt on the map. Read a book about its treasures.

Use question marks and exclamation marks where necessary.

M1b

Questions and Exclamations

Not all of the sentences we use are ordinary statements. Look out for the following:

(1) Use the question mark when a question signal turns a statement into a question. A **question mark** asks for an answer. We can turn any statement into a question by making our voice *go up* at the end (as shown by the arrows in the sentences on the next page):

SPOKEN: Fred locked the door ↗
WRITTEN: Fred locked the door?

SPOKEN: Your uncle sent you money ↗
WRITTEN: Your uncle sent you money?

Other question signals are question words like *when, where, why, how, who, which,* and *what.*

> *Who* took my glass?
> *What* did he say?
> *How* did he get in?
> *Where* are the eggs?

In many questions, an *auxiliary* has traded places with the subject:

> *Are* they still waiting?
> *Have* you heard from him?
> *Did* the store refund your money?
> *Will* we always be at the end of the line?

(2) Use the exclamation mark when you want a statement to stand out for special attention. When we are especially excited about something we say, we turn up the volume or make our voice shriller. Use the **exclamation point** to mean "special attention":

SPOKEN: The *Martians* are coming
WRITTEN: The Martians are coming!

SPOKEN: A *wheel* came off
WRITTEN: A wheel came off!

Note that many shouts, orders, and similar exclamations are shorter than a complete sentence. They do not need a subject and a verb:

> Hurray!
> Silence!
> One more time!
> What a beautiful day!

EXERCISE 1

After the number of each sentence write the punctuation mark you would use for that sentence. Be prepared to explain why you chose the mark you did. (You and your classmates may *dis*agree on one or two of these.) Use the question mark only if there is a clear question signal in the sentence.

1. We won the game as usual _____
2. How did you win the game _____
3. For the first time in ten years we won the Big Game _____
4. You really lost your book _____
5. Did you lose your book _____
6. Billy is my brother _____
7. He has found his long-lost brother _____
8. Have you ever baked a cherry pie _____
9. Have you seen the girls _____
10. Give me liberty or give me death _____
11. Which road should I take _____
12. Are these mushrooms poisonous _____
13. Could they have taken the wrong turn _____
14. We have won the trip to Hawaii _____
15. Why do you always ask me for help _____
16. We took our usual route home _____
17. Do you know the way to their house _____
18. We have lived there for many years _____
19. Stay away from the fire _____
20. Where did Columbus first land in the New World _____

Check the use of end punctuation in each of the following passages. Put *S* after the number if the punctuation is satisfactory. Put *U* for unsatisfactory if a mark has been used incorrectly or left out.

UNIT REVIEW EXERCISE

EXAMPLE: Why does he always complain.
(Answer)   *U*

1. How much do you know about tigers?
2. Only about 6,000 of these animals are left in the world.
3. They first lived in Siberia they later moved south.
4. Have you see pictures of a full-grown tiger.
5. It has beautiful yellow or red fur with black stripes.
6. It has strong claws and teeth. It will attack any animal.
7. A tiger may eat 200 pounds of meat at one meal!
8. Tigers are good hunters. With a keen sense of smell.
9. Their ears are very sharp. Their eyesight is poor.
10. They track down fast animals. Deer and antelope.
11. Do tigers attack people.
12. Old tigers cannot hunt well. They may attack human beings.
13. We've read about wounded tigers. Turning on hunters.

14. We often see tigers in movies about the jungle.
15. Actually strong heat bothers tigers they cool off in water.
16. They are good swimmers. A tiger may swim two or three miles.
17. The cubs soon hunt on their own. After about six months.
18. Tigers are beautiful animals. They also do much damage.
19. Governments often put a price on their heads.
20. Do you think this is right.

M2
LINKING PUNCTUATION

Use linking punctuation to help join two statements in a larger combined sentence.

Our language has many ways to join two statements together to make a larger combined sentence. When the two statements are joined in one unit without the seam showing, we use *no* punctuation. When there is a slight break between the two, we use a *comma*. When there is a heavier break, we use a *semicolon*. In each of the following, a second statement has been added to the first:

SEPARATE: I saw her. *She walked right on.*

COMBINED: I saw her *when she left the house.*
I saw her, *but she walked right on.*
I saw her; *however, she ignored me.*

When separate statements become part of a larger sentence, we call them **clauses.** Clauses are the partner sentences that join to make up a larger combined unit. In each of the examples above, each of the two clauses has its own subject and verb. Know what punctuation to use when you join two clauses in a larger combined sentence.

M2a
Linking Independent Clauses

Use a comma or semicolon between two independent clauses.

When two clauses are joined only loosely, we call them **independent** clauses. We could easily separate them again and put a period between the two:

JOINED: We feared a flood; however, the dam held.
SEPARATE: We feared a flood. However, the dam held.

How do we punctuate such "separable" clauses? Punctuation depends on the connecting link. Remember:

(1) Use a comma before a coordinating connective. Such **coordinators** make two statements "work together." We then have only a slight break between the two. Use the **comma** before one of the coordinating connectives *and, but, for, or, yet,* or *so:*

My cousins rowed, *and* I steered.
I am feeling fine, *but* my sister is sick.
Harry left school early, *for* he had a doctor's appointment.
We must repay the money, *or* he will charge us interest.
Polly sings well, *yet* she can't read music.
It was snowing heavily, *so* the driver put on chains.

(2) Use a semicolon before an adverbial connective. We have a heavier break if the link is one of the **adverbial connectives,** such as *however, therefore, furthermore, nevertheless, besides,* or *in fact.* Use a **semicolon** when two clauses are linked by one of these:

We asked for tickets; *however,* the show was sold out.
The deadline has passed; *therefore,* we are returning your
    money.
She sent the package early; *nevertheless,* it arrived late.

Remember an important difference between these adverbial connectives and the first kind of link: Coordinators always come at the point where the two statements join. But words like *therefore* can move in the second clause. They can interrupt the second statement, or they can come at the end. The semicolon, however, stays in place:

The deadline has passed; we are, *therefore,* returning your
    money.
She sent the package early; it arrived late, *nevertheless.*

(3) Practice using the additional comma (or commas) with adverbial connectives. A word like *therefore* often causes a double break. A comma often sets it off from the rest of the second clause. (If it interrupts the second clause, *two* commas set it off.) This additional punctuation appears in much serious, formal writing. It is not required, however, and often left out in modern books and magazines:

RIGHT: We rushed to the box office; the concert, *however,* was
                    sold out.
ALSO RIGHT: We rushed to the box office; the concert *however* was
                    sold out.

EXERCISE 1

In each of the following, two clauses have been joined in a larger combined sentence. Look at the blank space in each sentence. Put *C* after the number of the sentence if there should be a comma. Put *SC* after the number of the sentence if there should be a semicolon.

EXAMPLE: We wrote Uncle Ed a letter _____ but he never answered.

(Answer) *C*

1. We were planning a picnic _____ but it rained.
2. Contestants must be sixteen _____ therefore, we have no chance.
3. The buses were stalled _____ so we all missed school.
4. The team was losing _____ and fans were leaving the stadium.
5. The ice was thin _____ the boat was trapped, nevertheless.
6. The manager was gone; however _____ she had left a note.
7. We never heard the record advertised _____ yet it sold many copies.
8. Should I buy the set _____ or should I save my money?
9. The shoes are too expensive _____ besides, the store is closed.
10. We were very sad _____ for our friends were leaving.
11. The restaurant is closed; the snack bar, however _____ is open.
12. Come inside _____ or close the door.
13. The car had been fixed _____ so we continued our trip.
14. You ordered the article _____ and you should pay for it.
15. The day was a holiday _____ the post office, therefore, was closed.
16. We like this town _____ in fact, we come here often.
17. The builders used aluminum _____ for steel is too heavy.
18. Only a dozen people signed up _____ therefore, the trip was canceled.
19. The article was damaged _____ so we returned it to the store.
20. I liked the book _____ however, I was disappointed in the movie.

EXERCISE 2

Words like *and* and *for* do not *always* add a second clause to a sentence. (They also have other uses.) The following sentences need added punctuation only if the connective actually joins two clauses, each with its own subject and verb. How would you fill the blank space in each sentence? After the number of the sentence, put the right abbreviation:

C   for comma
SC for semicolon
No for no punctuation

1. I had not done my homework _____ therefore I was not prepared.
2. We love horseback riding _____ so we ride nearly every day.
3. We stayed at the camp _____ for several days.
4. Patricia wanted a mynah bird _____ but she got a canary.
5. We wanted to go to the mountains _____ all members of the family, therefore, saved their money.
6. They knew the road was dangerous _____ besides, they were driving an old car.
7. It is no use crying _____ for I cannot help you.
8. I read a dozen short stories _____ and three novels last summer.
9. I understand the question _____ but I forget the answer.
10. His sister has been ill _____ however, she will be at the graduation.
11. The janitor turned out all the lights _____ and left the building.
12. I haven't seen her lately _____ in fact, I saw her last three weeks ago.
13. The shortstop made his third error _____ the coach, therefore, took him out of the game.
14. The pitcher retired twenty-seven batters in a row _____ in fact, she pitched a perfect game.
15. Fred cooked _____ and Jim did the dishes.

EXERCISE 3

Combine the sentences in each of the following pairs in a larger sentence. Write each combined sentence twice: The first time, use a coordinator. The second time, use an adverbial connective. Each time use the right punctuation.

EXAMPLE: It was getting dark.
We pitched our tent.
(Answer) *It was getting dark, so we pitched our tent.*
It was getting dark; therefore, we pitched our tent.

1. Martha loved fishing.
Her sister preferred swimming.

2. Bertha did not speak plainly.
No one understood her.

3. Ellen wrote a good story.
The magazine accepted it.

4. We lost the game.
We congratulated the other team.

5. We understood the directions.
   We could not fit the pieces together.

6. The play ended.
   Everyone applauded wildly.

7. They followed the doctor's orders.
   We cannot blame them.

8. They never answer my letters.
   I sent a telegram.

9. The road has many curves.
   It is uphill most of the way.

10. We need the money.
    We need it badly.

M2b

Linking Dependent Clauses

Know when to use commas with dependent clauses.

When we join two clauses, they often become locked together for good. One of them becomes **dependent** on the other. It can no longer stand by itself. In each of the following pairs, the second line shows a dependent clause left standing alone It no longer has the **main clause** it needs for support:

COMBINED: The crowd booed *when I dropped the ball.*
SEPARATE: *When I dropped the ball* . . . (Then what happened?)

COMBINED: I can reach the branch *if you lift me.*
SEPARATE: *If you lift me* . . . (Then what?)

With some dependent clauses, we need a comma. With some, we use no punctuation. Two different kinds of connectives start a dependent clause, but the same basic rule applies to both. Remember:

(1) Use a comma before a subordinator only if the dependent clause could be left out. Subordinators, or subordinating connectives, are words like *if, when, where, because, unless, before, after, while, until, though,* and *although.* When you see such a word, ask: How important or necessary is the information it brings into the sentence? Often the information is essential—we cannot do without it.

Essential information blends into the sentence without a break—no break in speech, no punctuation in writing. You can tell that a dependent clause is essential when you can change *if* or *where* to *only where:*

ESSENTIAL: Astronauts can survive *if they take along oxygen.*
    (*only* if they do)
ESSENTIAL: Rice will grow *where water is plentiful.*
    (*only* where it is)
ESSENTIAL: I will return *after you apologize.*
    (*only* after you do)

Sometimes the added information is *not* essential. We can do without. The main point of the sentence would still be true if the dependent clause were left out. Nonessential information is added to the sentence after a slight break. In writing, it is set off by a **comma.** We usually find this comma before *though* or *although* and also before *whereas.* You can tell that the information is nonessential when you can put *anyway* or *regardless* before the dependent clause.

NONESSENTIAL: He was hungry, *although he did not say so.*
    (He was hungry *anyway.*)
NONESSENTIAL: We went outside, *though it was raining.*
    (We went outside *anyway.*)

(2) *Use a comma when the dependent clause comes first.* A clause that starts with a subordinator can move to the beginning of a sentence. We then use a comma to show where the main clause starts. Use this comma regardless of how important the dependent clause is:

If they take along oxygen, astronauts can survive.
When I get my allowance, I will pay you back.

(3) *Use a comma only with nonessential relative clauses.* Relative clauses start with a relative pronoun like *who, which,* and *that.* (Remember that a relative pronoun does not only *link* two clauses. It also *takes the place of something* in the second clause.)

Relative pronouns give us essential information when the clause they start tells us *which one.* In the following examples, there are *no breaks* and *no commas:*

ESSENTIAL: We stared at the truck *that followed us.*
    (*Which* truck? The one that followed us.)
ESSENTIAL: He congratulated the student *who won the prize.*
    (*Which* student? The one who won the prize.)
ESSENTIAL: The boys *who broke the windows* will be prosecuted.
    (*Which* boys? The ones who broke the windows.)

The relative pronoun brings in *non*essential information if we already know *who* or *which one.* We then hear a break in speech. We need a **comma** in writing. Notice that we know *who* when the relative pronoun points back to a name:

NONESSENTIAL: I talked to Jean Gable, *who had just arrived.*

Note that *two* commas are needed when the dependent clause *interrupts* the main clause:

NONESSENTIAL: Jim Snepp, *who had won the contest,* read his prize poems.

NONESSENTIAL: Japan, *which was badly defeated in World War II,* is again a leading industrial nation.

(4) Do not use a period to separate a dependent clause from its main clause. If you break it off from the main clause and put a period in front of it, you are left with a sentence *fragment.* Avoid such sentence fragments:

JOINED: The village was flooded *when the dam broke.*

FRAGMENT: The village was flooded. *When the dam broke.*

EXERCISE 1

Study the difference between the sentences in each of the following pairs. Which sentence needs a comma, or commas? Put *C* after its number. Which sentence should have no added punctuation? Put *No* after its number.

EXAMPLE: The stranger smiled broadly _____ after I apologized.
(Answer) *No*

1. My family kept a big guard dog _____ although the neighbors complained.
2. My family kept a big guard dog _____ until the neighbors complained.

3. My grandmother admired President Eisenhower _____ who was a Republican.
4. My grandmother admired every President _____ who was a Republican.

5. We always go inside _____ when it rains.
6. When it rains _____ we always go inside.

7. The road was open _____ unless snowfall was very heavy.
8. The road was open _____ though snowfall was very heavy.

9. The people _____ who lived here _____ have moved away.
10. Cora's parents _____ who lived here _____ have moved away.

11. She lent me *Robinson Crusoe* _____ which she had been reading.
12. She lent me the book _____ that she had been reading.

13. My aunt ran the store _____ whereas my uncle did the farming.
14. My aunt ran the store _____ when my uncle did the farming.

15. We drove up to the peak _____ that is the highest mountain there.
16. We drove up to Pikes Peak _____ which is the highest mountain there.

17. The owner will call the police _____ if the fight starts again.
18. If the fight starts again _____ the owner will call the police.

19. They invited us to Kent Harbor _____ where they had rented a cabin.
20. They invited us to the place _____ where they had rented a cabin.

EXERCISE 2

Each of the following sentences contains a main clause and a dependent clause. What punctuation would you use in the blank spaces? Write *C* if the sentence should have a comma. Write *No* if there should be no punctuation.

1. The American Revolution began _____ when British soldiers fired on a mob in Boston.
2. The result was the Boston Massacre _____ which was the first use of weapons against the colonists.
3. The soldiers fired on a crowd _____ that had harassed a British sentinel.
4. The leader of the crowd was Crispus Attucks _____ who was probably a sailor.
5. Attucks was a slave _____ until he escaped from his master.
6. Attucks and two companions fell dead _____ after the British fired.
7. These three were the first Americans _____ who died in the struggle for independence.
8. You see a monument in their honor _____ if you travel to Boston.
9. Attucks is remembered _____ although his two companions are forgotten.
10. He was the first black American _____ who died for the country.

Mechanics

Rewrite the following sentences twice. Add a dependent clause each time. The first time use a *subordinator*. The second time use a *relative pronoun*. Use the right punctuation between the two clauses.

EXAMPLE: My friends were frightened.
(Answer)   My friends were frightened *when the weather turned bad.*
My friends, *who had never sailed before,* were frightened.

1. Jimmy blew the trumpet.
2. The comedian threw the pie in the guest's face.
3. The audience laughed at the joke.
4. The plane skidded across the runway.
5. My friends hitchhiked.
6. Captain Cook traveled around the world.
7. Jean never smiled.
8. García came from Puerto Rico.
9. The man was my friend.
10. The bridge collapsed.

What punctuation should appear in the blank space in each of the following sentences? After the number of the sentence, put the right abbreviation:

C   for comma
SC   for semicolon
No   for no punctuation

EXAMPLE: We brought everything inside _____ before the storm broke.
(Answer) *No*

1. People who cut their own wood _____ are warmed twice.
2. When you drink the water _____ think of the source.
3. The train ride was beautiful _____ however, it took several days.
4. The holiday had started _____ so the streets were crowded.
5. Helen Keller became famous _____ although she was blind.
6. The creek will be filled in _____ if the new houses are built.
7. It had turned very cold _____ nevertheless, many people stood in line.
8. The rules had been changed; our request, therefore _____ was turned down.
9. I called several times _____ but nobody answered.
10. She was always practicing _____ when I saw her.

11. Millions of people read *Roots* ——— which was written by Alex Haley.
12. Many people saw the television series ——— that was made from it.
13. A sign marked the spot ——— where the first city hall stood.
14. Annie is busy tonight ——— besides, she hates horror movies.
15. Jamaica ——— which was once British, is now independent.
16. We followed the directions ——— that came with the package.
17. After they heard the announcement ——— the people cheered.
18. Stranded trucks blocked the road ——— therefore, we abandoned the car.
19. Missouri was a state ——— whereas Oklahoma was a territory.
20. They will take back the set ——— unless the bill is paid.

Use punctuation marks to show breaks inside a sentence.

M3

INSIDE PUNCTUATION

A simple sentence holds together *without* punctuation. We do not put a comma between the subject and its verb, or between the verb and an object.

Our dog had buried the bone.
We give the cat leftovers.
The hungry dogs ate the meat.

When *do* we use punctuation inside a sentence?

Use commas where necessary to set off modifiers.

M3a

Commas for Modifiers

As long as a sentence uses only the most basic parts, we need no commas or other marks to help us find our way:

The clerk offered the customer a seat.
A plane has been circling the field.

Punctuation may become necessary when we add attachments to the basic parts of such a sentence. We call such attachments **modifiers.** Some modifiers blend into a sentence without a break. Others are set off by commas. Remember:

(1) Use the comma when a nonessential modifier causes a slight break in a sentence. A modifier is essential when we *must have* it to complete our message. It then blends in with the rest of the sentence. There is no break in speech and *no punctuation* in writing.

USING THE COMMA
An Overview

The comma has more uses than any other mark. Put it to good use in the following situations:

(1) With coordinators like *and, but, or, for, yet,* or *so:*
The audience became quiet, *and* the speaker started.

(2) With some subordinators *(though, although, whereas):*
We enjoyed the trip, *although* it was a foggy day.

(3) To show where the main clause starts:
If we get up early, we can watch the sunrise.

(4) With a nonessential relative clause:
We saw Santa Cruz Mission, *which dates back to Spanish days.*

(5) With a nonessential modifier:
Oldham Castle, *perched on a hill,* is now a hotel.

(6) With an introductory modifier:
After a brief intermission, the concert continued.

(7) In a series:
Football, baseball, and *basketball* are popular sports.

(8) With dates and addresses that have several parts:
She was born *Monday, January 5, 1976.*
They had moved to *Nashville, Tennessee.*

(9) With tag openings and tag questions:
Yes, that is true.
They helped you, *didn't they?*

(10) With other interrupters:
Your ticket, *James,* has been lost.
She is always too busy, *it seems.*

(11) Between two things lined up for contrast:
They live in Chicago, *not Detroit.*

(12) Between a credit tag and a quotation:
She said, "You are telling us nothing new."

In each of the following, the added part answers the question "which one?" It tells us "*only* this one" or "*only* these":

ESSENTIAL: Arrest the man *in the red shirt*.
(Leave the one in the green shirt alone.)

ESSENTIAL: Any person *sleeping on the job* will be fired.
(But no one else.)

Nonessential parts are added to a sentence in which the main point has already been made. They add something that the audience might *also* want to know. They could be left out. Use **commas** to mark off such nonessential parts.

In the following examples, can you hear the slight break in speech?

NONESSENTIAL: We found him in the storeroom, *sleeping on the job*.
(But the main point is that we found him.)

NONESSENTIAL: His sister, *reading by the window,* gave us a mean look.
(The mean look is the important part of the sentence.)

NONESSENTIAL: Teresa stayed by the telephone, *waiting for a call*.
(The essential part is that she *stayed* there. The rest is added explanation.)

NOTE: When nonessential words *interrupt* a sentence, you need two commas. The first shows where the modifier starts. The second shows where it ends:

The holdup man, *smiling politely,* took the day's receipts.

(2) Set off introductory modifiers. Use the comma to show where the main part of the sentence starts. Prepositional phrases with three words or more are usually set off from the main part:

LONG PREPOSITIONAL PHRASE: *With his new walking stick,* he started off again.

LONG PREPOSITIONAL PHRASE: *At the seashore in the summer,* we hunt for seashells.

This comma is often necessary for clarity. In each of the following examples, the comma helps us see where the main part of the sentence starts:

CONFUSING: In the evening trains run frequently.
CLEAR: *In the evening,* trains run frequently.

CONFUSING: At our school books are never thrown away.
CLEAR: *At our school,* books are never thrown away.

At the beginning of a sentence, *–ing* verbals are always set off from the subject that follows them. This rule applies whether the verbal carries other words with it or not:

INTRODUCTORY VERBAL: *Whistling,* Jack stepped out into the hall.
INTRODUCTORY VERBAL: *Taking careful aim,* she hit the ball.

(3) Set off modifiers that go with the sentence as a whole. Expressions like the following give us a comment or an explanation that goes with the sentence as a whole:

Considering her age, she did very well.
To be quite frank, we need no additional help.
I never liked him, *to tell you the truth.*

Words and expressions like *generally, obviously, unfortunately,* and *for example* also usually go with the sentence as a whole. They are often set off by a comma, especially in formal writing. Two commas are needed if the expression comes in the middle of a sentence.

RIGHT: *Unfortunately,* our tickets were lost.
ALSO RIGHT: *Unfortunately* our tickets were lost.

RIGHT: People in Brazil, *for example,* speak Portuguese.
ALSO RIGHT: People in Brazil *for example* speak Portuguese.

EXERCISE 1

Look at the blank space in each of the following sentences. Put *C* after the number of the sentence if there should be a comma. Put *No* if there should be no punctuation.

EXAMPLE: People living in Maine _____ are used to cold winters.
(Answer) *No*

1. We lost the note _____ giving us directions.
2. After a long hike _____ we reached the camp.
3. My parents, born in Canada _____ grew up in Michigan.
4. The neighbors put out food _____ for their cats.
5. The driver backing out of the driveway _____ barely missed the post.
6. The article was about a car _____ running on batteries.
7. Leaving the house _____ I remembered my appointment.
8. The stranger said good-bye _____ shaking my hand.
9. A rolling stone _____ gathers no moss.
10. To be honest with you _____ the money is gone.
11. The picnic, unfortunately _____ was rained out.
12. A new mechanic _____ is working at the gas station.

13. The usher counted the people _____ waiting in line.
14. Considering today's prices _____ the table was a bargain.
15. The package on the top shelf _____ is for you.
16. My brother John _____ waiting outside, got impatient.
17. The Mississippi, rising over its banks _____ flooded the fields.
18. The police aided residents _____fleeing from the fire.
19. The food was bad _____ to tell you the truth.
20. Gathering speed _____ the plane rumbled down the runway.

EXERCISE 2

In some of the following sentences, a comma should appear after an introductory modifier. In some, a comma should come after an introductory clause to show where the main part of the sentence starts. Look at the blank space in each sentence. Put *C* after the number of the sentence if there should be a comma. Put *No* if there should be no punctuation.

EXAMPLE: In the old days _____ storytellers knew many tales.
(Answer)   *C*

1. In a folktale from Africa _____ we hear about the girl with the large eyes.
2. Her tribe _____ had gone without rain for months.
3. Walking far _____ the girl searched for water.
4. If she found an old water hole _____ she would scoop water from the mud.
5. In one almost dry water hole _____ she saw a beautiful fish.
6. The skin of the fish _____ resembled the colors of the rainbow.
7. Helping the girl _____ the magic fish filled her pitcher with clear water.
8. The clear water _____ was a big surprise for the tribe.
9. Her parents _____ sent her brother after the girl as a spy.
10. When the parents learned about the fish _____ they were afraid.
11. With fear in their hearts _____ the people killed the fish.
12. Carrying the fish _____ the girl waded into the largest water hole.
13. After she disappeared _____ large water lilies floated on the water.
14. The listeners _____ can guess the end of the story.
15. The beautiful lilies _____ looked like large eyes.

Use commas where necessary to show minor breaks in a sentence.

Several kinds of repetition or interrruption cause minor breaks in a sentence. Look for the following. Listen for the slight break (or breaks) when each sample sentence is read aloud.

M3b

Commas for Minor Breaks

**LANGUAGE
IN ACTION**

GOLD IN THEM THERE HILLS

Complete each of the following sentences. Use the punctuation already shown. Fill in materials of your own choice that fit the blank spaces. (Write on a separate sheet.)

EXAMPLE: The old newspaper was dated _____ , _____ .
(Answer)   The old newspaper was dated December 13, 1849.

1. On our _____ , we went to the museum.
2. In _____ , the tools of the early miners were on display.
3. We looked at the crude picks, _____ , and _____ .
4. On _____ , we saw an old photograph of a miner.
5. Other pictures showed abandoned ships in San Francisco, _____ .
6. News of the gold rush had spread from Chicago, _____ , to New Orleans, _____ .
7. Sailors, _____ , and _____ left their jobs.
8. Boom towns sprang up with stores, _____ , and _____ .
9. These places had names like Frenchman's Gap, _____ , and _____ .
10. Prospecting was a job for strong, _____ , and _____ people.
11. Most of them found only hard work, not _____ .
12. We cannot blame them for _____ , can we?
13. Some searched the hills with only a mule, _____ , and _____ .
14. Others scooped wet sand from a river into pans, _____ , and _____ .
15. After the end of _____ , many boom towns became ghost towns.

(1) Use commas between sentence parts that have been repeated. The verb in the sentence below has *three* subjects. Note the commas that go with this **series** of subjects:

SERIES: *Mrs. Smith, Mr. Fox,* and *Ed* had an argument.

Most sentences have a single subject, a single verb, and, in some cases, a single object. But each of these parts can be repeated. You can have several subjects, or verbs, or objects in the same sentence. When you have *three or more* of any major part, separate them by commas:

SERIES OF SUBJECTS:	*The boy, the girl,* and *the dog* went for a walk.
SERIES OF VERBS:	The crowd *laughed, shouted,* and *cried.*
SERIES OF OBJECTS:	We saw *the skyscrapers, the department stores,* and *the theaters* of New York.
SERIES OF MODIFIERS:	This is a job for *strong, healthy,* and *adventurous* people.

(2) Use commas in dates, addresses, and measurements with two or more parts. Notice how the commas in the following sentences keep the main items separate from each other. With dates and addresses, a comma is used *after* the last main item if the sentence continues:

DATES: My lucky day was May 27, 1980.
May 27, 1980, was my lucky day.

ADDRESSES: Our address was 5946 Michigan Avenue, Chicago, Illinois.
We lived at 5946 Michigan Avenue, Chicago, Illinois, before moving south.

With measurements in two or more parts, no additional comma is used after the last item:

MEASUREMENTS: Jill weighed 105 pounds, 12 ounces on the scale.
I measured 5 feet, 4 inches in bare feet.

(3) Use commas to set off parts that are not built into the structure of the sentence. Such **interrupters** are set off from the main sentence with a comma or commas. In speaking to someone, we often hold up the rest of what we are saying to call the person by *name:*

James, bring me your book.
You have to get dressed now, *Pat.*
Your advice, *doctor,* will be followed.

Here are other tags and comments that are set off:

OPENING TAGS: *Yes,* I will lend you a pencil.
Well, I guess I will leave now.
Oh, I forgot.

TAG QUESTIONS: You found the book, *didn't you?*
He can eat everything now, *can't he?*
I'm a fool, *am I?*

COMMENTS: Tryouts, *it seems,* will be held on Friday.
The trip, *they agreed,* had been a success.

CONTRAST: We meet Tuesday, *not Monday.*

EXERCISE 1

The following sentences show different kinds of punctuation inside a sentence. Each sentence shows *how things are done right.* Study the examples carefully. Be prepared to explain why punctuation was used the way it was.

1. After the long trip, the crew was dead tired.
2. You will be at the graduation, won't you?
3. The trouble with you, George, is your shyness.
4. No, I have not been invited.
5. Son, you will have to do better than that.
6. You would never lie to me, would you?
7. Lloyd, Lisa, and Ed played tennis.
8. I wrote the letter on June 14, 1981.
9. Everyone was cheering, clapping, and laughing.
10. A neighbor, it seems, reported the accident.
11. In the mountains in the summer, time moves slowly.
12. Where have you been, old friend?
13. Yes, now I see.
14. People arrived by car, by boat, or by train.
15. They had moved to 1301 Washington Avenue, Provo, Utah.
16. Saturday, December 29, had been circled in red.
17. The fish weighed 13 pounds, 12 ounces.
18. Why, nobody drives that kind of car anymore.
19. The park, we were told, was closed.
20. They always traveled by car, never by plane.

EXERCISE 2

Check the following sentences for needed punctuation. Which of the sentences need one or more commas? On a separate sheet of paper, write *C* after the number of each sentence that does. Write *No* if no punctuation is necessary. (Be prepared to explain in class where you would put the commas, and why.)

EXAMPLE: Her parents had come from Baltimore Maryland.
(Answer)   *C*

1. The student put a sandwich a heavy sweater and a notebook in the locker.
2. The note they found in the bottle had been written on February 17 1756.
3. The shopper bought 12 pounds of potatoes.
4. The monster was huge ugly and toothless.
5. The doctor took my temperature ordered me to stay in bed and wrote out a prescription.
6. Your time is up George.
7. The artist was studying the picture.

8. You know my friend Ralph don't you?
9. A new mechanic they told me is now working at Henderson's service station.
10. We hiked up the hill and down the other side.
11. The pitcher struck out one batter walked the second and hit the third.
12. We showered got dressed and had a good breakfast.
13. No one had ever asked George for his autograph.
14. Well perhaps they will change their minds.
15. Park your car in the driveway not in the street.
16. We had never before seen the sunset from the very top of the mountain.
17. A weight of 6 pounds 3 ounces is unusual for this fish.
18. You could always take the bus couldn't you?
19. Boston Massachusetts has a beautifully renovated waterfront.
20. The stage had been decorated in red white and blue.

Know when to use inside punctuation other than commas.

M3c
Colons, Dashes, and Parentheses

Follow these guidelines for the use of colons, dashes, and parentheses:

(1) Use the colon to introduce lists and explanations. Use the colon when it takes the place of an expression like *namely* or *as follows:*

We had visited three states: *Kansas, Texas, and New Mexico.*
He had forgotten the most important thing: *the key.*

(2) Use dashes to signal strong breaks. Dashes make things stand out:

They had only one goal—*to win.*
The gate was open—*what luck!*
Their house—*a mansion on the hill*—was for sale.

Use dashes when *a whole sentence* interrupts and breaks up another sentence:

Your uncle—*this is the truth*—has never helped us.

(3) Use parentheses around added comments or explanations. Parentheses may show that an explanation or comment is not very important:

We had worked hard all spring *(with a few days off for Easter).*
Her book *(published in 1976)* told a marathon swimmer's story.

But we also use parentheses when we add exact details for readers who may want them:

It was the highest peak in the range *(8,765 feet)*.
Her birthday *(June 8)* will be on a Sunday.

Sometimes material in parentheses is a *separate sentence.* The following example has its own period at the end:

The whole family was hot. *(The dog was panting like a long-distance runner.)*

EXERCISE 1

Complete the following sentences. Use the punctuation shown. Find material of your own to fill the blank spaces.

EXAMPLE: The new unit of measurement was the meter (_____).
(Answer)   The new unit of measurement was the meter *(3.28 feet)*.

1. The United States shares long borders with two neighbors: _____ .
2. My birthday (_____) should be a happy day.
3. I want one thing most of all— _____ .
4. I remember the names of several recent Presidents: _____ , _____ , and _____ .
5. Most Americans know the street where the President lives (_____).
6. The number of this page (_____) appears at the bottom.
7. People in cities often see only a few kinds of birds: _____ .
8. My favorite place—_____—has much to offer.
9. Many young people like pizza (_____).
10. I enjoy my favorite holiday: _____ .

EXERCISE 2

Most of the following sentences show the right way to use colons, dashes, and parentheses. Put *S* for satisfactory after the number of each such sentence. Put *U* for unsatisfactory if something has gone wrong.

EXAMPLE: Her grandparents had come from Latvia (now a part of Russia).
(Answer)   *S*

1. It was a very short book (128 pages).
2. Everyone was waiting for the same thing: rain.
3. My aunt—you won't believe this won a car in a raffle.
4. The picture showed the world's highest mountain: Mount Everest).

5. Oklahoma—then a territory—was little known.
6. Leningrad (the former St. Petersburg) is a beautiful city.
7. Rachel Carson wrote a famous book about pesticides: *Silent Spring*.
8. We talked about famous parks: Yosemite and Yellowstone.
9. We rented a car. (The buses did not run on Sundays)
10. They expected the worst—a major repair job and a long delay.
11. My parents were always talking about a trip to Mexico. (We never went.)
12. We had several animals: cats, a dog, and a turtle.
13. The encyclopedia (a very old edition) did not mention rockets.
14. The warehouse was on Bond Street (near the waterfront.
15. You will find her in the new building (Room 201B).

What punctuation should appear in each blank space in the following sentences? After the number of each blank, write one of the following abbreviations:

C   for comma;
CL for colon;
D   for dash;
P   for parenthesis;
No for no punctuation.

EXAMPLE: People have hunted animals for food _____ for safety, and for pleasure.
(Answer)   *C*

1. A refuge (also called a sanctuary _____ offers shelter.
2. In a wildlife refuge _____ wild animals are protected from human beings.
3. Animals living there _____ can breed in peace.
4. Hunters—with some exceptions _____ are banned.
5. Theodore Roosevelt set up the first refuge _____ Pelican Island.
6. It protected the brown pelican _____ once hunted for its feathers.
7. Now most states _____ have safe areas for wildlife.
8. Some areas can be found in the prairies _____ in marshes, and along our beaches.
9. The buffalo _____ the eagle, and the pelican might not have survived without them.
10. An island in the Pacific shelters saltwater birds _____ gulls, petrels, and cormorants.
11. It is about thirty miles from San Francisco _____ California.
12. Birds _____ traveling south need safe places to stop.
13. One such place is north of the Great Salt Lake _____ Utah.

14. Mallards (a kind of duck _____ need safe places with much water.
15. The government has set aside lakes _____ and deltas for them.
16. Hunted without any limits _____ some animals are gone forever.
17. You have heard about the passenger pigeon _____ haven't you?
18. These birds, living together in huge flocks _____ have disappeared.
19. Considering their huge numbers _____ this seems unbelievable.
20. We should study _____ cherish, and protect our remaining wildlife.

M4
CAPITALS AND SPECIAL MARKS

Learn to use capitals and special marks of punctuation.

Periods, commas, and semicolons are the basic traffic signals on the written page. They tell us when to stop, when to go, and when to slow down. In addition to these basic signals, we use special marks for special purposes.

M4a
Using Capitals

Use capital letters for proper names, for most of the words in a title, and for the first word of a sentence.

Unlike many punctuation marks, capital letters are not signaled in any way in speech. But capital letters do "speak" to the reader, just as punctuation marks do. The most important job of a capital letter is to start a **proper name**. A proper name sets an individual or a group off from other examples of the same kind. In a group of children, probably only one may be called *Cynthia*. In a soccer league, only one team is likely to be called the *Earthquakes*.

Look at the difference between general words and proper names in the following examples:

GENERAL WORD: boy, girl, neighbor
PROPER NAME: Brian Jones, Linda, William A. Mack

GENERAL WORD: river, mountain, park
PROPER NAME: Snake River, Pikes Peak, Acadia Park

GENERAL WORD: family, nation, people
PROPER NAME: Americans, Canadians, Mexicans

Remember:

(1) Capitalize the pronoun I: my brother and *I;* you and *I.*

(2) Capitalize the first word in a sentence or a direct quotation:

The coach said, "Let's try again."

(3) Capitalize the names of people. Remember to use capital letters to start the names of your friends, people in the news, or people in history:

Cynthia, Thomas Friendly, my brother Jim
Martha Graham, Craig F. Callahan, Jean McCormick
George Washington, Martin Luther King, Jr.

Capitalize the *title or rank* of the person when it goes with the name:

Senator Smith, Mayor Young, Sergeant Wiley, Dr. Mardici

When titles or ranks are mentioned without a person's name, they are usually not capitalized. Only in a few cases does the title of a person already point to that person: the *President* of the United States, the *Pope:*

Several *generals* were photographed with the *President*.
The *cardinal* had just talked to the *Pope*.

NOTE: Capitalize family words like *mother, father, uncle,* or *brother* only when the word is the name that you would call that person. Study the differences in the following pairs:

My mother worked for the post office.
You are right, *Mother*.

She had two *brothers* and one *sister*.
He said, "Well, *Brother,* you were wrong again."

His dad was cleaning the fish in the kitchen.
Remember to ask *Dad* about the trip.

(4) Capitalize the names of places. Use a capital letter to start the names of all countries, states, cities, towns. Capitalize the names of all oceans, lakes, rivers, mountains. Capitalize all of the words in the name except prepositions *(of, at)* and articles *(the, a, an):*

COUNTRIES:	Canada, Brazil, the United States of America, the Soviet Union, Nigeria
STATES:	Oklahoma, Maine, New Hampshire, South Dakota, Alaska
COMMUNITIES:	Chicago, Los Angeles, New Orleans, Kansas City, Salem
STREETS:	Pontiac Avenue, First Street, Michigan Boulevard, Elm Lane
MAP NAMES:	Pikes Peak, Sacramento River, Lake Erie, Saratoga Creek

CAPITALS FOR NAMES
An Overview

PERSONAL NAMES	PEOPLE:	Claire Moos, Jefferson Davis, Douglas MacArthur, Abigail Adams, Helen Keller
	TITLES:	The Reverend Martin Luther King, Jr., Senator Friendly, the President, Ms. Murphey
	IMAGINARY PEOPLE:	Ulysses, Mother Goose, Little Red Riding Hood, Johnny Appleseed, Wonder Woman

	CONTINENTS:	Africa, South America, Europe, Asia, the Antarctic
	COUNTRIES:	United States of America, France, China, Greece, Brazil, Egypt, the Netherlands
	REGIONS:	New England, the Orient, the South, the Northwest
PLACE NAMES	STATES:	California, Massachusetts, Ohio, Texas
	CITIES:	Atlanta, Kansas City, New Orleans, Las Vegas, Philadelphia
	SIGHTS:	Grand Canyon, Lake Michigan, Mount Washington
	ADDRESSES:	Elm Street, Roosevelt Boulevard, Union Square, Cottman Avenue

CALENDAR NAMES	MONTHS:	February, May, August, November
	WEEKDAYS:	Tuesday, Thursday, Saturday, Monday
	HOLIDAYS:	Christmas, Hanukkah, Labor Day, Father's Day, Easter

	INSTITUTIONS:	the Congress, the Treasury Department, the Central Intelligence Agency
INSTITUTIONAL NAMES	BUSINESSES:	General Motors, Bell Telephone Company
	SCHOOLS:	Central High School, Eisenhower Middle School, University of California
	GROUPS:	the Democratic Party, Veterans of Foreign Wars, the Peace Corps

	PROPER NAMES:	the Virgin Mary, St. Patrick
RELIGIOUS NAMES	FAITHS:	Christian, Jewish, Muslim, Protestant
	DENOMINATIONS:	Roman Catholic, Quaker, Episcopalian, Baptist

Directions like north, south, or west are not usually capitalized. But capitalize these and similar words when they are used as names for a part of the country or the world:

REGIONS: the Midwest, the Near East, the deep South, cities in the East, a town in the Southwest

DIRECTIONS: go *north* on this highway; a place *south* of here

(5) *Capitalize calendar names.* Make sure to use a capital letter for the days of the week and the months of the year:

DAYS: Monday, Wednesday, Friday, Sunday

MONTHS: February, March, July, December

Do *not* capitalize the names of the seasons:

SEASONS: spring, summer, fall, autumn, winter

(6) *Capitalize the names of all nationalities and languages.* Treat the names of tribes, religious groups, and the like the same way:

NATIONS: Italian, French, English, Cuban, Russian

TRIBES: Cheyenne, Navaho, Sioux, Ojibwa

RELIGIONS: Christians, Muslims, Jews

We always capitalize the names of languages. But capitalize the names of other school subjects only when you give the name of an actual course:

COURSES: I will take Biology I, General Math II, History III, and English next semester.

SUBJECTS: I will take biology, math, history, and English next semester.

(7) *Capitalize the names of other things and ideas that have proper names of their own.* Look out for the following:

CAR:	Ford, Chevrolet, Volkswagen
SHIP, TRAIN, PLANE:	the *Nautilus,* the *Congressional Limited,* the *Spirit of St. Louis*
COMPANY, INSTITUTION:	General Mills, Bedrock High School
ORGANIZATION:	American Legion, the Boy Scouts of America, the FBI
BUILDING:	the Empire State Building, the White House
HISTORICAL EVENT OR PERIOD:	the Second World War, the Ice Age
DOCUMENT:	the Declaration of Independence
TRADE NAME:	Xerox, Palmolive, Pepsi-Cola
SACRED FIGURE OR WRITING:	God, the Holy Ghost, the Koran

(8) Capitalize words that are made from proper names. We capitalize not only the word *Britain* but also words like *British* and *Britisher*. We capitalize both *Africa* and *African*. Look at the capitalized words in the following examples:

> a *Japanese* camera, my *Californian* friends, several *New Yorkers*

We sometimes need a capital letter for things that were *named after* a person or a place:

> a *Winchester* rifle, a *Pullman* car, the *Morse* code

(9) Capitalize important words in titles. Use a capital letter for the *first word in titles* of books, movies, poems, articles, songs, plays, television shows, and so on. Also, use a capital letter for all other words in the title except articles, prepositions, and connectives that have fewer than five letters:

The Once and Future King	"The Waltons"
West Side Story	"Bridge over Troubled Water"

The rule for capitalizing titles applies to the titles of your own papers, too. Remember that verbs are always capitalized in titles, even when they are very short.

> Seeing Is Believing
> Dogs Are Superior to Cats
> I Am Young and Carefree

NOTE: When titles are mentioned in print, titles of *whole publications*—books, magazines—are italicized. (Use underlining in a typed or handwritten paper.) Other titles are put in quotation marks.

EXERCISE 1

After the number of each sentence, write down (and *capitalize*) each word that should start with a capital letter.

EXAMPLE: Pat wilson came to our company from central junior college.
(Answer) *Wilson, Central Junior College*

1. Last tuesday we celebrated halloween.
2. My friend charles comes from sweden.
3. We just moved from the country to market street.
4. The visitors from england were greeted by mayor white.

5. When school ends in june, we have the summer off.
6. She lived in baltimore, maryland, for two years.
7. I go to king junior high school.
8. The president will speak to the congress tomorrow.
9. The republican party did well in the last election.
10. We camped in the great smokies.
11. My family loves new england in the fall.
12. We read about hercules, a famous greek hero.
13. My mother joined the american federation of labor.
14. They took a plane from australia to asia.
15. My older sister works for the acme casting company.
16. He was a methodist but later became a unitarian.
17. The department of motor vehicles issues license plates.
18. We drove from chicago to denver in two days.
19. Athletes came from the united states and the soviet union.
20. Penn state university played the university of oklahoma.

After the number of each sentence, write (and *capitalize*) each word that should start with a capital letter. If there are no words in the sentence that should be capitalized, write *No* next to the number of the sentence.

EXERCISE 2

1. Nancy is transferring to abington junior high school.
2. His brother will go to college in the fall.
3. Susan was hired as a manager by general electric.
4. Zelda was headed west in her english ford.
5. The washington monument is an outstanding memorial.
6. Have you ever visited yellowstone national park?
7. I have good grades in history, spanish, and english.
8. My favorite relative is aunt lucy.
9. The doctor sent my father to the hospital.
10. Later doctor staub sent father to grandview hospital.
11. Everyone said that judge parsons was a fair judge.
12. In july this summer, we are going to new jersey.
13. On thanksgiving day we saw the *mayflower* at plymouth, massachusetts.
14. The son goes to the methodist church; his father is a unitarian.
15. Judy garland sang "somewhere over the rainbow" in *the wizard of oz*.
16. The book about general macarthur was called *american caesar*.
17. Not enough girls are studying biology or engineering.
18. The meeting, mother, is next tuesday.
19. She had come to new york from puerto rico.
20. The class had read a poem about paul bunyan.

LANGUAGE
IN ACTION

THE FRENCH IN MISSOURI

Capitalize those words that should be capitalized, and write them after the number of the sentence.

(1) the state of missouri does not usually make us think of french people. (2) but the french once used the mississippi as a trade route between their canadian possessions and new orleans. (3) the city of st. louis was the first outpost of the french territory of louisiana. (4) it had been a spanish settlement earlier. (5) the map shows normandy and bellefontaine as the names of nearby towns. (6) major streets in the city are named after early french families, for example, laclede and chouteau.

EXERCISE 3

In the following sentences, some words are used twice. Each word is used once as a general word and once as a proper name (or part of a proper name). After the number of each sentence, write the words that should be capitalized in that sentence. Use capital letters as needed.

1. We liked father because he was the most generous of all fathers.
2. The united states is made up of fifty separate states.
3. Tim was bitten by a snake in the red snake mine.
4. Yes, moore high school is the largest high school in town.
5. I learned everything I know about math in math 1.
6. The *popetown news* is just another small-town paper.
7. Our stadium has been compared with tiger stadium.
8. At the time, general grant had not been a general very long.
9. The red river is the most often flooded river in the country.
10. The church on the corner is st. joseph's church.

M4b

Using Apostrophes

Use the apostrophe to show contractions and the possessive of nouns.

We cannot *hear* the apostrophe when sentences are read out loud. But like capital letters, it is a standard feature of the way we write. Be sure to recognize the places where an apostrophe is needed in a written sentence:

(1) Use the apostrophe to show where letters have been left out. In speech we often shorten (contract) words by leaving out sounds. We say *I'd* for *I would, she'll* for *she*

will, don't for *do not.* Look at the use of the apostrophe in the **contractions** shown in the brief chart.

I am → *I'm*	are not → *aren't*
I will → *I'll*	do not → *don't*
he will → *he'll*	does not → *doesn't*
she would → *she'd*	cannot → *can't*
he is → *he's*	will not → *won't*
we are → *we're*	would not → *wouldn't*
you are → *you're*	has not → *hasn't*
they are → *they're*	had not → *hadn't*
could have → *could've*	is not → *isn't*

CONTRACTIONS

Some contractions sound exactly like other words that do *not* have an apostrophe. Be sure you can tell the difference. Study the following:

- *It's* always means *it is. Its* without the apostrophe means *of it.*

it's	*It's* (it is) time to go home.
	I know *it's* (it is) true.
its	The team lost *its* coach. (the coach *of it*)
	Honesty is *its* own reward. (the reward *of it*)

- *They're* always means *they are. Their* without the apostrophe means *of them.* (*There* means "in that place.")

they're	*They're* (they are) leaving tomorrow.
	She says *they're* (they are) gone.
their	We visited *their* house. (the house of them)
	Their car was new. (the car of them)
there	here and *there,* over *there*

- *Who's* always means *who is. Whose* without the apostrophe means *of whom.*

who's	*Who's* (who is) on the phone?
	I'm not sure *who's* (who is) right.
whose	*Whose* idea was it? (the idea of whom)
	I want to know *whose* pen this is. (the pen of whom)

Remember the following contractions especially. Make them part of your list of "unforgivables"—the "must-know" words that you should never misspell. All of them use a shortened form of *not* (*n't*):

doesn't   don't   isn't   hasn't

NOTE: We often use contractions, or shortened forms, in personal letters or in quoting what someone has said. The more serious or more formal our writing becomes, the fewer contractions we use. In a formal report or a serious business letter, use *cannot* for *can't, will not* for *won't, do not* for *don't,* and so on.

(2) Use the apostrophe and an added s *('s) to show the possessive of nouns.* The **possessive** form of nouns shows where or to whom something belongs: my *sister's* car, her *uncle's* house. We often use this form when talking about people or groups. It answers the question: "*Whose* is it?" Sometimes, it answers a different question: "By whom was this activity done?"

WHOSE?	*Jim's* shoes	the *family's* savings
	her *aunt's* farm	our *team's* record
	the *driver's* gloves	the *city's* debts
	Maria's job	a *customer's* package
	the *mayor's* office	my *friend's* house
BY WHOM?	the *President's* speech	the *dog's* barking
	our *coach's* advice	the *team's* workout
	the *champion's* victory	your *friend's* behavior

We often use the possessive form in expressions that show *time, value, or measurements:*

HOW MUCH?	a *day's* work	an *hour's* drive
	a *dollar's* worth	at *arm's* length
	a *minute's* thought	a *week's* growth

To make sure that the word with the *s* at the end is a possessive, see if you could use an expression beginning with the word *of* instead:

the car *of my brother* = *my brother's* car
the doctor *of her father* = *her father's* doctor
the trophy *of his mother* = *his mother's* trophy
the savings *of my family* = *my family's* savings
the work *of one day* = *one day's* work

(3) Use only the apostrophe to show the possessive if a noun already has the −s ending. Most plural nouns already have an −s that shows there are several: many *girls,* seven *brothers,* two *families.* The apostrophe alone, added at the end, then shows us "Whose?" or "By whom?" or "How much?"

WHOSE?   She went to a *girls'* school. (many *girls*)
          I was banned from my *brothers'* bedrooms. (several *brothers*)
          The two *families'* houses faced each other. (two *families*)

BY WHOM? Our *musicians'* performances were great.
          The *girls'* races had already been run.

HOW MUCH? All the *books'* linings were worn.
          We had planned a two *weeks'* vacation.
          He owed me several *days'* pay.
          We bought three *dollars'* worth of bait.

Not all plural nouns have the −s at the end. They then use the normal possessive with *'s:*

the *children's* uncle
the *women's* caucus

NOTE: When a proper name ends in −s, *either* of the following is acceptable: *Charles'* letter, or *Charles's* letter.

HOW WE USE SPECIAL MARKS

**Look at the following sample of language in action.
Explain all uses of apostrophes in these examples.**

It's Guaranteed

Don't Wait—Buy Now

Your Money Back
If You're Not Satisfied

Tomorrow's Car Today

A Traveler's Dream

Mario's Restaurant

30 Days' Trial

You'll welcome its sparkle.
You'll relish its taste.

(4) Do not use the apostrophe with the possessive forms of personal pronouns. In addition to *my, your,* and *our,* we sometimes use possessive forms like *yours, ours, hers,* and *theirs.* None of these ever have the apostrophe. *Its,* when it means *of it,* is also used without the apostrophe:

> They left their car and took *ours.*
> The team celebrated *its* victory.
> That car is not really *hers.*

The ordinary rules for the possessive do apply to the *indefinite* pronouns like *somebody (someone), everybody (everyone),* and *nobody (no one):*

everybody's friend	*someone else's* job
nobody's fault	*anyone's* guess

(5) Use 's to form the plural of numbers and letters:

> There were two *7's* in the telephone number.
> Use two *m's* in *recommend.*
> Rock music became popular in the *1950's.*

EXERCISE 1

A. Write the contracted forms of the italicized words in the following sentences.

1. *I cannot* agree with his opinions.
2. He *does not* give us much support.
3. Frank decided that *he would* become a mechanic.
4. I know that *she will* succeed.
5. I *do not* know how to solve that problem.
6. Donald *is not* here.
7. *I would* rather be right than President.
8. You *have not* seen her at all?
9. *I am* not surprised.
10. *Who is* your new friend?

B. Write down the complete words for the shortened form in each of the following sentences:

11. We're leaving now.
12. They're not at home.
13. I've seen her before.
14. He'd seen her before, too.
15. You'll never regret it.
16. I'd rather not play.
17. You can't go home again.

18. He doesn't know me.
19. I don't know the answer.
20. They aren't ready.
21. I'm not a hero.
22. You're a real friend.
23. He's a good student.
24. She's not afraid.
25. It's over here.

Choose the form that fits the sentence. Write it after the number of the sentence.

1. *(They're/Their)* friends were waiting.
2. Every nation has *(it's/its)* own national heroes.
3. *(They're/Their)* waiting for us in the car.
4. *(They're/Their)* leader had lost the election.
5. *(It's/Its)* true in spite of his denials.
6. Do you know *(who's/whose)* next?
7. The band was ready for *(it's/its)* performance.
8. We never visit *(their/there)*.
9. The government announced *(it's/its)* decision.
10. I think *(it's/its)* too expensive.

For each word that appears in parentheses, write down the possessive form that would fit into the sample sentence. Write on a separate sheet of paper.

EXAMPLE: (player) There is no question about this _____ skill.
(Answer) *player's*

1. (fans) The golf _____ favorite in 1978 was Nancy Lopez.
2. (Nancy) It was _____ first year on the pro tour.
3. (women) She won five tournaments in a row, setting a record for the _____ golf tour.
4. (Ladies) Among her victories was the _____ Professional Golf Association championship.
5. (year) Her first _____ earnings broke all records.
6. (men) She broke the _____ record for most money earned as a rookie.
7. (Nancy) Her followers have been called _____ Navy.
8. (Arnie) This puts her on a level with Arnold Palmer, whose followers are called _____ Army.

9. (pro) Like Palmer's, this _____ putting eye is deadly.
10. (player) This young _____ first tournament came at the age of ten.
11. (family) She had her _____ support.
12. (parents) She was her _____ pride as she won by 110 strokes.
13. (father) It was through her _____ efforts that she learned how to play golf.
14. (crowd) The _____ response was very encouraging.
15. (everybody) Her performance exceeded _____ expectations.
16. (months) Her first six _____ earnings were over $150,000.
17. (man) Golf used to be a rich _____ game.
18. (President) Newspapers wrote about the _____ golf partners.
19. (everyone) Golf still is not _____ favorite sport.
20. (players) Famous _____ faces are becoming familiar to the television audience.

EXERCISE 4

For each of the following, choose the form that is right for the sentence. Write down the correct form after the number of the sentence.

EXAMPLE: I had forgotten my (brother's/brothers) birthday.
(Answer)   *brother's*

1. People used to ask for a *(dollar's/dollars)* worth of gas.
2. Now we pay several *(dollar's/dollars)* for gas for a short trip.
3. The two *(friend's/friends')* families lived close together.
4. My *(cousin's/cousins)* hobby was stamp collecting.
5. There were several telephone *(call's/calls)* for me.
6. Her employer owed her one *(week's/weeks')* pay.
7. People who were laid off received two *(week's/weeks')* pay.
8. I studied my *(family's/families)* history.
9. The students were studying their *(families/families')* histories.
10. Several Dutch *(family's/families)* founded the town.
11. She accepted *(everybody's/everybodys)* apologies.
12. The crowd did not like the *(umpire's/umpires)* decisions.
13. Why don't you borrow your *(sister's/sisters)* bicycle?
14. The principal handed out the *(students/students')* diplomas.
15. It was about an *(hour's/hours')* walk to the farm.
16. A *(pet's/pets)* burial was a big event for my little sister.
17. She always said it was *(nobody's/nobodys)* business.
18. My *(aunt's/aunts)* letters were usually cheerful.
19. I have several *(aunts/aunts')* in South Dakota.
20. The mayor opened a new *(children's/childrens)* playground.

Use quotation marks to mark off a person's exact words.

When we quote someone, we repeat that person's exact words, exactly as we remember them. When we quote what someone has written, we make sure to copy word for word what a passage says. **Quotation marks** help us show such word-for-word quotations. They are always used in pairs: Be sure to put marks where the quotation begins and ends.

To use quotation marks right, remember the following:

(1) Learn the difference between direct and indirect quotations. You are using **direct quotation** whenever you report someone's *exact* words. You are using **indirect quotation** whenever you repeat what someone has said but use your own words. Notice the differences between the two in the examples below. Only the direct quotations are quoted word for word. Only direct quotations appear in quotation marks:

DIRECT: She said, "I don't know the answer."
INDIRECT: She said that she didn't know the answer.

DIRECT: Dad suggested, "Let's start at seven o'clock."
INDIRECT: Dad suggested that we start at seven o'clock.

Indirect quotations are usually easy to identify because they commonly begin with an introductory word. *That* is the most popular introductory word to begin indirect quotations. It is used in the examples above. Sometimes, however, the *that* is not included:

DIRECT: The stranger said, "I am very hungry."
INDIRECT: The stranger said (that) he was very hungry.

DIRECT: She said, "Your cat is in my tree again!"
INDIRECT: She said (that) our cat was in her tree again.

When we quote questions, both the direct and the indirect quotation may begin with a question word like *who, which, what, why, how,* or *where:*

DIRECT: He asked me, "Why do you want to know?"
INDIRECT: He asked me why I wanted to know.

DIRECT: They asked, "Who will be in charge there?"
INDIRECT: They asked who would be in charge there.

NOTE: Indirect quotations are *not* set off by quotation marks or any other punctuation.

QUOTATIONS
Special Marks

Writers using quotation marks sometimes need special marks for special situations. Study the following examples of special cases:

(1) A colon instead of a comma often introduces a *long or formal* quotation:

> I looked in the guide, and the rule said: "Once you touch one of the pieces on the chessboard, you must move that piece and no other."

(2) Three dots (an **ellipsis**) show that something has been *left out:*

> The memo said, "The funds for our music program . . . have dwindled and may dry up altogether before the end of the school year."

(3) **Square brackets** show something that has been *added* to the quotation by someone other than the original speaker or author:

> The diary continued: "Since the storm broke on March 3 [actually March 4], we have been cut off from the rest of the world."

(4) Sometimes the person who is quoted is *quoting someone else* in turn. We use a special set of single quotation marks to show such a quotation that is part of another quotation:

> The coach turned to me and said: "I want you to say after me, 'I hate to be last.'"

(5) Quotation marks sometimes call attention to *difficult words*—technical terms, or words from a foreign language. **Italics** (underlining on a typed page) are often used for this purpose:

> The school held a "walkathon" to raise funds for the annual senior class trip.
> The town had an annual *fiesta* that brought in many visitors.

(2) Use a comma to separate a direct quotation from its credit tag.   A **credit tag** is a short statement that tells us who the speaker or the author is. If the credit tag comes first, put the comma before the first quotation mark:

> She said, "At least we tried."
> The mayor answered, "We have no record of it."

If the credit tag comes last, put the comma *inside* the second quotation mark:

> "It has always been this way," she said.
> "We are out of food," the diary said.

You need *two* commas if the credit tag comes in the middle of a quoted sentence:

> "This problem," the report said, "is far from solved."
> "First of all," Joyce said, "my name isn't Jean."

NOTE: Sometimes the credit tag comes between two complete sentences. You then need a period before the beginning of the second quoted sentence:

> "We like this place," her letter went on. "The sun shines every day."
> "It's just as well," Helen answered. "There are many rattlesnakes here."

(3) Learn where to place other marks of punctuation when you are using quotation marks.   When a period comes at the end of a quoted statement, it goes *inside* the final quotation mark:

> She shouted, "I can't hear you. We have a bad connection."

Question marks and exclamation marks usually go inside the last quotation mark:

> Tony asked, "Who told you that?"
> The swimmer shouted, "Help! Save me!"

Sometimes you may be asked a question *about* a quotation. The question mark then goes outside the quotation:

> Did he really say, "I will pay for everything"?

(4) Start most quotations with a capital letter.   Exceptions are short quotations that become a part of a longer sentence:

> We all laughed when he told us about his "permanent pet."

Mechanics

EXERCISE 1

In each of the following pairs, which is the direct quotation? After the number of the pair, write the direct quotation and punctuate it correctly. (Study the differences between the direct and the indirect quotation in each pair.)

EXAMPLE: He asked me why are you here.
            He asked me why I was here.
(Answer)   He asked me, "Why are you here?"

1. She told us that we needed a special permit.
   She told us you need a special permit.

2. I asked my brother why do you always tease me.
   I asked my brother why he always teased me.

3. The principal said that everyone needed the test.
   The principal said everyone needs the test.

4. My friend asked who our new coach was.
   My friend asked who is your new coach.

5. She answered I always come here on Fridays.
   She answered that she always came there on Fridays.

6. The sign said that the library would be closed.
   The sign said the library will be closed.

7. The stranger asked which road would take him back to town.
   The stranger asked which road will take me back to town.

8. The voice said the plane has landed safely.
   The voice said that the plane had landed safely.

9. My sister always says I do as I please.
   My sister always says that she does as she pleases.

10. She asked how we could pay for the car.
    She asked how can you pay for the car.

EXERCISE 2

What punctuation is missing in each of the following? After the number of the sentence, put the missing mark or marks in the right order. Write *No* if no additional punctuation is needed. (Write on a separate sheet.)

EXAMPLE: He always said, "It can't be helped ＿＿＿
(Answer)   ."

1. The report said ＿＿＿ There is little chance of rain."
2. "It's too late now ＿＿＿ she said.
3. Jim asked, "Have you paid the bill ＿＿＿
4. Did he really say, "No school on Monday ＿＿＿

5. "On Sundays," the letter went on ____ we go to the beach."
6. "The beach was crowded," she wrote ____ People were everywhere."
7. Cora shouted ____ Watch out for the truck!"
8. My uncle asked me ____ who my new friend was.
9. "That's too bad ____ I told him.
10. She asked me, "Why are you always in a hurry ____
11. The teacher asked, "Are you going toward the office ____
12. She told us ____ that something was wrong with our car.
13. "I know," the mechanic said ____ where you can get your car repaired."
14. Shakespeare wrote ____ All the world's a stage."
15. Tim asked, "Has anybody seen my friend ____
16. The guide suggested that ____ Route One was more scenic than the turnpike.
17. "I know her very well," Don said ____ She's my sister."
18. Which of you said, "I don't care ____
19. The child screamed, "Get me out of here ____
20. Ted said ____ he himself would plan all the details.

Use hyphens with compound words and some prefixes.

Observe the following guidelines:

(1) Use the hyphen with compound words that are shown with hyphens in your dictionary. The hyphen says, "Read these words as a single unit":

bull's-eye	mother-in-law	a drive-in movie
cave-in	in-laws	teeter-totter
hocus-pocus	great-aunt	six-pack

(2) Use hyphens in some compound numbers. Combined numbers from twenty-one to ninety-nine need hyphens.

thirty-three   sixty-five   forty-eight   twenty-one

Hyphens are also used with *fractions used as modifiers:*

The theater was only *one-third* occupied.
The tank was *three-quarters* full.

(3) Use hyphens with some prefixes. Hyphens are used with the prefixes *all–, self–,* and *ex–* (when *ex–* means "former"):

ex-President	self-control	all-powerful
ex-champion	self-conscious	all-American

Hyphens are also used between a prefix and a capitalized proper name:

un-American   pro-Catholic   anti-German

(4) Use hyphens with group modifiers. Put hyphens between words used as a combination to modify a noun. Such combinations take the place of a single adjective:

> an *up-to-date* directory
> a *well-designed* painting
> a *person-to-person* call

NOTE: Words that are often used together may finally become a single word: *teenager, kindhearted.* Only an up-to-date dictionary can tell you for sure which combinations are written as single words and which are written with a hyphen between them. Use the dictionary when you are in doubt.

EXERCISE 1

In each of the following sentences, find the combination that needs one or more hyphens. Write the hyphenated word or expression after the number of the sentence.

EXAMPLE: We had a heart to heart talk.
(Answer)   *heart-to-heart*

1. Twenty eight people signed up for the drill team.
2. He always asked for a yes or no answer.
3. The ex President was invited to the White House.
4. They had always kept their self respect.
5. Her father in law was from Ireland.
6. The movie was being shown at a drive in theater.
7. The hero was played by a good looking actor.
8. There had been some anti American feeling in the country.
9. We had only seventeen tickets for thirty one people.
10. We read a story about a man eating tiger.
11. We all went to a Chinese American dinner.
12. It had been a well planned outing.
13. We needed up to date information.
14. The gas tank was already three quarters empty.
15. We were looking for a medium sized car.
16. She went to Africa as a good will ambassador.
17. Their curious looks made me self conscious.
18. They ignored our well meant advice.
19. They both liked old fashioned clothes.
20. The announcer gave a play by play report.

KEEPING UP WITH GREAT-GRANDFATHER

Where would you use apostrophes and hyphens in the following passage? Rewrite the passage, using apostrophes and hyphens where they belong.

My great grandfather is eighty three years old. He is an ex coach and has been retired for twenty three years. Its a full time job keeping up with him. In an ordinary days schedule, he first runs my mothers errands and even makes the childrens beds. Later he goes next door to Sams house to see if he can get into the afternoons basketball game. He is not the teams leading scorer, but he really doesnt interfere with the boys fun. They call him Bulls Eye Bailey. Then he goes across the street to Karens house to watch the teenagers practice the latest steps. Great grandfather is not the worlds best dancer, but he tries. Its something to see.

How should each of the following be spelled—separate words, one word, or hyphenated? Find the answer in a dictionary.

baby sitter
gun shy
labor union
news letter
short range (plans)
short story
short sighted
time out
time honored
blue collar (worker)

Check the sentences on the following page for the use of capitals and for other special marks. In most of the sentences, these have been used right. Put *S* for satisfactory after the number of each such sentence. Put *U* for unsatisfactory if something has gone wrong.

EXAMPLE: The student from Nigeria was improving her English.
(Answer)   *S*

1. Charlotte said, "You told us all this before."
2. He preferred English and music to math.
3. They enjoyed remembering how they had crossed the Rocky Mountains in an old ford.
4. Linda's father doesn't approve of late hours.
5. She asked "why I did not help her."
6. The athletes from Canada and Cuba heard the spectators' cheers.
7. The leader of the group asked, "Why are you late?"
8. I don't know my cousins address in Miami.
9. My sister Eileen always had a smug self satisfied look.
10. The first Tuesday in March is my birthday.
11. The woman's ex-husband worried about the children's future.
12. Several of the students spoke polish or russian.
13. Who said, "Free pizza for everybody"?
14. My father wont give me permission to go downtown.
15. The fire captain shouted, "This is not a drill!
16. Most of our neighbors were Methodists or Lutherans.
17. "Go upstairs," she said. "I will talk to you later."
18. He had some Spanish-speaking friends from Mexico.
19. I hope to have my degree in a years time.
20. The Ford Motor Company sells it's cars in England and Germany.

M5

SPELLING

Work on your spelling regularly.

With a few exceptions, English spelling is an either-or matter. Like a telephone number you have dialed, the spelling you have written down is either right or wrong.

Follow these guidelines in order to improve your spelling:

(1) Do not guess at the spelling of a word—look it up in a dictionary. Make this a habit. The more often you spell a word correctly, the better the chance that the correct spelling will stay in your mind.

(2) Look at the word carefully. Many people have a good memory for things they see. If you merely glance at a word, you cannot print it in your mind. If you pay close attention to the individual letters and then to the whole word, you may lock the proper spelling in your mind.

(3) Say the word distinctly. Then spell aloud each letter individually: R-E-C-E-I-V-E. Many people have a good memory for what they hear.

(4) Write the word clearly, in large letters. Many people have a good memory for things they have done. Remember what it *feels like* to write the word.

(5) Make use of memory aids. Does *definitely* have an *i* or an *a* in the third syllable? You will remember that it has an *i* if you think something like: "I *definitely* want to *finish*." You will find many such memory aids in this unit.

(6) Become aware of common spelling problems. Make a list of the common words that give you difficulty and practice them. A list of commonly misspelled words is included in this chapter. After you learn which of them are your special enemies, write them out in a notebook. Keep after them.

The ten words in the following list account for a large share of the spelling problems that students have. Make these part of your list of "unforgivables." These are "must-know" words. Read the list over until you know each word inside out. Memorize the memory aids.

WORD	MEMORY AID
a lot	Always *two* words: a few, a little, *a lot*
believe	Don't *believe* LIES.
definite	I *definitely* want to FINISH.
friend	I brought FRIES for my *friend*.
perform	He *performed* PERsonally.
receive	I *received* the RECEIPT.
separate	We had *separate* RATions.
surprise	The SURfer was *surprised*.
used to	They *used to* sell USED cars.
writing	Make your *writing* inVITING.

Learn how to spell simple words that are commonly misspelled.

A demon is an evil spirit or devil. The words in the list below are spelling devils: They seem easy to spell but often cause more trouble than longer, more uncommon words.

Study the memory aids. Do not let these words cause trouble in your writing. Take up one group at a time.

	WORD	MEMORY AID
GROUP 1	accept	When you *accept* something, you *join in*. (The word *except* takes something out. We use it to make an *exception*.) REMEMBER: Everyone *accepted except* Judy.
	again	When you pronounce this word, it may sound like "a-gin." REMEMBER: There is a GAIN in again.
	all right	Always *two* words. REMEMBER: *All right* means ALL is RIGHT.
	always	This word is a combination of *all* and *ways*, but the second *l* has been dropped. REMEMBER: AL *always* knows the way.
	among	The *o* in this word sounds like a *u*. REMEMBER: Tarzan lived *among* the MONKEYS.
	answer	The *w* in *answer* is not sounded. Originally, the word was related to *swear*. REMEMBER: I SWEAR the *answer* is true.
	awful	This word adds *–ful* to the word *awe*, with the *–e* dropping out: No *e*, one *l*, in *awful*. REMEMBER: Her LAWFUL spouse was *awful*.
	beginning	We do not hear the second *n*, but it must be there in writing. REMEMBER: The INNING is *beginning*.
	busy	The *u* in this word sounds more like an *i*. REMEMBER: They put US on a *busy* BUS.
	business	Remember to put the *i* in: The word is a combination of *busy* (with the *y* changed to *i*) and *–ness:* busy + ness = business. REMEMBER: They use a BUS in their *business*.
GROUP 2	coming	The *–e* is dropped from *come* when *–ing* is added, but the *m* is *not* doubled: No *e*, one *m*, in *coming*. REMEMBER: We are *coming* to WyoMING.
	country	REMEMBER: The COUNT lived in the *country*.
	does	This word sounds as if it should be spelled d-u-z: Remember that it is related to *do*. REMEMBER: *Does* John DOE exist?

done	Here again, the word is related to *do*. REMEMBER: It was *done* by ONE.
early	The *a* is not sounded in this short but difficult word. REMEMBER: The EARL lost his EAR *early*.
easy	The *s* has a *z* sound and the *a* is not sounded in *easy*.
enough	REMEMBER: To be TOUGH and ROUGH is not *enough*.
every	Put in the second *e*. REMEMBER: To trust *every*one is NEVER CLEVER.
government	Pronounce the word distinctly: gov-ern-ment. REMEMBER: VERN is studying *government*.
guess	The *u* is not pronounced and the *s* is doubled. REMEMBER: *Guess* how the GUESTS DRESSED.

GROUP 3

half	We do not hear the *l*. REMEMBER: ALFRED took *half* of the cake.
having	This word is spelled exactly as it is pronounced: hav-ing. Remember not to add an –*e*.
just	When *just* is pronounced quickly, it often does not rhyme with *must*. REMEMBER: We MUST have a *u* in *just*.
library	This word has an *r* on both sides of an *a*. REMEMBER: The LIBRARIANS BROUGHT BRICKS for the *library*.
making	The word comes from *make*, but drop the –*e* when writing *making*. REMEMBER: The KING was *making* the laws.
many	Do not double the *n*. Use *a* for the first vowel sound. REMEMBER: *Many* a MAN doesn't have ANY money.
meant	This is the same word as *mean*, only in the past. REMEMBER: I still MEAN what I *meant*.
minute	Remember the –*ute* at the end. REMEMBER: He ate a NUT a *minute*.
none	A shortened form of *no* plus *one*. REMEMBER: I want ONE or *none*.
often	The *t* is often not heard in *often*. REMEMBER: We *often* lost five out of TEN.

GROUP 4

once	The word means *one* time. REMEMBER: Put a *c* in ONE to spell *once.*
perform	Pronounce the word distinctly: per-form. REMEMBER: *Percy* will *per*form.
probably	*Three* syllables. REMEMBER: The bottle is *probably* dispos ABLE.
ready	The *a* is unsounded in this word. REMEMBER: He was *ready* for READING.
said	This word sounds as if it should be spelled *sed,* but it is related to *say.* REMEMBER: He *said* he would send AID.
says	Remember that to spell *says* right you have to add an *s* to SAY.
seems	The problem here is the vowel sound, spelled with a double *e.* REMEMBER: She *see*ms to SEE well.
similar	The ending is *–lar.* REMEMBER: It was *similar* to a LARGE LARK.
since	Don't spell this word as if it were the plural of *sin.* REMEMBER: *Since* rhymes with MINCE.
studying	*Studying* combines *study + ing.* REMEMBER: I was studying in the STUDY.

GROUP 5

success	Both the *c* and the *s* must be doubled in this word. Pronounce it carefully: suc-cess. REMEMBER: Double *c,* double *s,* in su*ccess.*
through	*Through* is spelled like *though* except for the *r.*
tired	This word is sometimes confused with *tried.* REMEMBER: The *tired* driver changed the TIRE.
together	Look at the second syllable: to-geth-er. REMEMBER: Let's GET *together.*
tonight	This word was originally two words: *to* plus *night,* but they have grown together. REMEMBER: Join TO with NIGHT to spell *tonight.*

trouble	The demon-letter here is the *o*. REMEMBER: His DOUBLE is in *trouble*.
truly	REMEMBER: Drop the *e* from *true* to spell *truly*.
used	When this word is directly followed by *to*, we often do not hear the *–d*. Make sure it is there when the word is written: He use*d* to live in Camden; I use*d* to like her.
writing	The forms of this verb are *write, wrote, writing, written*. Remember to double the *t* of *write* only with *written*.
wrong	Do not forget the *w* at the beginning of this word. The only vowel is an *o*. REMEMBER: He wROte the *wrong* address.

How well do you remember the common spelling problems you have studied? After the number of each sentence, write down the familiar spelling demon that has been left out in that sentence. (Write on a separate sheet.)

EXERCISE 1

EXAMPLE: The opposite of late is _____ .
(Answer)   *early*

1. Sometimes it rains too much but sometimes not _____ .
2. Books are kept in a _____ .
3. Firs and pines are not exactly the same but only _____ .
4. The opposite of failure is _____ .
5. A telephone number is either right or _____ .
6. We tell meddling people to mind their own _____ .
7. The people who govern us are our _____ .
8. Some tests are difficult and others _____ .
9. Study halls are not for talking but for _____ .
10. After a hard day's work, people feel _____ .
11. In a cafeteria, people may sit separately or _____ .
12. Sixty seconds make up a _____ .
13. A fifty-fifty split gives each person _____ .
14. We see some people too seldom and others too _____ .
15. Belgium is a small _____ in Europe.
16. When we do not know for sure, we _____ .
17. We ask a question and expect an _____ .
18. The opposite of the end is the _____ .
19. A ghostwriter was _____ the speeches for the President.
20. Sometimes there are too few students and sometimes too _____ .

Mechanics

EXERCISE 2

The following sentences include many of the spelling demons you have studied. Have someone dictate these sentences to you. Then check your spelling of the italicized words. Make a special list of the words you missed, and give them special attention.

1. We *often guess wrong.*
2. He is *probably studying* in the *library.*
3. *Every country* has a *government.*
4. She *always seems* to have the *answer.*
5. The *awful* news *meant trouble.*
6. I'll be *all right again* in a *minute.*
7. My *busy friend* felt *tired.*
8. They *used to* be in *business together.*
9. She *said* it *just once.*
10. They are *beginning early enough.*
11. *None* of them were *ready* to *perform.*
12. He *says* that *easy does* it.
13. *Many* others had a *similar success.*
14. The *writing* we had *done* was *easy.*
15. We *accept* if we *receive half.*

EXERCISE 3

Many words cause trouble because they are not spelled the way they sound. Study the following groups of ten.

GROUP 1	GROUP 2	GROUP 3
ache	embarrassed	justice
aisle	entrance	knowledge
athlete	exaggerate	marriage
beauty	extremely	message
civilized	February	opinion
competition	foreign	quantity
concrete	ideal	salary
courage	importance	silence
debt	impossible	strictly
doubt	increase	visible

EXERCISE 4

Have someone dictate one or more groups from the following list of one hundred words. Which of them do you have difficulty spelling? Write in a spelling notebook the words that give you trouble. Study these words over a period of a week or more. At the end of the time period, have them read to you again, and cross off the words you have mastered.

GROUP 1	GROUP 2	GROUP 3	GROUP 4	GROUP 5
ability	consider	future	mystery	scratch
action	content	governor	nervous	secret
actual	continue	guest	occur	serious
admit	crazy	horrible	operate	service
ancient	custom	however	original	similar
apply	defense	human	payment	solution
balance	deliver	identity	planet	spirit
beyond	democracy	immediate	popular	stranger
borrow	discover	information	positive	student
calm	discussion	invention	primary	substitute
camera	distant	judge	private	suggest
career	duty	lawyer	problem	system
chapter	dying	legal	progress	therefore
collect	enjoyable	liquid	purpose	tomato
column	example	loyal	rebel	traffic
command	excellent	major	regret	treasure
commit	experience	manner	relative	valuable
compare	explain	mercy	require	victory
conclusion	familiar	midnight	resign	wreck
connect	freedom	movement	result	youth

Know basic spelling rules.

The advantage of learning spelling rules is obvious: By learning one rule, you can learn to spell many words. The following rules will help you with many different words:

(1) Know when to choose ei *or* ie. We often have to choose between *ei* and *ie* for the long *ee* sound. Write *i* before *e*—except after *c*. All of the following words have the long *ee* sound:

I BEFORE E:	believe achieve piece chief grief
EXCEPT AFTER C:	receive receipt ceiling conceited deceit

The following words are exceptions to this rule: *either, neither, species, weird, leisure, seize.*

(2) Know when to double the last letter of a word. Double a *final consonant* when adding endings to words—if the ending starts with a vowel. Make sure the final letter of such a word is a *single* consonant that comes after a *single* vowel:

DOUBLED CONSONANT

big	bigger, biggest
fat	fatter, fattest, fattening
hop	hopper, hopped, hopping
hot	hotter, hottest
plan	planner, planned, planning
red	redder, reddening, reddest
run	runner, running
scrap	scrapped, scrapping
slip	slipper, slipped, slipping
win	winner, winning

Do *not* double the consonant if the final syllable has a double vowel *(oo, oa, ea,* etc.*)* or a silent *e:*

DOUBLE VOWEL	SILENT E
heat—heated, heating	*hate*—hated, hating
read—reading, reader	*plane*—planed, planing
neat—neater, neatest	*love*—lover, loving
sleep—sleeper, sleeping	*hope*—hoped, hoping
loot—looted, looting	*scrape*—scraped, scraping

The syllable with the doubled consonant must be the one *stressed* when you pronounce the word. Read the following out loud and make sure you hear the difference:

DOUBLING	NO DOUBLING
beGIN, beGINNing	BENefit, BENefited
forGET, forGETTing	deVELop, deVELoping
adMIT, adMITTed	exHIBit, exHIBited
overLAP, overLAPPing	WEAKen, WEAKening
reGRET, reGRETTed	ORBit, ORBiting

If the stress shifts *away* from the syllable, doubling does *not* take place:

reFER, reFERRed	REFerence
preFER, preFERRing	PREFerence

(3) Know when to drop a final e. Drop a silent *e* before an ending that starts with a vowel. Keep the silent *e* if the ending starts with a consonant:

	VOWEL	CONSONANT
love	loving	lovely
bore	boring	boredom
fate	fatal	fateful
like	likable	likely
state	stating	statement

SILENT *E*

This rule has important exceptions:

−e dropped: *argument, awful, duly, judgment, truly, wholly*
−e kept: *mileage*

NOTE: Sometimes the final *e* comes after *c* or *g*. Keep the *ce* or *ge* before *a* or *o*. The *e* then shows that the *c* or *g* has the soft sound: *changeable, courageous, noticeable.*

SPELLING CHANGES
A Reminder

Many words change their spelling when we add an ending. Add the following pairs to your list of "unforgivables." These are "must-know" words.

beauty—beautiful
city—cities
begin—beginning
family—families
plan—planned
carry—carrying
occur—occurred
study—studies
hurry—hurries
happy—happiness

(4) Know when to change a final y. Change a final single *y* to *ie* before *–s*. Change it to *i* before most other endings. Keep the *y* before *–ing*.

	ie:	try–tr*ies*, dry–dr*ies*, city–cit*ies*, carry–carr*ies*, hurry–hurr*ies*, family–famil*ies*
FINAL Y	*i:*	beauty–beaut*i*ful, copy–cop*i*ed, dry–dr*i*es, easy–eas*i*ly, happy–happ*i*ness
	y:	carrying, copying, hurrying, studying

A final *y* that follows a vowel usually does not change:

days, delays, enjoyed, grayness, employer, joys, valleys

A few exceptions to this rule are the following:

day–daily, gay–gaily, lay–laid, pay–paid, say–said

(5) Know how to spell words with added prefixes or suffixes. When you add a *prefix* to a word, do not change the spelling of the word. The following prefixes are common in English: *dis–, im–, in–, mis–, re–,* and *un–*. When you add them to words you do not double the last letter of the prefix:

dis + agree = disagree	mis + apply = misapply
dis + appear = disappear	mis + inform = misinform
im + patient = impatient	re + state = restate
im + possible = impossible	un + able = unable

If the original word begins with the same letter with which the prefix ends, you will have *a double letter* in the new word:

dis + satisfied = dissatisfied	mis + spell = misspell
im + moral = immoral	re + enlist = reenlist
im + mortal = immortal	re + enter = reenter
in + numerable = innumerable	un + natural = unnatural

When you add *–ly* to a word ending in *l*, keep the double *l*. When you add *–ness* to a word ending in *n*, keep the double *n*.

legal + ly = legally	foreign + ness = foreignness
actual + ly = actually	mean + ness = meanness
central + ly = centrally	thin + ness = thinness
final + ly = finally	even + ness = evenness

Write the complete words called for in the following instructions:

A. Fill in *ei* or *ie:*

1. bel____ve	6. conc____ted
2. ach____vement	7. rel____f
3. s____ze	8. n____ther
4. rec____ve	9. rec____pt
5. dec____ve	10. p____ce

B. Add *–ing* to the following words:

1. hit	6. shoot
2. plan	7. bat
3. float	8. hate
4. begin	9. run
5. hop	10. hope

C. Add *–s* to the following words:

1. day	6. try
2. city	7. carry
3. hurry	8. study
4. valley	9. delay
5. family	10. copy

D. Add *–able* to the following words:

1. break	6. prefer
2. forget	7. regret
3. notice	8. change
4. enjoy	9. read
5. like	10. dispose

E. Add *–ness* to the first five words and *–ly* to the second five:

1. happy	6. final
2. mean	7. easy
3. gray	8. cruel
4. lonely	9. day
5. heavy	10. cheerful

Read the sentences on the next page. Look at the words in parentheses. Add the endings that would make each fit into its space in the sentence. Change the spelling of the word as necessary. (Write on a separate sheet.)

EXAMPLE: (happy) She wished us much success and _____ .
(Answer) *happiness*

1. (family) Several _____ were living in the house.
2. (win) He was a poor loser but a generous _____ .
3. (begin) The concert was just _____ .
4. (argue) The players and the umpire got into an _____ .
5. (copy) I need three _____ of the report.
6. (plan) We are _____ an outing for the weekend.
7. (notice) There had been a _____ change in the color.
8. (occur) A very unusual accident had _____ .
9. (final) We _____ got our money back.
10. (pay) They had already _____ for the tickets.
11. (beauty) A _____ tree shaded the lawn.
12. (hurry) We were always _____ to the next class.
13. (city) Many big _____ have subways.
14. (bore) We saw a very _____ movie.
15. (prefer) Customers were asked to state their _____ .
16. (regret) I have always _____ not knowing her.
17. (forget) He was always _____ his car keys.
18. (worry) My friend eats a lot when he _____ .
19. (courage) She was praised for her _____ act.
20. (try) We gave up after three more _____ .

M5c

Confusing Pairs

Watch out for confusing pairs of words.

Words using the same root word are often spelled differently. Look out for the following especially:

(1) Know how to spell different words using the same word root.   Study the following list of familiar troublemakers:

accident	BUT	accident*ally*
basic	BUT	basic*ally*
curi*ous*	BUT	curiosity
disas*ter*	BUT	disas*trous*
e*x*p*l*a*i*n	BUT	expl*an*ation
four, *four*teen	BUT	forty
gener*ous*	BUT	generosity
nin*e*, nin*e*ty	BUT	nin*th*
pron*ou*nce	BUT	pron*u*nciation
sp*ea*king	BUT	sp*ee*ch
*thr*ough	BUT	*tho*rough
ti*ll*	BUT	unti*l*

Sometimes the spelling of a word changes as it changes its role in a sentence:

SINGULAR:	A *woman* answered the phone.
PLURAL:	Two *women* owned the store.
PRESENT:	We *choose* a new leader today.
PAST:	We *chose* Juanita last year.
PRESENT:	We *use* cheap paper.
PAST:	We *used* to live there.
VERB:	We *passed* the station an hour ago.
NOUN:	My uncle lives in the *past*.
NOUN:	His *prejudice* against us was strong.
ADJECTIVE:	He was *prejudiced* against us.

NOTE: Include the *–ed* ending in the following expressions: an *old-fashioned* hayride; she was *supposed to* meet me; I *used to* like baseball.

(2) *Know how to spell words that sound similar or alike.* Study the following confusing pairs very carefully to make sure you can use them correctly:

GROUP 1

been	*Been* is a form of the verb *to be*. EXAMPLE: You should have *been* there.
bin	*Bin* is a noun naming a place for storage. EXAMPLE: Put the dirty clothes in the clothes *bin*.
buy	This word means to get by paying money. EXAMPLE: We went to the grocery store to *buy* milk, butter, and bread.
by	This word is a common preposition. It is also an adverb meaning "near, beyond, past." EXAMPLES: The opening game was won *by* the home team. A huge flock of birds was flying *by*. I like the white house *by* the river best of all.
dear	*Dear* is usually an adjective. It means expensive or valued. EXAMPLE: All of my favorite vegetables are *dear* this season.
deer	*Deer* is a noun naming an animal. EXAMPLE: Most American zoos have many *deer*.

grate	The verb means to rub against a rough surface or irritate. EXAMPLES: We will *grate* some onions. The static on the radio *grated* on my nerves. As a noun, *grate* usually names a frame made of bars. EXAMPLE: There was a *grate* in the fireplace.
great	This word is usually an adjective referring to large size, number, or importance. EXAMPLE: The California redwood grows to a *great* size.
hear	We use our ears to hear. EXAMPLE: We could *hear* the train when it was still miles away.
here	*Here* means in this place or at this point. EXAMPLE: We were standing *here,* not there.
heard	*Heard* is a form of the verb *hear.* It may stand alone as the simple past, or it may come after helping verbs. EXAMPLES: I *heard* that. I have *heard* that her ankle is better now.
herd	*Herd* is a noun for animals gathered together. It also may be used as a verb meaning to bring together. EXAMPLES: The *herd* of cattle was grazing. I was hired to *herd* the cattle.
knew	*Knew* is the past of the verb *to know.* EXAMPLE: The doctor *knew* how to treat the patient.
new	*New* is usually an adjective meaning recent or modern or different. EXAMPLE: He bought a *new* suit.
know	We know something we have learned. EXAMPLE: I *know* their telephone number.
no	This word means not any or not so. EXAMPLES: *No,* I cannot find it. He had *no* way to get home.
loose	*Loose* means not tight, free. EXAMPLE: The scout tied a *loose* knot.
lose	*Lose* means to miss; it is also the opposite of *win.* EXAMPLES: Do not *lose* your books. The team will *lose* without its best hitter.
plain	A *plain* is a level stretch of land. As an adjective, *plain* means obvious or simple. EXAMPLES: The *plain* stretched for miles. I spoke in *plain* words.
plane	The noun *plane* stands for an airplane or a carpenter's tool. EXAMPLE: We did not hear the *plane.*

GROUP 2

principal	The *principal* is the head of a school. EXAMPLE: Go to the *principal's* office.
principle	A *principle* is a basic rule. EXAMPLE: Cheating is against my *principles*.
quiet	*Quiet* is the opposite of noisy. EXAMPLE: We had to be *quiet* in the hospital.
quite	*Quite* means completely or really. EXAMPLE: We were *quite* tired after the hike.
than	*Than* is usually used in a comparison. EXAMPLE: Charlie is shorter *than* Tommy.
then	*Then* means at that time. EXAMPLES: We met them *then*. First we heard screams; *then* there was silence.
their	*Their* is a possessive pronoun; it must be followed by a noun. EXAMPLE: *Their* packs were easily carried on *their* backs.
there	*There* is an adverb meaning in or at that place. EXAMPLE: I see you hiding *there*. *There* is also used as a sentence starter. EXAMPLE: *There* is a fly in your soup.
they're	*They're* is a contracted form of *they are*. EXAMPLE: *They're* really angry now, those bees.
to	This word is a preposition when it is followed by a noun or a pronoun. It also appears before verbs. EXAMPLES: She went *to* the North Shore. He wanted *to* live on the North Shore.
too	*Too* is an adverb meaning also. It also shows degree: *too* hot, *too* much. EXAMPLES: I want to go, *too*. You're *too* young to go.
two	Remember that the number *two* is spelled with a *w*. EXAMPLE: *Two* boys were walking down Pennsylvania Avenue.
way	This is the word for route or path. EXAMPLE: I know the best *way* to Boston.
weigh	We *weigh* something to see how heavy or important it is. EXAMPLES: Tubby *weighs* himself three times a day. After *weighing* all the ideas, he decided his own was the best.

weak	*Weak* is the opposite of strong. EXAMPLE: The little boy was too *weak* to resist the infection.
week	*Week* is a unit of time. EXAMPLE: They were given a *week* to complete the work.
wear	*Wear (wore, worn)* usually means to carry on the person. EXAMPLE: *Wear* slacks to the picnic.
where	*Where* is usually a question word or a connective that has to do with a place. EXAMPLES: *Where* do you live? Show us *where* you caught the fish.
weather	The noun *weather* refers to rain, wind, air temperature, and other conditions of the atmosphere. As a EXAMPLES: The *weather* is bad; I *weathered* the storm.
whether	*Whether* is the connective that means "whether or not." EXAMPLE: I asked *whether* he was going.
who's	This word is a contraction of *who is.* Do not write it unless you can substitute *who is.* EXAMPLE: *Who's* (who is) at the door now?
whose	This word is a relative pronoun or a question word that means "of whom." EXAMPLES: Someone *whose* grades are good will be given the award. *Whose* coat is this?

(3) Know how to spell words with suffixes that sound similar or alike. Look for the following especially:

–able	accept*a*ble, cap*a*ble, port*a*ble
–ible	poss*i*ble, terr*i*ble, vis*i*ble
–ance	attend*a*nce, mainten*a*nce, perform*a*nce
–ence	experi*e*nce, exist*e*nce, excell*e*nce
–ant	attend*a*nt, brilli*a*nt, radi*a*nt
–ent	differ*e*nt, excell*e*nt, independ*e*nt
–er	farm*e*r, lead*e*r, shoemak*e*r
–or	doct*o*r, tail*o*r, operat*o*r

NOTE: Spell out *have* in combinations like the following:

would *have* agreed	(NEVER: *would of agreed*)
could *have* learned	(NEVER: *could of learned.*
must *have* spoken	(NEVER: *must of spoken*)

In each of the following expressions, one word appears with one or more letters left out. Add any missing letters and write the completed word after its number.

EXAMPLE: hard to expl—n
(Answer) *explain*

1. a very strong curi—sity
2. the eighth and ni—th chapters
3. found it acciden—ly
4. free to ch—se
5. a disast—ous misunderstanding
6. hard to pron—nce
7. well-known for her gener—sity
8. the wrong pron—ciation
9. old-fashion— clothes
10. a clear expl—nation
11. the gas station attend—nt
12. a crowd of wom—n
13. f—rty years old
14. basi—ly correct
15. my sp—ch teacher
16. unti— we meet again
17. a differ—nt size
18. invis—ble ink
19. an independ—nt candidate
20. low attend—nce

After the number of each sentence, write the choice that fits the sentence best.

EXAMPLE: She has *(been/bin)* in Mexico several times.
(Answer) *been*

1. The painting showed a *(heard/herd)* of buffalo.
2. Her arrival was a *(great/grate)* surprise.
3. My friends *(no/know)* nothing about sources of energy.
4. We lived peacefully on a *(quiet/quite)* side street.
5. The *(dear/deer)* were protected until the hunting season.
6. Several people had parked cars *(there/their)*.
7. The school hired a new *(principal/principle)*.
8. My grandmother preferred *(plane/plain)* clothes.
9. They drove much *(to/too)* fast.
10. You can *(by/buy)* the same model cheaper elsewhere.
11. Trains *(used/use)* to pass by there in the night.
12. He looked at me and *(than/then)* ran away.

Mechanics

13. They were *(suppose/supposed)* to be here.
14. The neighbors are reseeding *(there/their)* lawn.
15. The book compared the *(past/passed)* and the present.
16. Blood is thicker *(than/then)* water.
17. Everyone in town *(new/knew)* about the burglary.
18. You should *(of/have)* notified me.
19. What did you *(wear/where)* to the party?
20. He always talked about what might *(of/have)* been.

EXERCISE 3

In this exercise, you will find words you have studied and additional confusing pairs. After the number of each sentence, write the choice that fits the sentence best.

1. I am *(to/too)* tired to help you.
2. *(Who's/Whose)* going to accept that excuse?
3. We did not have a *(quiet/quite)* place to read.
4. Perhaps I can make it up next *(week/weak)*.
5. You have already wasted a *(hole/whole)* hour.
6. A *(road/rode)* runs through Rocky Mountain National Park.
7. At various stops along it, one can *(see/sea)* for miles.
8. High altitudes make some people *(weak/week)*.
9. *(You're/Your)* car must be in good condition.
10. *(Their/There/They're)* are no service stations along the road.
11. She went horseback riding for an *(hour/our)* yesterday.
12. Part of the time, she let the horse's reins hang *(loose/lose)*.
13. She galloped wildly across the *(plain/plane)*.
14. She could *(hear/here)* the wind whistling in the trees.
15. The mourners prayed for his *(sole/soul)*.
16. The girls enjoyed the picnic more *(than/then)* the last time.
17. They ate lunch in the shade *(by/buy)* the stream.
18. They had packed *(their/there/they're)* own lunches.
19. Decide *(who's/whose)* turn it is.
20. I have *(heard/herd)* that the road is closed.

UNIT REVIEW EXERCISE

In the following sentences, find any letter or letters missing at the space shown. After each number, write the *completed word.* (No letters are missing in some words.)

EXAMPLE: We have had terrible w____ther.
(Answer) *weather*

1. It is better to be safe th____n sorry.
2. She is a dependable fr____nd.
3. I real____y love her more than anybody.

4. His head nearly touched the c_____ling.
5. I was surprised that he mis_____pelled that word.
6. How much is four times f_____rty?
7. Lou was so t_____red that he went to bed.
8. I expect to rec_____ve a call at nine.
9. It is al_____ways easier to talk than to act.
10. Our princip_____ rushed to the lunchroom.
11. Ginny _____new the answer but kept quiet.
12. Many students l_____se things at school.
13. I bel_____ve everything you say.
14. Have you h_____rd from Phyllis?
15. They laughed at my pron_____nciation.
16. Tell me who_____ idea it was.
17. My sister use_____ to help me.
18. He loved beaut_____ful scenery.
19. Take the books back to the lib_____ry.
20. Several famil_____s shared the cabin.

Make sure your papers are attractive to the eye and easy to read.

Before you hand in any paper, put yourself in the reader's place. Does the appearance of the paper make you want to read it, or does it turn you away from it? Are the individual letters distinct, or do you have difficulty telling an *o* from an *a,* an *i* from an *e?* Is there plenty of space between lines so that your eye moves easily from line to line? When you have finished reading the paper, which do you feel: "That was a pleasure," or "I'm glad that is done"?

Here are some general guidelines:

• *Use standard-size paper* (eight and one-half by eleven inches). Use unlined paper if you type. Use paper ruled in wide lines if you handwrite. Use blue or black ink.

• *Use margins on all four sides.* Your teacher may give you directions about margins. If not, use about one and one-half inches at the top and left-hand side, and about an inch at the bottom and right-hand side. *Indent* the first line of a paragraph an inch in writing and five spaces in typing.

• *Leave space between words and more space at the end of sentences.* If you are typing, leave one space between words and two spaces after end punctuation. Double-space between lines so there is room for corrections.

• *Follow your teacher's instructions about the heading for your papers.* A common practice is to place your name at the upper right-hand corner of the first page, the name and number of the course beneath this, and the date on a third line. Pages are typically numbered in the upper right-hand corner, but do *not* number the first page.

• *Use standard form for titles.* Titles of papers are normally placed on the first page, about two spaces below the heading. Center your title, and do not underline it or put it in quotation marks (unless it is a quotation from some other source). Unless your teacher tells you to, do not use a separate title page except for papers longer than three or four pages. When you do use a title page, center the title in the middle of it and place the heading in the upper right-hand corner. You may use a question mark or exclamation mark at the end of your titles, but do not use a period:

Where Did the Fish Go?
Save Our Eagles!
I Need a Friend

LAST-MINUTE CORRECTIONS

The following corrections are permissible on your final copy if they are neat and few in number:

(1) Draw a line through words or phrases that you want to leave out. (Do not use parentheses for this purpose.)

```
I knew that if I backed down that things could only
```

(2) To correct a word, draw a line through it and write the corrected word in the space immediately above. Do not cross out or add individual letters:

```
                      accept
We should never except other people's opinions without
```

(3) To add a missing word or phrase, insert a caret (∧). Then write the word or phrase immediately above:

```
                whose
She asked me∧car it was that was parked outside
```

(4) To change the paragraphing of a paper, insert the symbol ¶ to indicate an additional paragraph break. To show that an existing paragraph break should be ignored, insert *no* ¶ in the margin.

Use hyphens to divide words at the end of a line.

A paper looks neater if the right-hand margin is reasonably straight. In order to make it straight, you will have to divide words. The dictionary is the surest guide to where words should be hyphenated. Here are some general guidelines:

(1) Break up words into their smaller building blocks. The following are examples of words correctly divided between a prefix and a root or between a root and a suffix:

dis-agree	non-stop	un-able	re-pay
talk-ing	wash-able	happi-ness	agree-ment

(2) Divide words with double consonants between the consonants. Note the examples below:

neces-sary	paral-lel	ten-nis	hap-pen
shal-low	com-mit	cot-tage	mar-ried

But when a double consonant is immediately followed by the suffix *–ing,* the division is usually made where the suffix begins:

call-ing   fill-ing   spell-ing

(3) Divide words between pronounceable parts only. When you divide a word at the end of a line, you should be able to pronounce each part of the word comfortably. Study the following examples:

no-tice (not not-ice)	ex-plore (not exp-lore)
be-tween (not bet-ween)	develop-ment (not develo-pment)
im-portant (not imp-ortant)	op-erate (not ope-rate)

(4) Do not divide words with only one syllable. Put the whole word on one line or the next. Do not divide such words as the following:

played (not play-ed)	school (not sch-ool)	read (not re-ad)
does (not do-es)	bought (not bo-ught)	

(5) Do not divide words so that a single letter stands alone. Also, try to avoid carrying only two letters over to the next line. This rule applies even when the single letter or the two letters represent a syllable of the word:

around (not a-round)	emerge (not e-merge)	unite (not u-nite)
idea (not i-dea)	over (not o-ver)	

Use the divisions on the left-hand side, not those on the right:

pris-oner	(rather than prison-er)
eventu-ally	(rather than eventual-ly)
no-tify	(rather than noti-fy)
al-lergy	(rather than aller-gy)

EXERCISE

Write the following words with hyphens showing where the words may be divided. If a word may be divided in more than one place, show all possible divisions. If a word should not be divided, write the word without hyphens. Check your dictionary if you are unsure of an answer.

1. across	6. important	11. asleep	16. able
2. vessel	7. suppose	12. collect	17. asked
3. distance	8. repeat	13. remember	18. fished
4. argument	9. darkness	14. imagination	19. terrible
5. message	10. morning	15. awaken	20. frequently

M6b

Abbreviations

Know which abbreviations are acceptable in ordinary writing.

Many abbreviations are acceptable only in special kinds of writing. The following rules will tell you which abbreviations are appropriate for *ordinary* writing:

(1) Abbreviations of titles should come before or after a person's name. Such titles as *Mr., Mrs., Ms., Dr.,* or *Rev.* before a name, and *Jr., Sr., M.D.,* and *Ph.D.* after a name, are acceptable in ordinary writing. Do not use them, however, if you do not use a person's name with them:

ACCEPTABLE: The Rev. and Mrs. J. D. Spooner, Jr., will be the sponsors.

UNACCEPTABLE: The Mrs. asked if there was a Dr. in the house.

(2) Some abbreviations are used in ordinary writing only before or after specific dates or times. The acceptable abbreviations are A.M., P.M., A.D., and B.C.

ACCEPTABLE: It was once predicted that the world would end at 2:30 P.M. in A.D. 435.

UNACCEPTABLE: I got up in the P.M.

(3) Many abbreviations for the names of agencies, business firms, technical processes, and the like are in common use. If you are familiar with an abbreviation, you may assume that it is in common use. The following are some examples of acceptable abbreviations. Notice that periods are not used between the letters:

FBI   (Federal Bureau of Investigation)
IBM   (International Business Machines)
TWA   (Trans-World Airlines)
SCLC   (Southern Christian Leadership Conference)
UN   (United Nations)

(4) Do not abbreviate the names of countries, states, months, or *days of the week.* In business records or in addresses on letters some of these abbreviations are acceptable, but not in ordinary writing:

UNACCEPTABLE: I spent three days in N.Y.
ACCEPTABLE: I spent three days in New York.

UNACCEPTABLE: I was there on Fri., Nov. 21.
ACCEPTABLE: I was there on Friday, November 21.

Some exceptions: Washington, *D.C.; USSR.*

(5) In ordinary writing, do not *abbreviate words standing for measurements.* In scientific writing, business writing, and in lists, you may find abbreviated words such as *inch* (in.), *foot* (ft.), *pound* (lb.), *minute* (min.), *second* (sec.), and so on. Spell out such words in ordinary writing:

UNACCEPTABLE: I waited 3 min. and 40 sec.
ACCEPTABLE: I waited 3 minutes and 40 seconds.

UNACCEPTABLE: He said the fish weighed 18 lbs. and 12 oz.
ACCEPTABLE: He said the fish weighed 18 pounds and 12 ounces.

In each pair, which sentence is acceptable in ordinary writing? Write the letter for the acceptable choice after the number of the pair.

EXERCISE

1. (a) A Gen. and a Capt. were on the committee.
   (b) Ms. Myers and Mr. Parsons were on the committee.
2. (a) I have to see the doctor Mon. morning.
   (b) I have to see Dr. Tillson Monday morning.

3. (a) Several doctors were called for the consultation.
   (b) Several M.D.'s were called for the consultation.
4. (a) The meeting was adjourned until the P.M.
   (b) The meeting was adjourned until 3:30 P.M.
5. (a) Mrs. Stern assigned pages 31 to 45 for homework.
   (b) Mrs. Stern assigned pgs. 31 to 45 for homework.
6. (a) For three yrs. I lived in San Francisco, Calif.
   (b) For three years I lived in San Francisco, California.
7. (a) The monument is over 555 ft. high.
   (b) The monument is over 555 feet high.
8. (a) The headquarters of the FBI is in Washington.
   (b) The headquarters of the Federal Bureau of Investigation is in Wash.
9. (a) He will have a three-week vacation in August.
   (b) He will have a three-wk. vacation in Aug.
10. (a) We waited for two hrs. on the corner of Fifth Ave.
    (b) We waited for two hours on the corner of Fifth Avenue.

M6c

Numbers

Learn which numbers should be spelled out and which written in figures.

The following advice will help you to decide when to spell out numbers and when to use figures:

(1) Spell out a number that begins a sentence:

POOR PRACTICE: 25 is my lucky number.
GOOD PRACTICE: Twenty-five is my lucky number.

(2) Spell out numbers from one to ten and round numbers with no more than two words:

POOR PRACTICE: We invited 5 men and 4 women.
GOOD PRACTICE: We invited five men and four women.

POOR PRACTICE: We sent out 200 invitations but only 40 persons came.
GOOD PRACTICE: We sent out two hundred invitations but only forty persons came.

(3) Use figures for long numbers and exact figures:

The room seated about 450 people.
The population was 112,504.
They received a check for $2,877.54.

NOTE: With shorter numbers, you may find both "18" and "eighteen," both "104" and "one hundred and four."

(4) Use figures for dates and years; street, room, telephone, and page numbers; percentages and figures with decimal points. All of the following are good practice:

Nina was born on October 5.

David lives at 929 Valley Road; his telephone number is 885-4052.

Its weight should be between 2.2 and 2.5 grams.

The poll shows that 44 percent of the people are for Brand XX and 36 percent are for Brand X; the remaining 20 percent are undecided.

(5) Spell out fractions and numbers with suffixes such as st, nd, rd, *and* th:

POOR PRACTICE: He found ¼ of the treasure missing.

GOOD PRACTICE: He found one-fourth of the treasure missing.

POOR PRACTICE: Carry your answer to the 2nd or 3rd decimal place.

GOOD PRACTICE: Carry your answer to the second or third decimal place.

After the number of each pair, write the letter of the sentence that illustrates acceptable practice for the writing or spelling out of numbers. Assume that all the sentences are to be used in ordinary writing. (Your teacher may ask you to correct those sentences that do not represent acceptable practice.)

EXERCISE

1. (a) Forty-six students joined in the rally.
   (b) 46 students joined in the rally.

2. (a) I thought that there were fifty-six on hand.
   (b) I thought that there were 56 on hand.

3. (a) The fan cost $12.50.
   (b) The fan cost twelve dollars and fifty cents.

4. (a) The Williams family has two cats and three dogs.
   (b) The Williams family has 2 cats and 3 dogs.

5. (a) They live at twenty Main Street.
   (b) They live at 20 Main Street.

6. (a) Our track team finished 2nd in the ¼ mile relay and fourth in the ½ mile relay.
   (b) Our track team finished second in the quarter-mile relay and fourth in the half-mile relay.

7. (a) I had only ½ of the answers right.
   (b) I had only half of the answers right.

8. (a) We stayed near New York from June 19 to June 21.
   (b) We stayed near New York from June nineteenth to June twenty-first.

9. (a) The mixture was made of three percent acid, twenty percent alcohol, and seventy-seven percent water.
   (b) The mixture was made of 3 percent acid, 20 percent alcohol, and 77 percent water.

10. (a) We found the answer on the 3rd line of the 5th page.
    (b) We found the answer on the third line of the fifth page.

UNIT REVIEW EXERCISE   Most of the following sentences show the right use of abbreviations or numbers in ordinary writing. Put *S* for satisfactory after the number of each sentence that shows how things are done right. Put *U* for unsatisfactory after the number of the sentence if something has gone wrong.

1. Her family lives on Lamont St. in Hartford, Conn.
2. The plane was scheduled to leave at 2:30 p.m.
3. In 1981, we had seven feet of snow.
4. The candidate collected 54.6 percent of the vote.
5. The school had only two hundred sixty-five students.
6. I had seen 3 or 4 movies about the FBI.
7. Mrs. Hansen had seen Dr. Fielding several times.
8. Thirteen is often considered an unlucky number.
9. The YMCA raised ten thousand dollars for the project.
10. ¼ of the money from the concert was for the band.
11. We need a check for $125.35.
12. Jr. had an appointment in the p.m.
13. The city had been founded around 1500 B.C.
14. Their offices were on Grant Street in Des Moines, Iowa.
15. The population of our town was 12,358.
16. The largest fish we caught measured 3 ft., 2 in.
17. We lived at twenty-one Michigan Avenue.
18. Her 1948 Dodge had become a collector's item.
19. The meeting will be held on Apr. 7 in the afternoon.
20. We chartered a bus for the trip to Washington, D.C.

Chapter 6

Oral Language
Speaking to a Group

Chapter Preview 6

Learn to speak confidently to a group.

Speaking in public is not basically different from speaking to friends and neighbors. Just like an individual, a group of people will laugh at something funny. They will be puzzled by something that is difficult or new. They will get angry when they are insulted. The difference is that in public speaking you usually have to wait your turn. And when your turn comes, you try to make the most of it. You make sure you are prepared, and you try to make your words count.

When you speak in class or at a club meeting, do you make your voice heard? Do you make your points clearly enough so that people will remember what you have said? Have you ever tried to *explain* something to a group of people, the way a teacher does? Have you ever tried to *persuade* a group of people?

The materials in this chapter are designed to help you make the most of your turn when you speak to a group.

01
THE WAY WE TALK

Learn how to make yourself heard.

A friend who knows us well, and who is standing or walking right next to us, can usually make out what we are saying. If not, he or she can always say "Huh?" or "What was that?" But someone who is listening to you from the back row of a meeting room must be able to *hear you clearly* the first time. Your message will be wasted if it does not reach the receiver. The most basic rule of public speaking is: Make sure the audience gets the message.

Vary your voice to help get your message across.

O1a
Using Your Voice

When written down, a message may seem to state a simple fact. But we can use our voices to give the same message many different meanings. By shouting the message, we can say: "This is important!" By whispering the message, we can say: "This is a secret!"

Use only your voice (and your face) to show the different meanings indicated below for the same message. (You may want to use this message for a contest to choose the student with the "most expressive voice.")

"There's a dinosaur in the science building."
(along with other important exhibits.)

"There's a dinosaur in the science building."
(and we are *very* proud of it!)

"There's a dinosaur in the science building!"
(Horrors—a prehistoric monster come back to life!)

"There's a dinosaur in the science building."
(Yeah—a likely story!)

"There's a dinosaur in the science building."
(Great—finally some excitement around here!)

"There's a dinosaur in the science building."
(Big deal—that kind of thing happens around here all the time.)

"There's a dinosaur in the science building."
(Don't tell anybody—nobody is supposed to know!)

Learn to use the full range of your voice. We find it hard to pay attention when a speaker speaks in a droning tone. A good speaker makes full use of the breaks, and changes in tone, that make speech lively. Three features especially give speech variety:

(1) Sometimes we turn up the volume for a word or a syllable (and also draw it out longer than usual). We are putting **stress** on it. Stress makes something stand out for special attention. It affects the meaning of the statement. Read the following out loud:

1. I like Jean.
   (That's the simple truth.)

   I like Jean.
   (I—not Bill Schwartz.)

   I *like* Jean.
   (But I don't *love* her.)

   I like *Jean*.
   (But not her sister Ann.)

2. The glass is on the table.
   (A simple statement of fact.)

   The *glass* is on the table.
   (The pitcher is somewhere else.)

   The glass *is* on the table.
   (So don't ask me to put it there!)

   The glass is on the *table*.
   (Not on the sink.)

(2) Sometimes we make our voice go up higher. We raise its **pitch.** When you want to turn a statement into a question, you can simply make the pitch go up *one* step at the end. If you really want to show how ridiculous the statement is, you can make pitch go up *two* steps at the end. Read the following out loud:

1. I like Jean.
   (That's a simple fact.)

   I like *Jean?*
   (Don't you believe it!)

   I like *Jean??!!!*
   (But that's *ridiculous!*)

2. He gave the baby beer.
   (That's what he did.)

   He gave the baby *beer?*
   (Did I hear that right?)

   He gave the baby *beer?????*
   (He must be completely out of his mind!!)

(3) A break in the middle of a sentence can show hesitation. We may not really be sure what to say, or how to say it. But a break can also signal that something important is coming. Read the following out loud:

1. He is a—friend.
   (I don't really know what to call him.)

   He has always been—a friend!
   (Something extra special!)

2. What you need is a—vacation.
   (I wish I could be sure.)

   What you need is—a vacation!
   (Isn't this a brilliant idea?)

A. Read the following sentences out loud. Bring out the differences in meaning as clearly as you can.

Jim laughed at me.	Jim *laughed* at me?
Jim laughed at me.	Jim laughed at *me?*
Jim *laughed* at me.	Jim laughed at *me?!!*
Jim laughed at *me.*	

B. Read each of the following statements as if you were repeating a *false* accusation to show how ridiculous it is.

I have stolen the dandelions!
My snoring keeps everyone awake!
My friends ate the crust off the apple pie!
I barked at the neighbor's bulldog!
I check books out of the library to keep you from reading them!

Try one or more of the following experiments. (Your class may want to vote on who performed each task best.)

1. Write several sentences about something the President, the mayor of your community, or some other public official has recently done or is about to do. First, *whisper* your sentences as if you were telling a secret. Then, read your sentences *loudly* and firmly, as if you were making an important announcement.

2. Write several sentences listing many of the meat dishes offered at a favorite restaurant. Read them first in such a way that

they will make the listener's mouth water. The second time read the *same* sentences but pretend you are a vegetarian or a visitor from a country where eating meat is considered a horrible crime.

3. Pretend you are a tourist guide showing familiar sights in your community. Write several sentences describing the sights. Read them first in the monotonous voice of someone *bored* with the job. Then read them with feeling—show that you want your listeners to appreciate what they see.

O1b
The Language of Gestures

Use natural gestures to give your words added force.

Talk is not all words. While we talk, we "make faces." We gesture with our hands. Everybody understands a shake of the head to mean "no," a nod to mean "yes." Your head thrown back may show happiness or joy. Your head bowed may show sorrow or respect.

Pretend you are teaching a student from Japan or Korea who has learned English mostly from books. Can you teach the gestures that go with the words? How many of the following can you say *without* words? (TEST: Act out one or more of these, and see whether your classmates get the message.)

"Who, me?"	"I'm amazed!"
"Go away!"	*"This* is supposed to be great?"
"Oh, I forgot!"	"This tastes terrible!"
"Come here!"	"I feel sick to my stomach!"
"That's no good!"	"It's too loud!"
"What can I do?"	"Let me think!"
"I'm scared!"	"Sorry, I really don't know."

Your gestures show your audience that you really believe and feel what you are saying. If you stand stock-still, your words will sound like something you have memorized. Use the gestures that come naturally to us when we describe something, or when we argue with a person.

EXERCISE 1

How good are you at talking with your hands? Pantomime a demonstration of how to build a doghouse. Be sure to make people see the nails, the hammer, and the saw. Show how to measure and saw the wood, how to assemble and nail it together, how to put the roof on. Finally, show

how you coax the dog to try out the finished doghouse. (You and your classmates may want to select other additional tasks that could be pantomimed, and that would test a speaker's ability to talk with his or her hands.)

Read each of the following lines with the right use of voice and gestures. (The class may want to hold a contest to determine who can read the lines most convincingly.)

1. "All of you in this room . . ."
2. "The pumpkin was this big."
3. "He lived over there, beyond the hills."
4. "It was the biggest bear I'd ever seen."
5. "Please, give to the Red Cross."
6. "We must not fail."
7. "I am speaking to you and you and you."
8. "Now, hold on. Let's stop and think a moment."
9. "It shot up like a rocket."
10. "It drifted up like a lazy balloon."
11. "It wasn't I. I swear it."
12. "Please, Mom, just this once."
13. "Well . . . that's life."
14. "Oops, I'm sorry. It's washable ink."
15. "Would you mind getting off my toe?"
16. "Oh, boy, really?"
17. "Please, don't shoot."
18. "I don't believe it."
19. "Welcome back to Kent Manor!"
20. "We don't need anything today."

Choose one of the following poems. Study it carefully and practice reading it aloud. Try to make your voice and gestures convey the right mood or the right atmosphere.

The Spider and the Fly

"Will you walk into my parlor?" said the Spider to the Fly.
" 'Tis the prettiest little parlor that ever you did spy;
The way into my parlor is up a winding stair,
And I have many curious things to show when you are there."
"Oh no, no," said the little Fly, "to ask me is in vain;
For who goes up your winding stair can ne'er come down again."

—Mary Howitt

Wind-Wolves

Do you hear the cry as the pack goes by,
The wind-wolves hunting across the sky?
Hear them tongue it, keen and clear,
Hot on the flanks of the flying deer!

Across the forest, mere, and plain,
Their hunting howl goes up again!
All night they'll follow the ghostly trail,
All night we'll hear their phantom wail.

For tonight the wind-wolf pack holds sway
From Pegasus Square to the Milky Way,
And the frightened bands of cloud deer flee
In scattered groups of two and three.

—William D. Sargent

Night Clouds

The white mares of the moon rush along the sky
Beating their golden hoofs upon the glass Heavens;
The white mares of the moon are all standing on their hind
legs
Pawing at the green porcelain doors of the remote Heavens.
Fly, mares!
Strain your utmost,
Scatter the milky dust of stars,
Or the tiger sun will leap upon you and destroy you
With one lick of his vermilion tongue.

—Amy Lowell

Silver

Slowly, silently, now the moon
Walks the night in her silver shoon
This way, and that, she peers, and sees
Silver fruit upon silver trees;
One by one the casements catch
Her beams beneath the silvery thatch;
Couched in his kennel, like a log,
With paws of silver sleeps the dog;
From their shadowy cote the white breasts peep
Of doves in a silver-feathered sleep;
A harvest mouse goes scampering by,
With silver claws and a silver eye;
And moveless fish in the water gleam,
By silver reeds in a silver stream.

—Walter De la Mare

Learn to give a short planned talk.

What is a speech? A speech is communication between one person and an audience. Thus, giving a speech is simply communicating with an audience. You as a speaker have something to say, and you say it to a group of people who are gathered to listen to you.

Sometimes, there is little difference between a short speech and a conversation in which you play the central role. Imagine that you have just returned from an exciting vacation. You meet some of your friends and begin telling them about your trip. Soon more of your friends gather round, and you may find yourself talking to eight or ten people. In such a situation, though, the conversation may soon move on to other topics. And you may later remember things that you should have mentioned but forgot.

The main thing that makes a short speech different from such a conversation is that a good speaker *plans ahead*. Remember:

(1) A speech often has a definite purpose. It does not ramble on from one subject to another, like a conversation. The speaker concentrates on *one* topic, like "Violence in Current Movies," or "The Mineral Treasures of Canada's Frozen North." The speaker has a definite *job* to do: to satisfy our curiosity, to persuade voters, or to win support.

(2) A good speaker takes time to collect material. The speaker reads background materials, looks up important names and facts. You yourself may gather material for a short speech from an encyclopedia or an article in a newsmagazine.

(3) A good speaker arranges the material in a clear order. When you prepare a short talk, fix the three or four major points clearly in your mind in the order in which you will take them up. Usually you will have some *written notes* in front of you to remind you of your major points, and of important facts and figures.

NOTE: Avoid the "canned speech" that is completely written out or memorized. Learn to speak freely on the basis of your written notes. The audience likes to see that you are still thinking about what you are saying—still adding things, or choosing a better word for an important idea.

O2a

The Portrait in Words

Give a short talk about a person who should be better known.

Nearly everybody is familiar with the names of our great Presidents and our most famous generals. But many people who have made other kinds of important contributions are not well known.

In a short speech, remind your audience of one of these "unsung heroes." Include the essential facts about the *contribution* the person made. But also include some material that shows something about the *kind of person* you are describing. If possible, include a quotation, in words the person actually said. Your speech will serve as a short "portrait in words" of someone who is not as well known as he or she should be.

Here are some ideas that might help you select such a person:

• Today it is common to see black athletes win top honors. When did blacks first make their way in the world of sports? Who, for instance, was the first black heavyweight champion?

• Most of us have heard the names of famous male scientists such as Louis Pasteur and Albert Einstein. What women have you heard about who played important roles in major scientific discoveries?

• Spy movies and television programs have long been popular with American audiences. True stories about *real* spies are often as exciting as the stories writers create for movies and television. Do you know anything about real spies who risk their lives in the service of their country?

• Doctors who perform daring new operations often receive much publicity. Have you ever heard or read about any of the pioneers of modern medicine?

The following passage provides the kind of information that you might use in a short speech about a person. It deals with one of the first leaders of black Americans in their battle for dignity and justice. By reading more about the man, can you add some touches to your speech that would reveal the man's character and personality? Can you add one or two quotations from his speeches?

Frederick Douglass was the son of a Negro slave. He became a famous American author and journalist. At an early age he was sent to Baltimore as the property of a Mrs. Auld, a learned woman who secretly taught him to read. Later he became the property of a tough master who was unable to break his spirit. Eventually, Douglass escaped to New York. He became an agent of the Massachusetts Anti-Slavery Society. This was a job which gave him the opportunity to deliver numerous addresses against slavery. He conducted the *North Star,* an anti-slavery weekly journal. Douglass was a staunch supporter of the Union and urged the United States to use Negro troops in the Civil War. Douglass served the United States in many posts. He was the American consul-general in the Republic of Haiti from 1889 to 1891. Frederick Douglass was one of the best orators of his time.

Tell a brief story to help support a major point.

O2b

**The Story
with a Point**

One of the oldest and best-known kinds of stories is the beast fable as told many hundreds of years ago by Aesop. Aesop first told many familiar stories about the sly fox, the proud lion, and the vain crow.

Aesop used his stories to *make a point*. He wanted people to *learn* something from each one of his fables. For instance, Aesop told the story about the bat. When the birds had a war with the four-footed beasts, the bat took advantage of the fact that it could fly like a bird, and yet was really a mammal, like a rat or a mouse. When the birds seemed to be winning, it fought on their side. But when the beasts were winning, it crossed over to their side. Can you figure out what the point of the story is? When peace finally came, *neither* side wanted to have anything to do with the bat. This story explains why bats live all by themselves in dark caves.

Prepare a short speech in which you use a fable (or other brief story) to support a point. Suppose your message is as follows: "Persuasion is more effective than violence." The outline for your speech would look like this:

MAIN POINT: Persuasion is more effective than violence.
SUPPORT: Fable of North Wind and Sun

This simple plan could provide you with material for a two-minute speech. Of course, the speech would seem rather blunt to the audience if you merely stated your main idea and told the story. You would want to think of some way to introduce the topic.

Study the way the speaker presenting the following sample speech *leads up* to the story. Also notice the way the speaker sums up the main point.

The Power of Persuasion

Most of us have had the urge to smash somebody at one time or another. Some people give in to this urge rather frequently—sometimes at the expense of being smashed themselves.

There's a better way to solve disputes—persuasion.

A Greek slave many years ago learned this fact and set it down for us in the form of a story.

The North Wind and the Sun were having an argument one day over which of them was the more powerful. They realized that their talk wouldn't prove anything, so they decided upon a contest. Whichever could get the jacket off a man walking up the road would be victor. The North Wind tried first and blew a blast of cold air. The man's jacket flapped open with the gust, but he grasped it with his hands and drew it tightly around him. Once again the North Wind sent a cold blast at the man, and once again the man bent forward into the wind and drew his jacket tighter around him. This continued for quite some time, the North Wind tearing at the jacket with violent fury. But with every icy blast the man grew more intent upon clinging to his jacket. Finally, in disgust, the North Wind submitted to the Sun. The Sun shone gently on the man. Within a few moments the man himself removed his coat and flung it over his shoulder, and he continued happily on his way.

The next time the urge to violence comes over you, remember the frustration of the North Wind. Try using the Sun's recipe, a little human warmth.

EXERCISE

People often have fun by bringing a familiar story *up to date.* They can then give it a new moral that may be the opposite of what the audience expects.

Can you see how James Thurber has fun with a familiar story in the following example from his book *Fables for Our Times?* Choose one of Thurber's modern fables for retelling. Or make up your own modernized version of a familiar fable or tale.

The Little Girl and the Wolf

One afternoon a big wolf waited in a dark forest for a little girl to come along carrying a basket of food to her grandmother. Finally a little girl did come along and she was carrying a basket of food. "Are you carrying that basket to your grandmother?" asked the wolf. The little girl said yes, she was. So the wolf asked her where her grandmother lived and the little girl told him and he disappeared into the wood.

When the little girl opened the door of her grandmother's house, she saw that there was somebody in bed with a nightcap and nightgown on. She had approached no nearer than twenty-five feet from the bed when she saw that it was not her grandmother but the wolf, for even in a nightcap a wolf does not look any more like your grandmother than the Metro-Goldwyn lion looks like Calvin Coolidge. So the little girl took an automatic out of her basket and shot the wolf dead.

Moral: It is not so easy to fool little girls nowadays as it used to be.

Explain something difficult, or show how something works.

The most practical kind of speech explains something the listener needs to know. Prepare a three-minute speech in which you demonstrate how to do something or explain how something works. Choose a topic with which you are familiar and in which you are interested. It may be a favorite pastime or hobby, such as knitting, archery, rock collecting, or ceramics. It may be a technical topic, such as the workings of a light bulb or steam engine. If you wish, use visual aids such as models and sketches.

Watch out for the following:

• Explain *terms* that the beginner does not know. When you use a word like *detonator* or *filament,* make sure your listeners know what you are talking about.

• Do not cover *too many steps* or operations too fast. Have you ever had difficulties with directions that go: "Turn right, then left, then right, then straight ahead." Give your listeners a chance to grasp one thing at a time.

• Keep your eye on your *audience*. If they frown or fidget, they did not understand something you said. *Go back* over it; make sure they follow your explanation.

THE ART OF LISTENING

A good speaker is a good listener. Develop your listening skills:

(1) Listen for *information*. When you speak to a group, mention events you heard about on a news program. Remember important statistics used by another speaker.

(2) Listen to the *questions* other people ask. Find out what their interests and their problems are. Then when you talk to a group, they can feel you are talking to *them*. You can talk about what interests them, or what troubles them.

(3) Listen to other speakers in order to study them as *models*. When someone gives a good informative talk, ask: How did the speaker lay out the material? How did the speaker keep the audience interested?

The following assignments will give you a chance to find out how good a listener you are. They will give you a chance to *improve* your skill as a listener.

ACTIVITY 1

Do you ever have a chance to listen to speakers who talk about a career, or about their community? The next time you have the opportunity, take *notes* during such a talk. Give a summary of the most important information as an oral report.

ACTIVITY 2

Listen to a television *news* program. (Choose one that runs between five and fifteen minutes.) In what *order* do the speakers present the major news events of the day? Do they show which they consider really *important*? Do you think they are good speakers? Why, or why not?

Your teacher may ask all the members of your class to watch the same program, so that you can compare your evaluation with that of your classmates.

You and your classmates may want to stage an imitation news program on current school news.

Study two or three current *commercials* that make effective use of the spoken word. Describe some of the features that make a commercial effective. Can you imitate the punch lines of several current commercials?

ACTIVITY 3

Have you ever listened to a conversation between two people who do not really *say* anything? People often talk mainly to show they feel friendly. Write the lines for a friendly or polite conversation between two people —neighbors, family members, friends, or the like. Then act out the conversation with a classmate.

ACTIVITY 4

Chapter 7

Resources
The Library, Study Skills, Taking Tests

R1

USING THE LIBRARY

Make full use of the library.

Libraries offer us good stories or novels for leisure reading. They are also storehouses of facts and information. Do you want to repair something on your family car? You can learn how in a library. Do you want to learn more about vitamins? You can learn it in a library. Do you want to know the world record for the fifty-yard dash? You can find it in a library.

R1a

Finding Library Materials

Learn where to find things in your library.

Most libraries are very well organized. You can use them most effectively by learning how they are organized.

Probably the first thing you will see as you enter your library is the **circulation desk.** This is where you sign books and other library materials in and out. This is also where you should go if you have a question to ask. Usually, a librarian or library aide stationed at the desk will help you find the information you are seeking. Don't hesitate to ask these library workers for help; you can learn much about the library from them.

The **card catalogue** is also usually near the entrance. It is a cabinet full of small drawers. In these drawers are cards which tell what books are in the library. The cards will also tell you where to find the books.

See **R1b** for further information about the card catalogue.

Other catalogues may tell you where magazines, records, and the like, are kept.

To make proper use of the catalogues, you will have to know the main divisions of your library. Most libraries are organized in the following sections:

(1) *Fiction* (book-length stories) is usually kept in a separate place. It is arranged alphabetically by the last name of the author. If there is more than one book by the same author, they will be arranged alphabetically by title. A sign reading "fiction" will usually direct you to this section of the library.

In the fiction section, you may find a separate place for collections of short stories. These are also arranged according to the author's last name. For example, *The Good Deed* is a collection of short stories written by Pearl S. Buck. You would find this collection in the "B" section of the short-story shelves.

Sometimes a collection of short stories may contain the work of several authors. *Fifty Best American Short Stories, 1915-1965* is one of these. You would find this book under the name of its *editor,* Martha Foley.

(2) *Biographies* and *autobiographies* are kept in another place. These are books about the lives of individuals. They are also in alphabetical order. But the order does not necessarily depend on who wrote the book. It is based on the name of the person the book is about. . . . *Sting Like a Bee,* for example, was written by José Torres. But you would not find it under "Torres." You would find it under "Ali," because it is about Muhammad Ali. With autobiographies, of course, the author and the subject are the same. *Mr. Citizen,* an auto-biography of Harry S Truman, would be found under his name.

(3) Another section of the library may contain *reference books.* These include encyclopedias, dictionaries, atlases, almanacs, biographical reference books, and the like. These books are used often. For that reason, they usually may not be taken out.

See **R1d** for further discussion of reference books.

(4) *Nonfiction* or factual books that may be taken out form another section of the library. These books will have a code number on their spine. The code number tells you what the book is about. Below is the code used today by most secondary school libraries. The code is known as the **Dewey decimal system.**

000-009 general reference works
100-199 philosophy, psychology
200-299 religion, mythology
300-399 social sciences (economics, government, etc.)
400-499 language
500-599 pure science
600-699 applied science (aviation, medicine, etc.)
700-799 arts, recreation, sports
800-899 literature
900-999 history, geography, travel

This system is called a *decimal* system because after the main number there will often be a decimal point followed by another number or numbers. The number of "Red" Auerbach's book on basketball, for example, is 796.24.

(5) In addition to books, most libraries contain *magazines, pamphlets, newspapers,* and *nonprint materials,* such as records, filmstrips, microfilm, and the like. Find out if your library carries such materials.

Magazines are in the **periodical section.** Current issues are usually easy to find because they are displayed on open shelves or reading racks. They are arranged alphabetically by the name of the magazine. Back issues of magazines may be stored elsewhere in the library. Current issues of newspapers are usually on a wooden rack. This may be in or near the periodical section.

Pamphlets and papers that cannot be put on shelves are stored in a metal filing cabinet. This is called the **vertical file.** In the vertical file, you will find manila folders. Each folder will be labeled according to the topic of the papers and pamphlets it contains. The folders will be in alphabetical order.

Your local or school library may or may not contain nonprint materials. Ask your librarian, and find out where such material is stored.

EXERCISE 1

Visit your local or school library, according to the direction of your teacher. Draw a floor plan of the library you visit. Label the sections on your floor plan, using all of the following labels, if possible:

REFERENCE COLLECTION
BIOGRAPHY COLLECTION
PERIODICAL COLLECTION
NEWSPAPERS
VERTICAL FILE
CIRCULATION DESK
CARD CATALOGUE
FICTION COLLECTION
NONFICTION COLLECTION
SHORT-STORY COLLECTION
(if separate from fiction)

Here is a sample map:

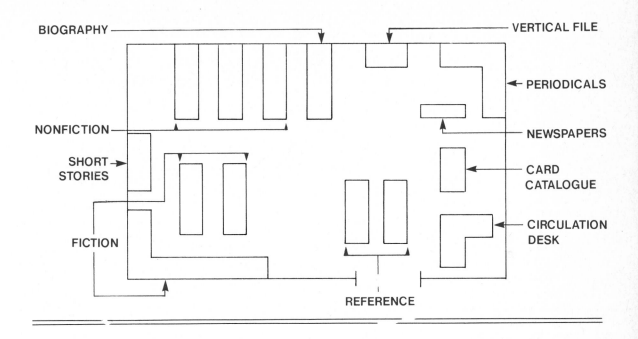

BIOGRAPHY — VERTICAL FILE

PERIODICALS

NONFICTION — NEWSPAPERS

SHORT STORIES — CARD CATALOGUE

CIRCULATION DESK

FICTION

REFERENCE

EXERCISE 2

Explore your local or school library. Take notes on what you discover. Talk to a librarian also. Look especially for unusual things, like records, back issues of magazines, the vertical file, and nonprint materials. After your exploration, write a composition on "Things I Discovered About the Library."

EXERCISE 3

Find a book in any *four* of the ten divisions of the Dewey decimal system. On your paper, write the full call number (the number on the spine of the cover), the title, and the author of each of the four books.

EXERCISE 4

Arrange the books of fiction listed on the next page in the order in which you would find them on the library shelves. (When alphabetizing by title, do not use "a," "an," or "the" when they are the first word in a title.)

1. Robert Newton Peck, *A Day No Pigs Would Die*
2. Marjorie M. Prince, *The Cheese Stands Alone*
3. Marjorie Kellogg, *Tell Me That You Love Me, Junie Moon*
4. Robert Louis Stevenson, *Treasure Island*
5. William Saroyan, *Boys and Girls Together*
6. Richard Peck, *Representing Super Doll*
7. Hannah Green, *I Never Promised You a Rose Garden*
8. William Saroyan, *My Name is Aram*
9. Walter Scott, *Ivanhoe*
10. John Steinbeck, *The Pearl*
11. William Saroyan, *Mama, I Love You*
12. John Steinbeck, *Of Mice and Men*
13. Charles Dickens, *A Christmas Carol*
14. Robert Louis Stevenson, *Kidnapped*
15. Paula Fox, *The Slave Dancer*
16. S. E. Hinton, *The Outsiders*
17. James Forman, *My Enemy, My Brother*
18. Charles Dickens, *Oliver Twist*
19. Kenneth Roberts, *Northwest Passage*
20. Kenneth Graham, *Wind in the Willows*

EXERCISE 5

Use the Dewey decimal code on page 367 for this exercise. Number your paper from one to ten. After each number write the hundred in the Dewey decimal system under which you would find the book.

EXAMPLE: *The Story of Religion*
(Answer)   200

1. *A Traveler's Guide to Europe*
2. *The Art of Politics*
3. *Greek Gods and Goddesses*
4. *How to Play Field Hockey*
5. *Introduction to Biology*
6. *The Guitar and How to Play It*
7. *How to Avoid Heart Attacks*
8. *Understanding Poetry*
9. *A Brief History of the United States*
10. *Teaching Yourself Spanish*

R1b

Using the Card Catalogue

Learn how to use the card catalogue.

The card catalogue tells you where to find books. It is a cabinet with small drawers. Each drawer has 3 x 5 cards arranged alphabetically. On the front of the drawers are letters. The letters tell you what part of the alphabet is in that drawer. For example, a drawer marked C-DE would contain all cards beginning with C. It would also contain all D cards up to DE. Thus you would find "DESSERTS" in that drawer. But you would not find "DIETS."

There are four basic types of cards in a card catalogue. These are title cards, author cards, subject cards, and "see"/ "see also" cards.

(1) **Title cards.** If you know the title of a book you want, you can look for it under the first word of that title. (Remember, however, that "a," "an," and "the" do not count. If the title of your book begins with one of these words, go on to the next word to find the title card.)

Suppose that you want to read *Life on the Run,* a book about basketball. First, you find the drawer that contains the L or LI cards. Then look in that drawer for the word "life." If there is more than one book or subject with "life" as its first word, go on to the next word, "on." If the library has the book, you will find a title card. It will look something like this:

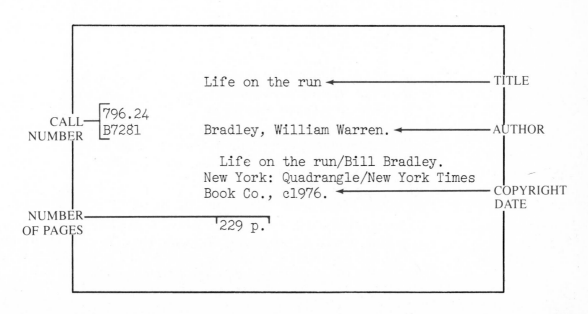

Notice the **call number** in the upper left-hand corner of the card. This tells you that the book is in the 700 section of the nonfiction collection. If the book had been a work of fiction, you would find "Fiction" in this place. If it had been a biography or a reference book, you would find a "B" or "Reference."

Other kinds of information may be found on title cards. For instance, a book may have illustrations, a bibliography (a list of books and articles on the same subject), or an index. These facts will be noted on the card. Some cards also give brief descriptions of a book.

(2) **Author cards.** Each book in the library will also have an author card. These will look much the same as title cards, except that the name of the author will be the first item on the card.

Author cards are useful if you know the name of the author but do not know the title of the book you are seeking. Naturally, these cards are indexed by the *last* name of the author. Under the last name of an author, you will find individual cards for all the books the library has that were written by that author. You will also find cards for all books written *about* that author.

(3) **Subject cards.** Subject cards look like title and author cards, too, but the first line of a subject card will contain the subject of the book, printed in capital letters. Bill Bradley's book, for example, will have a subject card beginning "BASKETBALL."

Subject cards are useful if you are doing a research paper on a subject. To find them, however, you have to have the right key word. Suppose, for example, that you are doing a report on measles and mumps. You probably will not find either of these headings on subject cards. Think of a more general heading under which these illnesses might be listed. You will find a subject card headed "DISEASES" or "COMMUNICABLE DISEASES."

(4) **"See" and "see also" cards.** A "see" card directs you to another part of the card file. For example, if you were reading about American writers and were to look up Mark Twain in the card catalogue, you would probably find a card like the one at the top of the next page.

```
Twain, Mark

        see

Clemens, Samuel Langhorne
```

This card tells you that all information about Mark Twain will be found under "Clemens," which is Twain's real name. Other "see" cards may simply tell you to look under a different subject. Here is an example:

```
WEED KILLERS

    see

HERBICIDES
```

This card tells you that information about weed killers will be found under the subject "HERBICIDES."

"See also" cards are like "see" cards. The only difference is that "see also" cards direct you to *additional* information on a subject.

Below is a drawing of the front of a card catalogue. Notice that each drawer contains the letters of the cards in that drawer. Also note that each has a number. Look at the authors, titles, and subjects below the drawing. Write on your paper, next to each author, title, or subject, the number of the drawer in which you would find the card.

EXAMPLE: LIFE ON OTHER PLANETS
(Answer) #7

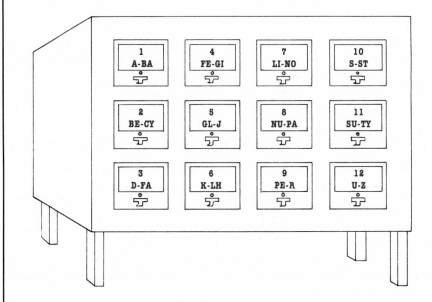

1. *Miracle on Thirty-fourth Street*
2. Edgar Allan Poe
3. CYCLONES AND TORNADOES
4. MOUNTAIN CLIMBING
5. *Young Pioneers*
6. Janis Joplin
7. WASTE, DISPOSAL OF
8. *The Cat Ate My Gymsuit*
9. Roberto Clemente

10. *Lilies of the Field*
11. *Babbitt*
12. Frances Perkins
13. DEAFNESS
14. *The Iliad*
15. UNITED STATES, GOVERNMENT OF
16. *A View from the Rim*
17. RELIGIOUS FAITHS
18. Roger Kahn
19. *Dolley Madison, Her Life and Times*
20. *Stories in Verse*

EXERCISE 2

Look in your library card catalogue for author cards for each of the writers below. If you find a card, write the title of one of his or her books. Also write the call number of the book if one is given. Write these on your paper next to the name of the author. If you find no cards, write "none" after the name of the author.

1. Agatha Christie
2. Claude McKay
3. Michael Crichton
4. Emily Dickinson
5. Frederick Douglass
6. Linus Pauling
7. Harriet Beecher Stowe
8. Agnes de Mille
9. Red Smith
10. Rachel Carson

EXERCISE 3

Look in your library card catalogue for title cards for each of the books below. If they are in the catalogue, write the full name of the author (or authors) and the call number of the book if one is given. Write these on your paper next to the name of the book. If the book is not in your library, write "no" next to the name of the book.

1. *The Amateur's Guide to Caves and Caving*
2. *Bicycle Touring*
3. *Island of the Blue Dolphins*
4. *Edgar Allan Poe*
5. *The Man Who Bought Himself*
6. *The Story of Art*
7. *Climbing Ice*
8. *Citizen of New Salem*
9. *Kon-Tiki*
10. *Famous Scientific Expeditions*

EXERCISE 4

Look at the subject cards in your library to find a book on any *five* of the following subjects. (If you find a "see" card, go to one of the other headings listed on it.) Write the title, author, call number, and copyright date for each of the five books you find.

1. Baseball
2. Africa
3. Gardening
4. Architecture
5. Games
6. Photography
7. Pollution
8. Space Exploration
9. Police
10. Sculpture

R1c
Finding Magazine Articles

Learn how to use the *Readers' Guide*.

The card catalogue lists all the books in the library. But another important source of information is the magazines in the periodical section of the library. Where do you go to find what is contained in these magazines? The answer is the *Readers' Guide to Periodical Literature,* known as the *Readers' Guide,* for short.

This reference book indexes all articles, stories, and poems that have appeared in close to 200 magazines. It is published twice a month, except in February, July, and August—when it is published once a month. A bound cumulative volume is published each year. If you do not already know, ask your librarian where the *Readers' Guide* is kept in your library.

The *Readers' Guide* has a combined author and subject index. Therefore whether you are looking for a topic or an author, simply look for the listing in alphabetical order. Here is a sample subject listing. The author listing for the article would look much the same, except you would find it under its author—"Shaw, D."

VIOLENCE
Violent movies create violent kids. D. Shaw.
il Today's Health 52:10-11+O '74.

Notice that the subject is in capital letters. Then the title is given, followed by the name of the author. The abbreviation, il, means that the article is illustrated. The article appeared in *Today's Health,* in October (O), 1974. The number 52 refers to the volume number of the magazine. This is followed by a colon and the page numbers on which the article appeared. The plus sign after the page numbers means that the article was continued on some later pages in the same issue.

To save space, the *Readers' Guide* uses many abbreviations. You will find a list of them and their meanings in the front of every issue.

EXERCISE 1

Pick a personality or a subject that interests you. Then look through the *Readers' Guide* for articles on that person or subject. Pick three articles that you would like to read. Write a list of those articles, giving complete information on each one. Be prepared to tell the class the title, author, magazine, date, and page numbers of each article. In other words, be sure you completely understand each entry. Check the front of the *Guide* if there are abbreviations you do not understand.

EXERCISE 2

On another personality or subject, find some articles that you would like to read. Then check to see which of the magazines your library has. Read at least one article and write a report on the main points that interest you. Write the title of the magazine and the title and author of the article on your report.

Learn how to use reference books.

R1d
Finding Reference Materials

When you want a brief answer to a question, an overview of a subject, or a short biography, the place to go is the reference section of your library. You will probably find many kinds of books there. Here are the main three types:

(1) Encyclopedias. **Encyclopedias** have articles on a broad range of subjects of general interest. So complete is their coverage that the best ones are several volumes long. These include the *Encyclopaedia Britannica,* the *Encyclopedia Americana, Collier's Encyclopedia,* and the *World Book Encyclopedia.*

In encyclopedias, topics are arranged in alphabetical order. Guide letters located on the binding of each volume will tell you which part of the alphabet is included in that book. For example, if the letters on the first volume of one encyclopedia are A-ANNO, the next volume might be labeled ANNU-BALTIC.

Guide letters will usually help you to find the main article on your topic. But it is even better to use the index. (Large encyclopedias have a separate volume index.) There you will find all references to your topic contained in the entire encyclopedia.

An encyclopedia is a good starting point for a report. It will give you a bird's-eye view of a subject. But it cannot include as much information as, for example, a whole book on a subject. Never just copy a report from an encyclopedia. (Never even copy passages from an encyclopedia without using quotation marks and noting where the information comes from.)

(2) Biographical Reference Books. You will find some biographies in encyclopedias. But **biographical reference books** generally cover more names and include more detail. They usually limit themselves to factual details about persons. They will not try to judge the person or explain her or his character. For that kind of information, you should go to biographies or autobiographies.

The following list includes some of the most important biographical reference books.

> *Dictionary of American Biography*
> *Who's Who in America*
> *Who's Who of American Women*
> *Current Biography*
> *The Junior Book of Authors*
> *American Men and Women of Science*
> *Grove's Dictionary of Music and Musicians*
> *World Biography*

(3) Atlases. **Atlases** contain detailed maps and a great deal of information about countries and cities. From an atlas you can learn the location of places, mountains, rivers, lakes, and the like. You can also learn many facts about countries, such as population, natural resources, climate, industries, and so on. Atlases usually have alphabetical

indexes listing places and topics. These indexes help you find quickly the information you want. Some useful world atlases are the following:

The Encyclopaedia Britannica Atlas
Hammond's Ambassador World Atlas
Rand McNally Cosmopolitan World Atlas

EXERCISE 1

Which type of reference book interests you most—encyclopedias, biographical reference books, or atlases? Pick one of these three reference book categories. Then go to your library and write down the names of at least three in that category that your library has.

EXERCISE 2

Which type of reference work would you find most useful for answering each of the following questions? Write "E" if an encyclopedia would be the best place to look. Write "B" if the information could most likely be found in a biographical reference book. Write "A" if the information could probably be found in an atlas.

1. What is the annual rainfall of Egypt?
2. Who is John Tunis?
3. How did the Girl Scouts originate?
4. What is the latitude and longitude of Peking, China?
5. Who was the 21st President of the United States?
6. Where does a certain prominent person currently live?
7. What is your state's nickname, motto, and flower?
8. For what college did Earl Campbell play football?
9. What is Brazil's leading industry?
10. What was the "Gunpowder Plot"?
11. How many symphonies did the composer Henry Cowell write?
12. Where is the Hellespont Channel?
13. How do automobile batteries work?
14. Where was Tracy Austin born?
15. Who invented dynamite?
16. What country has the largest oil production?
17. What are the rules for the game of cricket?
18. How old is Charles Schultz?
19. What is the population of Anchorage, Alaska?
20. In what country is Mount Everest?

UNIT REVIEW EXERCISE

Number your paper from 1 to 15. Find the definition in the right-hand column below that matches each item in the left-hand column. Write the letter of that item on your paper next to the appropriate number.

1. TITLE CARD

2. CIRCULATION DESK

3. "SEE" CARD

4. "SEE ALSO" CARD

5. VERTICAL FILE

6. DEWEY DECIMAL SYSTEM

7. SUBJECT CARD

8. CALL NUMBER

9. *THE READERS' GUIDE*

10. AN ATLAS

11. CARD CATALOGUE

12. AUTHOR CARD

13. AN ENCYCLOPEDIA

14. PERIODICAL SECTION

15. A BIOGRAPHICAL REFERENCE BOOK

A. A cabinet containing 3 x 5 index cards

B. A card whose top entry lists the name of a book

C. A series of numbers appearing on the spine of a book

D. A set of books containing information on a variety of subjects

E. A place where books are signed out

F. A book containing information on well-known persons

G. A book listing articles that have appeared in magazines

H. A book containing maps

I. A card directing you to additional information in a card catalogue

J. A card whose top entry lists the name of a writer

K. A place where pamphlets are kept

L. A method for classifying books by numbers

M. A card directing you to another place in the card catalogue

N. A card whose top entry lists a topic

O. A place where magazines are kept

R2
IMPROVING STUDY SKILLS

Build good study habits.

This year and for many years to come, you will be a student. You will spend a great deal of your time in that role. You may or may not be pleased about it, but you certainly will be happier if you play the role well. Of great help to you will be good study habits. Build a firm foundation now, and later studying will seem easy and natural. Pay special attention to the following points:

- Study in a *quiet place*. No one can study well with one ear and eye fixed on a TV set. Actually, if you concentrate on studying, you will find you have more time to watch television and do other things. Try to find a place where you will not be interrupted by others. If there is no quiet place in your home, try to do at least some of your studying in your school or local public library.

- Set aside a *definite time* for study. Always study during that time. Even if you have no homework on an evening, find something to study. Reread a chapter in a textbook. Reread your notes. Write about what you have been studying. Or do some extra problems. Of course you may have to study more at some times than at others. But if you study *regularly,* you should find that you will not have to cram before tests.

- *Budget* your study time. Make lists of what you have to do. Cross items off as you complete them. Tackle your most difficult assignments first rather than last. Do not study right up to bedtime. Allow some time to relax before going to bed.

- Keep a *notebook*. Some students like a separate book for each subject. Others divide a single book into parts. Naturally, your notebook should be neat, at least neat enough that you can read it. Assignments may be kept in your notebook, or in a separate assignment book.

- Take notes *in class* and *when you read*. Do not trust your memory—a note taken while something is being said is far more reliable. Take notes while you are reading, too. That way, the information is registered twice—in your mind and on paper.

- *Read your notes* from time to time. Do not wait until the night before a unit test. If you do, you will not be able to ask your teacher questions about material that you do not understand.

R3

Learn how to take tests of basic skills.

TAKING TESTS   Many states or school districts require schools to give tests of minimum competency. These tests measure basic skills or "proficiencies." They measure things that the student should know before going on to the next grade in school or before graduating. In some states a student must pass such a test before receiving a high school diploma. Some states require the student to pass a test in elementary school before going on to junior high school or middle school. Some states require the student to pass a test in junior high school before entering senior high school, or in middle school before going on to high school.

In some states the minimum competency tests are the same throughout the state. In other states each school district prepares its own tests of minimum competency.

Several different names have been given to these tests beside "minimum competency." Some of these names are: (1) everyday skills test; (2) test of survival skills; (3) test of life skills; and (4) basic skills competency tests.

The basic skills are usually considered to be reading, writing or composition, and arithmetic. Tests of life skills or survival skills often include reading of labels, timetables, telephone books, traffic signs or other public signs, repair manuals, and newspaper ads. Often the students are asked to fill out forms and to write memos, accident reports, or letters. The letters may be complaints about faulty products, letters applying for jobs, "thank-you" notes, or recommendations.

Learn to take tests so that the tests will show what you know and what you can do. Remember the following advice when taking tests:

(1) Read the directions carefully. Ask questions if you do not know the meanings of the words in the directions. Ask questions, too, if you do not understand the directions.

(2) Keep working. Do not spend too much time on one question or on one part of the test. If you find one part is hard, go on to the next part. Then, if you have time later, come back to the hard part.

(3) Use guessing wisely. If the directions say that your score will be the number of correct items, it is safe to guess. If wrong answers lower your score, do not guess wildly.

(4) Reread and correct all of your written paragraphs. If you are asked to write something, make notes before you begin to write. After you have finished writing, go back and read what you wrote. Correct the spelling errors that you find. Check the capitalization and punctuation. Check the agreement of subject and verb and other basic relationships in a sentence.

Learn the ways your knowledge of word meanings is measured in tests of basic skills.

R3a

Vocabulary
Tests

Tests of word meanings are used in all grades of school from kindergarten through high school. Such tests are also given after high school. People may take such tests when in college or when applying for a job.

(1) **SYNONYMS**

The most common tests of word meanings ask you to find synonyms. For a test word, you select the word that is closest in meaning to it. In each of the following examples, the right answer has been circled:

A	EMPLOY	B	SCHOLAR
	(1) sing		(1) teacher
	(2) quit		(2) school
	(3) hire		(3) test
	(4) run		(4) student
C	IMP	D	ANTENNA
	(1) ant		(1) aerial
	(2) rascal		(2) uncle
	(3) bird		(3) radio
	(4) man		(4) insect

NOTE: Synonyms are not always *exactly* alike. The two words often produce different reactions in the reader or listener. *Shy* and *bashful* are such a pair. They are very close in meaning, but many people would rather be called *shy* than *bashful*. Nevertheless, the two words are synonyms.

② ANTONYMS

A test of antonyms makes us look for a word with the *opposite* meaning. In each item of the following sample, there is a word in capital letters, followed by four answer choices. From the four choices, circle the one whose meaning is *opposite* to the meaning of the word in capital letters. In each of the following examples, the right answer has been circled:

E INTERNAL	F SUPERB
(1) alone	(1) above
(2) devilish	(2) bad
(3) external	(3) below
(4) inside	(4) breakfast
G FINAL	H BUY
(1) top	(1) distant
(2) examination	(2) sell
(3) first	(3) purchase
(4) last	(4) hello

Authors of antonym tests items often include synonyms among the wrong choices. In sample E, *inside* is a synonym for the word *internal*—not an antonym. In sample G, *examination* is a possible synonym for *final*—not an antonym. In sample H, *purchase* means the same as *buy*.

The right choice for sample E is *external*. Notice that one of the wrong choices is *devilish*. The author included this for students who might confuse *internal* and *infernal*.

In sample F, the word *superb* means excellent or very good. The word that is opposite to this is *bad,* the right answer choice. Notice how the author picked the other answer choices. A prefix *super-* means *above*. The opposite is *below*. The choice of *breakfast* may be picked by someone who confuses *superb* with *supper*.

In sample G, the word that is opposite in meaning to *final* is *first,* the right answer choice.

In sample H, the author used *distant,* which is opposite to *by*—spelled differently. *Hello* is opposite to *bye*—again spelled differently. The right answer choice is *sell,* which is opposite in meaning to *buy*. Remember: Antonym tests will often test your ability to tell confusing words apart.

I. SYNONYMS

In each test item, there is a word in capital letters followed by four answer choices. From these four choices, pick the word that is most nearly like the meaning of the word in capital letters. Write the letter of your choice in the space next to the number of the item.

_____ 1. FLAME
    A air
    B smoke
    C water
    D fire

_____ 2. PACES
    A throws
    B words
    C steps
    D spaces

_____ 3. PARDON
    A excuse
    B hurt
    C part
    D separate

_____ 4. ERROR
    A mirror
    B horror
    C terror
    D mistake

_____ 5. QUICK
    A slow
    B fast
    C quit
    D quite

_____ 6. LEAP
    A jump
    B walk
    C peel
    D sleep

_____ 7. WEALTHY
    A healthy
    B wise
    C pretty
    D rich

_____ 8. FATIGUED
    A tired
    B chubby
    C funny
    D guessed

_____ 9. PLUMP
    A fat
    B lump
    C plumber
    D prune

_____ 10. SHY
    A heavens
    B bashful
    C showy
    D tricky

II.

ANTONYMS

In each test item, there is a word in capital letters followed by four answer choices. Select the answer choice whose meaning is most nearly *opposite* in meaning to the word in capital letters. Write the letter of your choice in the space next to the number of the item.

_____ 1. RETREAT
A desert
B advance
C medicine
D discomfort

_____ 2. MINIATURE
A tiny
B soft
C sweet
D large

_____ 3. SILLY
A afraid
B wise
C foolish
D slow

_____ 4. STRENGTHEN
A shorten
B extend
C weaken
D brighten

_____ 5. CAREFUL
A timid
B helpful
C careless
D fruitful

_____ 6. LEADER
A reader
B child
C silver
D follower

_____ 7. LOCK
A pick
B unlock
C latch
D hair

_____ 8. HUBBUB
A bubble
B bustle
C rim
D quiet

_____ 9. SUBTRACT
A thin
B foolish
C add
D sunny

_____ 10. AMBITIOUS
A lazy
B long
C curious
D quick

Learn how tests of basic skills test your command of written English.

Basic skills tests often measure the student's ability to write standard English. Some items test punctuation or capitalization. Others include problems of usage. The following pages provide a sampling of test questions that you may be asked to answer.

① **REVISING PARAGRAPHS**

The students are asked to check a paragraph for usage problems or errors in mechanics. Portions of the paragraph are underlined and numbered.

The student is asked to use the following code to mark each numbered, underlined phrase:

- *U* for usage problem
- *P* for punctuation error
- *C* for capitalization error
- *NC* for no change

Read the following example:

> James michener called Bora Bora the "most beautiful
> ‾‾‾‾‾‾‾‾‾‾‾‾‾‾   ‾‾‾‾‾‾‾‾‾‾‾‾‾‾
>   1   2
>
> island in the world." Every year it attracts more tourists
>
> than it did the year before. Its three mountain peaks is
>   ‾‾‾‾‾‾‾‾
>   3
>
> often hidden in the clouds. Its white sand, beaches sur-
> ‾‾‾‾‾   ‾‾‾‾‾‾‾‾‾‾‾‾‾‾‾‾‾‾
>   3   4
>
> round a large lagoon, whose colors vary from deep blue to
>
> pale yellow.

To answer test items like these, remember what to look for: a punctuation error, a capitalization error, or a usage problem. For each item, read the whole sentence first. Then see if the underlined phrase uses any punctuation. If it does, ask yourself if it is the right mark. If it is not, mark *P*. If there is no punctuation, decide if you think it needs some punctuation: a comma, an apostrophe, quotation marks, or some other mark. If it does, mark *P*.

If there is no error in punctuation, look for an error in capitalization. Is there a capital letter in the underlined section? Is the capital letter correctly used? If not, mark the item with a *C*.

If there is no capitalized word in the phrase, check each word to see if one of the words should be capitalized. If a capital letter is needed, mark the item *C*. If not, go on to check for usage problems.

All sentences should be written in standard English. Check each word or phrase for nonstandard English or slang. If there is a usage problem, mark the item *U*.

If you conclude that there is no problem in the underlined portion, mark the item *NC*.

Here are the answers for the sample paragraph:

- Item 1: There is no punctuation, and none is needed. However, the man's last name is Michener. A capital letter is needed. The answer is *C*.
- Item 2: There is no punctuation, and there are no capital letters. No punctuation is needed, and no capitalization is needed. There is no usage problem. The answer for this item, therefore, is *NC*.
- Item 3: There is no punctuation, and there are no capital letters. No punctuation is needed, and no capitalization is needed. However, the sentence has a plural subject: *peaks*. The verb, therefore, should also be plural. The word *is* is not plural. So, there is a usage problem in this underlined portion. The answer should be *U*.
- Item 4: There is a comma. There is no need for a comma after *sand*. The answer is *P*.

② BEST-SENTENCE TESTS

One type of test item that is used to measure writing ability lists three sentences. Each sentence says roughly the same thing. Your job is to read the sentences carefully and select the sentence that is best.

Look at the following sample items and try to choose the *best* sentence for each item.

5 A Harold borrowed his friend's car.
     B The car of his friend was borrowed by Harold.
     C Harold borrowed the car that belonged to his friend.

6 A Sue's cousin is a plumber.
     B The cousin of Sue became a plumber.
     C In Sue's family, one of her cousins is a plumber.

7 A If the witches are wicked, they are very ugly.
     B Witches, if they are wicked, are very ugly.
     C Wicked witches are very ugly.

8 A A youngster is needed to deliver papers about fourteen years old.
     B A youngster, about fourteen years old, is needed to deliver papers.
     C To deliver papers, a youngster about fourteen years is needed.

Often the best choice is the sentence that is most direct. A sentence that is brief and clear and has an active verb is usually better than a longer one with a passive verb. Modifiers should point clearly to what they modify. The answer to the four examples follow:

• Item 5: The most direct statement is sentence A, the right answer. This sentence uses only five words, whereas B uses a passive verb and needs nine words. Sentence C is roundabout, using a separate clause to show that the car belonged to a friend.

• Item 6: Again, sentence A is brief, clear, and direct. It is the right answer.

• Item 7: The right answer is sentence C. The other two sentences say the same thing but are unnecessarily long.

• Item 8: The best sentence is B. In sentence A, the modifying phrase is badly placed: the *papers* are not fourteen years old. In sentence C, the word *needed* is far away from the words that tell us what the need is.

③ PARAGRAPH ORGANIZATION

On the following page are two examples of the kind of test items that test your ability to develop a paragraph. Each item has a list of four numbered sentences. You are asked to put these four sentences into the order that would result in the best paragraph.

---

9 1 After a period of childhood, they go through adolescence from age 9 to age 14.

    2 The life cycle of chimpanzees is very much like that of humans.

    3 Old age sets in at about 35 years.

    4 Their period of infancy is about five years.

        A 1–4–3–2
        B 2–4–1–3
        C 4–1–3–2

10 1 It was named in honor of the actor John Wayne shortly after his death.

    2 He is remembered especially for playing the "good guy" in Westerns.

    3 The second busiest airport in California is the John Wayne Airport, Orange County.

    4 He will be remembered, too, for a long time to come as his movies are shown over and over again on TV.

        A 2–4–3–1
        B 3–1–2–4
        C 3–2–4–1

- Item 9: Three sentences mention ages. These can be arranged according to the ages: 4–1–3. This leaves sentence 2 to be placed either first or last. It alone would make either a good topic sentence or a good closing sentence. But, when we look at sentence 4, we see the pronoun *Their,* which must point back to something in an earlier sentence. *Their* refers to *chimpanzees* in sentence 2, which then must be placed before sentence 4. Sentence 2 then becomes the opening sentence. The answer is B.

- Item 10: Look for words in each sentence that point back to something in the previous sentence. Sentence 1 starts with the word *It.* This word refers to the airport mentioned in sentence 3, and so sentence 1 follows sentence 3. Sentence 2 starts with *He,* which must point back to some male mentioned earlier—John Wayne. Therefore, sentence 2 must come after sentence 1. Sentence 4 also starts with *He* and could follow sentence 1. However, the words *remembered, too,* tell us that something else was remembered first. So, sentence 4 should follow sentence 2. The answer, therefore, is B.

④ **PRACTICAL SKILLS**

Learn how to take tests of those practical skills that are sometimes called "everyday," "survival," or "life" skills. These tests may ask questions about package labels, timetables, pages of telephone books, newspaper ads, recipes, road signs, pages of a driver's manual, maps, charts, library cards, a TV guide, indexes, and the like. They may ask you to fill in application forms, tax forms, and other printed forms that you are likely to see and to use often outside school.

Look at the following application for a library card. Copy this card on a piece of paper and fill in the blanks.

APPLICATION FOR A LIBRARY CARD

Print the following:

Name _____ Date _____
       Last   First

Address _____
        Street & No.   City   Zip Code

Age *(if under 18)* _____

Signature _____ Telephone _____

Parent's Signature *(necessary if applicant is under 18)*

_____

In the first blank space, did you *print* your last name followed by your first name? Did you include the month, the day, and the year in the space marked *Date?* Did you include two letters to name your state in the space for the Zip Code?

In the space marked *Signature* did you *write* your name as you usually write it? If you were filling out this card to apply for a library card, which space would you *not* complete?

**SAMPLE
TEST B**

I. PERSONAL LETTER

Read the following letter all the way through. Then go back and read it again carefully. When you come to a numbered, underlined section, look at the three answer choices whose number corresponds to that of the underlined section. Decide which of the three responses is the best choice. If you think the underlined material is correct, mark the letter of the "No Change" response. If you think one of the other two answers is best, mark the letter of that choice. Write the letter of your choice in the space next to the number of the item.

<u>2909 Patricia st.</u>
1

Marion, IN 46952

<u>July 6 1980</u>
2

<u>Dear Marty,</u>
3

Next month I'll visit my grandmother again <u>in shelby</u>. I hope
4

that <u>me and you</u> can go on another overnight camping trip, as we
5

did last year. I'll bring along the same pup tent that <u>we use then</u>.
6

Do you <u>still got</u> the sleeping bags and <u>the stove.</u>
7   8

I'll arrive in Shelby <u>on august 7.</u> Can we go on our camping trip
9

on the evening of <u>August 10?</u>
10

Cordially yours,

Lynn

_____ 1. A 2909 Patricia St.　　　　_____ 2. A July, 6, 1980
       B 2909 patricia st.　　　　　　　　 B July 6, 1980
       C No Change　　　　　　　　　　　 C No Change

_____ 3. A Dear Marty—　　　　　　　_____ 4. A in Shelby
       B Dear Marty?　　　　　　　　　　 B to shelby
       C No Change　　　　　　　　　　　 C No Change

_____ 5. A you and I
       B me and Marty
       C No Change

_____ 6. A we used then
       B we use last year
       C No Change

_____ 7. A have got
       B still have
       C No Change

_____ 8. A the stove!
       B the stove?
       C No Change

_____ 9. A on August 7.
       B on August 7!
       C No Change

_____ 10. A of august 10?
        B of August 10.
        C No Change

II. PARAGRAPH ORGANIZATION

Read all four sentences in each of the following test items. Decide in which order these sentences would make the best paragraph. Mark the letter of your choice in the space next to the number of the item.

_____ 1. 1 The Waltons have three children.
     2 The oldest, a girl named Ann, was born in 1967.
     3 Then five years later they had another son and named him Mark.
     4 Two years later, in 1969, they had a boy, whom they named Troy.
        A 1–2–4–3
        B 2–4–3–1
        C 2–3–4–1

_____ 2. 1 We had a delicious lunch.
     2 This was followed by grilled cheese sandwiches.
     3 We started with mushroom soup.
     4 Then we finished with a dessert of chocolate pudding.
        A 1–3–2–4
        B 3–1–4–2
        C 3–4–2–1

_____ 3. 1 First, the lemons are squeezed.
     2 Finally, ice is added to make it cool.
     3 Then water is added to the lemon juice, and it is sweetened with sugar.
     4 Making lemonade is very easy.
        A 1–2–3–4
        B 1–3–4–2
        C 4–1–3–2

_____ 4. 1 Often it is found in the form of crystals.
    2 Iron pyrite is a mineral found in several parts of the country.
    3 For this reason it is called "fool's gold."
    4 These crystals have a metallic luster and a brass-yellow color.
      A 1–4–3–2
      B 2–1–4–3
      C 2–3–1–4

_____ 5. 1 In 1839 the Hudson Bay Co. took over the post and changed the name to Fort Stikine.
    2 Wrangell is the fourth name given to a small Alaskan fishing village.
    3 Russians built a post there in 1834 and called it Fort St. Dionysus.
    4 When the U.S. Army built a military post there in 1868, they called it Fort Wrangell; later the word _Fort_ was dropped.
      A 2–3–1–4
      B 3–1–4–2
      C 4–1–3–2

_____ 6. 1 Then Clifford Ray, a professional basketball player, was called to help.
    2 A dolphin named Mr. Spock playfully snatched an iron bolt from a diver and swallowed it.
    3 With his long arm, he reached nearly four feet into Mr. Spock's gullet and pulled the bolt from his stomach.
    4 Two days of attempts to get the bolt out of the dolphin's stomach were unsuccessful.
      A 1–3–2–4
      B 2–1–4–3
      C 2–4–1–3

III. PRACTICAL SKILLS

A. _Application for a Credit Card_

Edna A. Thornton is applying for a credit card. She is 19 years old and is a sophomore at Whitely College. She lives at 247 Lawton Lane, Whitely, MN 55199 in Lake County. Her telephone number is 713-4992. Her cousin, Mary Stewart, recommended the B. L. Thompson card.

Complete the following application for credit as it would be correctly completed by Edna Thornton today.

Instructions:
   Print in capital letters.   Begin printing in the first tinted box in each section.   Bring or mail the application to the store.   Your card will be sent to you by mail.

APPLICATION FOR B. L. THOMPSON CREDIT CARD

Last Name   *First Name*   *Initial*

Home Address   *Home Phone*

City   *County*   *State*   *Zip Code*

Employer

School, if Student   *Age, if Student*

Year in College (check one)

Fresh. ☐   *Soph.* ☐   *Jr.* ☐   *Sr.* ☐

Referred to **B. L. Thompson** *by* _____

Applicant's Signature _____ *Date* _____

B.   *Change of Address Notice*

Walter Bradley, a bachelor, will move to a new home at 2113 Sunnyvale Avenue, Cincinnati, OH 45230 a week from today. He lives alone at 414 Shady Lane, Holgate, OH 46810. Before moving he should complete a Change of Address Order and mail it to his present post office in Holgate. Complete both sides of the form on the next page as it should be filled out by Walter Bradley today.

U.S. GPO: 1980–726-981

THIS ORDER PROVIDES for the for-warding of first-class mail and all parcels of obvious value for a period not to exceed 1 year.		Print or Type *(Last Name, First Name, Middle Initial)*	
CHANGE OF ADDRESS IS FOR: ☐ Entire Family (When last name of family members differ, separate orders for each last name must be filed) ☐ Individual Signer Only	**OLD ADDRESS**	No. and St., Apt., Suite, P.O. Box or R.D. No. *(In care of)*	
I AGREE TO PAY FORWARDING POSTAGE FOR MAGAZINES FOR 90 DAYS. ☐ NO ☐ YES		Post Office, State and ZIP Code	
USPS USE ONLY CLERK/ CARRIER ENDORSEMENT	**NEW ADDRESS**	No. and St., Apt., Suite, P.O. Box or R.D. No. *(In care of)*	
		Post Office, State and ZIP Code	
CARRIER ROUTE NUMBER		Effective Date	If Temporary, Expiration Date
DATE ENTERED		Sign Here ▶	Date Signed

PS Form 3637, June 1980   *Signature & title of person authorizing address change. (DO NOT print or type)*

CHANGE OF ADDRESS ORDER

MAIL OR DELIVER TO POST OFFICE OF *OLD* ADDRESS

AFFIX
FIRST-
CLASS
POSTAGE
IF MAILED

POSTMASTER

TO_____

CITY_____

STATE_____ ZIP_____

ILLUSTRATION CREDITS

ACKNOWLEDGMENTS

Harcourt Brace Jovanovich, Inc. for permission to reprint the definition of the word "gill" from *The Harcourt Brace Intermediate Dictionary*. Copyright © 1968 by Harcourt Brace Jovanovich, Inc. Reprinted by permission of the publisher.

Harper & Row, Publishers, Inc. for permission to reprint an excerpt from *A Choice of Weapons* (pp. 204–205) by Gordon Parks. Copyright © 1965, 1966 by Gordon Parks. Reprinted by permission of Harper & Row, Publishers, Inc.

Harper & Row, Publishers, Inc. for permission to reprint "When I Went Out," (page 8), from *In the Middle of the Trees* by Karla Kuskin. Copyright © 1958 by Karla Kuskin. By permission of Harper & Row, Publishers, Inc.

Houghton Mifflin Company for permission to reprint "Night Clouds" from *The Complete Poetical Works of Amy Lowell*. Copyright © 1955 by Houghton Mifflin Company. Reprinted by permission of the publisher.

Nancy N. Jones, Editor, for permission to reprint "A Friend," by Bev Albertson, an excerpt from *I Can't Write*.

Little, Brown and Co. for permission to reprint "The Face Is Familiar," Stanza Five of "Introduction to Dogs," by Ogden Nash. Copyright 1938 by Ogden Nash.

The Literary Trustees of Walter De la Mare and The Society of Authors as their representative for permission to reprint "Silver" by Walter De la Mare.

Macmillan Publishing Co., Inc. for permission to reprint the definitions of "resist" and "hack" from the *Macmillan Dictionary,* William D. Halsey, Editorial Director. Copyright © 1977, 1973 Macmillan Publishing Co., Inc.

Random House, Inc. for permission to reprint an excerpt from *Life in the Middle Ages* by Jay Williams. Copyright © 1966 by Random House, Inc.

Acknowledgments

Random House, Inc. for permission to reprint the definition for "short-sighted." *Random House School Dictionary*. Copyright © 1978 by Random House, Inc.

Scholastic Magazines, Inc. for permission to reprint "Wind-Wolves" by William D. Sargent. Copyright © 1926 by Scholastic Magazines, Inc. Reprinted by permission.

Scott, Foresman and Company for permission to reprint pronunciation key and entries from *Thorndike-Barnhart Advanced Dictionary* by E. L. Thorndike and Clarence L. Barnhart. Copyright © 1973 by Scott, Foresman and Company. Reprinted by permission.

Scott, Foresman and Company for permission to reprint entry from *Thorndike-Barnhart Advanced Junior Dictionary* by E. L. Thorndike and Clarence L. Barnhart. Copyright © 1968 by Scott, Foresman and Company. Reprinted by permission.

Scott, Foresman and Company for permission to reprint entries from *Thorndike-Barnhart High School Dictionary* by E. L. Thorndike and Clarence L. Barnhart. Copyright © 1968 by Scott, Foresman and Company. Reprinted by permission.

Viking Penguin Inc. for permission to reprint an excerpt from *The Red Pony* by John Steinbeck. Copyright 1938; Copyright © renewed 1966 by John Steinbeck.

Viking Penguin Inc. for permission to reprint an excerpt from *Travels with Charley: In Search of America* by John Steinbeck. Copyright © 1962, Viking Penguin Inc.

The H. W. Wilson Company for permission to reprint an excerpt from the *Readers' Guide to Periodical Literature*. READERS' GUIDE TO PERIODICAL LITERATURE Copyright © 1974, 1975 by The H. W. Wilson Company. Material reproduced by permission of the publisher.

INDEX

Numerals in italics indicate illustrations. Charts are identified in the Index.

2 3 4 5 6 7 8 9 10 DODO 88 87 86 85 84 83 82 81

HANDBOOK KEY